Language Development in Exceptional Circumstances

Edited by

Dorothy Bishop
Medical Research Council
Applied Psychology Unit, Cambridge, UK

and

Kay Mogford
Department of Speech
University of Newcastle-upon-Tyne, UK

Psychology Press
a member of the Taylor & Francis group

First published by Churchill Livingstone, Edinburgh 1988

Reprinted in paperback 1994 and 2000

Psychology Press Ltd, Publishers
27 Church Road
Hove
East Sussex, BN3 2FA
UK

British Library Cataloguing in Publication Data

Language Development in Exceptional Circumstances. — New ed
    I. Bishop, Dorothy II. Mogford, Kay
    401.9

  ISBN 0-86377-308-7

Printed and bound by Bookcraft Ltd, Midsomer Norton, Somerset

LANGUAGE DEVELOPMENT IN
EXCEPTIONAL CIRCUMSTANCES

Preface

In conceiving of this book, we had from the start two rather different readerships in mind: first, those who are interested in the intellectual problems posed by the study of language development in its own right, and second, those whose primary interest is in development under exceptional circumstances — speech therapists/pathologists, pediatricians, clinical and educational psychologists, and those working in special education. We hope that the contents of this book will show these two groups, theoreticians and practitioners, how much they have to offer one another. Our aim has been to make the book comprehensible to readers from a wide range of backgrounds, to avoid jargon, and to assume little specialist knowledge, without oversimplifying complex issues.

One of the frustrating facts that researchers in developmental psycholinguistics must contend with is that the topic under investigation, language development, is seldom amenable to experimental manipulation. In the main, researchers in language development are in much the same position as astronomers: they can observe and describe the phenomena of interest in minutest detail, but they have little opportunity to influence them. The example of astronomy illustrates that this constraint need not limit theoretical development. It does, however, frequently make it difficult to subject theories to adequate test. With this book we aim to demonstrate that although we can seldom design experiments to manipulate variables thought to affect language learning, we can resolve many of our difficulties by considering language acquisition in children who are developing in exceptional physical or environmental circumstances.

Ever since attempts have been made to describe and explain normal language development, references to exceptional circumstances have been made. Initially these referred to anecdotal incidents, single case studies, and one-off investigations of isolated phenomena. These variations in the conditions in which language is acquired can be regarded as natural experiments which would not be feasible or ethical under normal circumstances. The quality and quantity of evidence cited in early accounts were often inadequate, but in recent years there has been an increase in the volume of research accompanied by a greater sophistication in methodology. The time appears right to review the accumulating evidence and address issues and examine assumptions that underlly our understanding of language development. In Chapter 1 we raise five theoretical questions about language acquisition on which exceptional circumstances can throw some light. Chapter 15 returns to reconsider these questions in the light of the evidence supplied by the other chapters.

Exceptional circumstances can have important implications for theories of language development, but this is not the only motivation for studying them. Knowledge of the variations in the pattern of language development that can occur when children develop in exceptional circumstances is important for those concerned with the provision of services to meet special educational and developmental needs.

Over the past two decades research in this area has proliferated. Many studies have built upon research on normal language development, using techniques and concepts which were developed in the study of children reared in conditions typical for their language community, whose mental and physical development was unremarkable. The ultimate motivation in many cases has been the practical one of developing intervention techniques based on a sound empirical knowledge of how development may be affected by disadvantage or handicap. However, this common aim has not led to uniformity in experimental methods or theoretical approaches, which have tended to vary, depending on the parent discipline of the researchers and the particular circumstances under investigation. For these reasons the resulting research appears in a variety of specialized publications, and this has limited the opportunities for relating work concerned with different types of child. In some cases the quantity of accumulated evidence is large and apparently contradictory, and so requires a balanced, critical and objective evaluation before it will yield a useful framework for practitioners. This we aim to provide here.

Although the meeting of the disciplines of psychology and linguistics has revealed new insights into language development, it has also made this field less accessible for those with a practical interest in the subject but without familiarity with linguistic terminology. To help remedy this situation, a brief introduction to developmental psycholinguistics is included in Chapter 1. In addition, a glossary is provided to help readers unfamiliar with specialist medical and linguistic terms, as well as an appendix which describes some of the more commonly used assessment procedures referred to in the text.

We would like to thank those colleagues who so willingly gave time to read and comment on individual chapters: Lesley Milroy, Brian Neville, and June Robson. Thanks are also due to Anne Stals for her cheerful assistance with secretarial tasks throughout the gestation period of this volume.

One of the disadvantages of an orally-based language is that it is sequential rather than simultaneous, so whenever two editors work together, one must be listed first and the other second. The order of mention of editors and the ordering of authorship for Chapters 1 and 15 were determined by the toss of a coin.

Manchester and
Newcastle, 1988

DB
KM

Contributors

Ursula Bellugi EdD
Director, Laboratory for Language and Cognitive Studies,
The Salk Institute for Biological Studies, La Jolla, California,
USA

Amy M. Bihrle BA
Research Associate, Laboratory for Language and Cognitive
Studies, The Salk Institute for Biological Studies, La Jolla,
California, USA

Dorothy Bishop MA MPhil DPhil
Senior Research Scientist, Medical Research Council Applied
Psychology Unit, Cambridge, UK

Warren H. Fay PhD
Professor of Speech Pathology, Oregon Health Sciences
University, Portland, Oregon, USA

Fred Genesee PhD
Associate Professor, Department of Psychology, McGill
University, Montreal, Canada

Susan K. Klein MD
Research Fellow, Department of Neurology (Pediatrics),
Albert Einstein College of Medicine, Bronx, New York, USA

Diane C. Lillo-Martin PhD
Department of Linguistics, University of Connecticut, USA

Shelly Marks MS
Research Associate, Laboratory for Language and Cognitive
Studies, The Salk Institute for Biological Studies, La Jolla,
California, USA

Anne E. Mills DrPhilHabil
Senior Lecturer, Department of Language Studies, College of
Ripon and York St John, York, UK

Kay Mogford MCST PhD
Department of Speech, University of Newcastle-upon-Tyne,
UK

Lucinda O'Grady
Research Assistant, Laboratory for Language and Cognitive
Studies, The Salk Institute for Biological Studies, La Jolla,
California, USA

Isabelle Rapin MD
Professor, Department of Neurology and Pediatrics
(Neurology), Albert Einstein College of Medicine, Bronx,
New York, USA

Jean A. Rondal PhD
Professor of Psychology, Psycholinguistics and Logopedics,
University of Liege, Belgium, Scientific Adviser to the
Belgian Down's Syndrome Association (APEM)

Helene Sabo MA
Cornell Medical Center, Division of Cognitive
Neurosciences, New York, USA

Naomi Schiff-Myers PhD
Associate Professor, Department of Communication Science
and Disorders, Montclair State College, New Jersey, USA

David H. Skuse MB ChB MRCP MRCPsych
Wellcome Trust Senior Lecturer and Honorary Consultant in
Child Psychiatry, Institute of Child Health, University of
London, UK

Karen van Hoek
Research Assistant, Laboratory for Language and Cognitive
Studies, The Salk Institute for Biological Studies, La Jolla,
California, USA

Contents

Glossary

acute—of short duration and severe (cf. *chronic*)

affix—a *morpheme* added to a word stem for the purpose of inflection or derivation. Prefixes come in front of the stem (e.g. *un*important), and suffixes come after the stem (e.g. hope*less*)

affricate—a sound in which a complete closure is made at some point in the vocal tract and then slowly released so that friction occurs at the same place of articulation, e.g. initial sound in 'cheese', 'juice'

age-equivalent score—a test score expressed in terms of the age at which that score would be the average. For example, if the mean *raw score* is 30 for 4-year-olds and 40 for 5-year-olds, then a 5-year-old child who obtained a raw score of 30 is assigned an age-equivalent score of 4 years

agreement—the marking of an expression to agree with another expression of the same category; e.g. in 'this house' vs 'these houses' the form of the determiner agrees with the number (singular or plural) of the noun. In 'I go' vs 'he goes' the form of the verb, 'go' or 'goes', agrees with the subject for person and number

alveolar plosives—consonants made by stopping the oral air stream by contacting the tooth-ridge with the tongue tip or blade, followed by an explosive release. E.g. first sound in 'tooth', 'dark'

American sign language (ASL)—the major language used by the deaf in the United States, in which words are represented by manual signs. It has its own morphology, syntax and semantics, quite distinct from English

anaphora (adj. **anaphoric**)—use of a pronoun to refer back to someone or something that has already been mentioned in a conversation. E.g. 'I met the girl's mother. *She* said . . . . . .'

Apgar scores—a scale developed by Dr Virginia Apgar in 1952 to aid objective assessment of the state of the newborn infant. Appearance/colour, pulse/heart rate, reflexes, activity/muscle tone and respiration are rated on a scale, 0–2, with maximum total score of 10

apical—at the tip or apex

aspirate—(medical) to suck or siphon body fluids from a body cavity

aspirate—(phonetic) to add a small quantity of air to the release of a plosive consonant

assimilation—a process where the production of a speech sound is influenced by another sound in the word, as when 'doggie' is pronounced 'goggie'. Assimilation can be regressive, where a later sound influences an earlier sound, as in the example above, or progressive where an early sound influences a subsequent sound (e.g. 'kettle' pronounced as 'kekkle')

1

audiogram—graphic representation of hearing threshold at different frequencies. See also *decibel*

bilirubin—a pigment derived from the breakdown of hemoglobin from the red blood corpuscles in the spleen. Normally the substance is excreted through the digestive system. It is harmful in high concentrations in the blood, particularly to the nuclei of the immature brain

Blissymbolics—a system of iconic symbols originally designed as an international language, but now widely used as a means of communication by children unable to articulate or read. The symbols are displayed on a chart and can be indicated in a variety of ways. The printed word is written beneath the symbol

centile score—see *percentile score*

cerebellar—belonging to the cerebellum

cerebellum—part of the brain above and behind the medulla at the top of the spinal cord, responsible for smooth and co-ordinated movement

chronic—opposed to *acute*. Lingering, lasting

clause—a term used in grammatical analysis to refer to units consisting of a verb together with the optional elements subject, complement and adjunct

cluster reduction—a phonological process which is typically found in the speech of children during the course of phonological development. Consonant clusters are simplified by reducing the number of consonants realised. E.g. 'string' becomes 'ting' or 'tring'

cluttering—a disorder of speech and language, the main symptom of which is over-rapid, arrhythmic speech which impairs intelligibility in the absence of a disorder of phonology. It is considered a disorder of fluency but is often associated with a cluster of language difficulties in the absence of intellectual impairment

code-switching—the ability to move from one linguistic code or language to another. The term is also used for switching between different styles of speech within a language, e.g. from formal to informal

concrete nouns—words which refer to objects in the real world (e.g. dog, house, tree). The opposite of concrete is abstract (e.g. liberty, fear, illness)

concrete operations period—in Piagetian theory, a stage of development, corresponding approximately to 7 to 11 years of age, in which the child becomes capable of intellectual operations that involve being able to process information from several aspects of a situation simultaneously, to understand reversibility of operations, and to take the view of others

conductive hearing loss—hearing impairment caused by any affection of the conducting apparatus, i.e. the external auditory canal, the middle ear, or the labyrinthine windows (cf. *sensorineural hearing loss*)

content word—an item from one of the open classes in the lexicon: nouns, verbs, adjectives and adverbs (cf. *function word*)

contrastive analysis—an approach to the study of language in which those units that are used to produce contrasts in meaning are identified. This process is used, for example, to identify the phonemes in a child's phonological system

coreferential—referring to the same entity. For example, the phrases: 'the man in the black suit', 'John Smith' and 'him' are coreferential in: 'The man in the black suit is John Smith. You'll like him.'

cranial nerves and nuclei—nerves arising in the brain stem from within the cranium (skull). Conventionally numbered I–XII, the nerves are responsible for all the major sensory and motor functions of the head and neck including vision, smell, taste, hearing and speech

critical period—a period during which an organism has to receive appropriate stimulation if development is to proceed normally

CT scan—computerized transaxial tomography

scanning. A noninvasive method which uses X-rays to produce images of the brain

decibel—a unit on a logarithmic scale which measures the intensity of sounds. In a pure tone audiogram the hearing loss on each of the frequencies sampled is expressed in terms of the decibel increase in sound required to make a signal audible. As a rough guide, one may say that for a person with normal hearing, the threshold is at 0 dB, whispered speech is heard at 30 dB above threshold, a conversational voice at 60 dB above threshold, and a shout at 90 dB above threshold

deictic terms/deixis—terms such as 'me' and 'you', 'here' and 'there', 'this' and 'that', 'yesterday' and 'tomorrow', for which the referent depends on the situation of the utterance. (See Ch. 1, p. 18)

derivational morphology—formation of new words by addition of meaningful affixes, or *derivational morphemes*, e.g. a + moral → amoral; a + sexual → asexual; non + nuclear → non-nuclear. Some derivational morphemes change the grammatical class of words to which they are affixed, e.g. pure + ify → purify; simple + ify → simplify; accept + ance → acceptance

dichotic listening—an experimental procedure in which competing auditory messages are fed simultaneously to both ears. The task has been used to provide an index of cerebral lateralization

discourse—a stretch of conversation or written language extending beyond a single sentence

distinctive features—features that distinguish two phonemes. Some phonemes are distinguished by a single feature, others by several features. The initial sounds in 'tow' and 'sew' are distinguished by the distinctive feature of manner of articulation (plosive versus fricative), whereas the initial sound in 'tow' is distinguished from the initial sound in 'go' by two features (place of articulation and voicing)

dyad—term used to describe a pair of people who are interacting

dyadic—describing interaction between two persons. (Also triad/triadic to refer to three persons in interaction)

dysarthria—articulatory difficulty caused by weakness, inco-ordination or paralysis of the speech musculature. This definition is sometimes expanded to include speech problems caused by structural defects of the speech apparatus

edematous—swollen

EEG—Electro-encephalography—a technique that monitors the electrical activity of the brain by recording on paper impulses picked up by electrodes applied to different areas of the skull. The technique is used to help diagnose epilepsy. (See also *evoked responses*)

effusion—an escape of fluid (not necessarily containing bacteria) into body tissues or cavities. (See also *purulent*)

electromyography—recordings of electrical activity from muscle fibres to measure muscle activity

etiology—the origin or cause of a condition or disease

evoked responses—technique devised to investigate functioning of sensory systems and brain function. A stimulus is presented and the electrical activity of the brain is monitored to detect changes that correlate with stimulus presentation, thereby indicating the status of the sensory system. The technique is used to test hearing and vision in children too young or disabled to co-operate in behavioural testing

filtered speech—recorded speech that has been treated so that some bands of frequencies have been removed. As the amount of filtering is increased perceptible distortions begin to occur, but normally hearing individuals can tolerate some filtering without intelligibility being affected

fine motor skills—manipulative skills of the hands and fingers (cf. *gross motor skills*)

formant—a narrow band of acoustic energy,

which appears as a horizontal stripe on a *spectrogram*. Each vowel sound has a characteristic pattern of formants

formant transitions—transitions occur as articulators move from one position to another moving the energy concentrations from one frequency band to another. The result is distinctive perceptual qualities

fricative—a sound made by bringing two articulators close together without forming a complete closure, so that friction occurs as air passes through the vocal tract, e.g. initial sound in 'fat', 'see'

functor—see *function word*

function word (functor)—a word whose role in a sentence is to indicate a grammatical relationship, rather than to convey semantic content. Roughly equivalent to items from closed sets, such as pronouns, prepositions, verbal auxiliaries and determiners. (cf. *content word*)

fundamental frequency—in speech, the rate of vibration of the vocal folds, which determines the pitch of the voice

glossing—interpreting the meaning of an utterance

glottal stop—sound made by stopping the air stream and releasing it at the *glottis*

glottis—the space between the vocal folds

grades—in the US educational system, a group of pupils working together in the same year. Grades range from grade 1 in the first year of elementary school, usually begun at age 6, to grade 12 for the last year of high school, usually completed at age 18. The correspondence between age and grade is not perfect, as gifted children may skip a grade, whereas slow learners may repeat a grade

grapheme—the minimal contrastive unit in the writing system of a language. Also defined as a letter or letter group corresponding to a phoneme

grammatical morphemes—morphemes which serve a predominantly grammatical rather than a semantic function. This class includes inflections denoting contrasts such as past and present tense, singular and plural, comparative and absolute, as well as articles, auxiliary verbs and prepositions. (See Ch. 1, p. 15)

gross motor skills—control of large muscles concerned with balance and whole body movements such as walking and hopping (cf. *fine motor skills*)

haptic—relating to the sense of touch

hemiplegia—motor paralysis affecting the left or right side of the body

holophrase/holophrastic—a term describing a grammatically unstructured utterance in the earliest stage of language learning, consisting of a single word e.g. more, there, 'allgone', which is taken to represent a whole sentence where the other elements are understood from context and non-verbal behaviour

hydrocephalus—an excess of cerebrospinal fluid inside the skull due to an obstruction to normal circulation of the fluid. Surgical intervention is usually required to create drainage so that pressure in the skull does not result in brain damage

hyperbilirubinemia—excessive *bilirubin* in the blood, found in jaundice of the newborn

hyperlexia—surprisingly well-developed and precocious ability to read written text, in the context of impairment of other mental functions. There may be an obsessive quality to reading, with a tendency to read aloud any written material that is encountered. Comprehension of what is read is invariably poor

hypotonia—reduced muscle tone

iconicity (adj. *iconic*)—in sign language, the tendency for signs to resemble in form some aspect of what they denote. For example, in American Sign Language, the sign for BIRD is made with the thumb and index finger in front of the mouth resembling the movement of the beak of a bird. In the sign for TREE, the arm and hand supposedly represent the trunk and branches of a tree

illocutionary act—the social function which the speaker intends to communicate. Also referred to as the *illocutionary force* of an utterance. (See Ch. 1, p. 19)

imagery—elicitation of a visual image by a word, or use of visual images in memory

inflection—a word ending attached to a word stem that expresses a grammatical relationship: e.g. plural -s. See also *grammatical morpheme*

intervocalic—between vowels

intonation—the pattern of pitch changes produced by a speaker saying a phrase

ipsilateral—on the same side

kinesthesis—the muscle sense of movement

labials—consonant made with the lips

lexicon—mental dictionary or word store

magnetic resonance imaging—a noninvasive brain-imaging technique which gives a much higher level of contrast between grey and white matter than *CT scan*

manual language—see *sign language*

memory span—the maximum number of verbal items (usually digits) that a person can repeat back immediately after hearing them

metalinguistic awareness—ability to think about and reflect on language, its structure, function and nature. For example the ability to recognise that some words sound the same even though meanings are unrelated, that words and non-words can be created by permuting initial phonemes on a common stem, awareness of dialectal variation

microcephaly—a condition in which there is defective development of the brain and the head is abnormally small

mixing—production of utterances containing elements from two different languages

morpheme—the most basic element of meaning, which cannot be analyzed into simpler elements. See also *grammatical morpheme*

morphology—the study of the underlying structure of words and their decomposition into elements of minimum meaning, or *morphemes*

Motherese—term used to describe the variety of a language that mothers typically use to their children. Over 100 characteristics have been described, including high frequency of questions, repetition and redundancy. In general Motherese contains short, well-formed utterances, delivered slowly with exaggerated intonation, increasing in complexity as children get older

myelination—process whereby nerves become covered in a sheath of fatty substance called myelin, which improves the efficiency of nerves as conductors

nasal—a sound in which there is a closure in the oral cavity, and the soft palate is lowered allowing air to escape through the nose, e.g. initial sound in 'man', 'nice'

nativist—theoretical approach identified with Noam Chomsky that stresses the inborn rather than acquired characteristics of an individual

nominal—a noun or noun phrase

nuclei (adj = nuclear)—accumulations of nerve cells in the central nervous system associated with a particular function: in the sensory pathways to the brain interconnections between nerve cells occur at nuclei in the brainstem

nystagmus—involuntary and jerky movement of the eyeballs

organ of Corti—the sense organ of hearing, situated in the cochlea

overextension—the use of a word in a more general sense than that adopted by adults, as when a child refers to all four-legged animals as 'doggie'

percentile score (centile score)—score expressed in terms of the percentage of the normal population obtaining a score at or below that level. E.g. if a person scores at the 20th percentile, this means that 20% of the normal population would be expected to score at or below that level, and, conversely, 80% would score above that level

perceptive hearing loss—see *sensorineural hearing loss*

perinatal hypoxia—diminished amount of oxygen in the tissues during the process of birth

pharynx—portion of vocal tract behind the tonsils, above the larynx and below the opening to the nose in the throat

phonation—production of voice by vibration of the vocal cords

phone—a phonetic unit or segment. Phones are defined in terms of phonetic characteristics rather than ability to signal contrasts in meaning (cf. *phoneme*)

phoneme—the smallest segment of sound that can be distinguished by its contrast within words. (See Ch. 1, p. 11)

phonetic inventory—list of speech sounds employed in the speech of a single speaker

phonetics—the study of articulatory and acoustic specification of speech sounds

phonological process—the substitution of an alternative class for a class of sounds or sound sequences. The substituted class is identical except in those features presenting a specific difficulty to the speech capacity of the individual. (See Ch. 1, p. 13)

phonology—the study of how speech sounds function to signal contrasts in meaning in a language. (See Ch. 1, p. 11)

phrase—a term used in grammatical analysis for a part of a sentence, containing one or more words but without the subject-predicate structure of a clause. There are different kinds of phrases: adverbial ('in the street', 'before the war'), verb phrase ('didn't want', 'should have been'), noun phrase ('the big man'), and adjectival ('nice and sweet')

plosive (also referred to as *stop*)—a speech sound made by a complete closure at some point in the vocal tract. Air is compressed behind this closure, and then abruptly released

posterior fossa—hollow at the base of the rear of the skull which houses the cerebellum

pragmatics—the study of how utterances are used to convey meaning in different social and environmental contexts. (See Ch. 1, p. 19)

prelinguistic—before the child is producing spoken language

preoperational period—in Piagetian theory, a stage of mental development corresponding very roughly to 2 to 7 years of age, in which the child can deal mentally with objects and events that are distant in both time and space, but there is a tendency to focus on only a limited amount of information in a situation, and a corresponding limitation in the ability to perceive relationships

prevalence—number of instances of a given condition in a given population at a specified time

prognosis—prediction of the course of a disease or condition

pronoun reversal—use of 'you' to refer to the self, and 'I' or 'me' to refer to others

prosody—the *suprasegmental* aspects of phonology

prospective study—research study that involves identifying a population who are followed over time with the aim of contrasting those who develop a disease or other condition and contrasting them with those who remain unaffected

psychomotor—relating to the mental origin of muscular movements, to the production of voluntary movements

purulent—relating to or resembling pus, i.e. a liquid containing bacteria secreted during infections. (See also *effusion*)

quadriplegia—motor paralysis of all four limbs

raw score—an untransformed score, e.g. in

terms of number of items correct (cf. *scaled score*)

reaction time—time taken to react to a stimulus, usually under experimental conditions. Reaction times vary with the complexity of the intervening mental processes

receptive aphasia—language impairment in which comprehension is affected. Usually used to refer to an acquired disorder associated with brain damage, but sometimes also used for children with selective comprehension problems, normal nonverbal abilities and no history of brain damage

reference—the relationship between words and the things that they stand for. *Referent*—the 'thing' or 'quality' that a word or phrase refers to

relative clause—a type of subordinate clause which acts as a post-modifier within the structure of a noun phrase, often introduced by a relative pronoun such as 'that', 'who' or 'which', e.g. 'the man *who came yesterday*'

resonance—vibrations in the walls of cavities that enhance the quality and duration of a sound. Oral and nasal cavities act as resonators for the human voice

reticular formation—a diffuse arrangement of neurons in the brainstem that receives input from most of the sensory systems and plays an important role in regulating arousal states

retrospective study—a research design used to test etiologic hypotheses by comparing characteristics and past experiences of individuals who have a disease or condition with those who do not

scaled score—a linear transformation of a *standard score*, designed to result in all scores being expressed as whole, positive numbers. The best known example of a scaled score is the deviation IQ, in which scores are represented in terms of a population mean of 100 and standard deviation of 15. Thus an IQ of 130 corresponds to a score two standard deviations above the mean, and one of 85 to a score one standard deviation below the mean

semantic relations—aspects of meaning determined by the relationship of words within a sentence. (See Ch. 1, p. 17)

semantics—the study of meaning. (See Ch. 1, p. 17)

semiotic—having a signalling or symbolic function

sensorimotor—having to do with control of voluntary movement, and the sensations involved in control of movement (i.e. touch, joint position sense)

sensorimotor period—in Piagetian theory, a stage of development covering the period from birth to approximately 18–24 months, during which infants acquire knowledge by acting on their surroundings, manipulating the objects around them and noting the sensory consequences

sensorineural hearing loss (perceptive hearing loss)—hearing impairment caused by any affection of the perceiving apparatus, i.e. the cochlea (sensory) or the auditory nerve (neural) (cf. *conductive hearing loss*)

serous—containing, secreting or resembling watery fluid

short-term memory—part of the memory system that can retain a limited amount of information for a brief period of time with the aid of rehearsal

sign language—language that uses manual gestures rather than sounds. Natural sign languages (e.g. American Sign Language, British Sign Language) have their own syntax, morphology, and semantics, quite distinct from spoken languages. In contrast, artificial sign languages (e.g. Signed English, Paget Gorman Sign System) are not true languages in their own right, but are designed to represent spoken languages in signed form

sociolinguistics—a branch of linguistics that studies the relationship between language and society including social attitudes to language, and language use in relation to social situations and to social relationships

sonograph—see *spectrogram*

spectrogram (also spectrograph/sonograph)—an acoustic analysis of the properties of speech sounds in which the distribution of sound energy across speech frequencies is represented as a function of time. (See Ch. 14, p. 226)

speech act—the act performed in making an utterance. (See Ch. 1, p. 19)

speech blocks—a symptom of *stuttering*. The speaker is unable to continue speaking and the speech organs exhibit tension

stammering—see *stuttering*

standard score (z-score)—a score expressed in terms of how many standard deviations that score deviates from the population mean. Where the population mean is M, and the population standard deviation is S, then a *raw score,* X, corresponds to a standard score $z = (X - M)/S$. Standard scores have the advantage that they make it possible to compare results from different age groups, and across different tests on a common scale. See also *scaled score*

standardized test—a test for which the level and range of performance in a normal population have been established, making it possible to express *raw scores* as *standard scores*

strabismus—squint

striate cortex—an area of cortex at the back of the brain concerned with processing of visual input

stuttering (stammering)—a speech impairment in which fluency is disrupted by involuntary hesitations, repetitions and prolongations of words or parts of words. The speaker is capable of fluent speech under certain conditions. See also *speech blocks*

subtractive bilingualism—learning of a second language at the expense of a first language. Frequently brought about when schooling and upward social mobility depends on success in the second language

suprasegmental—concerned with aspects of phonology above the level of the individual segment, i.e. stress, tone, length and intonation

syntax—a system of rules which accounts for the ways in which different parts of speech may be legitimately combined to form sentences in a language. (See Ch. 1, p. 14)

telegrammatic speech (telegraphic speech)—speech that resembles the style typically used for economy in telegrams. *Content words* and word order are preserved but *function words* and *grammatical morphemes* are omitted

total communication—a method of communication used in the education of the deaf. Manual, auditory and oral systems of communication are used simultaneously to give as much information as possible about an utterance. The manual communication may be finger spelling and/or signs

trachea—windpipe

transparency—the extent to which relationships between meaning and language form are straightforward and readily detectable. The opposite is *opacity*. Transparency is high when there are consistent one-to-one mappings between meaning and sequences of sound

underextension—use of a word in an overrestricted fashion, e.g. use of the term 'dog' to refer only to one type of dog

velar plosives—consonant sounds made by stopping the oral airstream at the the velum (soft palate) by contact with the back of the tongue, followed by an explosive release. E.g. initial sounds in 'go', 'car'

velopharyngeal—in the area of the soft palate (velum) and the pharynx; refers to the space between the back of the throat and the mouth. When the soft palate is raised, the passage through the nose is cut off. The soft palate and the pharyngeal wall together are called the velopharyngeal sphincter

verbal auxiliary—term used in the grammatical description of the verb phrase to refer to nonlexical verbs, subordinate to the main verb, that help to make distinctions in mood, voice and aspect. In English the auxiliaries are: do, be, have, can/could, may/might, shall/should, will/would, must, ought, used to

verb inflections—affixes to verbs that signal plural and change of tense, e.g. walks, walked

visuo-spatial—term to describe motor and perceptual abilities or tasks involving visually perceived stimuli, patterned in space, e.g. recognizing and copying shapes drawn on paper

voice quality—perceived characteristics of phonation, e.g. hoarse, strident, breathy

Wernicke's area—area in temporo-parietal cortex of the left hemisphere, damage to which results in impairment of language comprehension. (See Ch. 13, p. 204)

WH-question—question introduced by question word such as 'who', 'what', 'which', 'how', which requires a response containing specific information, rather than just 'yes' or 'no'

word association—experimental task used to explore the relationships between words. Word associations are elicited by instructions to say or write 'the first word that comes into your head' after another word is given

working memory—a postulated component of the memory system, thought by some to be identical to short-term memory, used to hold crucial information in temporary store while mental operations are carried out

yes-no question—a question, usually signalled by inversion of the subject and auxiliary verb, which requires 'yes' or 'no' as an answer, e.g. 'did you go out last night?'

z-score—see *standard score*

1

Language development in unexceptional circumstances

K. Mogford & D. Bishop

When psychologists first attempted the task of describing the pattern and course of language development in young children, they used a number of common-sense measures to record observable changes in language behaviour at different ages. McCarthy (1930), for example, in a study of children aged from 2 to 5 years, measured the length of children's sentences, the frequency of different parts of speech, the number of words in a child's vocabulary, and the proportion of speech that was used for social and non-social purposes. The picture of language development that emerged was one of gradual increase in verbal skill as children added new items to their language repertoire, reducing the number of errors in their speech, and gradually narrowing the gap between their imperfect imitations and the adult models to which they were exposed. In the early 1960s, however, the study of child language was transformed in conception and approach under the influence of linguists, who argued that research on language acquisition had largely ignored developments in linguistics, and had, as a result, been quite inadequate at portraying the nature of the task that faced children acquiring language.

Methods of linguistic analysis and description had already been applied to different aspects of child language in diary studies of individual children (Leopold 1939, 1947, 1949a, 1949b, Velten 1943), but these were not widely known nor easily comparable with the psychological descriptions. When psychologists began to adopt linguistic methods, the hybrid discipline of developmental psycholinguistics was born, and a different picture of language development began to take shape. To a linguist, one of the most fundamental notions about language is that it is a system organized in a regular and predictable way such that it is possible to write a set of rules that describes the regularities of the system. Rather than documenting verbal errors, which gradually decrease with age, linguists approached children just as they would approach speakers of a hitherto unknown language, treating their verbal productions as evidence of a language system susceptible to linguistic analysis and description. This approach to language acquisition meant that the process could then be described as a series of structural changes within a system that could be inferred from observing and recording the child's attempts to understand and express meaning through language. There are a number of different levels on which the system may be said to be organized, each dealing with a different unit of analysis. These are *phonology, grammar, semantics,* and *pragmatics.*

PHONOLOGY

Phonology is the study of how speech sounds function to signal contrasts in meaning in a language. Our familiarity with English orthography tends to make us think of speech sounds as discrete and immutable segments: thus we learn that there are three sounds in 'pat', and the same three sounds occur in a different order in 'apt' and 'tap'. Only when we study other languages do we learn that the way in which we classify speech sounds is not universal. For example, there are articulatory differences in how English speakers usually produce stop sounds (such as the 'p' sound), depending on whether the sound occurs as a single consonant (as in 'pat') or in a syllable-initial consonant cluster (as in 'spat'). A stop preceding a vowel is usually produced with a puff of air (aspiration), except when in a

cluster. However, in some languages (e.g. Thai and Hindi) the two variants of stop sounds (aspirated and unaspirated) can both occur at the start of words, but the meaning of the word will depend on which is used. Thus, for the speaker of Thai, there is just as much difference between an aspirated and unaspirated stop as there is for the English speaker between a pair of sounds such as /b/ and /p/. Conversely, English distinguishes between some sounds that are treated as a single sound in other languages. There is, for example, no distinction between /r/ and /l/ in Japanese.

Ladefoged (1975) defines *phonemes* as the smallest segments of sound that can be distinguished by their contrast within words. In English, 'pat' and 'bat', or 'cap' and 'cab' are different words: therefore we regard /p/ and /b/ as different phonemes. However, 'pat' is perceived as the same word, regardless of whether it is produced with an aspirated or unaspirated initial stop: therefore the aspirated and unaspirated forms of /p/ are treated as different versions of the same phoneme.

Table 1.1 Phonetic symbols used for phonemes: Received Pronunciation

Consonants	Vowels
/p/ as in *pill*	/i/ as in *see*
/b/ as in *bill*	/ɪ/ as in *sit*
/t/ as in *till*	/ɛ/ as in *set*
/d/ as in *dill*	/a/ as in *sat*
/k/ as in *kill*	/ɑ/ as in *calm*
/g/ as in *gall*	/ɒ/ as in *not*
/m/ as in *men*	/ɔ/ as in *taut*
/n/ as in *net*	/ʊ/ as in *put*
/ŋ/ as in *long*	/u/ as in *boot*
/f/ as in *fail*	/ʌ/ as in *duck*
/v/ as in *veil*	/ɜ/ as in *bird*
/θ/ as in *think*	/ə/ as in *about*
/ð/ as in *though*	/eɪ/ as in *play*
/s/ as in *sail*	/ʊ/ as in *no*
/z/ as in *zoo*	/aɪ/ as in *my*
/ʃ/ as in *show*	/aʊ/ as in *cow*
/ʒ/ as in *measure*	/ɔɪ/ as in *coil*
/tʃ/ as in *church*	/ɪə/ as in *here*
/dʒ/ as in *gem*	/ɛə/ as in *there*
/l/ as in *line*	/uə/ as in *cruel*
/r/ as in *right*	
/w/ as in *will*	
/j/ as in *yet*	
/h/ as in *hat*	

Note that the phoneme is an abstract unit, defined according to how sounds affect meaning, and not just in terms of acoustic and articulatory characteristics. *Phonology*, the study of sound patterns of language, may be contrasted with *phonetics*, which is concerned with articulatory and acoustic specification of speech sounds.

The phonemes used in the standard form of English spoken in Great Britain (known as Received Pronunciation) may be grouped into 24 consonant and 20 vowel sounds, as shown in Table 1.1. The main phonological difference between Received Pronunciation and other dialects and varieties of English is in the vowel system (see Hughes & Trudgill 1979 for an account of English dialects used within the UK, and Ladefoged 1975 for an introduction to American/British differences).

Early studies of articulatory development

How do children learn the phonological system of their native tongue? Early studies in this field concentrated on motor proficiency in speech sound production. These studies documented which sounds were within a child's repertoire at different ages. In English, for example, it was noted that plosives and nasals were among the first consonants to appear, with fricatives, affricates and clusters developing later. Table 1.2 shows the ages of acquisition given by Berry & Eisenson (1956) for different phonemes.

These early studies did not pay much regard to how children used sounds meaningfully, their concern being principally with *articulation*. Whilst an articulation analysis classifies sounds produced by children according to whether the sound is phonetically accurate in terms of the adult system, a phonological analysis is concerned with how a child uses sounds to convey distinctions in meaning. To illustrate this point, consider three hypothetical children: Adam pronounces 'cup' as 'tup', 'cake' as 'cake', 'take' as 'cake', and 'time' as 'time'. Ben pronounces all these words correctly. Both children can articulate [t] and [k], but Adam, unlike Ben, does not make a phonemic distinction between these sounds, so both 'cake' and 'take' are pronounced the same. A third child, Chris, uses the non-English sound [x] in some contexts where [k] would be expected: 'cup' is pronounced correctly, 'cake' is [xeix] and 'take' is [teix]. Chris would be identified as making articulatory errors on a classic articulatory analysis, and his speech would undoubtedly sound odd, but a phonological analysis would show that he does maintain a consistent distinction between sounds which correspond to different phonemes in English.

The contribution of Jakobson

An important breakthrough in the conceptualization of development of speech sound production was Jakobson's 'Kindersprache, Aphasie, und allgemeine Lautgesetze', published in 1941 and translated into English in 1968. Jakobson adopted a phonological framework, studying children's language just as a linguist would approach a new foreign language. Thus he looked for regularities in the sounds and sound patterns used by young children, concentrating not on listing which sounds the child could produce, but on documenting which sounds the child treated as distinctive in signalling meaning. He concluded that children build up a repertoire of phonemes by a series of binary splits. First the child would make a broad distinction between consonants and vowels (but would not initially distinguish between sounds within either of these categories). Each of these classes would then be progressively subdivided: for example, a common pattern would be for consonants to be divided early on into nasal and non-

Table 1.2 Age of articulatory efficiency of 22 consonant sounds (after Berry & Eisenson 1956)

Age	Sounds mastered
by $3\frac{1}{2}$	b p m w h
by $4\frac{1}{2}$	d t n g k ŋ j
by $5\frac{1}{2}$	f
by $6\frac{1}{2}$	v ðʃʒ l
by $7\frac{1}{2}$	s z r θ

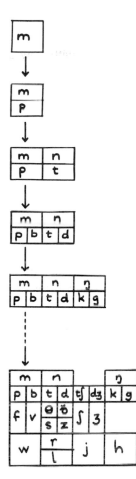

Fig. 1.1 Postulated stages in the development of a system of contrasts between English consonants

Menn 1985). Nevertheless, his work remains an important influence, and has led to a fruitful line of investigation into development of speech sounds in children, moving away from phonetic error analysis to consider the phonological systems of young children.

Phonological processes

Space prohibits a comprehensive review of theories and research in this area (see Grunwell 1982), and forces us to restrict consideration of later work to one particularly influential theory. This is Stampe's (1969) proposal that children's developing phonology should be described in terms of simplifying processes, affecting whole groups of sounds rather than single phonemes, and determined by ease of articulation. For example, Stampe maintained that young English-speaking children can perceive the distinction between velar stops (/k/ and /g/) and alveolar stops (/t/ and /d/), and their internal representations of words differing on this distinction would not be the same. However, because alveolar sounds are easier

Table 1.3 Phonological processes commonly observed in child language (from Grunwell 1982)

Process	target word	child's production
weak syllable deletion	banana	['nɑnɑ]
	pyjamas	['dɑməd]
final consonant deletion	juice	[du]
	bed	[bɛ]
reduplication	bottle	['bɒbɒ]
	pudding	['pʊpʊ]
assimilation (consonant harmony)	dog	[gɒg]
	neck	[nɛk]
cluster reduction	plate	[peɪt]
	drum	[dʌm]
fronting (velar → alveolar)	girl	[dɜl]
	cup	[tʌp]
stopping (fricative → plosive)	face	[peɪt]
	shoes	[dud]
gliding	red	[wɛd]
	telly	['tɛjɪ]
context-sensitive voicing	party	['bɑdi]
	peg	[bɛk]

nasal, later divisions being based on contrasts corresponding to different places of articulation (lips, alveolar ridge, or velum). Jakobson's theory likens phonological development to embryological development: an initial undifferentiated sound class subdivides into two: each of these subdivides further, this process being repeated until a fully differentiated system is arrived at (see Fig. 1.1).

Later workers have questioned many of Jakobson's conclusions, particularly insofar as he proposed that the order of acquisition of contrasts was consistent across different languages, and consistent for all children (e.g.

to produce, a *process* of 'fronting' operates, affecting velars as a class, so that 'cup' is pronounced as 'tup', and 'girl' as 'dirl'. This is an example of a process which involves substituting one type of sound for another. Other processes involve the influence of one sound upon another within the same word. Thus there is a tendency to maintain the same place of articulation for successive segments, so that articulation of one consonant is affected by the phonological context in which it occurs. A child who can pronounce /t/ accurately in 'table' may pronounce 'kettle' as 'kekkle' because of the influence from the preceding consonant (a process known as *'assimilation'*). The influence may also operate in the opposite direction, as when 'doggie' becomes 'goggie'. Table 1.3 lists processes that are commonly found in the language of young children.

Perception of phonemic contrasts

Over the years there has been much debate as to whether the order of acquisition of speech sounds is determined by perceptual factors, ease of articulation, or both or neither of these. As we have noted, process theory regards ease of articulation as the most important determinant of phonological development, but there is little direct evidence for this.

Many investigators have dismissed the notion that perceptual factors are important in determining acquisition on the grounds that even very young infants are well able to discriminate speech sounds differing by a single distinctive feature (see Aslin et al 1983 for a review). However, it is a large step from being able to discriminate two speech sounds to perceiving them as distinct phonemes. The perceptual challenge for children learning a language is not just that of discriminating different sounds: they must also learn to categorize sounds so they know which sounds to treat as variants of the same phoneme, and which as distinct phonemes capable of signalling a difference in meaning (Kuhl 1986).

Methodological problems inherent in studying phonemic perception limit our understanding of those factors which determine order of acquisition in normal children, let alone in abnormal populations (see Yeni-Komshian et al 1980). It seems likely that visual as well as auditory characteristics of speech sounds are implicated, and that children make use of lip-read as well as auditory information in learning a phonological system (Dodd 1987b).

Suprasegmental phonology

So far, we have concentrated on the development of ability to produce and perceive individual phonemes or speech segments: this is the domain of *segmental* phonology. Another branch of phonology is concerned with the analysis of larger units: this is known as *suprasegmental* phonology. The principal suprasegmental features are stress, length, tone and intonation. These *prosodic* aspects of language are often thought of as relatively minor and unimportant, but ability to perceive and produce prosodic features appropriately is crucial for effective communication. Prosodic features can convey a distinction in meaning (e.g. 'green house' vs. 'greenhouse'), indicate the speaker's emotional attitude (interested, bored, frightened, and so forth), specify the speaker's intention (e.g. making a statement vs. asking a question), and indicate which parts of an utterance convey new information (compare 'JOHN is coming with us' vs. 'John is coming with US') (Cutler & Fodor 1979).

GRAMMAR: SYNTAX AND MORPHOLOGY

The linguist's conception of grammar is very different from the layman's. To many people, 'grammar' refers to a prescriptive set of rules for correct language, such as the rule that states it is wrong to insert an adverb between the two parts of an infinitive (e.g. 'to boldly go'). Such rules generate much emotive debate, but often bear little relationship to natural usage of language (see Crystal 1984). When linguists talk about grammatical rules (or indeed linguistic rules generally), they are not concerned with setting a standard of usage to be attained. The rules they talk of *describe* regularities in how sentences are organized, rather than *prescribing* what kinds of structure are right or wrong. Furthermore, when a linguist says that, for example, in English there is a rule which determines how an active sentence is transformed into a corresponding passive sentence, this does not imply that speakers have any conscious awareness of this rule. Rules describe regularities in linguistic behaviour of which speakers are often unaware. For example, native speakers of English have no difficulty in deciding that 'He should have been gone long ago', 'Shouldn't he have gone long ago?', 'Has he been gone long?' are grammatical sentences, whilst 'He have should been gone long ago', 'Should he haven't gone long ago?' and 'Has been he gone long?' are ungrammatical. However, few readers without a background in linguistics would find it easy to state any general rule which describes positional restrictions on the occurrence of auxiliaries in English. *Syntax* is concerned with formulating rules to account for the ways in which different parts of speech may be legitimately combined to form sentences in a language.

Morphology is the study of the underlying structure of words and their decomposition into elements of minimum meaning, or *morphemes*. Thus 'excite' consists of one morpheme, 'exciting' of two morphemes ('excite' and 'ing'), 'unexciting' of three morphemes, and so on. Inflectional morphemes serve a grammatical function and are used in English to denote such contrasts as between past and present tense, singular and plural, comparative and absolute. Other grammatical morphemes include articles, auxiliary verbs and prepositions.

Confusion can arise in this field because there is some variability in how linguistic terms are used in the study of language acquisition. Some authors use 'syntax' when referring to development of inflectional morphology as well as rules of word order. Also, strictly speaking, *morphology* encompasses all aspects of word formation, but in the context of language development the term is often used as a shorthand for inflectional morphology.

How do children learn grammar?

Early investigations of children's learning of grammar involved simple counts of sentence length, number of words of different types, and proportions of grammatical and non-grammatical sentences. Studies such as those of McCarthy (1930) and Gesell and his colleagues (1950) established that, not surprisingly, utterance length increases with age, as does the proportion of sentences conforming to adult grammar. What was not understood was how children progressed from the earliest single word utterances to full adult competence. Do young children just emit words at random? Do they perhaps imitate those sentence elements that are most frequent or most stressed in adult speech? Psycholinguistic studies, beginning with the pioneering work on acquisition of English by Roger Brown (1973), make it clear that the young child does not just reproduce arbitrary fragments of adult language. Even in the earliest combinations of two words, there is order and regularity in children's utterances, both in terms of the types of words produced and in the order in which they are combined. The earliest accounts of child language attempted to account for this regularity purely in grammatical terms, by specifying broad classes of words and documenting the sorts of combinations of these that did and did not occur. Dissatisfaction with this approach led to the view that one could not capture the regularities of children's first word combinations purely in grammatical terms. Meaning was also important (Bloom 1970). If we were to write a grammar for the child, taking into account only features like word classes and word order, then we would have to assign the same grammatical structure to sentences like 'Daddy car', said by a child who saw her daddy's car, and 'Daddy car' uttered by a child who wanted Daddy to give her a toy car. This seems unsatisfactory, as the context indicates that the child intends different meanings by the two utterances, the first being interpreted as 'Daddy's car', whilst the second means 'Daddy give me the car'. Bloom argued that in formulating a grammar for the child we need to represent these different meanings, and assign a different underlying structure to sentence pairs like these, on the basis of our interpretation of the child's meaning. We will return to this point below, in the section on semantic relations.

As children's utterances increase in length, their productions can be described in terms of a simplified grammar which becomes increasingly complex as the child matures. The rule-governed nature of children's early utterances becomes particularly apparent when we trace the development of particular sentence types in English, such as negatives and questions. Children go through a stage of producing forms which are not mere contractions of adult forms: e.g. there is a point at which negation is expressed by sentence forms such as 'I no want it' or 'no wipe finger', and question forms may lack the inversion of subject and auxiliary verb, e.g. 'what you are doing?', 'where he is going?' (see Tager-Flusberg 1985 for a review).

Further evidence that children are learning rules rather than merely imitating parts of adult utterances emerges from the study of grammatical morphemes. As children learn to produce inflectional endings, they often over-generalize these inappropriately to irregular words; so we hear phrases such as 'two mouses', and 'I goed'. As they do not hear these forms in adult speech, we can infer that children have learned a basic rule such as 'attach -s to noun to form plural' and 'attach -ed to verb stem to signal past tense'.

Increase in grammatical complexity

As children mature, the grammatical complexity of their utterances increases in many different ways. These have been documented in some detail in an assessment procedure published by Crystal et al (1976). The sorts of changes that occur are:

1. An increase in use of grammatical morphemes (see de Villiers & de Villiers (1973) for data on order of acquisition of different grammatical morphemes).
2. An increase in average phrase length, achieved by inclusion of determiners (e.g. the, a, this) and adjectives in noun phrases, and expansion of verb phrases to include verbal auxiliaries (have, be, do, can, should, etc.).
3. Number of elements in a clause increases gradually from one element (e.g. 'dog'), to two elements (e.g. Subject + Verb: 'big dog bite'), then three elements (e.g. Verb + Object + Adverbial: 'see mummy in garden'), and subsequently increasing to four elements and more.
4. Both phrases and clauses are expanded by processes of co-ordination and postmodi-fication: e.g. co-ordinated clauses: 'Jane came to my house and we made cakes'; postmodifying phrase: 'find the ship *with the flag*'; postmodifying clause: 'I got the one *that you gave me*'.
5. An entire subordinate clause can act as a single element in a main clause: e.g. 'Can I come with you *when you go to the shops?*'

Most children are using co-ordinated and subordinated clauses by 4 years of age, with full mastery of most basic sentence types of English by the age of 5 (Wells 1985).

Comprehension of grammatical structure

Expressive language ability can be studied simply by tape-recording and analyzing a child's speech. Discovering which grammati-cal structures the child does and does not understand is much more complicated, and involves setting up situations which allow one to test for comprehension of the contrast in meaning between two or more grammatical forms. An ingenious study by Fraser et al (1963) used a technique in which the child was presented with pairs of pictures depicting a particular contrast (see Fig. 1.2), and asked to point to the picture that corresponded to a particular sentence. They found that, in

Fig. 1.2 Item used to test imitation, comprehension and production of grammatical contrasts. Reproduced with permission from Fraser et al (1963): 'The sheep is jumping' vs. 'The sheep are jumping'

general, ability to comprehend a contrast preceded ability to use that contrast appropriately in expressive language. The multiple choice technique that they used has been adopted in many clinical tests of language comprehension (Lee 1971, Carrow 1975). An alternative approach to the study of comprehension has involved asking children to act out commands with toys or other objects. Bever (1970), for example, studied children's comprehension of the active/passive distinction by giving the child a set of toy animals and asking them to 'make the horse kiss the cow', 'make the horse be kissed by the cow', and so on. One thing that has emerged from such studies is that the grammatical structure of the test sentence is not the only factor to affect performance. Plausibility of alternative interpretations plays a crucial role. Children often have response biases to behave in particular ways with objects: it has been shown that children's responses will depend on the toys used (Chapman & Kohn 1978) and on the particular verb in a reversible sentence (Sinclair et al 1971). They may also adopt some general strategy such as picking up the first-named object and using it in the role of agent (Huttenlocher et al 1968).

Techniques for assessing comprehension can be useful for documenting the acquisition of sentence structures that are relatively rare in spontaneous speech, such as 'not only. . . but also', or 'neither. . . nor' constructions. Such studies show that mastery of grammar continues well past the age of 4 years, with some structures continuing to give difficulty

to children aged 8 years or above (Bishop 1983a).

SEMANTICS

Semantics is that branch of linguistics concerned with the study of meaning in language. There has been much debate in linguistics concerning the degree to which grammar and semantics can be studied independently. Chomsky's (1957) famous sentence 'colourless green ideas sleep furiously' was used by him to illustrate the point that a sentence can be judged as grammatically well-formed while being devoid of meaning (cf. 'sleep green ideas furiously colourless', which is neither grammatical nor meaningful).

Semantic relations

However, although a sentence can be grammatical without being meaningful, meaning is not independent of grammar. The grammatical structure of a sentence will determine the semantic relationships between sentence elements, so that in:

John killed Mary

John is 'agent' and Mary is 'patient', whilst in:

Mary killed John

these roles are reversed and the meaning is quite different.

There is no one-to-one correspondence between grammatical roles, such as subject and object, and semantic roles, such as agent and patient. For instance, 'Mary' is grammatical subject but semantic patient in the sentence:

Mary was killed by John

We have already mentioned the work of Bloom (1970), who stimulated interest in the study of semantic relationships expressed in young children's first word combinations. Bloom used the example 'mummy sock' to argue that utterances with the same surface structure were used by the child to express different meanings: e.g. 'mummy's sock', or 'mummy, put my sock on'. She proposed that we could infer these different meanings by studying the context in which the utterance occurred ('rich interpretation' of utterance meaning). Studies using this method have shown that children learning grammar tend to use word order fairly consistently to express the same basic set of semantic relations in their early utterances, as follows:

agent + action: man kick
action + object: drive car
agent + object: Mummy bike
agent + locative: sit chair
entity + locative: cup shelf
possessor + possession: Timmy hat
entity + attribute: ball blue
demonstrative + entity: there car

Brown (1973) noted that children progress from the two-word stage by stringing together two relations and omitting the common word, so that, for example, we get:

'dad kick'   +   'kick ball' → 'dad kick ball'
(agent action) (action object) (agent action object)

Alternatively, one element of a relation is expanded, so that the expansion of an object (e.g. 'helicopter') into possessor + possessed ('my helicopter') results in a sentence such as 'bring my helicopter' (action + possessor + possessed).

Lexical semantics

So far, we have concentrated on analysis of meaning at the level of the sentence. Another branch of semantics is the study of meaning of individual words, or lexis. De Villiers & de Villiers (1978) divide words into four categories according to the complexity of their conditions of use.

1. The simplest level is that of proper names, where there is only one referent for each word. Many of children's first words are proper nouns, like 'Mummy' and 'Daddy'.

2. The next level is that of common nouns, where a word refers to a whole class of objects. With these words children must learn appropriate conditions of usage, and appreciate similarities and distinctions which are often quite subtle, so that they can, for example, refer to a range of animals, big and small, hairy and smooth, as 'dog', distinguishing these from similar animals such as cats, foxes, or goats. Young children do not always learn the meaning of a common noun all at once. They often use words in a way that indicates they have only a partial understanding of their meaning. It is not uncommon for a word like 'dog' to be used in too general a way, to refer to goats, cats and foxes as well as dogs. This has been termed *overextension*. *Underextension* can also occur, as when, for example, a child accepts as 'dog' only one particular breed of dog, or even only one familiar dog, such as the family pet.

3. The next level of complexity includes relational words, such as dimensional adjectives (big, little, tall, short), where correct use depends on reference to some standard.

4. All languages contain terms such as 'me' and 'you', 'here' and 'there', 'this' and 'that', for which the referent depends on the situation of the utterance. These are known as *deictic* terms, and they pose a complex cognitive problem for the child learning to use them: for example, the child is always addressed as 'you' and never as 'I', yet must learn to refer to others as 'you' and to the self as 'I'. One might imagine that these deictic expressions should be among the latest to be acquired by the child, but this is not the case: by the age of 3 children are adept at understanding terms like 'here' and 'there', and the

use of personal pronouns is mastered even earlier than this (de Villiers & de Villiers 1974).

PRAGMATICS

To communicate effectively, the child needs to know far more than just the phonology, grammar, and semantics of a language. Pragmatics covers a huge domain, which may be broadly defined as the appropriate *use* of language in different contexts.

Speech acts

The meaning of an utterance is determined not simply by the meanings of words in the sentence and semantic relationships between them. Part of the meaning is what the speaker achieves in making an utterance, and this will depend not just on the literal meaning of the sentence, but also on the context of that utterance. Hurford & Heasley (1983) illustrate this with the sentence 'there is a piece of fish on the table'. In uttering this sentence, the speaker may be carrying out any one of a variety of different *speech acts*, such as complaining (to a waiter in a restaurant), warning (not to let the cat into the kitchen), or reassuring (one's spouse that there is something for dinner). In each of these cases the *communicative function* of the utterance is different, according to the context of the utterance, even though the sequence of spoken words remains the same.

The relationship between type of speech act and grammatical type of sentence is by no means entirely predictable. In general, it is true that declarative sentences are used to *assert*, interrogative sentences to *ask a question*, and imperatives to *give a command*. However, consider this example:

Lady Hamilton: Would you mind opening the window?

Servant: Yes, of course

If we analyse this pair of utterances purely in syntactic and semantic terms, it seems that we have a standard yes/no question, with a positive reply, which would seem to indicate that the servant would indeed mind opening the window. Yet this exchange does not strike us as odd. What we do is to interpret Lady Hamilton's question not as a request for information but as a command to open the window, to which the servant assents.

Such examples of mismatch between speech act and grammatical category of sentence are by no means uncommon, e.g.:

declarative sentence acting as command:
  (adult to children) 'I'm fed up with your squabbling'

declarative sentence acting as question:
  'I suppose you have lots of people coming to see you'.

Perlocutionary effects and illocutionary acts

In speech act theory, a distinction is made between two types of effect which an utterance can have. A *perlocutionary effect* is the effect the utterance has on others, regardless of the speaker's intention. For example, a teacher may give his class a stern talking to about their disgraceful behaviour, but the effect he has is simply to bore them. A student who says: 'I'm sorry I didn't do the essay, but I was out all night at a party', may intend to mollify his tutor with an apology but succeeds only in making her angry. The perlocutionary effects achieved by these two utterances are to cause boredom and anger, respectively.

In contrast the *illocutionary act* performed by a speaker making an utterance (or the *illocutionary force* of the utterance) is determined by the social function which the speaker intends to communicate. Examples of illocutionary acts include apologizing, complaining, congratulating, condoling, and many others. In the two examples given above, the illocutionary acts performed by the speakers are admonishing and apologizing.

A further distinction may be made between direct and indirect illocutionary acts. In the example of Lady Hamilton and the servant, the direct illocution of Lady Hamilton's utterance is a request for information about how the servant feels about opening the window. The indirect illocution is a command.

Speech act theory and language development

Speech act theory has been applied to language development in several ways. One line of study has been concerned with cataloguing the range of speech acts used by children, the ways in which similar functions are carried out nonverbally in the preverbal children, and the relationship between the two (Bruner 1975a). Even when the child's syntactic abilities are minimal, simple conversational-type exchanges can occur between adult and child. Bates et al (1975) maintained that prior to 10 months of age, the child's impact on others is only perlocutionary. Thus the mother responds to the baby's cries, cooing, and other behaviours, but the child does not behave intentionally to achieve this outcome—although parents often attribute intentions to young infants. By 10 months of age, the infant has become aware of the communicative value of behaviour, and learns to control this. In speech act terminology, the child's behaviour develops illocutionary force. Bates et al further argued that those communicative intentions that are first to be expressed nonverbally are also the first to be realised verbally later in development.

Another line of work has looked at how children learn to use and understand socially acceptable forms of language, such as utterances which perform indirect illocutionary acts. De Villiers & de Villiers (1978) report an unpublished study by Shatz, who looked at the responses of 2- to 4-year-olds to requests from their mothers and found that even the youngest children usually responded appropriately to indirect requests. Bates (1976a) found that the ability to produce simple indirect commands developed around 3 to 4 years of age.

A further branch of research has looked at children's developing ability to modify the way in which they speak according to whom they are with. The analysis above should make it clear that a particular illocution can be made in a variety of ways. Suppose one is with a companion and wants to offer them an ice-cream: one might say: 'Would you like an icecream', 'I was thinking of buying an ice-cream', 'Do you want an ice-cream', 'How would you feel about an ice-cream now', and so on. The appropriateness of these different forms will depend on the social relationship between speaker and listener: deferential and polite forms are used to adults in authority, but not to little children, where it is more important to keep one's language simple. Sachs & Devin (1976), and Dunn & Kendrick (1982) have shown that children as young as 4 years are able to simplify their language for younger children and siblings.

What about children interacting with others of the same age? Garvey (1977) studied children's conversations with their peers and found that by the age of around 3 years they were sufficiently skilled to be able to play verbal games with partners, such as deliberately saying something stupid. For such utterances to work as a game, rather than merely causing confusion, children must be able to be aware of and use subtle social rules in communication so that they appreciate the joke when the rules are broken.

Discourse analysis

If we look at any stretch of conversation, we can see that the sequence of utterances is not random. Speakers relate what they say to what has gone before. Conversation quickly breaks down if one partner does not give the other a chance to talk, or, conversely, if one person maintains long silences at points when they are expected to respond. Nor can conversation proceed if two people are talking about completely different topics, if one person assumes knowledge that the other does not share or conversely, if one person does nothing but tell the other something they already know.

Discourse analysis has been defined as the analysis of the structure of naturally occurring language at a level above that of the sentence or clause (Stubbs 1983). It is an attempt to investigate the organization of larger linguistic units, such as conversational exchanges or written texts. One aim is to classify utterances in terms of particular functions they fulfil, and then to specify which sequences of functions make for coherent conversations.

In developmental studies most attention has been given to conversations between mothers and their children because this is usually the major context for early language learning. Among the skills the child needs to master are the abilities to function in both speaker and listener roles, to alternate these (turn-taking), to share a topic of conversation, recognize topic shifts, initiate a new topic, and maintain and develop it. In addition, the child must learn to recognize when communication has broken down, and to clarify and repair conversation when this occurs. To do all these things, one must be able to signal one's intentions to a partner in a recognizable form, and to appreciate the communicative intents of a speaker. As with research on speech acts, the focus has been both on specifying the range of skills the developing child acquires, and in studying the relationship between prelinguistic behaviours and later conversational skills. For example, it has been argued that before children are able to speak, mothers structure interactions with their infants in a way that encourages the development of conversational turn-taking (Snow 1977a).

Bloom et al (1976) looked at the development of four children (aged 19 to 36 months) in conversation with adults. As the children progressed in syntactic ability their utterances became increasingly more related to the preceding adult utterances, with a substantial increase in the proportion of utterances sharing the same topic. As children developed they learned to reply to an adult utterance by repeating a part of that utterance (usually the verb), elaborating or replacing other parts, for example:

adult: what did I draw

child: draw a boy

There was evidence that the adults as well as the children changed in conversational strategy as the child developed. At a certain point, parents start following up topics initiated by their child with questions. Children recognize the obligation to reply and adults can further develop the conversation by commenting on the reply and adding another question. In this way parents can be said to help structure conversations with young children.

Studies of older children have considered how they come to master such skills as telling a narrative story. In adult language, organization of discourse above the level of the sentence is particularly clear in this context. *Cohesive devices*, such as pronouns and definite and indefinite articles, are used to link sentences together. For example, this would be a very odd story:

> a boy went in a garden
> a boy met a monster
> a monster ate up a boy

Rather we would say:

> a boy went into the garden
> he met a monster
> the monster ate him up

Note that the choice of article, and of pronoun rather than noun, is made here on the basis of the position of the sentence in the story. When characters are first introduced, the indefinite article is used, but for later mentions, the pronoun or definite article is needed. However, temporal organization of the discourse is not the only factor affecting selection of definite or indefinite reference. This also depends on what the listener does and does not know. We would find it very strange if a cricket commentator were to say:

> 'A batsman has just hit a ball into the air'

Rather, we would expect to hear:

> 'The batsman has just hit the ball into the air'

or

> 'He has just hit the ball into the air'

The definite article is appropriate because it is assumed the listener *knows* that cricket involves a batsman and a ball. The only time indefinite articles would be used would be if one were describing the game for the first time to someone who had never encountered it, e.g. 'You have a ball, and the man who hits the ball is called a batsman'.

Mastery of these discourse devices develops relatively late in children. Both in spontaneous speech and in written language, children of 8 years and above tend to use definite articles and pronouns in situations where it is not clear to the listener (or reader) what is being referred to (see Perera 1984 for a review).

The area of pragmatics is one that is relatively young in child language research and involves abilities that are not yet fully conceptualized in psychological terms, such as the ability to infer another's intention, and to clothe one's own intention in words.

VARIABILITY IN LANGUAGE ACQUISITION

Our brief review of normal language acquisition gives the impression of uniformity in pattern of development for children learning the same language. Indeed, much research on language acquisition has been conducted from a theoretical stance that stresses the invariant nature of language development, not only for a particular language, but also, at a more abstract level, between languages (e.g. Slobin 1966). Nevertheless, that there is considerable variability in rate of language development can be seen from the data from Wells' (1985) longitudinal study of British children (Fig. 1.3).

Consider, for example, the data on 4-year-olds. Some 16% of children will score at or below a level corresponding to one standard deviation below the mean (i.e. midway between the line showing the mean and that showing 2 s.d. below). If we trace horizontally across to discover at what age this is the *average* score, we find it corresponds to around the 3-year-old level. Thus around one in six 4-year-olds have language skills one year

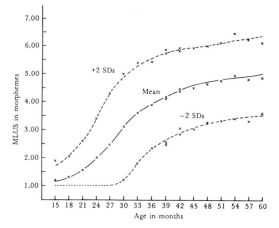

Fig. 1.3 Mean length of structured utterances by age in the Bristol Language Development Study: reproduced with permission from Wells (1985)

or more below age level. What sounds like a substantial delay (after all, a year is a long time!) is not statistically abnormal. Individual differences exist not just in rate but also in pattern of acquisition. Nelson (1973), for example, pointed out that there are differences in the types of words first learned by children, with some children (the 'referential' type) using predominantly words that named objects, and others (the 'expressive' type) having a majority of words that expressed personal desires or were used for social interaction. While individual variation is less striking than similarities in development, it is important for what it can tell us about the nature of language acquisition. Variations in pattern or rate of development can indicate to what extent language development is free to vary or is constrained by factors such as the characteristics of the language to be learned, and of the language learner, and the verbal environment (see Goldfield & Snow 1985 for a review). Early studies on individual differences looked at small numbers of children, deliberately excluding those whose development was atypical, or whose language learning opportunities were exceptional in any way. These exclusions were quite justifiable in terms of the aims of these studies, but we would argue that much can also be learned by looking at variation in language acquisition in atypical as well as typical children.

Social variations in language

In looking at variation in language acquisition, it is important to distinguish non-standard forms of language from impaired language. Language development should not be assessed purely in terms of one's own language usage nor in terms of the dominant language in a given culture: there is a range of social variation that can lead to the development of effective communicative skills. Prejudiced attitudes operate in particular in relation to differences in language usage by different social classes, or where an ethnic minority learns a different first language from the rest of the community. The Cockney child who says: 'We was goin' to bring our sandwiches wiv us but we ain't got no bread left' is using language in a way that is totally appropriate for the speech community in which he was brought up, and he communicates his thoughts effectively. Neither he nor his parents are language disordered or grammatically impaired. As Tizard & Hughes (1984) have shown, it simply is not valid to make generalizations about working-class mothers providing 'less adequate' language input to children than middle-class mothers.

This issue is complicated by the fact that in many societies, one form of the language has more status than others, and is regarded as the correct form to use in educated speech and in written communication. If this variety does not coincide with one's own dialect, then one must learn to use the standard form in written communication or run the risk of being thought ill-educated. Thus although nonstandard forms are not inferior on any linguistic criteria, users of these forms frequently find themselves at a social disadvantage. Sociolinguistics, the study of the social implications of variations in language use, is an enormous topic in its own right, and one which we cannot do more than allude to here (see Hudson 1980 for an introduction). The point we wish to stress is that one must

beware of regarding languages or dialects as *linguistically* inferior just because they are associated with low social status. Attention has focussed on this issue in the U.S.A, where sociolinguists have made detailed studies of Black American English, and noted that some features of this dialect have been regarded as signs of language disorder by teachers and other professionals. In a recent study, however, Seymour & Miller-Jones (1981) asked speech pathologists to judge language samples from Black American children and found that the converse now occurred: language that really *was* disordered was rated as typical Black English! Clearly, we need to be aware of the dangers in making linguistic judgements about dialects we are not familiar with. Having said that minority languages and dialects should not be thought of as linguistically inferior, we must stress that this does not make their users immune from language disorders.

EXCEPTIONAL CIRCUMSTANCES AS 'NATURAL EXPERIMENTS'

For practical and ethical reasons, researchers in developmental psycholinguistics can seldom manipulate the conditions under which language is learned. There are notable exceptions, as in Cazden's (1965) experimental attempts to manipulate language development by altering adults' talk to the child, but these have met with limited success. In general, researchers in language development can observe and describe the phenomena of interest, but they have little opportunity to influence them. This frequently makes it difficult to subject theories to adequate tests. Numerous theories of language acquisition are based on the logically shaky foundation of correlational data: we find that A is associated with B, and therefore postulate that A has caused B. Suppose, for example, we find that length of mother's utterances is positively correlated with rate of language development in the child. A plausible explanation is that the quality and quantity of speech directed to the child influences rate of language develop-ment. However, the correlational data alone do not allow us to reject competing expla-nations. It is also possible, for example, that a mother might adapt her speech to suit her perception of the child's language abilities. In that case, there would be a causal explanation for the positive correlation, but it would operate in the opposite direction from that proposed. Alternatively, shared factors affecting mother and child might influence both the quantity and quality of language used by both. These could be environmental factors (e.g. overcrowding, housing circumstances, etc.) or biological ones. Mother and child have 50% of their genes in common, so if, as seems reasonable, genetic factors play any part in determining cognitive or linguistic skills, then we would expect significant correlations between maternal language and the child's verbal development, without needing to suppose that one directly influenced the other. Correlational data alone do not allow us to unravel these alternative explanations.

The same problems of interpretation arise for theories that propose that development of A is a prerequisite for B. Suppose we wish to argue that a child must first learn to communi-cate particular sorts of messages nonverbally before going on to express them verbally. For example, we might postulate that the refer-ential ability manifest in the nonverbal activity of pointing is a prerequisite for referring to objects verbally. Unfortunately, we are usually restricted to considering correlational data when evaluating this sort of hypothesis, yet these cannot provide an adequate test. Suppose we note that shortly before children produce their first words they typically *do* go through a stage where they make extensive use of pointing at objects of interest. In the course of child development numerous factors change simultaneously. As the child is learning language, he or she is also devel-oping in many other ways, including physi-cally. One might therefore expect to find that the attainment of a particular shoe size was associated with the subsequent use of the child's first words. Yet we would not find it

plausible to conclude that feet of a certain size were a necessary prerequisite for language development. Is there any way we can escape from such logical difficulties and subject our theories to more rigorous tests? Although we can seldom design experiments to manipulate variables thought to affect language learning, we can resolve some of these difficulties by turning to 'nature's experiments'.

Early accounts of language development in exceptional circumstances referred to anec-dotal incidents, single case studies, and single, one-off investigations of isolated phenomena (e.g. Eisen 1962, Lenneberg 1962, Fry 1966). These variations in the conditions in which language is acquired can be regarded as natural experiments that would not be feas-ible or ethical under normal experimental conditions, but which allow us to dissociate factors that are usually associated in normal development.

A word of caution is, however, necessary. In regarding exceptional circumstances as 'natural experiments' one must beware of an over-simplistic approach that ignores the interaction of factors that occurs when environ-mental or organic context of development is disturbed or atypical. For example, one cannot assume that the only difference between a profoundly deaf child and a hearing child is in their responsiveness to sound. The child's handicap will affect the language environment. Thus some profoundly deaf children will have a signed language as their first language: others will not. In either case, the child's educational experiences are likely to be very different from those of a hearing child. Furthermore, the factors that caused the hearing loss might have other consequences: rubella, for example, has effects on the nervous system that typically extend beyond the auditory pathways. An understanding of such interactions is vital if we are to interpret 'natural experiments' meaningfully.

It is often assumed that normal conditions are essential for adequate language develop-ment, and that any variation in physical status or environmental conditions must be disadvantageous. However, we must beware of regarding exceptional as synonymous with inferior. As we shall see, not all unusual circumstances result in impairment: development can be different without necessarily being defective.

THEORETICAL ISSUES ADDRESSED BY STUDYING CHILDREN IN EXCEPTIONAL CIRCUMSTANCES

Exceptional circumstances can provide important evidence relevant to a number of major issues in language development.

1. What language input is necessary for the child to learn language?

Studies on the impact of quality and quantity of maternal speech on rate of language development have tended to concentrate on correlations between maternal language and child development for children developing in unexceptional environments. Much can be learned by going beyond these limits to look at language development in children whose verbal environment departs from the norm.

Chapter 2 considers language development in children who suffer from chronic neglect or abuse and for whom language input is severely limited in quality and/or quantity for several years. Typically, such children are subjected to such a range of physical and emotional deprivations that it is impossible to attribute any abnormalities of language development specifically to the inadequate verbal environment. Cases where children develop normal language despite such adverse circumstances, however, do provide important evidence of resilience of language acquisition.

Chapter 3, in contrast, considers the impact of a naturally occurring circumstance in which a child is exposed to severely defective spoken language from a parent, in the context of otherwise normal social, communicative and environmental stimulation, i.e. when a hearing child is brought up by a congenitally deaf parent.

Such children provide an important limiting case of language development in the face of severely restricted verbal stimulation. Many theories would predict that this verbal environment should result in severely impaired language development in the child.

Bilingualism is sometimes regarded as an unusual and possibly disadvantageous circumstance for language development, where confusion might result because the child is exposed to too much conflicting linguistic information. Chapter 4 considers the impact on language development of exposure to more than one language during the early years of life.

Twins provide an interesting test case for theories concerned with the impact of early mother-child interaction on language development, for here we have a situation where typically one family's resources are shared between two infants at the same developmental level. Chapter 5 reviews the evidence for and against delayed language development in twins, and considers how far verbal impairments can be attributed to the sharing of parental resources between two children, and how far other factors, such as increased perinatal risk, or the close twin relationship, may be responsible.

Even where a child's parents provide adequate verbal stimulation, the quality of language received by the child may be degraded if hearing is impaired. In Chapter 6 we consider the impact of mild temporary hearing loss on language learning: does such degradation of the verbal stimulus result in language impairments, or is there sufficient redundancy in language to make this unimportant?

For the profoundly deaf child, visual cues are the predominant or sole source of information about language. This raises the question of how the modality through which a language is learned affects language development. There are two very different sides to this question. Many educators believe that their goal should be to teach deaf children to understand spoken language via the visual modality, through lip-reading and written language. Chapter 7 considers what limitations are imposed on the acquisition of spoken language when little or no auditory information is available. Other deaf children use visual information in a very different way. These are children who grow up learning a visual, signed language as their first language. How far do these children follow normal stages of acquisition, and to what extent is language acquisition affected by the modality in which the language is learned? These questions are addressed by Chapter 8.

Normal communicative interactions between mothers and their children involve visual as well as auditory exchanges. How important is it for language comprehension that the child is able to relate a verbal message to the visual context in which it occurs? One way of assessing how important visual information is in language learning is to consider language development in children with a visual handicap. Blindness is not generally thought of as a condition which results in language difficulties, but is this view correct? Chapter 9 reviews work on language development in visually handicapped children and considers how language learning proceeds when visual cues are not available.

2. What is the relationship between cognition and language?

The relationship between language and cognition has always been a topic of major interest to psycholinguists. Can language develop largely as an autonomous system, or are certain cognitive attainments necessary before verbal skills can be acquired? If, as in Piagetian theory, we propose that certain nonverbal cognitive skills are prerequisites for language development, then we should find that language should not be able to develop in children who lack those skills. It, therefore, is of interest to consider children whose sensory, motor, or mental development is impaired in various ways, in whom language and other aspects of cognitive development may be dissociated, making it possible to demonstrate logical independence of different systems. Chapters 7, 8 and 9 are concerned with the impact of a primary sensory impairment on cognitive and language development, whereas Chapter 14 looks at the impact of physical disabilities that make speech difficult or impossible. Chapters 10, 11 and 12 consider language development in three conditions, Down's syndrome, Williams syndrome and infantile autism, all of which are known to affect nonverbal mental development in rather different ways.

3. How independent are different components of the language function?

In unexceptional circumstances, phonology, syntax, semantics and pragmatics develop in an orderly fashion in step with one another. Is this a coincidental relationship, reflecting simultaneous maturation of independent systems, or are developments of these different aspects dependent on one another? When we investigate children whose development is exceptional, it is interesting to compare the level of development of different language skills, to see how far they can become dissociated. As Chapters 10 to 12 illustrate, conditions such as Williams syndrome and infantile autism contrast sharply with Down's syndrome in their psycholinguistic profile.

Where we find increased incidence or prolonged presence of abilities or facets of language acquisition in the disabled child this may provide clues to their explanation in the normal acquisition process, or may lead to the discovery of similar abilities in the normal child. For example, echolalia (the repetition of all or part of another's utterance by a child) was originally thought as a pathological sign of infantile autism. However, research studies found that many normal young children go through an echolalic phase (Nakanishi & Owada 1973). The difference between the normal and the autistic child is in the age at which this behaviour occurs, and in its duration (see Ch. 12).

4. Are there critical periods for language development?

Lenneberg (1967) popularized the notion that the child's capacity for learning language might not be constant, but might decline with age. One consequence of this is that if some factor interferes with language acquisition during the crucial early years it might not be possible to recover from the language deficit later on, even if the adverse factor is removed. In this book, the 'critical period hypothesis' is addressed from several different perspectives.

Chapter 2 deals with the case of severe neglect, isolation and deprivation in early life. If a child grows up in such a severely deficient environment, can the adverse effects be reversed later on by providing a caring and adequate home for the child?

The topic of intermittent conductive hearing loss is also relevant for this question. It has been suggested that the consequences of a mild hearing loss may be far more severe in the first one or two years of life than later on. Chapter 6 considers how far the evidence supports this viewpoint.

Not all conditions affecting speech production have permanent and life-long effects, but may last long enough to prevent certain stages of development being expressed. Chapter 14 considers development in children with long-term tracheostomies. These children are rendered unable to speak at a time when most children will be babbling or speaking their first words. Can the consequences of this period of speechlessness be reversed, or does interference with this particular stage of development have persisting effects?

The other side of the coin of the 'critical period' issue is the question of plasticity. Lenneberg proposed that in the early years of language learning, there was considerable plasticity in the neurological representation of language, so that if damage occurred to the left hemisphere, language could develop in the right hemisphere instead. This plasticity declined with age, so that the likelihood of persisting language impairment after a left hemisphere lesion increased with age.

More recent research has suggested that Lenneberg's position be modified, and indicates that persisting language impairment does occur after early left hemisphere lesions, although this may not be obvious unless neuropsychological tests are used. In Chapter 13 we consider the evidence for and against plasticity in the neurological basis of language.

5. Can we specify necessary and sufficient conditions for language impairment?

Question 1 was concerned with what were the limiting conditions that were still compatible with normal language acquisition. Question 5 is the converse: what conditions are known to impair language acquisition?

Here our main focus of interest is specific language impairment, defined as a selective disorder affecting language development in a child whose intelligence, hearing and environmental circumstances are adequate for language acquisition. By definition these are children in whom language acquisition goes awry for no obvious cause. To date we know very little about the etiology of specific language impairment. By examining the effects on language development in exceptional circumstances it may be possible to locate the most likely kind of explanation and to rule out others by seeing how far a particular circumstance gives rise to a pattern of language development that mirrors that found in specific language impairment.

REASONS FOR STUDYING EXCEPTIONAL CIRCUMSTANCES IN THEIR OWN RIGHT

As we have indicated, exceptional circumstances can have important implications for theories of normal language development and may provide the only means of testing particular hypotheses. This is not, however, the only motivation for investigating children developing in exceptional circumstances.

These children are interesting in their own right: a knowledge of the variations in pattern of language development that can occur in different circumstances is important for those concerned with the provision of services to meet special educational and developmental needs.

Research in. this field raises questions concerning the direction and nature of remedial intervention. In the absence of any alternative suggestions, the predominating strategy in language intervention is directed towards stimulating a normal developmental progression. However, individual variations within the normal population suggest that there is some flexibility within the system. Does this flexibility extend to variations in patterns of development seen in the case of children who are exceptional in physical or cognitive status? Can we learn anything about which variations are relatively adaptive as opposed to maladaptive? Another way of posing the question is to ask are there many or one routes to language competence?

When we analyse language development in different situations it becomes clear that it is unhelpful to talk simply of conditions that cause 'language delay'. Language is not a unitary skill, but rather a collection of component abilities that can be delayed or disordered in many different ways. 'Language delay' is a blunderbuss term that fails to communicate either the degree to which language development is disrupted or those aspects of language development that are most affected. A child with Down's syndrome may obtain the same low IQ score as another child with infantile autism and a third child with congenital hydrocephalus, but this does not mean that language will be similar in all three cases, although it is likely that some aspects of verbal functioning will be deficient in each child. We hope to demonstrate here that if we label a child as having 'language delay resulting from intellectual impairment' this is in no sense an explanation, nor even an adequate description, of the problem. We need to go much further in analyzing the nature of the difficulties the child has with language in order to offer the most appropriate remedial help.

2

Extreme deprivation in early childhood

D. H. Skuse

Many writers on the intellectual nature of man have attempted to supply a chapter for which human experience afforded no materials, by conjecturing what would be the condition of a being secluded, from infancy to youth, from all knowledge of the external world and from all intercourse with his species, and, therefore, destitute of the common experience, the appetites, and the acquirements, which result from the circumstances in which a human being is usually placed. The probable character of his feelings and perceptions on viewing the glories of nature which he had never witnessed, and his sensations amidst the business and forms of life of which he had no previous notion, (affords) matter for very interesting speculation.

So begins an account of the life of Caspar Hauser, in the Penny Magazine of the Society for the Diffusion of Useful Knowledge, published in 1834. Caspar Hauser was a mysterious young man, just over 16 years of age, who had been discovered in a street in Nuremberg, in Bavaria, in 1828. He was initially without comprehensible language or social skills, having allegedly spent the greater part of his life in a dark cramped cell with no human company, for reasons that were never discovered. Despite possessing a vocabulary at discovery of not more than six or so words he was able, after 15 months' tutelage under the guidance of a certain Professor Daumer, to comment on the night sky 'That is indeed the most beautiful sight I have ever seen in the world. But who has placed all those numerous beautiful candles there? Who lights them? Who puts them out?'.

Over many centuries man has considered that a careful analysis of the sequelae of extreme deprivation of human contact in early childhood might reveal valuable insights into how normal language develops. To this end children have occasionally been deliberately raised in conditions of extreme isolation. The Egyptian pharaoh, Psammetichos, the Holy Roman Emperor Frederik II and King James IV of Scotland all allegedly attempted such experiments (Curtiss 1981a), in the latter instance the purpose being to discover which was the more ancient language, Latin or Greek. In our times, the development of twin sisters under conditions of minimal perceptual and social stimulation was studied by psychologists (see Dennis 1941) from the first to the fourteenth month of life. There are in addition a number of reports concerning individual children who spent their early years in conditions of exceptional impoverishment and deprivation as the result of deliberate action by nefarious, ignorant or incompetent caretakers (Davis 1940, Mason 1942, Koluchova 1972, 1976, Curtiss 1977, Douglas & Sutton 1978, Skuse 1984, Thompson 1986). Before considering those case histories in detail an account will be given of some valuable observations that have been made on children whose environmental deprivation resulted from an upbringing in neglectful and unstimulating institutions.

STUDIES OF CHILDREN IN INSTITUTIONS

One of the earliest descriptions of the impact of poor institutional care upon children's mental abilities was given by Harold Skeels. In his well-known and celebrated study Skeels (1966) reviewed the outcome of developmentally delayed children who had spent their earliest years in an unstimulating orphanage, back in the 1930s. His follow-up study contrasted the fortunes of 13 who were rehabilitated to an institution for mentally retarded adults (at an average age of 20 months) with a contrast group who remained in the orphanage. Those orphans who were rehabilitated were actively encouraged to make close relationships with one mother figure; later all but two were removed and placed in adoptive homes. The contrast group of 12 children, initially higher in intelligence, were exposed to the relatively unstimulating atmosphere of the orphanage for a prolonged period. Both groups were followed into adulthood, 21 years later. Their outcomes were strikingly different. Those who had been adopted were functioning normally, both in terms of mental and socio-emotional development. Many of the contrast group were still in institutional care and they presented a sorry picture. One important message to remember from this study is that within the 'experimental' group major gains in mental abilities were made *before* adoptive placement, in the relatively brief period (an average 19 months) the children spent with their temporary foster mothers. It should be pointed out that a damning article was published a few years ago by Longstreth (1981) in which the entire Skeels' project was criticized and pronounced worthless. However, it is arguable that Longstreth did not undermine Skeels' main conclusion, that infants from a very poor and deprived background can make a substantial and lasting recovery when removed to stimulating environments.

Other studies along the same lines include Dennis's (1973) report on a terribly impoverished foundling home in Beirut, Lebanon. He discovered a temporary, apparently environmentally induced developmental retardation which began around 3 months of age and reached a maximum by 12 months, when the mean 'behavioural quotient' of the subject infants was said to be 50. If the children were subsequently adopted by the age of 2 years they developed intellectually at a normal rate, but those who were adopted after 2 years did not make a full recovery despite follow-up to 10–14 years of age. Incidentally, the comparable findings from the Skeels' (1966) project (pp. 10, 22) show a correlation between duration of early follow-up (range 38–81 months) and gains in IQ (range 2–58 points) of 0.59.

Hakimi-Manesh and colleagues (1984) also reported on an orphanage, this time in Iran, which provided good physical nurturance but little mental stimulation for the infants in its care. An intervention study demonstrated that with relatively simple environmental manipulation for a brief interval, appreciable progress could be made in the mental and psychomotor functioning of the children and that gains attained persisted over a six month follow-up period.

One general caveat that should be borne in mind when interpreting the results of all these orphanage studies is that those infants or children who were adopted were unlikely to be a random selection. Prospective adoptive parents were likely to choose a more appealing or lively infant within an orphanage. Additionally, the staff would not promote the adoption of children they considered to have physical handicaps or stigmata (such as congenital syphilis) or even 'evident mental retardation' (see Longstreth 1981).

THEORETICAL IMPLICATIONS

Findings both from the institution-reared children and from the case studies raise important theoretical issues regarding the resilience of potential mental abilities in the face of extreme environmental adversity. For example, language development would seem to be achieved, with varying degrees of success, over a wide range and variety of upbringings.

Shatz (1985) suggested that the processes of language development are controlled by a genetic programme that has evolved to ensure success, in the sense of acquiring the power of communication (an adaptive skill) under a broad but bounded range of environmental circumstances. Evidence in favour of this hypothesis comes from a variety of sources,

many of which are discussed in this book (e.g. the acquisition of sign language by deaf children). But some of the most striking corroborative findings have been made by those who have studied formerly extremely deprived and neglected children; such scientifically-minded observers' interest is excited by age old but still unanswered questions. What makes us human? To what extent does heredity determine the development of human personality and intellect? How plastic or perfectable is the human organism?

Certain features are common to both recent victims and their historical counterparts. First, they are initially lacking basic human attributes such as speech or social skills; skills that are ubiquitous except in severely retarded or dysphasic children or those with autistic features. Secondly, removal from the impoverished conditions is often followed by a remarkable and usually relatively rapid recovery of their cognitive and other faculties.

These findings bear on a number of issues that are still exciting the interest of developmental psychologists, but have implications that go far beyond the rarified atmosphere of the psycholinguistic laboratory. Given the complexity of language and its importance to humans, the ability to develop language (gestural and/or spoken) must at some level be robust and resilient in extreme conditions. In general, children in a wide variety of settings achieve that skill, and, except for the most severely congenitally mentally handicapped children, retarded individuals appear to follow patterns of language development similar to those of normal children, although at a slower rate (Morehead & Ingram 1976).

At the earliest stages of development (up to two-word combinations) children seem to acquire language according to a predetermined trajectory; the path they follow may be fairly independent of higher cognitive processes (see Corrigan 1979) and the frequency with which they are exposed to certain aspects of a particular language.

The conundrum, as stated by Shatz (1985), is that since children usually do manage to learn the particular language and dialect to which they are exposed, the system has to be responsive to a variety of environmental influences. Accordingly, the acquisition system must be both sensitive to changing circumstances but also robust, in the sense that ultimately the goal of language competence must be achieved by one means or another.

Reviewing the evidence for relevant early environmental influences upon cognitive development Clarke & Clarke (1976) comment that there is now unequivocal evidence that a poor environment that improves in middle or even late childhood can lead to major gains in language capacity. Kagan et al (1978) concur with their opinion, adding that persistent defects imply a persistence of adverse experiences. It follows that the language acquisition system, whatever its nature, must possess and retain a good deal of adaptive flexibility all the way through to puberty. Yet it must also be sufficiently robust to withstand insult, whether environmental or biological.

The concept of adaptive flexibility is often referred to as *plasticity* (Siple 1985). The term implies that the organism retains the capacity to compensate for adversity in such a way that little functional deficit results from insults to the system, whether these are biological (such as overt brain damage) or environmental (such as a perceptually impoverished upbringing). In both cases the child possesses the *potential* for functional recovery up to certain limiting or boundary conditions. It might be easier to understand the concept of *plasticity* by considering the impact of biological insults to the central nervous system. For example, left hemisphere lesions acquired very early in life do not selectively impair language development, whereas those acquired in adulthood frequently cause aphasia. The concept of a 'critical period', during which unilateral lesions do not lead to persistent aphasic impairment and after which they invariably do so, is now regarded as an oversimplification. Studies of brain-damaged children have enabled provisional delineation of the boundary conditions for biological insults. For a fuller discussion of the impact on language devel-

opment after focal brain damage see Chapter 13.

It should also be possible to establish boundary conditions by looking at language development in atypical environments; under what circumstances does the organism lose the capacity to 'catch-up' to normal levels of language competence on removal from impoverished to adequately stimulating conditions, given an intact central nervous system? The human organism is equipped with both homeostatic mechanisms (such as those that maintain the body's temperature) and homeorhetic mechanisms (such as those that maintain a trajectory of growth in stature). We can conceive of such mechanisms as being under the control of a genetic programme, guiding their application to attainment of a goal which is, broadly speaking, adaptation to the environment (see Waddington 1977).

No doubt our capacity to acquire language is under genetic control, ensuring success under a broad but bounded range of environmental circumstances. These issues have recently been discussed by Shatz (1985) and MacDonald (1986). In the remainder of the chapter a detailed presentation of the findings from case reports on language development under conditions of extreme environmental deprivation will serve as the basis for a discussion about what current knowledge allows us to conclude about these important issues.

CASE STUDIES OF EXTREME NEGLECT AND DEPRIVATION

The findings on groups of children raised in unstimulating institutional care are complemented by a small number of intensive case studies on individuals or sibling groups. All but one report concern children who were brought up in what were nominally home environments rather than institutions. Detailed information is presented about the circumstances both before and after removal from adversity, and about outcome at follow-up. Briefly the facts of each case are as follows:

Anna (Davis 1940, 1947)

On 6 February 1938 the New York Times reported that a girl of more than 5 years had been found tied to an old chair in a storage room on the second floor of her farm home 17 miles from a small Pennsylvania city. She had apparently been there since babyhood. The child, Anna, was wedged into the chair which was tilted backwards to rest upon a coal bucket, her spindly arms tied above her head. She was unable to talk or move, and was dressed in a dirty shirt and napkin. Her hands, arms and legs were just bones, with skin drawn over them, so frail she could not use them. This state of cachexia was due to the fact that she had never had enough nourishment. Anna never grew normally and the chair on which she lay, half reclining and half sitting, was so small she had to double her legs partly under her. Immediately following her discovery Anna was removed to a children's home, where she was noted to be completely apathetic and lay in a limp supine position, immobile, expressionless and indifferent to everything. She was believed to be deaf, possibly blind.

Anna was placed initially in a county home for the aged and infirm. Nine months later she was transferred to a foster home. Although little progress had been made in the original establishment, where one nurse cared for over 300 inmates, the 'unremitting attention' of her foster mother led to rapid improvement in a wide variety of motor and cognitive skills. After a further nine months she was, for reasons that remain obscure, placed in a private home for retarded children. Few further advances were made at first, although she began to develop speech after two years had passed there. Shortly before her death from jaundice 12 months later, Anna was reported to be repeating single words and able to try and carry on a conversation.

Isabelle (Mason 1942; Davis 1947)

Born just 1 month later than Anna, another extremely deprived girl (who has been given the pseudonym Isabelle), was discovered in November 1938. At the time she was approximately $6\frac{1}{2}$ years old. She was an illegitimate child and had been kept in seclusion for that reason. Her mother was deaf and mute and it seemed that she and Isabelle had spent most of their time together in a dark room shut away from the family who had rejected them. Lack of sunshine and inadequacy of diet had caused Isabelle to develop rickets and her legs were 'so bowed that as she stood erect the soles of her shoes came nearly flat together', and she got about with a skittering gait. Isabelle's mother eventually escaped with her child after nearly 7 years' seclusion and the girl was brought to the Children's Hospital in Columbus, Ohio on 16 November 1938 for orthopaedic surgery and physiotherapy. Her behaviour towards strangers, especially men, was found to be that of a 'wild animal'. She manifested much fear and hostility and, in lieu of speech, made only a strange croaking sound.

Once in hospital Isabelle seemed miserable and withdrawn, and she was initially entirely mute. However, after just one week she began to attempt vocalization, although she had formerly used only gesture to communicate with her mother. Acquisition of vocal competence was observed to pass through normal developmental stages but at a greatly accelerated pace, so that within two months she was singing nursery rhymes, and within a year was able to read and write with fair competence. After 18 months she had a vocabulary of 2000 words and could compose imaginative stories.

Koluchova twins (Koluchova 1972, 1976)

Jarmila Koluchova reported in 1972 the case record of monozygotic male twins, who were born on 4 September 1960. Their mother died shortly after giving birth and for 11 months they lived in a children's home. They then spent 6 months with a maternal aunt but were subsequently taken to live with their father and stepmother. For $5\frac{1}{2}$ years, until their discovery at the age of 7, the twins lived under most abnormal conditions, in a quiet street of family houses in Czechoslovakia. Because of the actions of their stepmother, who had her own children whom she actively preferred, the boys grew up in almost total isolation, never being allowed out of the house but living in a small unheated closet. They were often locked up for long periods in the cellar, sleeping on the floor on a plastic sheet, and they were cruelly chastized. When discovered at the age of 7 they could barely walk and suffered from acute rickets. They showed reactions of surprise and horror to objects and activities normally very familiar to children of that age, such as moving mechanical toys, a TV set or traffic in the street. Their spontaneous speech was very poor, as was their play.

After discovery and removal the boys were placed at first in hospital, where they remained for a few weeks before going to a small children's home. Their mental age was initially around the 3 year level, whereas their chronological age was 7 years 3 months. After approximately 18 months in the children's home they were placed with a foster family with whom they remained until adulthood. Tremendous gains in cognitive attainments were made within a few months of rescue, and a further significant increase in the rate of improvement occurred on transfer to the foster home. The long-term outcome was excellent and the boys developed above average linguistic skills as well as making good socioemotional adjustment to adolescence.

Genie (Curtiss 1977)

One of the most extraordinary cases of severe deprivation yet reported is that of Genie, who was born in USA in April 1957. She was found at the age of 13 years 7 months, a painfully thin child who appeared 6 or 7 years old. From the age of 20 months she had been confined to a small room under conditions of extreme physical restraint. In this room she received minimal care from a mother who was herself rapidly losing her sight. Genie was physically punished by her father if she made any sound. Most of the time she was kept harnessed into an infant's potty chair but at night she was confined in a homemade sleeping bag fashioned like a strait jacket and lay in an infant's crib covered with wire mesh. She was fed only infant food. Genie's father was convinced that she would die; he was positive that she would not live past the age of 12 and promised that the mother could seek help for the child if she did so. But when the age of 12 had come and gone and she survived, the father reneged on his promise. It was not until Genie was $13\frac{1}{2}$ years old that her mother managed to get away, leaving home and husband to stay with the maternal grandmother. Several weeks later, whilst her mother was seeking welfare benefit, the child's strange demeanour was noticed by a clerk who alerted the authorities. Genie was admitted to hospital immediately. At this time Genie could not stand erect and could walk only with difficulty, shuffling her feet and swaying from side to side. Having been beaten for making any noise she had learned to suppress almost all vocalization save a whimper. She salivated copiously, spitting onto anything at hand, and was incontinent of urine and faeces. Curtiss comments 'Genie was unsocialized, primitive, hardly human'.

Genie was admitted to a children's hospital where she gained rapidly in height and weight, entered puberty and showed considerable cognitive achievements. Within seven months she was passing items on the Vineland and Leiter scales (nonverbal cognitive development tests) at virtually a 4 year level. She subsequently went to live with a foster family where slow progress continued. Genie never acquired true linguistic competence, nor was her social adjustment ever reported as approaching age-appropriate levels.

Alice and Beth (Douglas & Sutton 1978)

This was another pair of deprived twins. For the first three months of their lives their mother was working to support herself and they had no contact with her at all. She had separated from her husband, an itinerant musician, whilst pregnant. Alice and Beth were initially looked after by friends and then some distant relatives took charge and planned to adopt them, but their own marriage broke up. The twins were then taken into care for a few weeks, after which an aunt and uncle looked after them for the remainder of their first year. During that same year their mother returned to her husband for a time, became pregnant, and left him again after three months. Soon after that she moved with the twins into a council house, but it was damp, infested with mice and due for demolition. She suffered from depression badly enough to require medical treatment. It seems the girls received very little stimulation and, although they learned to walk at the normal time, they were very slow in learning to talk. When nearly 5 and due to move to infants school they still could not talk intelligibly, except to each other in a private language incomprehensible to others.

The parents were very co-operative with the intervention planned by the authors of this account and the children were not removed from home. The twins were separated at school and put in different classes, where they received language training for a period of six months. The greatest acceleration in acquisition of language abilities occurred when specific remedial help was being given. Within one year they had achieved close to normal scores on verbal and nonverbal intelligence test items and could readily cope with mainstream schooling.

Mary and Louise (Skuse 1984)

In the autumn of 1977 a little girl of almost 9 years was referred to the Children's Department at a large postgraduate teaching hospital. Over the previous year Mary had exhibited increasingly disruptive behaviour in the small children's home where she had lived for the previous 6 years with her sister Louise, who was 14 months her elder. When their early history was investigated further it transpired that these children had spent their early lives in a remarkably deprived environment on account of their having a mother (Patricia) who was not only mentally retarded and microcephalic but may additionally have been suffering from a serious psychiatric disorder. When discovered in March 1971 by the Social Services the comment was made that 'Louise and Mary are very strange creatures indeed'. Aged 3 years 6 months and 2 years 4 months respectively, they took no notice of anything or anyone except to scamper up and sniff strangers, grunting and snuffling like animals. They both still sucked dummies and no attempt had been made to toilet train them, so they remained in nappies. Neither child had any constructive play but picked up objects and handled, then smelt and felt them. Mary had no speech whatsoever and made no hearing responses. Her vocalization seemed limited to a few high pitched sounds. Later that year something came to light which had not been noticed by the authorities before but had apparently been going on daily ever since the children became mobile. The health visitor found them tied on leashes to a bed, a measure their mother had taken partly because she insisted on keeping the flat spotlessly clean and partly because she was worried they would fall off the balcony. If they became too noisy or active the children were put onto a mattress and covered with a blanket. They were subsequently removed from her and taken into care.

The sisters were later placed in a small children's home, run as a family unit. Their developmental achievements diverged, with very rapid initial gains being made in verbal and nonverbal abilities by both children but only Louise went on to achieve normal competence in language skills, and only she received mainstream schooling. Mary persistently displayed a number of autistic behaviours which were thought to be linked to an inherited predisposition, and she received special education throughout her childhood.

Adam (Thompson 1986)

Adam was abandoned, in 1972, in a small town in Colombia, South America. Nothing is known about his natural parents: he was placed in a girls' reformatory school where he remained until 16 months of age. During the day he lay in a windowless room on a single bed. He suffered repeated infections, including gastroenteritis and intestinal parasites, whooping cough and measles. His diet was limited to watery soup or porridge and he had no toys and no companions. On removal from these dire circumstances he had signs of marasmus (severe protein-energy malnu-

trition), was anaemic, and infested with parasites. His development was grossly retarded and he was emotionally withdrawn and passive; he cried when he was handled and resented being touched.

Adam was adopted aged 34 months and was followed up until nearly 14 years. By that time he was functioning very well in all aspects of social and scholastic adjustment, and his growth trajectories were age-appropriate.

ENVIRONMENTAL FACTORS IN SEVERE NEGLECT: CASE STUDIES

Table 2.1 illustrates the early environmental stimuli and influences upon these unfortunate children. The table is arranged so that those individuals whose outcome was relatively poor (Anna, Genie, Mary) may be relatively easily contrasted with those who had a good

Table 2.1 Early environmental stimuli and influences

Name	D.O.B.	Severe malnourishment	Maltreatment[+]	Longest period in normal environment	Consistent social contacts*	Exposure to Language	
						Spoken	Gesture
Anna (Davis) 1940	1.3.32	Yes	NRE	Birth– 6 months	MS	Minimal	Minimal
Genie (Curtiss) 1977	?.4.57	Yes	NREA	Birth– 1.8	MFS	Minimal	Minimal
Mary (Skuse) 1982	24.11.68	No	RE	None	MSF	Limited	Limited
Isabelle (Mason) 1942	?.4.32	Yes	E	None	M(Mute)	Minimal	Significant stimulation
Koluchova Twins (MZ boys) P.M. & J.M. 1972	4.9.60	Yes	NAE	Birth– 1.6	MFS(4)	Minimal	Minimal
Douglas & Sutton Twins (?Z) Alice Beth 1978	2.2.69	No	E	Birth– 1.0	MF (from 4 yr)	Limited	Limited
Louise (Skuse) 1982	30.9.67	No	RE	? Birth– 1.2	MS (from 1.2) F	Limited	Limited
Adam (Thompson) 1986	?.1.72	Yes	E	nil	None	Nil	Nil

[+]N = Gross neglect   E = Impoverished   *M = Mother
R = Physical restraint   environment   F = Father (inc. cohabitee)
A = Physical abuse/chastisement   with minimum stimulation S = Sib(s)

prognosis (Isabelle, Koluchova twins, Alice and Beth, Louise and Adam).

Malnutrition

The first point to consider is the fact that many of the children had been seriously malnourished. Now, the evidence for a direct link between malnutrition and the development of language is tenuous. When we attempt to relate acute and chronic nutritional deprivation to mental competence we should take account of a number of issues (Stein & Susser 1985): first, the timing and duration of malnutrition upon fetal development; secondly, the severity of malnutrition and the dietary constituents affected; thirdly, the precise cognitive deficits that result—in this case whether language is affected more or less severely than other aspects of mental competence; fourthly, the social context—the nature of the broad environment in which the malnourished child is raised.

With regard to the postnatal phase of mental development, in diverse studies, using different designs and outcome measures, malnutrition alone during this phase has not been shown to produce permanent mental impairment. However, in combination with a lack of intellectual and social stimulation mental performance *is* likely to be depressed. The question arises, is that depression reversible and if so under what conditions? Of the children reviewed in Table 2.1 five were definitely severely malnourished for varying periods. Despite this, the outcome for the Koluchova twins, Isabelle and Adam was good whereas Anna and Genie exhibited profound handicaps. There is no evidence that Mary and Louise were malnourished. Perhaps we should concur with John Dobbing (1984) when he concludes in a recent commentary on this subject, 'Malnutrition is beguiling in its pseudo-simplicity. Is it not possible that malnutrition may add to ninety nine other environmental disadvantages *when* they are present, . . . its functional ill effects can be compensated for by corresponding advantages when *not* enough of them (are present),

even though the malnutrition may have produced irreversible deficits and distortions . . . in the growing brain?'

Auditory-verbal stimulation

All the cases reported were brought up in conditions of abnormal auditory stimulation, although we lack exact information about the quality of experience which was available, except in the case of Genie where virtually the only sound she heard for 13 years was from an adjoining bathroom. In the case of Isabelle her sole companion was a deaf mute mother; Mary and Louise had each other for company as did the twins described by Douglas and Sutton. Anna, Isabelle and Mary were all thought to be deaf when first discovered (subsequently disconfirmed in all three cases), although there does not seem to have been that concern about the other children. Anna initially showed a peculiar pattern of hearing responses in that she would, for example, turn her head towards a ticking clock yet neither clapping hands nor speech produced a reaction. This behaviour is reminiscent of Bonnaterre's (1800) account of the wild boy of Aveyron, who would not flinch at a pistol shot yet showed immediate interest in the sound of a cracking nut.

Dennis (1941) commented, in his experimental study of deliberate deprivation of twin girls, 'we carefully refrained from baby talk and from babbling, as we wanted to know whether such vocalizations would occur without example'. Interestingly, it proved impossible for him to maintain the strict scientific objectivity he desired because 'from the 15th week onward they almost invariably greeted us with a smile and a vocalization . . . we decided in week 27 to return their smile of greeting and speak to them as we approached'.

A great deal of research has been published in the past decade on the importance of 'prelinguistic behaviour' in the context of the infant's earliest environment (e.g. Bruner 1983). Its relationship to the development of initial speech acts is not clear but a prelinguistic period in a stimulating environment may be of great importance if speech acquisition is to occur in the normal way. Psychosocial deprivation has been reported to impair preverbal vocalization and babble (Provence & Lipton 1962), but we do not have any reliable account of these phenomena in the children reviewed here. In Dennis's (1941) study, despite minimal opportunity for verbal interaction with their caretakers, by 12 months of age the twins had expressed a wide range of preverbal vocalizations, including ba-ba, da-da, la-la, by-by. However, neither child came to use any sound which corresponded to a real word within the 61 week period covered by the experiment.

In the series of children under review here only Mary, Isabelle and Adam suffered a persistently linguistically deprived environment from birth. Isabelle was in an exceptional situation because of the stimulation she recieved by gesture and interaction with her mute mother. This experience prior to discovery was almost certainly of benefit in facilitating her rapid later acquisition of spoken language.

Opportunities for play

Language development may be correlated with the development of spontaneous play: in Piaget's (1967a) term both are aspects of the same semiotic ability and as such, play may be considered to be a cognitive activity that contributes to the infant's knowledge of the world about him (Rosenblatt 1977). We may follow, through the development of play, the process by which the child learns that events, objects and ultimately symbols have an existence, function and purpose outside himself. In the strict Piagetian account of the emergence of language, although it is an essential instrument in cognitive constructions at the highest level, language is merely one particular instance of the semiotic or symbolic function. It is this function as a whole (including mental imagery, symbolic play and so on), and not language alone, which causes sensorimotor behaviour to evolve to the level of representation or thought (Piaget 1971). Thus Piaget would say that for a child to use any kinds of words at all requires quite advanced symbolic abilities; recent research has shown this view may be mistaken. The earliest use of words is usually in the context of, and refers to, a social relationship (Gopnik & Meltzoff 1985). This and similar research (Tomasello & Farrar 1984) has shown that children begin by using certain words such as 'there', 'no', 'more' and 'bye-bye' in social contexts, but later use them to refer to their own plans. Finally, in a third stage, they are used to refer to objects and events in the outside world. Accordingly, it is fascinating to learn that Genie's spontaneous productive vocabulary at the age of 13 years 7 months (Curtiss 1977) included only the holophrastic terms 'stopit' and 'nomore'. Of relevance here may be the view held by Vygotsky (1978) regarding the importance of social interaction as the source of the child's knowledge of the world, and his claim that all human abilities are first used in an interactive context and only later used alone. This claim can be seriously tested only by longitudinal data, to see whether activities displayed by an individual child first appear in interaction or in solitary activities. Data of relevance are provided by the findings on the play of these severely environmentally deprived children, who for the most part had little or no opportunity for interactive play during their confinement.

We can categorize play in developmental terms under three broad headings (Rosenblatt 1977). First, functional or sensorimotor play, which consists of no more than the manipulation of objects with reference to their attractive and inherent properties. Secondly, representational play, which includes using toys as if they were corresponding real objects, for example, where a miniature teaset is manipulated to simulate the child's real life experience of a tea party. Thirdly, symbolic play, which implies that the child is using an object in the play seen to stand for something else, its original meaning having been transcended as, for example, when the child uses a ruler as an aeroplane. It should be noted,

Table 2.2 Characteristics of extremely deprived children at discovery

Name	D.O.B.	Age at discovery	Physical stigmata at discovery	Motor * retardation (degree)	Speech		Formal psychometric assessment	Emotional expression & social behaviour
					Comprehension	Expression		
Anna (Davis) 1940	1.3.32	5;11	Cachexia	+++	Nil	Nil	SB <2;6	Profoundly withdrawn. Completely apathetic
Genie (Curtiss) 1977	?.4.57	13;7	Cachexia Dwarfed	++	PPVT 1;6	Echoes single words	LIPS (wide scatter on sub-tests) 4;9 VSM 1.05	Alert and curious. Eager for social contact. Silent tantrums
Mary (Skuse) 1982	24.11.68	2;4	Microcephaly Syndactyly	+	Nil	Nil	CJ (non-verbal skills) Nil	Withdrawn. Gaze avoidance. Temper tantrums
Isabelle (Mason) 1942	?.4.32	6;6	Rickets	++	Simple gestures only	Simple gestures only	SB 1;7 VSM 2;6	Withdrawn. Fearful of Hostile towards strangers
Koluchova Twins (MZ boys) P.M. & J.M. 1972	4.9.60	6;11	Rickets	++	(RE) 2 years	(RE) 1;6	CJ (non-verbal skills) 5;0	Timid and mistrustful
Douglas & Sutton Twins (?Z) Alice & Beth 1978	2.2.69	4;11	No	None	RDLS (at 5;4) Alice 3;4 Beth 3;8	Unintelligible	SB 3;7	Friendly. Amenable to adults
Louise (Skuse) 1982	30.9.67	3;6	No	+	CJ 1;0	CJ <1;0	CJ (non-verbal skills) <1;6	Affectionate. Happy. Temper tantrums
Adam (Thompson) 1986	?.1.72	1;4	Marasmus	+++	Nil	Nil	CJ 0;3	Passive, withdrawn, resented contact

CJ   — Contemporaneous clinical judgement
RE   — Retrospective estimation (from written reports)
SB   — Stanford-Binet intelligence scale
RDLS — Reynell developmental language scale

VSM — Vineland social maturity scale
LIPS — Leiter international performance scale
PPVT — Peabody picture vocabulary test

* +   = mild
+ +   = moderate
+ + + = severe

however, that this simple account of the stages which lead to truly symbolic play has been criticized on the grounds that the play activities of young children should not be interpreted as if the activities displayed served the same symbolic function for children as they would for adults (Zukow 1986).

Truly symbolic play usually begins around the age of 24 months and is well established by 30 months. Mary and Louise showed no play when first seen, although Louise made relatively good progress in her nursery group. Within 18 months she was using functional and occasional representational skills. Mary, on the other hand, was $4\frac{1}{2}$ years old when she began to display even the rudiments of functional play, two years after discovery. It was a further two years before representational play became established. Louise had reached this stage at five years of age, but for both girls the achievement was coincident with their having achieved a language comprehension age-equivalent of $2\frac{1}{2}$ years.

The close relationship between the development of a capacity for using symbolic functions and associations, and the onset of representational play, has been described by several workers (e.g. Rosenblatt 1977). It is also well known that autistic children suffer a severe handicap in both areas (Rutter 1985). Even so, children suffering from specific developmental language disorders may play with some representational features (Egan 1975). In normal children the correlation seems to exist between language comprehension (but not expression) and symbolic play (Largo & Howard 1979).

We have little information about the play of severely deprived children other than Mary and Louise. Anna's freedom of movement and the range of objects available for her tactile exploration were both certainly very limited. This was also true for Genie, whose 'toys' consisted of empty cheese cartons and two plastic raincoats. We do not know what toys were available to Isabelle, but the evidence suggests that they were few if any.

The Koluchova twins had only a handful of building bricks. Koluchova (1972) comments that the twins' spontaneous play was very primitive (functional/sensorimotor), but imitative (non-representational) play soon developed. Anna, just one year after discovery, was said 'hardly to play, when alone'. Isabelle on the other hand enjoyed undressing dolls very shortly after first being brought into hospital. Within a few months she was drawing and colouring with crayons and over the next two years play is said to have become 'highly imaginative'. Genie showed little in the way of play for several years. A little sensorimotor activity with toys or other materials plus an inclination to hoard is all that was observed, until $4\frac{1}{2}$ years after discovery she first engaged in an acting fantasy with Susan Curtiss. Adam was apathetic and withdrawn when rescued at the age of 16 months, but within two weeks was said to be 'smiling and reaching out for toys'. Intriguingly the historical figure Caspar Hauser had allegedly similarly been deprived of opportunities to play in his confinement:

> In his hole he had two wooden horses and several ribbons: with these horses he had always amused himself so long as he remained awake; and his only occupation was to make them run by his side, and to fix or tie the ribbons about them in different positions . . .
> whenever any trifle, a ribbon, a coin, or a little picture was given to him he cried 'Ross! Ross!' (horse) and expressed by his looks and motions a desire to hang all these pretty things upon a horse. This suggested to a police soldier the idea of giving him a wooden horse for a plaything. The possession of this toy seemed to affect a great alteration in Caspar. He lost his insensibility, his indifference, and his dejection, and he conducted himself as if he had found an old and long desired friend . . . He never ate his bread without holding any morsel of it to some one of his horses,—for more were given him,—nor did he ever drink water without first dipping their mouths in it, which he afterwards carefully wiped off . . . as the

powers of Caspar's mind opened, he became less interested by the playthings with which he had been at first so entirely absorbed. Even his love for horses was transformed from the wooden representation to the living animal, and in an amazingly short time he became a most accomplished and fearless horseman'.

CAN OUTCOME BE PREDICTED?

All the children reviewed had very limited language abilities at discovery but in most cases subsequent progress was very rapid indeed. One important question is, would it have been possible to predict which child would do well after rescue from the depriving environment on the basis of what was found at discovery. The evidence is not clear-cut, but the answer seems to be in the negative. Immediately upon discovery Mary was 2 years 4 months, and Louise 3 years 6 months. Yet in terms of their appearance and behaviour they were remarkably similar, both to each other and to other well-documented cases such as the Koluchova twins. At this early stage each child was said to exhibit 'autistic tendencies'. The subsequent development of these sisters is unusually well documented (Skuse 1984). After just 6 months in a

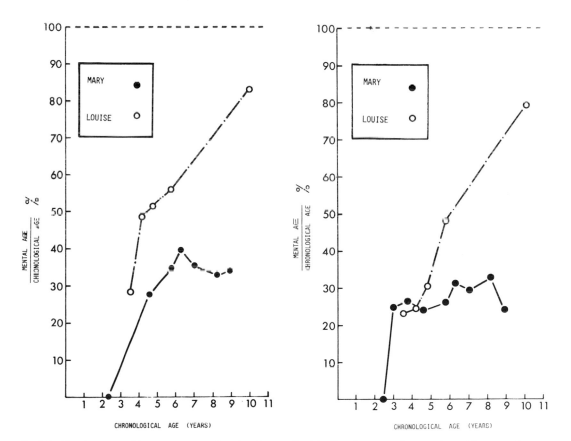

Fig. 2.1 Development of language comprehension from the time of the girls' discovery

Fig. 2.2 Development of expression of language from the time of the girls' discovery

preschool playgroup, which they attended irregularly for 2 hours a day, Louise was clearly making rapid progress in all aspects of her development, whereas Mary did not give the impression of being a normal child.

Louise's recovery of expressive and receptive language is contrasted with that of Mary in Figures 2.1 and 2.2. Her pattern of accelerated attainment is in keeping with the accounts of Isabelle and the Koluchova twins' own development of language after rescue. Recovery may have been aided by the consistent speech therapy she received. Acquisition of comprehension proceeded more rapidly than the facility to express herself, an observation which accords with the findings in several other accounts (e.g. Genie, Isabelle, the Koluchova twins, Alice and Beth). The course of Mary's development was, in contrast, less successful, but she was probably a child with constitutional anomalies which would have restricted her abilities to acquire certain cognitive skills in any event. She was a microcephalic child, as was her mother, who was herself mentally retarded, with a Stanford-Binet IQ of less than 50. Certain of Mary's nonverbal cognitive skills developed virtually as rapidly as those of her sister, but even the pattern of her achievements in these tasks was very uneven. She performed best on those items which were least verbally loaded. Additionally, Mary rarely used gesture or mime, never expressed social greetings or people's names, and the form of her language when it did develop was deviant. She exhibited recurrent echolalia and some stereotyped utterances, although no pronominal reversal. Her social relationships were disordered, she showed stereotypies of motor behaviour and in later years it became more obvious that she was expressing an autistic pattern of behaviour. The overall severity was rather less than in Kanner's classical (1943) description (see Ch. 12). She had, incidentally, a half-brother who was definitely autistic and severely developmentally delayed, and who had been fostered soon after birth.

Genie was not brought out of her hopeless social conditions until 13 years and 7 months of age, and she failed to develop any useful conversational speech although she did gain enormously in comprehension over the following five years. Lenneberg (1967) may have been correct when he suggested that language acquisition must occur during the first 12 years if it is to proceed normally, and Genie's history is often taken as evidence for his hypothesis (e.g. Rutter 1981, Curtiss 1981b). We do have good evidence that after unilateral brain damage children may switch cerebral dominance for various functions relatively easily, at least until puberty supervenes. In this connection Curtiss (1977) concludes, after a detailed account of her painstaking assessment of Genie's linguistic abilities, that the child is a 'holistic' right hemisphere thinker in respect of both verbal and nonverbal tasks. She believes this may be a direct result of Genie not acquiring language during the so-called 'critical' period. It seems a pity therefore that nowhere does she produce evidence to confirm that the left hemisphere of this unfortunate girl was functioning normally from a neurophysiological point of view.

Latest reports on the children's achievements in terms of language skills are summarized in Table 2.3. This shows that Isabelle, the Koluchova and Douglas and Sutton twins, Louise and Adam, reached virtually age-appropriate levels within a few years, despite the variety of ages at which they were removed from their formerly understimulating circumstances.

From the results of these studies one can reach a variety of conclusions about the nature of language development under extremely adverse environmental conditions. First, it seems to be more vulnerable than other cognitive faculties in view of the evidence of profound retardation at discovery in all cases reviewed, even when other features of mental development (such as perceptuomotor skills) have been relatively unaffected (e.g. Alice and Beth). Expressive speech is more seriously retarded at discovery, and develops less rapidly than comprehension after placement in a normal environment. The

Table 2.3 Latest available reports on the children's developmental level

Name	D.O.B.	Age at Discovery	Language Comprehension	Language Expression	Formal tests of cognition Performance	Formal tests of cognition Verbal
Anna (Davis) 1940	1.3.32	5;11	(C.A. 10;3) RE 2;6	(C.A. 10;3) RE 2;6	(C.A. 8;1) M-P 1;7	(C.A. 8;1)
Genie (Curtiss) 1977	?.4.57	13;7	(C.A. 16;10) ITPA Auditory Reception 5;0	(C.A. 16;10) ITPA Verbal Expression 3;8	(C.A. 17;9) RCPM 11;0 FGPT 11;0	(C.A. 18;9) PPVT 5;10
Mary (Skuse) 1982	24.11.68	2;4	(C.A. 13;0) RDLS 4;0	(C.A. 13;0) (RDLS 3;5)	(C.A. 8;11) WISC 94	
Isabelle (Mason) 1942	?.4.32	6;6	(C.A. 8;2) Reported as age appropriate		(C.A. 8;2) Reported as of normal intelligence	
Koluchova twins (MZ boys) P.M.	4.9.60	6;11	(C.A. 10;0) RE 9;0	(C.A. 10;0) RE 9;0	(C.A. 10;0) WISC 85	(C.A. 10;0) WISC 97
J.M. 1972	4.9.60	6;11	(C.A. 10;0) RE 9;0	(C.A. 10;0) RE 9;0	(C.A. 10;0) WISC 86	(C.A. 10;0) WISC 94
Douglas & Sutton twins Alice	2.2.69	4;11	(C.A. 6;4) RDLS <6;0	(C.A. 6;4) RDLS 6;0	(C.A. 6;4) WPPSI 108	(C.A. 6;4) WPPSI 102
Beth 1978	2.2.69	4;11	(C.A. 6;4) RDLS 5;1	(C.A. 6;4) RDLS 5;3	(C.A. 6;4) WPPSI 92	(C.A. 6;4) WPPSI 85
Louise (Skuse) 1982	30.9.67	3;6	(C.A. 14;5) Age appropriate (SR)	(C.A. 14;5)	(C.A. 10;1) WISC 80	(C.A.10;1) WISC 77
Adam (Thompson) 1986	?.1.72	1;4	(C.A. 13;10) Reported as age appropriate	(C.A. 13;10)	(C.A. 8;9) WISC 113 full scale	(C.A. 8;9)

ITPA	— Illinois test of psycholinguistic abilities	RCPM	— Ravens coloured progressive matrices
M-P	— Merrill-Palmer scale of mental abilities	PPVT	— Peabody picture vocabulary test
WISC	— Wechsler intelligence scale for children	RDLS	— Reynell developmental language scale
WPPSI	— Wechsler preschool and primary scale of intelligence	RE	— Retrospective estimation from written reports
FGPT	— Figure ground perception test	SR	— School report
C.A.	— Chronological age at assessment.		

exact role of environmental influences upon the form and pace of normal language acquisition is still a matter of debate (e.g. Kuczaj 1986), but there can be no disputing the primacy of *interpersonal* interaction as a necessary pre-condition.

In contrast, perceptuomotor skills are reported to be less retarded at discovery, and this could imply that they are relatively resilient to a lack of interpersonal interaction, as is gross motor development. In other words, the propensity perceptually to explore the environment that we see in normal infants is likely to be preserved despite gross deprivation, and the opportunity for practising these potential skills must be relatively more accessible even in the most impoverished and un-

stimulating settings. Because language develops in the context of *social* interaction, if opportunities for interaction are absent semiotic abilities seem to rest in abeyance.

If we try to predict which children will do well and which poorly on the basis of features at discovery, limited conclusions may be drawn. The complete absence of comprehension and expressive speech at discovery seems ominous, especially where there is a large discrepancy between nonverbal and verbal abilities (e.g. Anna, Genie, Mary). In view of the fact that initial social behaviour was highly variable between cases, correlations with later social adjustment are necessarily weak. Nevertheless, there are indications that the early combination of profound language deficit, and apathy or withdrawal from social contact which lasts more than a week or two, means that the child will have especial difficulties developing a normal range and quality of relationships in later life (see Anna and Mary). It may of course indicate that the child has a constitutional disorder which will limit the speed and quality of recovery.

Following removal from deprivation the evidence suggests that, if recovery of normal language ability is going to occur, rapid progress is the rule with substantial achievements being made within a few months (e.g. Isabelle and Adam). In those cases where it was several years before the children had caught up to age appropriate levels of language ability, improvements had nevertheless been noticeable and significant in the earliest months (e.g. Louise).

If a discrepancy is found between the rate of recovery of visuospatial skills and of speech, as was the case with Mary, this may be additional evidence in favour of the hypothesis that there exist constitutional limitations on achievement. Genie, for example, was subject to highly skilled education by Susan Curtiss for over four years, but developed few normal or appropriate acts of communication. Perhaps the few children, such as Genie, who did not make a full recovery after rescue should be considered exceptions to the general rule. If at least part of the explanation for their poor recovery is that some had suffered from a biological handicap, perhaps they had initially been maltreated because they were in some way abnormal; there is evidence that Genie was eventually found to have many features of childhood autism and that these had been recognized by her family years before discovery (Clarke, personal communication).

One is also reminded of Itard's valiant but ultimately unsuccessful efforts to teach Victor, the wild boy of Aveyron, vocal speech. Despite Lane's (1977) assertions to the contrary, it does not seem likely that his failure was entirely due to inadequate techniques of therapy, and the child was probably abandoned in middle childhood because he was found to have developmental features of childhood autism (Wing 1976a).

A striking contrast is also seen in these cases between those who were initially eager to attract adult attention and understanding at discovery and those who were apathetic and disinterested in social interaction. Perhaps the distinction is most striking in the case of the sisters, Mary and Louise; both girls did receive speech therapy soon after discovery, but when little progress was made with Mary it was abandoned. Her relative lack of social communication and language had become reminiscent of autism by the age of 9 years. However, it should be noted that four years later a remarkable transformation had taken place and she had made tremendous progress in both areas which was coincident with the disappearance of those autistic features. Despite having been placed in a variety of children's homes over that period she did receive some consistent and intensive speech therapy which, reports suggest, was successful in engendering a change in social attitudes. This observation is in itself important because it suggests that further progress may be made with children several years after removal from deprivation, even in cases when the obstacle to success is thought to consist of constitutional anomalies.

Koluchova (1976) comments; 'In spite of the fact that the twins had scarcely spoken at all until the age of 7 (their) development was quickest after the ninth year when they came to their foster family, which provided them with all the prerequisites, both in the development of speech and for the whole personality'. Although they did subsequently attend speech therapy, this seems to have been with the aim of improving pronunciation and articulation rather than in instilling a desire to communicate by vocal language. Similarly, Isabelle received nearly two years of intensive speech therapy from a team of therapists under the direction of Marie Mason, who capitalized on the child's motivation.

We can thus conclude that the general rule seems to be that the children either start to improve rapidly or that they do not recover the normal use of language at all. There is no lag before recovery of speech begins to occur in those cases with the best prognosis. This point is linked to the rapid development of social adjustment, and attachment behaviour, suggestive of the tremendously powerful need for otherwise normal children to form close relationships with their caretakers. Formation of an early focus of attachment onto one special adult seems to have distinguished Mary's from Louise's behaviour in their first nursery group. This urge to make a single loving relationship was commented on by Skeels (1966). He asserts 'This highly stimulating emotional impact was observed to be the unique characteristic and one of the main contributions of the experimental (i.e. first post-orphanage) setting' (p. 17).

Thus in the context of a loving relationship recovery of language begins almost immediately, without delay, and proceeds rapidly. The duration of deprivation prior to discovery does not predict how long recovery will take to become complete. Whether the age of the affected child at discovery is a limiting factor is uncertain, for there is contradictory evidence on that matter. The tale of Caspar Hauser presents us with a detailed account of a child who was discovered at the age of 16 years 1 month, and made a full recovery of language. Unfortunately, despite the vast literature about him it has never been clear whether his was a genuine case of deprivation or whether he was in fact an imposter (Curtiss 1981a). Genie, who was rescued at the age of 13 years 7 months may, as has already been discussed, have been an abnormal child in the first place.

INTERACTION OF GENETIC AND ENVIRONMENTAL INFLUENCES ON DEVELOPMENT

Recently, Money and his colleagues at the Johns Hopkins University (1983) reported an important series of children who had been seriously abused in early childhood and who had, as a consequence, excessively short stature and gross impairment of cognitive development. The age of the children at rescue varied between 2 years 4 months and 17 years 5 months, and follow-up was up to a maximum of 12 years 6 months. Tremendous gains in IQ over that period were seen, up to 90 points, and there was virtually linear relationship between the quantitative improvement in IQ and the duration of the post-rescue follow-up period.

The evidence both from the studies of extreme early deprivation followed by rescue and rehabilitation, and from studies of children who were raised in abusive and neglectful situations of lesser severity, goes completely against the notion of IQ constancy. The implication is that, although the polygenic mode of inheritance of intelligence is by now well established (e.g. Teasdale & Owen 1984), genes exert their effects 'indirectly' and those effects depend upon the particular environment in which individuals find themselves. For example, in a recent book, Wilson & Herrnstein (1986) suggest that 60% of the variation of IQ scores is in some way attributable to genetic variation. The correct interpretation of this figure is as follows. Since there is no practical method of separating the physical and social effects of genes, heritability estimates include both. This means that heritability estimates set a lower bound on the explanatory power of the environment, not an upper bound. If genetic variation explains 60% of the variation in IQ scores, environmental variation must explain the remaining 40%. But it may explain as much as 100%. It all depends *how* the genes affect IQ scores, and we are still a long way from knowing the answer to that riddle. In extreme environments, the role of environmental factors in determining the apparent IQ will be of greater importance than in an average environment (see Shields 1980).

DEGREE OF RECOVERY AND REMEDIAL STRATEGY

Finally, we need to consider whether degree

of recovery is influenced by specific remedial measures after rescue. In general, intensity of intervention does not seem to be of singular value in bringing about recovery. Qualitative rather than quantitative influences are paramount and Koluchova's (1976) conclusions are apposite: 'The most effective and integrative curative factor is (the) foster mother and the whole environment of (the) family' (p. 185).

In conclusion, extreme deprivation in early childhood is a condition of great theoretical and practical importance. Clinically it is essential that such children are recognized and differentiated from cases of global mental retardation, so that appropriate environmental mental manipulation and educational experience may commence as soon as possible. Fortunately, the evidence reviewed suggests that, in the absence of genetic or congenital anomalies or a history of gross malnourishment, victims of such deprivation have an excellent prognosis. Some subtle deficits in social adjustment may persist. Theoretical observations include the implication that most human characteristics, with the possible exception of language, are strongly 'canalised' (in Scarr-Salapatek's (1976) conception) and hence virtually resistant to obliteration by even the most dire early environments. On removal to a favourable situation, the remarkable and rapid progress made by those with good potential seems allied to the total experience of living in a stimulating home and forming emotional bonds to a caring adult. We may hypothesize that a caregiver's qualities of emotional availability, sensitive responsivity, encouragement and provision of perceptual stimulation shown to be important for normal infants' development (Moore 1968, Bradley & Caldwell 1976, Clarke-Stewart 1977) are also the salient influences bearing on later learning and maturation in these unfortunate children.

3

Hearing children of deaf parents

N. Schiff-Myers

INTRODUCTION

The central question which this book addresses is the extent to which the course of normal development is affected by the properties of the environment and by the innate abilities of the child. The language environment of hearing children of deaf parents presents a unique opportunity to examine speech and language development in an environment with 'exceptional' linguistic input but which theoretically should otherwise be normal. These children either hear no oral language from their parents, or if their parents do speak, the children hear limited syntax, deviant articulation, voice and stress patterns. Some of these children learn sign language as either their first language or simultaneously with oral language, which could possibly affect their early oral syntax (see Ch. 4). It has been argued that if these children develop language normally, then the innate abilities of the child should be considered to be the major contributory factor (Lenneberg 1967). If these children do not develop language normally, then crucial elements of the environment that contribute to normal language learning could be identified.

Several studies have shown that adults modify their speech to children, that it is simpler than their speech to adults and lacking in grammatical errors (Broen 1972, Drach 1969, Pfuderer 1969, Phillips 1973, Remick 1973, Sachs et al 1972, and Snow

1972,1977b). Children are therefore thought to abstract the structure of their language from the *regularities* in the stream of speech they hear. If the regularity of input is an important factor in language learning, then even if hearing children of deaf parents were exposed to normal language from others in their environment, their speech and language should somehow reflect the inconsistency in input. A review of the studies of the speech and language development of this population should help us to better understand what are the critical elements in the environment that are important for speech and language learning.

In this chapter, recent research of speech and language development of hearing children of deaf parents will be reviewed. The following questions will be addressed:

1. Do the majority of these children have language/and or speech problems at some stage in their development. If so, at what ages are problems most likely to occur?
2. Which aspects of speech/language are most likely to be affected?
   a. voice
   b. phonological system
   c. syntax
   d. vocabulary
   e. content (semantics or meanings encoded)
   f. use (conversational abilities).
3. Are there any factors in the environment that will predict who will have problems and who will not?
4. What influence does sign language have on the development of syntax?

RESEARCH FINDINGS

There have been several observational studies of hearing children of deaf parents. The results of these studies show that while some normal-hearing children of deaf parents appear to have speech or language difficulty, others develop normally.

There have been only two studies of large groups of children. Brejle (1971) administered the Templin-Darley Tests of Articulation and the Peabody Picture Vocabulary Test to 56 subjects, 13 of whom were preschoolers. He found receptive vocabulary to be the same as that of the general population and articulation development to be better than that of the normal population.

Schiff & Ventry (1976) evaluated 52 children of deaf parents who were reported to have normal hearing. These children came from 34 families and ranged in age from six months to 12 years. All children received audiological evaluations as part of this study. Standardized tests, developmental scales and informal conversation and play techniques were used to evaluate their speech and language. Of the 52 children evaluated, 23 were considered to be definitely developing speech and language normally. One child was too young to evaluate and five who were under four years of age had questionable difficulties (i.e. their Mean Length of Utterance [MLU] was age appropriate, but they scored slightly below age level on comprehension tasks and the semantic content of their speech appeared to be limited). 23 children had definite speech and language problems (six had speech and language problems related to previously undetermined hearing loss, and six had known factors other than the deafness of the parents contributing to the delay (psycho-motor retardation, emotional disturbance, and brain damage)). Children were considered to be speech or language delayed if they scored one year below age level on any speech or language test or developmental scale.

Eleven children (21% of the total sample) from seven different families were considered to have speech or language problems with no other known identifiable factors other than the deafness of their parents contributing to the problem. Four of these children were preschool (under the age of 5) while seven were school-aged. Of the 11 children, one had an isolated articulation problem, and two had a language problem only, while eight had language and speech problems. Speech problems included five with phonological delay, three with cluttering and eight with what appeared to be deviant stress and intonation patterns. The three children who cluttered were from the same family. The 10 children with language problems all had comprehension and vocabulary deficits. Seven children who were over 5 years of age did poorly on comprehension tasks which required prior information and on tasks dependent on knowlege of word meaning (Auditory Reception and Auditory Association subtests of the Illinois Test of Psycholinguistic Abilities [ITPA] and the PPVT). These children seemed to demonstrate some word-finding difficulty in their spontaneous speech. Three children who were below four years of age also scored below age level on receptive vocabulary tasks (PPVT), or on developmental scales (Anderson et al 1963, Doll 1966, Mecham 1971. Only two of the school-aged children's expressive language contained errors of syntax (errors of verb tense, subject-verb agreement and pronoun confusion).

The results of the Schiff & Ventry study indicated that the prevalence of speech and language problems and hearing losses seemed to be higher than in the population at large, but factors other than the deafness of the parents sometimes contributed to that difference. Where other possible contributory factors were absent, a statistical difference in incidence of speech and language problems was not clearly demonstrated The 11 children who had problems with no other known contributory factors came from seven families. There appeared to be a tendency for children from the same family to have similar speech or language problems.

Although speech-language pathologists have often used the criterion of one year below chronological age level to determine potential problems, the problem with using age equivalent scores has now been well documented; they fail to help the test user appreciate the range of performance that can be expected from normal children (McCauley & Swisher 1984a,b). Therefore, standard scores and percentile scores would have been far more

useful. Unfortunately, many of the measures used for evaluating children had only age-equivalent scores.

Schiff & Ventry made several other observations which were surprising:

1. Speech and language problems, if they existed in this population, did not necessarily disappear after the child had entered school at ages 5 or 6 and was exposed daily to normal speech. Of the 12 school-aged children who were evaluated, nine were identified as having some speech or language problem; eight of the nine had more than 2 years of classroom experience. However, two of these children were judged to come from an emotionally disturbed environment.

2. Sibling status and time spent with normal speaking adults were not predictive of which children had problems. Six children (from three families) in the problem group, with no other known confounding factors contributing to their deficit, had hearing grandparents living in the same building. 81% of the normal-speaking children were oldest or only children, while more than half (55%) of the 11 children who presented communication problems in the absence of etiological factors other than the parents' deafness were younger siblings. Four of the children had older siblings with similar speech or language problems, one child had older deaf siblings, and one child had an older sibling with normal speech and language.

3. Intelligibility of the mother was an important, but not essential component for normal language to develop in this population. All of the seven mothers of the 11 children in the problem group were considered unintelligible speakers. However, more than half of the mothers of the normal speaking group were considered to be unintelligible.

There have been several studies of smaller groups of children of eight or fewer. Critchley (1967) studied three school-age children and found one child who began school at 5 years of age to have deviant articulation and some reading difficulty in the first grade. As the child matured, these problems disappeared.

This child's spontaneous speech was also considered to be 'ungrammatical'. A second child's verbal IQ scores were significantly lower than her non-verbal scores. No problem was noted in the remaining child.

Mayberry (1976) measured the oral-language and manual-language skills of eight first-born hearing children of manually communicating deaf parents. The children ranged in age from 3 to 7 years and no normal hearing adults lived in any of the homes. The mode of communication used with the children was determined by questioning the parents and observations of the investigator. One articulation test and four tests of oral-language performance were administered to each child: Arizona Articulation Proficiency Scale, Auditory Association subtest of the ITPA (Kirk et al 1968), Utah Test of Language Development, PPVT and Developmental Sentence Scoring (DSS). The manual-language skills of the children were tested with the PPVT and the Utah Test of Language Development. As in the study by Schiff & Ventry (1976) the criterion used for normal development was a score on any of the tests of no less than 12 months below chronological age, with the exception of the DSS, where a child needed to score no less than the 10th percentile. However when evaluating the results, if a child scored below criterion on only one measure but other test scores were acceptable, the investigator considered the child's oral language to be normal. Four children scored below criterion on one test but normally on other measures. All of the children scored within normal limits on the articulation test. Mayberry concluded that the oral exposure outside the home together with the parents' use of a structured communication system (i.e. sign language) was sufficient for the acquisition of oral language.

Six children between the ages of 3;4 and 4;4 were evaluated by Murphy & Slorach (1983). Four were first born and two were fourth born. No hearing adults were living in the home and all siblings had normal hearing sensitivity. Five of the mothers reported using predominantly an oral system with their children, but two reported that they used signs

if their children could not understand their speech. One mother used only a manual system. Interaction between mother and child was not observed. Time spent with hearing persons (termed 'extra help') was calculated and ranked, but not reported. The following measures were used to evaluate the children: Reynell Devlopmental Language Scales—Comprehension Section, Enticknap Picture Vocabulary Test (Enticknap 1957), Developmental Abilities Screening Inventory (Du Bose & Langley 1978), Goodenough-Harris Drawing Test, Language Assessment Remediation and Screening Procedure and MLU. The criterion used for determining a problem from the results of standardized tests was a score below age expectation level; a definition of when a below-age-level score was considered to be problematic was not given. Four of the children were judged to be functioning at age level in MLU. Five scored below age level on the comprehension task; two scored below age level on the vocabulary test.

The authors used an unpublished assessment program by Boxx (1979) to judge that all six children had deviant language development; three were considered to have delayed language development as well. Deviant utterances as defined by Crystal et al (1976) are those sentences 'which would be both structurally inadmissible in the adult grammar, and not part of the expected grammatical development of normal children (insofar as this can be established by reference to the language acquisition literature)' (Crystal et al 1976 pp. 28–29). Using this criterion, between 13% and 26% of utterances were judged to be deviant. The investigators also looked at the appropriateness of the children's responses to conversational moves by the experimenters. They found that the children frequently failed to respond appropriately, particularly to questions. All of the children had some utterances that had deviant word order ('That a daddy bring my': Murphy & Slorach p. 124). Although the authors did not say so, some of these 'deviant' utterances may have resulted from combining of phrases ('That here put on' [that here/ put on/], 'I got my room my farm' [I got my room/ my farm/] p. 125), while some have been found ('What there is') in the normal child language literature (Brown 1968). The authors observed that the deviant utterances occurred when the children attempted to express rather complex ideas with their limited linguistic skills. They concluded that some of the unusual constructions were due to interference from the system used in signing. The investigators also observed an overabundance of the referents 'thing' and 'there' in the children's spontaneous speech. No correlation was found between the 'extra help' the children received, and their Reynell comprehension scores and syntactic skills, but extra help was positively correlated with cognitive development, development of semantic relations and MLU.

There are two longitudinal case studies of hearing children of deaf parents who were not randomly selected, but were studied because problems were observed in nursery school (Todd 1975, Sachs & Johnson 1976, Todd & Aitchison 1980, Sachs et al 1981). The child studied by Todd (1975) and Todd & Aitchison (1980), Victor, reportedly learned sign language as his first language. This child's parents communicated with him only in American Sign Language (ASL) and he heard little or no normal language until he was 3 years old. He did have a younger hearing sibling (Toby), but his speech and language were not studied. Both articles dealt with Victor's language when he was approximately four years old. Many of the child's utterances lacked the syntactical relationships typical of speech (e.g. inflections, prepositions, and articles), while others seemed to reflect structural features of sign language: (1) bracketing or copying around—ABA constructions such as 'You house you?'; (2) reduplication—repetition 'Round, it down, down'; (3) doubling—repetition with synonyms 'See, all-finish you Toby' where *you* and *Toby* both refer to the same person; (4) afterthought or tacking on 'See broken car/my' and (5) incorporation of subject-verb and/or object in a single word—holophrasis—and the combination of holophrases. 'My sick ambulance fire' was said

when Victor was pretending to be injured in a wreck and the utterance was interpreted to mean 'I'm sick (= injured), so I need an ambulance, and the car is on fire' (Todd 1975 p. 113). Victor frequently pretended that cars were on fire.

The simultaneous existence in oral language of elements of normal oral language development and of the structure of sign language led Todd (1975) and Todd & Aitchison (1980) to conclude that oral language was being learned as a second language. However, they did not examine Victor's sign language development or his use of sign in interaction with his parents, but based this conclusion on the comparison of the structure of the child's utterances with the structure of sign language.

Sachs & Johnson (1976) and Sachs et al (1981) reported on the language development of a child (Jim) beginning at age 3;9, when he was referred for a speech and language delay from a preschool program for handicapped children. His younger brother, Glen, was also seen (Sachs et al 1981). Like Victor, Jim was not exposed to any oral language from his parents or from adult normal hearing speakers, except from television, until he entered nursery school at age 3 years. He did play with other children. Unlike Victor's family, neither parent reported that they signed to the children although they communicated with each other using sign language. Neither brother was observed signing. According to the mother's report, Jim said his first words at 2;6 and these seemed to be words he heard on television. It was reported that the mother related to her children warmly but did not use any symbolic system.

The following assessment procedures were used: language sampling, probes, the PPVT, the ITPA, Menyuk sentences (Menyuk 1969), Stanford-Binet Intelligence Scale, Gesell Developmental Schedule. The Boehm Test of Basic Concepts and the Goldman Fristoe-Woodcock Test of Auditory Discrimination were administered when the children were of school age.

At the initial session, when Jim was 3;9, he produced no spontaneous utterances (only responses to questions), manifested severe articulation problems and spoke in a soft voice. He scored below age level on the Developmental Sentence Types analysis, Menyuk sentences, and ITPA Auditory Sequencing. On the Gesell Developmental Schedule, he was rated at 42 months for gross motor skills, but only at the 36 months level for fine motor skills. The relationship between Jim's delay in fine motor skills and speech development was not discussed. It was not possible to administer the PPVT because Jim could not grasp the instructions. The investigators found Jim to be an effective communicator, despite his limited oral language. When the semantic relations were compared with younger children with the same MLU, Jim's expression of meanings were similiar; however, the proportion of multiword utterance types that contained more than one semantic relation was higher. The authors noted that this might be due to the fact that Jim was older and was trying to express more complex ideas but did not use syntactic devices for combining relations (e.g. conjunctions) within one utterance boundary and he used few grammatical morphemes in relation to his MLU. In addition, the order of Jim's words often did not conform to English order. The authors stated that many of these features might have resulted from stringing together associated words or phrases ('My mommy my house [ə] play ball' Sachs et al 1981 p. 44). Another source of unconventional word order was a strategy of making a comment and then specifying the topic ('Off my mittens.', 'Where is it plane?' (Sachs et al 1981 pp. 44–45). Some of these types of idiosyncratic patterns have been observed in normal children (Braine 1976, Clark 1974 cited by Sachs et al 1981).

Some of the constructions reported resembled those of Victor, the child studied by Todd and Todd & Aitchison. However, because Jim did not produce signs himself, the authors concluded that it was unlikely that he had internalized the structure of sign and was using that structure to produce his oral utterances.

Jim was seen twice weekly for one month.

During these sessions, his language was further evaluated. At the end of the seventh observation session, before being enrolled in speech-language therapy, Jim's scores on all tests had improved and only one utterance had a non-English word order.

Jim was enrolled in speech-language therapy through the first grade. His performance in school was considered to be normal. At age 6;11 he scored in the 90th percentile on the school's reading test. The PPVT and several subtests of the ITPA were administered periodically. Some of these scores were below his chronological age with the most consistent low scores being on the Manual and Verbal Expression portions of the ITPA. These below-chronological-age scores were not thought by the authors to represent an underlying speech-language problem.

Glenn, Jim's younger brother, manifested no speech-language problems at age 3;9, the age when Jim was first evaluated. However, when Glenn was first seen at 1;8, he used a soft voice quality, as did his brother, and did not use single words till he was two. Like Jim, he continued to score below age level on the Manual and Verbal Expression portions of the ITPA. He repeated the first grade because of immaturity, but his academic progress was satisfactory with reading scores above the 90th percentile.

Schiff (1979) followed the language development of five normal hearing first-born children of profoundly deaf parents who had no other hearing adults living in the home. They were called John, Ron, Seth, Lisa and Mona. These children were approximately 2 years of age when first seen (between the ages of 22–28 months) and were videotaped each month for a period of 6 to 9 months while interacting with their mothers and with the investigator. Four children spent a minimum of 10 hours per week in the company of hearing speakers, primarily grandparents, while one child spent a minimum of 5 hours per week with hearing speakers. All visiting times were included regardless of whether any interaction occurred with the child. All of the children watched television 2 hours daily.

The three mothers of the boys were judged to be less than 15% intelligible and had MLUs of under 2.0. One mother (Ron's) had an MLU of under 1.5. Lisa's mother was the most intelligible (86%), but her MLU was only 2.19. Mona's mother was 66% intelligible with an MLU of 3.5 in interaction with her child, and it was possible that her MLU was even higher in other contexts.

Schiff (1979) compared the language development of these children with children reported in the developmental literature and found:

1. The children used the same categories of semantic-syntactic relations with as many different types as those found by Bloom et al (1975). In other words, the children did not use only a few stereotyped phrases to encode the semantic-syntactic relations. Their utterances were varied and creative.

2. The overwheming majority of the children's utterances were systematically combined. Only 3% or less of the syntactic utterances violated the subject-verb-object order of constituents.

3. All of the children increased their MLU. However two children (John and Ron) barely achieved an MLU of 2.0 after 9 months of observation.

4. The three children who had reached Stage 3 of development (MLU of 2.5) were using present progressive (ing), prepositions (in and on), and the plural form in 90% of required contexts. These were the only morphemes that reached 90% acquisition by Stage 3 in the speech of all three children studied by Brown (1973). Furthermore, these children were developing the grammatical morphemes in the same sequence as those described by Brown (1973) and de Villiers and de Villiers (1973).

5. Ron and John were slower in development and were beginning Stage 2 when the observations ended. However, they too were developing the grammatical morphemes and there was not sufficient evidence to indicate a delay in development in comparison with reports in the normal developmental literature. All of the children said their first words by the time they were 24 months old. McCarthy (1954) reported an average Mean Length of Sentence of 3.1 at 30 months of age. According to these averages, John and Ron could possibly be considered to be delayed in development at 30 months of age when their MLU was 2.0. However, Nelson (1973) reported a MLU range of 1.80–4.46 in 18 normal children at 30 months of age. One of the children (Sarah) studied by Brown (1973) did not pass into Stage two (MLU of 2.0) until she was 32 months old. In the Nelson study as well as in McCarthy (1954), rate of language acquisition has been correlated with sex, with boys being slower.

6. The development of discourse relations paralleled the development of normal children studied by Bloom et al (1974, 1976). Like the children studied by Bloom et al, all the children's spontaneous imitations decreased as they developed contingent speech. Contingent utterances shared the same topic with the preceding adult utterance and added information to it, while imitations were exact repetitions of all or part of a prior adult utterance. The majority of child utterances which followed adult utterances were related to that utterance by topic (i.e. they were imitations or were contingent). Of those utterances that were contingent, most of these were linguistically contingent. Both imitations and intraclausal linguistically contingent utterances (utterances in which the child used a verb relation of a previous utterance) indicated that the children were using forms from the adult utterances to formulate their own in conversation.

The children used at least as many spontaneous imitations and intraclausal linguistically contingent utterances with their mothers as they did with the normal speaking investigator. Despite the mother's unintelligibility to hearing strangers, the children imitated their mothers' utterances and used the verb relations of their mothers' utterances when formulating their responses. For example, when Seth's mother asked 'What you want?' Seth responded, I want ABC.' When Lisa's mother asked, 'Who drive the car?' Lisa replied, 'Woman drive the car.' (Schiff 1979 p. 598). Schiff suggested that the children were utilizing linguistic information from their mothers' utterances to communicate with them, and probably to learn language as well. She considered this to be evidence that the children were learning language from their mothers as well as from hearing speakers.

7. Evaluation of the mothers' speech indicated that only 2% violated subject-verb-object ordering of consitituents. Grammatical morphemes, for the most part, were omitted from all of the mothers' speech. Only the mothers of Mona and Ron produced any of the grammatical morphemes in 90% of the contexts in which they were required. All of the grammatical morphemes that appeared in the children's speech were found to occur (albeit infrequently) in their mothers' speech. These results showed that hearing inconsistent use of grammatical morphemes in required contexts need not affect the children's development of these forms.

8. One of the children (Ron) was thought to have adopted his mother's deaf articulation and stress patterns, and his phonological processes were investigated by Schiff-Myers & Klein (to be discussed later in this chapter).

Schiff concluded that hearing children of deaf parents do not need to hear much 'normal' language to learn to encode what they have learned during the sensorimotor period. They can develop language normally if their mothers communicate with them using some telegraphic speech which is ordered into subject-verb-object relationships and is related to context, provided they are in contact with hearing speakers for a minimum of 5 to 10 hours weekly and watch some television. She hypothesized that if language affected these children's development at all, it might do so in the later stages when the mothers would not have the capacity to encode information that older children need. Relatively little language is needed to code the information that a 2-year-old needs to develop the basic foundations of language (i.e. the semantic-syntactic relations expressed in children's early utterances). However, it is unlikely that the mothers would have the capacity to orally encode abstract concepts using complex syntactic structures.

It was not possible to follow all the children through the school years. One child's parents (Mona's) separated from each other shortly after the study and the child and mother moved in with hearing grandparents. A second child (Lisa) moved to California. All of the children reportedly did well in nursery school. However, only the three boys were re-evaluated, when they were between the ages of $7\frac{1}{2}$ to $8\frac{1}{2}$. They were the children of most concern, because their mothers' MLU and intelligibility were so poor. All three children were reportedly doing at least average work in school with no learning problems. Ron had been seen from Kindergarten through second grade for speech therapy because he stuttered. However, he was described as being a quiet, often non-verbal child. No language or reading problems were identified for any of the children.

The three boys were evaluated for language and articulation proficiency. These results have not been reported elsewhere. An informal language sample was collected. In addition, the following tests were administered: Test of Language Development [TOLD] to assess general language functioning; PPVT to assess receptive vocabulary; the McCarthy Scales of Children's Abilities to compare verbal development with general cognitive functioning; and the Templin-Darley Screening Test to assess articulation development.

None of the children's spontaneous speech contained articulation errors, nor did they make any errors on the Templin-Darley. During the spontaneous sample, only Ron's speech contained grammatical errors. These were errors in subject-verb agreement (e.g. 'She didn't believes it') and in the use of the irregular past and plurals. He often appeared to be searching for words. It was impossible to determine if this apparent search was a manifestation of his dysfluency or the cause of it. No secondary blocks were observed, but he was reluctant to talk and appeared to be self-conscious about his speech.

Table 3.1 Standardized test results on three hearing children of deaf parents

Child	Age	TOLD Language Quotient	PPVT Percentile	Language Age	McCarthy Scales General Cognitive Index	Scaled Scores* Verbal	Perceptual Performance
John	8;6	101	78%	9;4	107	55	41
Ron	8;4	98	24%	6;8	109	59	41
Seth	7;6	113	92%	10;2	150+	71	57

*Mean = 50, Standard Deviation = 10

All of the children scored within normal limits on the standardized tests (see Table 3.1). No child scored below one standard deviation on any subtest of any standardized test. Only Ron scored more than one year below his chronological age. At a chronological age of 8;4 he achieved a language age of 6;8 on the PPVT and 6;6 on the Sentence Imitation subtest of the TOLD. However, his highest scores on the TOLD were Oral Vocabulary (scaled score 13 and language age of >8;3 and Picture Vocabulary (scaled score of 10 and language age of 8;3). (The mean for this test is 10 with a SD of three). A surprising result was that all of the children, including Ron, scored better on the verbal portion of the McCarthy Scales than they did on the perceptual-performance subtests.

In summary, based upon the results of the standardized tests, (a) none of the three children could be considered to be language disordered and (b) their language skills were consistent with their cognitive skills. Ron, however, had more difficulty communicating than the other two. In addition to the fluency problem, his spontaneous speech contained syntactic errors and he appeared to have some vocabulary deficits. The test results revealed that the syntactic errors were within normal limits. However, as a speech-language pathologist, I recommended to Ron's school that he continue in therapy, because of the difficulties observed in his spontaneous communication and the limitations in his language environment at home.

We can only speculate as to whether Ron really would have done better if he had come from a normal speaking home. His scores on perceptual-motor and quantitative tasks were no better than on verbal tasks. In addition, there were other problems in Ron's environment that might have contributed to his communication difficulties. When I observed Ron when he was 2 years, his mother often corrected his speech and asked him to imitate her. Being asked to imitate deaf speech must have been confusing. When Ron was 5 years, his father died suddenly in a drowning accident and soon after that his mother began living with another man. When I visited the school to speak to them about the results of my evaluation, they reported to me that Ron had recently run away from home. The child study team felt that Ron's speech and language were consistent with his overall intellectual ability. However, they were concerned about his problems at home. Prior reports indicated concern about the high standards set for Ron by his mother and the problems observed in their relationship.

EFFECT OF DEAF SPEECH ON PHONOLOGICAL DEVELOPMENT

The results of the studies reported above indicate that while some normal hearing children of deaf parents have articulation problems many do not. Leonard et al (1980) described the phonology of a normal hearing child of deaf parents as he developed his first 50 words. Only some of the earliest productions could be attributed to the influence of the deaf mother. Within an experimental paradigm imposed by the investigators, the child heard some words beginning with /θ/, /g/, and /d/ only from his mother. He initially produced some of these with a nasal, as did his mother, rather than with the appropriate sound or with a *d* (a dominant phone class he often used in the place of other consonants he could not produce). After a few weeks *d* replaced the nasal. Leonard et al (1980) concluded that as phonological organization develops, phonetic regularities occur across lexical items regardless of the original lexical input.

Of the five children studied by Schiff (1979) one child (Ron) appeared to have articulation and stress patterns similar to those of deaf speakers (i.e. what seemed to be hyponasal speech with numerous omissions and inappropriate stress patterns) during the preschool years. This child spent less time with hearing speakers (5–10 h per week as compared with 10–15 h per week), and was often asked by his mother to imitate her productions.

In order to determine the influence of deaf speech on all the children's development Schiff-Myers & Klein (1985) compared the phonological processes of the children from deaf homes with those used by children from normal hearing homes (Ingram 1974, 1976, 1978; Klein 1981; Preisser 1983) and with the processes of their mothers. The phonological processes in the mothers' productions were determined from a phonetic transcription of the recorded reading of 22 CID Everyday Sentences (Barley Speechreading Test 1971). This was used rather than spontaneous speech so that the investigators could be certain of the gloss. The mothers' spontaneous speech was transcribed only when the children imitated their mothers' utterances.

None of the children, including Ron, adopted their mothers' idiosyncratic articulation patterns in their spontaneous speech or when they imitated their mothers. The children's modifications were more like those of other young children described in the normal developmental literature than they were like the models provided by their mothers. Ron was different from the other observed chil-

dren in that he applied a greater number of phonological processes with greater frequency. Greater frequencies were especially apparent for Final Consonant Deletion, Cluster Reduction, Stopping, Prevocalic Voicing and Postvocalic Devoicing. Ron only adopted his mother's more atypical productions in a few situations where he was pressed to imitate her.

Three of the children (Ron, Mona and Lisa) used faulty stress patterns, but Ron did so with greater frequency (34% of polysyllabic words contained unusual stress patterns) and this probably contributed to the appearance of 'deaf-like' speech. Although Ron did use faulty stress more frequently than the other children in this study, it was not clear whether his pattern was different from that of other normal children at early stages of development. Stress patterns reported for other children of this age have included misplaced stress and the use of level stress (Leopold 1947, Smith 1973, Allen & Hawkins 1978, 1980, Klein 1984). While deaf speech contains faulty stress patterns because vowels and consonants tend to be prolonged or added, the children in this study rarely added vowels or consonants.

The results of this study did not support Lenneberg's (1967) observation that the 'quality of vocalizations' of hearing children of deaf parents resembles that of the deaf during the preschool years. Not only did these children not adopt their mothers' deaf speech productions but none of the children adopted their mothers' voice quality. Schiff & Ventry (1976) also observed that voice quality was never affected by the deafness of their parents.

INFLUENCE OF SIGN LANGUAGE

Because of the limited and deviant oral input of the deaf parents, most anecdotal reports from hearing children of deaf parents indicate that they believe they learned sign language as their first language and learned oral language from hearing adults (Fant &

Schuchman 1974, Vernon 1974). When problems did occur in oral language it was assumed that these problems were related to mapping oral language on a sign language syntactic base (Todd 1975, Todd & Aitchison 1980, Murphy & Slorach 1983). This would be similar to reports of other children who are simultaneously acquiring two languages (McLaughlin 1981) who seem to go through a stage of language mixing (see Ch. 4). However, 'deviant' syntactic constructions have been found in children who reportedly did not communicate with their parents in sign language (Murphy & Slorach 1983 and Sachs et al 1981). As Sachs et al observed in the child they studied, some of these deviant constructions may have resulted from stringing together associated words and phrases because the children lacked the syntactic means to express their more complex thoughts. Bloom (1973) identified successive single word utterances in a normal child's speech in which more complex notions were expressed by stringing together single words with a slight pause in between. Braine (1976) observed a similar phenomenon which he described as a 'groping period' in which early syntax lacked order for a short period of time. It is, therefore, not unheard of in the normal developmental literature, at least at the one and two-word stage, that children may go through a transitional period as they learn syntax where utterances may lack order. In this section, the interaction between sign language and oral language will be discussed in conjunction with the reported use of sign language in the homes.

Todd (1975) and Todd & Aitchison (1980) identified several characteristics of the structure of American Sign Language (ASL) which they found in the oral speech of a speech-language delayed child, Victor. These characteristics were discussed above. Unfortunately, Victor's sign language development was not evaluated to determine if he was delayed in sign as well. The investigators reported that Victor sometimes produced speech and signs simultaneously, but for the most part he simply spoke (Todd & Aitchison 1980). In addition, there is no reported observation of communication between parents and child to verify that, in fact, Victor's first language was ASL. Nevertheless, the investigators present rather convincing evidence that this child was superimposing oral language onto an ASL syntax. Sachs et al (1981) were told by researchers in sign language that many of Jim's errors could be based on ASL since many of his utterances lacked conventional order. However, they concluded that this relationship could be one of chance, because Jim did not produce signs nor did his mother communicate with him in sign although ASL was used in the home. They concluded that most of Jim's syntactical errors resulted from attempts to express fairly complex ideas with limited syntax. Thus, he seemed to string together associated words and phrases. While Todd and Aitchison (1980) reported that Victor's strategy of using ASL syntax when speaking had resulted in a 'dead end', Jim made rapid progress and developed into a normal speaker.

When there is normal oral input as the child is learning ASL then there appears to be no detrimental effect. Prinz & Prinz (1979, 1981) reported on the development of a hearing child of a deaf mother and a hearing father. The mother reportedly communicated with the child using ASL while the father communicated orally. The child acquired signs sooner, but her oral language development paralleled that of normal children. However, she seemed to pass through a transitional period in which she often applied the same syntactic rules to both languages—sometimes using the rules of English when she spoke and sometimes using what seemed to be the rules of ASL. She used reduplication to express plurality, saying the same word twice (e.g. 'milk milk'). However, many of the utterances reported by Prinz & Prinz (1981) as having a sign language base were similar to those found in the normal literature (e.g. 'Where Anya?' 'Allgone gum' and 'Allgone the water', 'more up,' pp. 82, 83).

Two other studies of children from deaf homes have indicated that sign language need not interfere with normal development. Jones & Quigley (1979) investigated question formation in two hearing children of deaf parents. They found that the development of question forms was not impeded by deviant input and reflected no influence from ASL.

Mayberry (1976) found that all of the parents of the eight children she studied reported using more sign language than speech with their children. When she observed the parent-child interaction, however, she found that parents of two children used oral language with sign; four children heard oral language from one parent and received manual communication from the other; and two children heard no speech from either parent. The amount of oral language or manual language used in the home did not predict the child's scores on language tests. However, the manual-language test performances of the children who received a combination of oral and manual input were well below those of the children who received only manual input. Mayberry concluded that sign language did not interfere with oral language development; on the contrary, when both languages were used by the parents, the children focussed on the oral.

Schiff-Myers (1982) compared the oral and sign language development of the five children described above with the mothers' oral and sign input. All of the parents reported communicating with each other with ASL but reported using both sign and oral language with their children.

One hour of video tape for each child, half of which contained interactions between the child and mother and half with the investigator, was transcribed with the assistance of a deaf adult who was fluent in sign language. Signs in this study included gestures in common use by hearing people as well as signs of ASL. Therefore, some of the signs were not necessarily learned as arbitrary signals. Approximately 96% of the children's communication was encoded orally and at least 70% of their oral communication attempts were not accompanied by signs. Although the children tended to use pro-

portionally more signs with their mothers than they did with the investigator, they were still overwhemingly oral. Despite the mothers' severe oral linguistic deficits, they all used oral language as their primary means of communication with their children and ordered their oral language according to English syntax and not ASL. More than 85% of all the mothers' communication with their children contained oral speech, although some of this speech was whispered. Of the signs that were accompanied by spoken utterances that could be understood, 87% of the children's and 95% of the mothers' signs were redundant to spoken utterances; they added no new information. Very few of the signs used by children or the mothers were arbitrary and required knowledge of a special code (8% of the children's and 7% of the mothers'). It is possible that the mothers were using nonarbitrary iconic signs just as hearing mothers tend to use simpler words to their children. The deaf consultant reported that the mothers were 'cutting their signs' and referred to them as 'baby signs'. The results of this study and Mayberry's (1976) study indicate that parents who claim they are communicating in both sign and oral language may be underestimating the predominance of their oral input.

SUMMARY AND CONCLUSIONS

The research reported above indicates that some normal hearing children born to deaf parents have speech and language problems while others do not. Although the prevalence of problems in this population seems to be higher than in the population at large, factors other than the deafness of the parents have been identified as contributing to that difference (i.e. emotional disturbance, psycho-motor retardation, brain damage, etc.). Part of the problem in ascertaining whether there is a real difference in incidence of speech and language problems results from differences in criteria used to interpret test results. Unfortunately, age equivalent scores were used by most investigators and the criteria varied for defining a problem when a score fell below chronological age. In addition, some researchers disregarded test results if a child scored below criterion on only one test, while other researchers did not. Nevertheless, the literature clearly shows that some hearing children develop speech and language normally, and that there are some aspects of speech and language that are rarely affected by the parents' deafness, even in children where problems have been observed.

Aspects of speech and language affected by parents' deafness

There are several aspects of communication that have been reported not to be affected by deviant linguistic input. The use of language for interactional purposes, discourse development and the content of language (i.e. the semantic relations) have not been reported to be adversely affected; nor have any of the children studied developed deaf voice quality, although they may sometimes communicate using whispered speech. Delays in phonological development have been reported in this population and some of these children's speech patterns have been described as 'deaf-like'. However, when the phonological processes of the children and the productions of the mothers were systematically analyzed, it was found that the children did not adopt the idiosyncratic patterns used by the deaf. They rarely imitated or spontaneously produced the atypical productions found in their mothers' speech. If errors in production were made, these were simplifications typically found in normal children's productive systems (Schiff-Myers & Klein 1985).

Faulty stress patterns were found to exist in some children's speech, but thus far the incidence has not been shown to be different from those found in children from normal speaking homes. The prevalence of atypical stress in the normal population of children has not been studied sufficiently to determine if these errors reflect more than normal variation.

Problems in fluency (stuttering and cluttering) were also observed, but it is difficult to prove that these are directly attributable to the parents' deafness.

Delay in development of mean length of utterance, grammatical morphemes and receptive and expressive vocabulary were identified in some children, as well as syntactic constructions that seemingly lacked the conventional ordering rules of English. When problems have been identified, they have occurred in preschool as well as in school-aged children. However, errors in the ordering of sentence constituents have been reported primarily in children between the ages of 3;4 and 4;4 (Todd 1975, Todd & Aitchison 1980, Sachs et al 1981 and Murphy & Slorach 1983), but have not been reported in the language of older and younger children.

Effect of sign language on oral language development

The lack of English word order in these children's utterances has been attributed to the acquisition of the syntax of ASL and then the superimposition of oral language on this base. However, it is not at all clear that the observed children were acquiring sign language as their first language. All of the observed children communicated primarily verbally when they were studied, including Victor, the child studied by Todd. Despite the fact that many deaf parents say, and anecdotal reports of hearing children of deaf parents indicate, that sign language is learned as the first language of children of many deaf parents, this may not necessarily be the case. Both Schiff-Myers (1982) and Mayberry (1976) observed that the ratio of sign/oral input was not accurately reported by the mothers. Furthermore, some deaf mothers with limited spoken language nevertheless order their oral language according to English syntax and not ASL (Schiff-Myers 1982). This was observed even when their MLUs were under 2.0 and they were less than 15% intelligible.

Even if sign language is the primary input language, it need not negatively affect the child's syntax. Mayberry found that two children between the ages of 3;0 and 3;10 who were communicated with primarily in ASL did not develop any speech/language problems and scored within normal limits on Lee & Canter's Developmental Sentence Scoring Procedure. They did as well as children who heard oral language from at least one parent. Furthermore, children whose parents did not sign to them also have been observed to encode utterances that lacked order (Sachs et al 1981, Murphy & Slorach 1983). Therefore, there is insufficient evidence to say that knowledge of ASL negatively affects oral language. There may be a transitional period for some children where only one syntax is used for both languages (oral or sign) but this effect should only be temporary. It is more likely, as Sachs et al (1981) have suggested, that the lack of order that has been reported is due to the child's attempts to encode complex notions with limited syntax, resulting in the stringing together of short phrases. Further studies that include context to interpret the children's utterances may help to resolve the issue.

Environmental factors

Not surprisingly, children who have parents with unintelligible speech and limited syntax are more likely to have speech and language problems. However, the amount of time spent with hearing speakers has not been predictive of normal speech/language development. Schiff & Ventry (1976) found that problems existed even when hearing relatives were living in the home, and Murphy & Slorach (1983) found no correlation between the amount of time the children spent with hearing people and the children's comprehension and expression skills. In addition, problems were found in younger siblings even when a problem did not exist in the older siblings (Schiff & Ventry 1976).

Nevertheless, a certain amount of normal language exposure would seem to be necessary for children to develop speech and language adequately. At least two of the children studied (Todd 1975 and Sachs et al 1981) who experienced speech-language delays did not hear normal speech from adults, except from television, until they were 3 years old. In the studies by Schiff & Ventry (1976) and Schiff (1979), all of the children who developed normally were in the company of hearing speakers for at least five hours per week.

Oral language from a deaf parent may also facilitate normal language learning. The two children studied by Todd (1975) and Sachs et al (1981) reportedly did not receive any oral communication from either parent. Schiff (1979) found evidence that the children she studied in the early stages were learning oral language from their mothers as well as from normal speakers (i.e. they were imitating their mothers' utterances and utilizing the verb relations of their utterances when responding to them). She concluded that children will develop language normally in the early stages if their mothers communicate with them using syntax that is ordered into subject-verb-object relationships and encodes the cognitive relationships they have learned or are learning during the sensorimotor period. This language ability is within the capabilities of many profoundly deaf adults with limited speech. Therefore, in addition to outside exposure to normal speakers, oral communication from the deaf parents could facilitiate the development of basic syntactic structure.

While these children may be able to learn the basic components of language (subject-verb-object constructions) from their mothers as well as from hearing people, the children soon exceed their parent's syntactic capabilities. The children studied by Schiff (1979) surpassed their mothers' productions of grammatical morphemes before they were 3 years old. All of the forms produced by the children sometimes appeared in their mothers' speech, but not with any consistency. Therefore, the children were not necessarily learning the morphological rules because of the *regularities* in the language they heard directed towards them. In addition, these hearing children of deaf parents were exposed to two different phonetic renditions of words they were learning. Yet when they produced words, they tended to produce the standard adult models or used simplifications typically found in normal children's productive systems and not deaf speech.

However, some differences were noted when the children were communicating with deaf speakers. Schiff (1976, 1978) found that five normally developing 2-year-olds used proportionally more signs, more exaggerated and whispered speech and shorter utterances with their deaf mothers than they did with the normal speaking investigator. Therefore, at 2 years of age, the children were already making modifications in their utterances seemingly based upon the linguistic differences of the listener. In addition, these children showed some awareness that their parents did not hear (e.g. one child was observed telling her mother when a tea kettle whistled). These observations suggest that the children who develop speech and language normally might realize early on that their parents' speech and language system is different from the standard model they hear produced by others. It has been reported that older hearing children of deaf parents become bilingual and use two systems to communicate, one with the deaf and one with the hearing (Schiff & Ventry 1976, Lenneberg 1967). Perhaps children who learn Standard English without any problems or delays are those who realize early in development that they are learning two languages. Like the bilingual child who learns two languages simultaneously, the hearing child of deaf parents might need to identify one language (deaf speech +/− ASL) with their parents, and the second language (Standard English) with others (see Ch. 4). If the children perceive their parents' oral language as different, then they should not be confused by the seeming 'irregularities' in input in the oral language they hear.

In conclusion, many hearing children of deaf parents do develop speech and language normally if their family life is otherwise normal and they have some exposure to normal hearing speakers (approximately 5–10 hours per week seems to be sufficient). There are no other obvious factors in the environment that differentiate children who experience delays or deviant speech and language patterns from those who develop normally.

4

Bilingual language development in preschool children

F. Genesee

This chapter is about language development in bilingual environments. It will focus on preschool age children who learn two languages simultaneously in non-school settings. This can occur as a result of exposure to two or more languages in the home or to one language in the home and another language outside the home, for example, with friends, grandparents or daycare workers. What distinguishes these language learners from other second language learners is that they can be said to be learning both languages during the primary language learning years (1 to 5 years) and their language learning is untutored in contrast to that of older children, adolescents and adults who might learn a second language through formal instruction or schooling. In a later section, we will consider why it is necessary to differentiate between subgroups of second language learners.

Before doing this, let us first define some terms to be used throughout the remainder of this chapter and then consider in general terms theoretical issues in second language acquisition. The term *primary language development* will be used to refer to language acquisition during the first 5 years of life in order to allow for the possibility that more than one language might be learned. *Bilingual development* will be used to refer to simultaneous acquisition of more than one language during the period of primary language development. *First language acquisition* will be used when acquisition of only one language from birth is in question and *second language acquisition* will be used to refer to acquisition of a second language after the primary language development period. It is necessary to distinguish between simultaneous and successive acquisition of a second language since strictly speaking there is no second language during the simultaneous acquisition of two languages.

GENERAL THEORETICAL CONSIDERATIONS

Theories of second language acquisition and bilingual development are concerned with the same basic issues as theories of first language acquisition, namely, the rate, pattern and processes of language development. More specifically, all theories of language acquisition seek to describe the child's developing grammar or linguistic competence as evidenced by his or her pattern of manifest language behaviour and to discover the linguistic, cognitive and social processes which underlie this development. In the bilingual case, this is equally true whether the language learners in question are children, adolescents or adults.

Of additional interest to second language acquisition theorists, in contrast to first language acquisition theorists, is whether the patterns and processes of language learning are influenced in some way by learning two or more languages simultaneously or by learning a second language after a first language has been acquired. In other words, are there interactions between the two language systems that result in the pattern of language acquisition being different in comparison with monolingual development? The task is complicated by the possibility of specific interaction effects between particular language combinations. For example, children learning English and French might manifest a different pattern of language development than children learning English and Chinese or

than children learning each language separately. Whether or not different manifest patterns of language development reflect differences in the underlying processes of acquisition is the real question. The task is complicated further by the possibility that different processes might be involved in successive acquisition of more than one language versus simultaneous acquisition of two languages, for reasons to be outlined later. The possibility of interaction effects during simultaneous acquisition of two languages and their implications for language acquisition have been primary concerns of research on bilingual development among preschool children and, consequently, we will return to consider these issues in some detail shortly.

There are a number of other important issues associated with second language acquisition. Chief among these is the issue of individual differences. Even the casual observer notices that there are wide variations in level of proficiency achieved by different second language learners. This is especially evident in cases of successive second language acquisition and is much less evident among cases of simultaneous acquisition. Researchers have investigated factors associated with age, cognitive style, personality, type and amount of exposure, and attitudes and motivation (Gardner 1986) as explanations for these differences (see McLaughlin 1985, for a review). The emerging picture is not always simple and clear, but general patterns are discernible. For example, the age factor which has been particularly controversial has yielded consistent and interesting findings.

It has generally been found that second language learners who begin language acquisition during the primary language development period ultimately achieve higher levels of proficiency in the long term than learners who begin later (Krashen et al 1979, Genesee 1987). In most cases, they achieve native-like levels of proficiency, given adequate and 'naturalistic' exposure (in contrast to formal second language instruction), whereas most older learners do not. This difference has been explained in terms of a neurophysiologically-based critical period for language learning (Penfield & Roberts 1959, Lenneberg 1967). At the same time, it has been found that older learners (from approximately age 7 on) show more rapid progress for a given period of exposure than young learners when achievement is examined over short periods of learning (e.g. two years or less). This has been observed both in school settings (Genesee 1981) and in non-school settings (Snow & Hoefnagel-Höhle 1978), but is particularly evident in the former. The older learner's apparently more efficient learning has been attributed to greater cognitive maturity (Genesee 1987). In sum, these findings attest to the native-like proficiency possible when second language learning begins early and to the considerable language proficiency attainable by older learners who are often mistakenly attributed with limited language learning ability.

It is generally accepted that a comprehensive theory of second language acquisition will have to account for the evident differences in proficiency attained by individuals and subgroups of second language learners. In contrast, theories of first language acquisition have tended to focus on the universal, invariant aspects of first language acquisition and on the competence of the ideal speaker-listener (Chomsky 1968). While large individual differences have been recognized in rate of first language acquisition, they have generally been regarded as idiosyncratic variations of no theoretical consequence. Recently, some interest has been shown in different styles of first language acquisition (see, for example, Nelson 1981).

Another issue of some import in many theories of second language acquisition is the role of input. Early behaviourist theories of second language learning saw input as important in establishing new stimulus-response connections or in overcoming old stimulus-response connections established in the first language. Input has continued to occupy a prominent place even in recent theories of second language acquisition; witness Krashen's (1981) *Monitor Model.* According to the 'comprehensible input hypothesis', which is part of this model, input that is comprehensible and linguistically somewhat beyond the learner's current competence is necessary for second language acquisition to occur. Krashen emphasizes the importance of input over other aspects of second language learning; in particular, he has argued that output or opportunities to use the language productively are not necessary to develop production skills (i.e. speaking and writing). Others disagree and make a case for also attributing some significance to output (Swain 1985, Genesee 1987).

The general importance attached to input in thinking about second language acquisition can be traced perhaps to work and interest in second language teaching, which until recently has been regarded as the careful, systematic engineering of input in order to bring about learning. Second language acquisition researchers have examined the relationship between second language learning and amount of input or exposure to the target language, the nature of target language input addressed to second language learners, and learners' solicitations for modified input (see Gass & Madden 1985 for a comprehensive collection of papers on input in second language acquisition).

Research on so-called 'motherese' or caretaker speech and on social/verbal interaction as a basis for first language development attest to interest in input among first language acquisition researchers. Thus, issues concerning input have not been totally unimportant in thinking about first language acquisition. Rather it is a question of emphasis. Whereas theories of first language acquisition have tended to view input as playing a largely supportive role in first language development, theories of second language acquisition have tended to view input as serving a primary causal role.

Finally, there has been considerable theoretical speculation and research activity regarding the cognitive, social and linguistic consequences of being bilingual (see for example, Cummins 1976, Genesee 1985, Hakuta 1986). In each case, researchers have compared bilinguals with monolinguals for possible positive or negative side-effects that might result from learning and knowing two or more languages. Findings from this research have fluctuated, especially regarding cognitive consequences. Early studies generally found negative effects. For example, bilingual children in Wales and Hawaii were reported to be academically and linguistically inferior to monolinguals (see Cummins 1976, Diaz 1983 for reviews). These studies were often carried out in subtractive bilingual environments where the second language was learned at the expense of the first language. As a result, the bilingual subjects in these early studies were not fully proficient in one or both of their languages. And yet, the researchers did not take this fact into account when designing and administering their tests. It is more likely, therefore, that their results reflected less than native-like language proficiency rather than intellectual skills per se.

More recent studies have reported complex patterns either of no differences or differences favouring bilinguals. These studies have tended to examine bilinguals with high levels of proficiency in both languages or have systematically examined bilinguals as a function of their proficiency in their respective languages. Cummins (1981) has proposed that the cognitive consequences associated with bilingualism are correlated with level of language proficiency. He maintains that positive cognitive consequences, and especially enhanced metalinguistic awareness, are associated with relatively high levels of proficiency in both languages, whereas no differences are associated with lower levels of proficiency. This remains a highly controversial issue (Hakuta 1986).

Implicit in this work is a model of human development that associates monolingualism with normal development and bilingualism with exceptional development; that is to say, second language acquisition implicates processes and outcomes that are in some

sense extra-ordinary and therefore consequential for human development. While the possibility of differences between monolingual and bilingual individuals is a legitimate and interesting concern, it begs the question of normal versus exceptional language development.

IS BILINGUAL LANGUAGE DEVELOPMENT EXCEPTIONAL?

One might well ask whether language development in bilingual environments is in fact exceptional. This question can be addressed from a demographic point of view as well as from a psycholinguistic point of view. We will examine the demographic perspective in this section.

Although there are no hard statistics on the prevalence of bilingualism worldwide, it is not unreasonable to believe that simultaneous acquisition of two languages or dialects is commonplace. Many parts of the world are characterized by distinct language groups inhabiting different but neighbouring countries (e.g. Europe and southeast Asia) or the same country (e.g. India, South Africa). These sociopolitical circumstances are often associated with childhood bilingualism resulting from intermarriage between members of different language groups or from socioeconomic pressures for members of each group to learn the other's language for utilitarian reasons. In addition, massive international migration of people throughout the world during the twentieth century has resulted in large numbers of minority language speakers in all developed and developing areas of the world (e.g. U.S., Australia, South America). The first generation children of immigrants are often bilingual; in most cases, subsequent generations are monolingual in the majority language as they become fully integrated into the host society. In sum, simultaneous acquisition of two languages is probably very common. Moreover, while the language learning environments associated with these bi- and multi-lingual circumstances might be varied and in some cases unusual, there is no reason to believe that they are exceptional when viewed against the broad range of first language learning environments found cross-culturally throughout the world.

Bilingual language development is nevertheless often viewed as exceptional and in some cases even undesirable by the population at large because of political or sociocultural factors. This may be especially true in monolingual settings where the population may come to regard monolingualism as the norm and therefore 'normal'. Even in bilingual settings, individuals may view early bilingualism as exceptional because they believe that it threatens the child's native language development. In Canada, for example, some French Canadians express grave reservations about raising their children bilingually for fear that English, the nationally dominant language, will retard or displace their development in French. Thus, they tend to view the development of only the native language, French, during the primary language developmental years as normal and desirable. These fears may conflict with the desire to learn English for socioeconomic reasons.

A cursory examination of research on language acquisition in general might also give one the impression that bilingual development and second language acquisition are indeed exceptional as evidenced by the relative lack of research on them. In fact, the predominant focus in developmental psycholinguistics has been on first language acquisition. It is only recently that research on bilingual development and second language acquisition has become an identifiable and significant focus of activity—witness the recent publication of a number of texts on second language acquisition: Ellis (1986), Klein (1986) and McLaughlin (1978, 1985). Noteworthy exceptions to this are isolated case studies of individual children raised bilingually by Leopold (1949), Ronjat (1913) and others during the first half of this century. And yet, the Zeitgeist that the study of 'ordinary' language development includes only or mainly first language acquisition prevails— most contemporary introductory textbooks on psycholinguistics still lack coverage of issues in second language acquisition.

As noted earlier, whether language acquisition is *in fact* psycholinguistically different and therefore exceptional when a second language is involved in comparison with first language acquisition is an empirical question with important theoretical implications. Let us turn to this question now.

SIMULTANEOUS VERSUS SUCCESSIVE SECOND LANGUAGE ACQUISITION

When examining language development in bilingual evironments, there are a number of psycholinguistic reasons for distinguishing between preschool versus older second language learners. Differences in language development in these cases might be expected because of differences in: (1) language acquisition ability, (2) cognitive ability and general knowledge of the world, and (3) prior linguistic knowledge, including specific contextual knowledge of social relations and verbal communication.

Language acquisition ability

It has been postulated that first language acquisition is dependent on a separate linguistic faculty or language acquisition device that contains a set of linguistic principles referred to as Universal Grammar. It is thought that these principles apply to the structure of all languages and that they constitute part of the child's innate endowment (Chomsky 1965, McNeill 1970). They are thought to constrain the kinds of hypotheses that the developing child will consider for a given set of linguistic input, that is, they constrain the pattern of first language acquisition. It has been postulated further that the language faculty atrophies with age or changes to become more rigid as a result of first language acquisition (Chomsky 1966, Lenneberg 1967). It follows, therefore, that learning another language after the language faculty has begun to change will necessarily be different from language acquisition during the primary language development period when the language acquisition device is fully operative.

Schachter (1986) has argued on empirical grounds that Universal Grammar cannot possibly account for second language acquisition among post-pubertal and possibly even 4- to 12-year-old learners since, in fact, there are basic differences in first and second language acquisition. She cites evidence that older second language learners in contrast to first language learners: (1) seldom acquire complete competence in the target language; (2) often fail to acquire basic linguistic structures or acquire incorrect or incomplete forms; (3) do not acquire all languages equally easily; and (4) show considerable influence from the first language. These differences do not occur with acquisition of two languages simultaneously during the period of primary language development.

There is not agreement on the role of the language acquisition device or Universal Grammar in second language acquisition, however. McLaughlin (1985), for one, contends that all second language learners utilize processes that are universal to all language learning, including first language acquisition. At the same time, he allows for the possibility that other processes might also be implicated in certain learning environments. In particular, he suggests that 'classroom language learners are sometimes thwarted in their use of innate language-learning mechanisms because of the way language is presented in the classroom, and have to resort to more idiosyncratic problem-solving techniques' (p. 23). He refers to the innate processes as 'acquisitional heuristics' and to the idiosyncratic problem-solving techniques as 'operating procedures' (see also Seliger 1984 for a similar distinction). While the former are language-specific, universal and innate, the latter are not. Rather they are learned problem-solving strategies of a non-linguistic nature that serve to overcome immediate, temporary and idiosyncratic blocks to language learning. Operating procedures

are more likely to be found in the case of second language acquisition than first language acquisition or bilingual development; the latter implicate acquisitional heuristics or the language acquisition device. Whether or not one believes that the language acquisition device is or is not available during second language acquisition, it is generally believed that second language acquisition probably implicates acquisitional mechanisms or strategies not found during first language acquisition or bilingual development.

Cognitive ability and knowledge of the world

Notwithstanding the language acquisition device as the primary basis for first language acquisition, it is thought that first language acquisition depends in some significant ways on cognitive factors of a non-linguistic nature, such as the child's memory capacity or perceptual-motor abilities (Chomsky 1980a, White 1981, Lindfors 1987). These non-linguistic factors influence the child's ability to perceive and to produce particular linguistic structures. Thus, although, in principle, the whole of Universal Grammar is available to the child from the start, it cannot manifest itself in its entirety immediately because of general cognitive or perceptual constraints. For example, the 2 year-old's limited memory capacity restricts the first verbal utterances to single morphemes and, furthermore, the child's conceptualization of the world in largely concrete, experiential terms restricts first morphemes to words with immediate referential meaning (Brown 1973). With cognitive development, the child's manifest language performance will change to reflect more and more innate, underlying linguistic competence, or Universal Grammar.

Thus, it can be argued that the determining factors in primary language development are largely cognitive or conceptual in nature because the language acquisition device is a given whereas the determining factors in subsequent language learning are largely linguistic in nature since cognitive/perceptual maturity is a given (Hakuta 1974, Felix 1978).

Accordingly, one would expect first language acquisition and bilingual development to be fundamentally the same since there are no differences in these cases in the learners' cognitive abilities, nor in the state of their language acquisition devices for that matter. In contrast, one might expect differences between not only second and first language acquisition but also between second language acquisition and bilingual development because the cognitive abilities of the learners in question will differ.

First language knowledge

Another language-related factor that is thought to distinguish the bilingual development period from later second language acquisition is the learner's existing linguistic knowledge (see Keller-Cohen 1981, for example). In other words, the fact of already knowing one language may influence the older learner's pattern of second language acquisition. In the past, this interaction has been conceptualized according to contrastive analysis largely in terms of interference effects; that is, where differences between two languages exist, the learner will experience difficulty and will attempt to use structures from the first language (Lado 1964). It is now thought that similarities between first language structures and second language structures can also create interference effects (Ellis 1986). At the same time, prior linguistic knowledge may actually facilitate the acquisition of specific second language structures that are similar to first language structures. Wode (1976) argues that the conditions under which and the extent to which second language learners use their first language knowledge when processing the second language are important empirical questions.

Part of the older learner's knowledge base will include specific contextual knowledge of how social relations or interactions and, in particular, conversations take place in the social group or speech community. Second language acquisition after first language acquisition may be influenced in significant ways by this established knowledge of conversations. In some cases, this knowledge may be facilitating, for example when both languages encode the same functions or social features in the same ways; in other cases, it may interfere with language acquisition, for example, when different functions or features are encoded by the two languages or when the same functions are verbalized in different ways. In contrast, preschool age children acquire language in parallel with social knowledge and thus there is no question of the influence of established social knowledge on primary language acquisition.

On theoretical grounds then, one would expect few differences between second language acquisition and first language acquisition when they occur simultaneously. Clearly, one would expect superficial or surface structure differences because the bilingual child is learning two languages and the monolingual child only one. The thrust of the theoretical argument is that there are likely to be few differences in the processes underlying bilingual development and first language acquisition. In this sense language development in a bilingual environment would not be expected to be exceptional. On the contrary, it would be psycholinguistically the same as first language acquisition. In contrast, because of the possible influence of these three categories of factors, significant differences might be expected between second language acquisition and both first language acquisition and bilingual development when the second language is acquired after a first language has been acquired. Second language acquisition under these circumstances might then be regarded as exceptional.

Notwithstanding these theoretical arguments, researchers of childhood bilingualism have generally argued on empirical grounds that bilingual development is psycholinguistically distinct from monolingual or first language acquisition. In particular, they have argued that children acquiring two languages simultaneously initially go through a stage of extensive linguistic interaction when the two language systems are mixed. Researchers have characterized this stage as one of linguistic confusion or, at least, as evidence for a unitary, undifferentiated language system (e.g. Murrell 1966, Swain 1972, Volterra & Taeschner 1978, Redlinger & Park 1980, Vihman 1982). There are reasons for questioning these interpretations. Let us now examine the empirical evidence and interpretations of it.

LANGUAGE INTERACTIONS IN BILINGUAL DEVELOPMENT

In this section, the term *mixing* will be used to refer to interactions between the bilingual child's developing language systems. Mixing has been used by other researchers to refer to the co-occurrence of elements from two or more languages in *a single utterance*. The mixed elements may be phonological, morphological, lexical, syntactic, phrasal or pragmatic. This definition is problematic when discussing childhood bilinguals because it refers only to two-word and multi-word stages of development, thereby eliminating a consideration of mixing during the one-word stage. Therefore, it seems desirable to extend the term to include single word utterances from two languages during the same stretch of conversation between a child and caregiver.

It is important to point out that adult bilinguals also mix languages in the same sentence, a phenomenon referred to as code mixing (Sridhar & Sridhar 1980). Studies of code mixing in adults show it to be a sophisticated, rule-governed communicative device used by linguistically competent bilinguals to achieve a variety of communicative goals, such as conveying emphasis, role playing, establishing sociocultural identity. It has highly-structured syntactic and sociolinguistic constraints (Poplack 1979). In particular, mixing of linguistic elements from one language into another language is constrained so that the syntactic rules of *both* languages are respected. Poplack (1979) cites evidence to the effect that intra-sentential mixing increases in adult bilinguals as their competence in the

two languages increases. Adult bilinguals will also switch between languages as a function of certain sociolinguistic factors, such as the setting, tone and purpose of the communication or the ethnolinguistic identity of the interlocutor. This language behaviour is referred to as *code switching* (Sridhar & Sridhar 1980).

Bilingual mixing

The majority of empirical investigations of bilingual development have found mixing (see McLaughlin 1978, for a summary of early research). Phonological, lexical, phrasal, morphological, syntactic, and semantic mixing have all been reported. Phonological mixing in the form of loan blends has been reported by Murrell (1966) and Oksaar (1971). Loan blends are words made up of phonemic segments from two languages. For example, Oksaar has recorded the loan blend 'kats' from an Estonian/Swedish bilingual child: it consists of the Swedish word for cat (*katt*) and the Estonian word for cat (*kass*). Murrell reports similar blends consisting of Swedish and Finnish and Swedish and English sounds.

Mixing of grammatical morphemes has been noted by Murrell (1966), Burling (1978), Lindholm & Padilla (1978), Oksaar (1971) and Redlinger & Park (1980). Redlinger & Park report several morphological mixing by a German/English bilingual. 'Pfeifung' ('Whistling') and 'Die Mädchen's going night-night' ('The girl's going night-night'). Bergman (1976) reports that her Spanish/English bilingual daughter used the English possessive morpheme *'s* in Spanish utterances. Several investigators claim that the morphological development of bilingual children appears to lag behind that of monolingual children (see Murrell 1966; Imedadze 1978, Vihman 1982). Others report no such lag (Burling 1978, Leopold 1978).

By far the most frequent type of mixing to be reported involves whole lexical items, both content words and functors (see Swain & Wesche 1975, Burling 1978, Leopold 1978, Lindholm & Padilla 1978, Redlinger & Park

1980, Vihman 1982, 1985, and Goodz 1987). Some investigators have found that content words, and especially nouns, are the most frequently mixed lexical items (Swain & Wesche 1975, Lindholm & Padilla 1978), while others have found that functors are the most frequently mixed (Redlinger & Park 1980, Vihman 1982). Redlinger & Park have reported specifically that adverbs, articles, pronouns, pre-positions and conjunctions occurred in mixed utterances in descending order of frequency.

Mixing at the level of the phrase has also been found. Redlinger & Park give an example for a German/Spanish child: 'Putzen Zähne *con jabon*' ('Brushing teeth with soap'). Lindholm & Padilla cite an example from a Spanish/English bilingual child: 'I ask him *que yo voy a casa*' ('I ask him that I go home'). They also reported that when phrasal mixing occurred, the structural consistency of the utterances was maintained so that there were no lexical redundancies or syntactic errors (see also Padilla & Liebman 1975). To the extent that this is generally true, it would argue against an interpretation of mixing in terms of linguistic confusion.

Swain & Wesche (1975) have reported exam-ples of syntactic mixing, or what they refer to as structural interactions, in the case of a 3-year-old French/English boy: (a) 'They open, *the windows?*' (use of the noun apposition construction from French in an otherwise English utterance); (b) 'A house *pink*' (colour adjectives follow the noun in French). Neither of these constructions, however, need be regarded as peculiar to bilinguals—the former is frequent even among English-speakers, and the latter could be considered an instance of interlingual overgeneralization; intralingual overgeneralization of syntactic rules is found in first language acquisition (Goodluck 1986).

Swain & Wesche also report instances of semantic mixing: 'You want to *open* the lights?' (in French, the verb *open* is used in comparison with the English verb *turn on* when referring to lights). Once again, this construction is used by some anglophones in Montreal even though their proficiency in French is limited. This raises an additional equivocation in interpreting these results.

Without knowing what language models are available to the learner, it is difficult to inter-pret such utterances unequivocally as linguistic creations by the child that reflect an under-lying confusion or lack of differentiation of language systems. Rather, the child may simply be saying what has been heard from parents or other speakers in the environment. We will return to a discussion of the import-ance of input later.

Rates of mixing vary considerably from study to study and from case to case. Mixed utterances are reportedly more frequent in early stages of bilingual development and diminish with age and, concomitantly, increasing language proficiency (Fantini 1978, Volterra & Taeschner 1978, Redlinger & Park 1980, Vihman 1982). Summarizing the results from four case studies, Redlinger & Park found 20% to 30% mixing during Stage I (Brown 1973), 12% to 20% during Stage II, 6% to 12% during Stage III, and 2% to 6% during Stages IV and V. Vihman (1982) reports that the use of mixed utterances by her Estonian/English bilingual son dropped from 34% at 20 months, to 22% at 21 months, to 20% at 22 months, to 11% at 23 months, and to 4% at 24 months of age.

Reported rates of mixing are difficult to interpret or compare across studies owing to: (1) differential dominance in the two languages in question, (2) the possibility of unequal or inequitable sampling of the child's language use in different language contexts and/or with different interlocutors, (3) the lack of an acceptable metric of language develop-ment with which to identify children at comparable stages, (4) different operational definitions of mixing, and (5) different language histories. Moreover, there is no reason to suppose that mixing is symmetrical between languages. One would expect more mixing of the weaker language in utterances of the stronger language than vice versa. Thus, reporting a single estimate of mixing for a child tells only half the story.

The period of language mixing just described is generally thought to be followed by linguistic differentiation. At this time, the child is thought to have developed or to be developing separate representations of two language systems or, alternatively, to have overcome the linguistic confusion characteristic of the earlier stage. Investigators studying children with different language histories have reported that differentiation occurs during the third year of life. Fantini (1978) reports that his son Mario differentiated Spanish and English at 2;8 while his daughter Carlina differentiated them at 2;5; both children were exposed to English relatively late, between 2;0 and 3;0. Murrell (1966) reports that her daughter, who was exposed to Swedish and Finnish since the first year, differentiated the two languages at 2;8. Vihman (1982) reports that her son Raivio differentiated Estonian and English at 2;0; primarily Estonian was used at home while English was used at the nursery and to a limited extent at home with his older sister and her English-speaking friends. And Imedadze (1978) reports that two independent vocabularies were evident at the end of the second year in a boy who had heard Georgian at home from both parents and Russian from his grandmother and nurse.

At the same time, the bilingual child begins to switch systematically between languages as a function of the participants, the setting, the function of the message (e.g. to exclude others), its form (e.g. narration), and to a lesser extent the topic of conversation. Bilingual children are reported to be especially sensitive to their interlocutors so that initially when differentiation occurs they tend to rigidly use the language they associate with the speaker even though he or she may express a willingness to use the other language (Fantini 1978, Volterra & Taeschner 1978).

In sum, that mixing of two languages occurs during bilingual development is accepted by all investigators. More questionable are the explanations of it.

Explanations of mixing during bilingual development

A number of 'local' explanations as well as a general explanation or hypothesis have been suggested to account for mixing during bilin-gual development. The local explanations attempt to account for specific instances or categories of mixing. Although relatively minor in importance, they warrant scrutiny because of their implicit assumption that bilingual development differs from first language acquisition in specific ways. We will consider the local explanations briefly before turning to the general one.

Local explanations

By far the most frequent local explanation of mixing is that bilingual children mix because particular lexical items are lacking in one language but available in the other (Fantini 1978, Lindholm & Padilla 1978, Volterra & Taeschner 1978, Redlinger & Park 1980). The same argument could be made for other linguistic elements—morphemes, syntactic devices and pragmatic rules, although it is usually limited to lexical mixing. Such instances of mixing could be viewed as lexical overextensions of the type observed in monolingual children (Griffiths 1986), with the only difference being that bilingual children overextend inter-lingually while monolingual children overextend intra lingually. In the case of first language acquisition, it has been observed that particular overextensions of nominals usually cease once the child has learned what mature speakers of the language would consider a more appropriate word (Griffiths 1986). In other words, monolingual children make use of whatever vocabulary they have acquired; as their vocabulary grows they use increasingly appropriate, less overextended words. This also seems a reasonable interpretation of bilingual overextensions (see also Goodz 1987) and, in fact, corresponds with the tendency for bilingual children to mix less as their proficiency increases, as noted earlier.

While lexical gaps undoubtedly account for some lexical mixing, they may not account for all instances. Vihman (1985) argued that lexical deficits were not the only reason for lexical mixing by her bilingual son since 34% of his early word combinations were mixed even though there was a 40% overlap in his Estonian and English vocabularies. Other investigators have cited examples of lexical mixing that appear to be attention-getters or to emphasize a message and not to overcome lexical deficits (Goodz 1987).

In contrast to mixing that might result from overextension, it might also result from underextension. Imedadze (1978) and Swain & Wesche (1975) have suggested that in some cases bilingual children identify a referent with the lexical item in the language that was first or most frequently used to label it. They might insist on using that word at all times when talking about that referent regardless of the linguistic context. Similar underextensions have been observed in monolingual children (Griffiths 1986).

Another 'local' interpretation of mixing has been preferred in terms of linguistic factors. Vihman (1985) argues that her son's use of English functors in Estonian utterances was not due to lack of the appropriate item in Estonian, but rather reflected the phonological and morphological complexity of the respective linguistic elements. In particular, the English functors were phonologically easier to produce or morphologically simpler than the corresponding Estonian terms (see also Murrell 1966 and Tabouret-Keller 1962). Slobin (1973) has argued convincingly that the acquisition of specific linguistic elements by monolingual children is also influenced by their linguistic complexity or saliency.

Thus local explanations of specific instances of mixing by bilingual children can be interpreted in terms of acquisitional processes that have been identified in first language acquisition. This accords with the theoretical argument made earlier that few differences in acquisition would be expected between bilingual development and first language acquisition.

Unitary or differentiated language systems?

Language mixing during the early stages of bilingual development has been interpreted in general terms as evidence of a unitary language system with undifferentiated phonological, lexical and syntactic subsystems (but see Bergman 1976, Lindholm & Padilla 1978, and Goodz 1987). For example, Leopold, in one of the first and still most comprehensive studies of bilingual development, concluded that 'Words from the two languages did not belong to two different speech systems but to one . . .' (in Hatch, 1978, p. 27). More recently, Redlinger & Park (1980) write 'These findings suggest that the subjects were involved in a gradual process of language differentiation and are in agreement with those of previous investigators supporting the one system approach to bilingual acquisition.' (p. 344). Volterra & Taeschner (1978) have interpreted mixing in terms of a three stage model: (1) initial unification of both lexical and syntactic subsystems; (2) differentiation of the lexicon but continued unification of syntax; and (3) finally, differentation of both the lexicon and syntax. Swain (1977) has postulated a 'common storage model' of bilingual development according to which all rules of both languages are initially stored in a common location. Even rules that are specific to each language are initially stored in common storage and subsequently tagged as appropriate for a particular language through a process of differentiation. The title of Swain's 1972 thesis *Bilingualism as a First Language* exemplifies the unitary system interpretation of early bilingual development.

There are good reasons to question this interpretation. The evidence cited by the respective investigators is necessary but not sufficient to support the unitary language system hypothesis. In order to uphold this hypothesis, one would need to establish that, all things being equal, bilingual children indiscriminately use items from both languages in all contexts of communication, regardless of the predominant language in use in a particular context. In other words, there should be no differential distribution of items from the two languages as a function of context. In contrast, support for the differentiated language systems hypothesis would require evidence that the children use items from their two languages differentially as a function of context. Even in cases where the child might be more proficient in one language than the other, which is common, it would be possible to test the differentiated language systems hypothesis by observing the distribution of items from the weaker language. In particular, if the two language systems hypothesis were true, then one would expect to find more frequent use of items from the weaker language in contexts where that language is being used than in contexts where the stronger language is being used, even though items from the stronger language might predominate in both contexts.

In fact, most proponents of the one language system hypothesis do not present or analyze their data by context. Therefore, it is impossible to determine whether the children are using the repertoire of language items they have acquired so far in a differentiated way. For example, the evidence cited by Volterra & Taeschner in support of stage I of their model consists simply of isolated examples of lexical mixing in utterances addressed to the child's German-speaking mother. No evidence of language use with the child's Italian-speaking father is given. Redlinger & Park calculated the rate of mixing for four different bilingual children over a period varying from 5 to 9 months and found a decline in mixing over time. No systematic data of differential mixing of each language as a function of language context are provided. Evidence of declining rates of overall mixing does not constitute sufficient proof that the child has only one system. Mixing may decline with development, not because separation of the languages is taking place but rather because the children are acquiring more complete linguistic repertoires and, therefore, do not need to borrow from or overextend between languages.

Some investigators have examined mixing as a function of interlocutor or context, but their analyses are incomplete or questionable. Vihman (1985) reports the percentage use of multiword English utterances in English contexts versus an Estonian context, but she does not report corresponding values for multiword Estonian utterances. That the child used English utterances in the Estonian context (that is, the home) is perhaps not surprising given that the child's sister and parents all spoke English and were undoubtedly overheard using English in their home in Palo Alto, California. More convincing evidence of a unitary language system would include examples of Estonian multiword utterances in English contexts (the daycare centre, for example). Redlinger & Park cite isolated examples of conversations between their children and each parent separately. Contrary to the authors' interpretation of their data, one child (Marcus) in fact gives some evidence of using more Spanish with his Spanish-speaking mother than with his German-speaking father even though German predominated in both conversations (these language samples will be analyzed in greater detail in the next section).

The role of input

An alternative explanation in terms of input has not been considered or examined seriously. Bilingual children's mixed utterances may be modelled on mixed input produced by others in the environment. The effect of modelling does not exclude the other bases for mixing already discussed as local explanations. Modelling could affect the child's language mixing in two ways—in specific ways, such that particular instances of modelled mixed utterances are used by the child, or in a general way, such that frequent mixing by an adult or linguistically more mature children will result in the child mixing frequently and generally. Bergman's speculation, noted earlier, that her daughter's use of the English possessive marker 's in otherwise Spanish utterances could be traced to her nursery school teacher's use of this same construction is consistent with the first possibility. Also in this regard, Goodz (1987) cites evidence of parents using mixed utterances in response to their children's language choices. Parents might thereby present specific examples of mixing that children are particularly sensitive to since they are made in response to the children's solicitations.

Certainly one would expect children exposed to frequent and general mixing to mix frequently since there is no reason for them to know that the languages should be separated. Indeed, there are fully formed dialects which consist of elements of two languages (e.g. so-called Spanglish in the southern U.S., or Franglais in Quebec). Conversely, it is commonly advocated, although not documented, that the best way to avoid bilingual mixing in children is to have each parent speak only one language to the child—the so-called rule of Grammont, after the individual who first espoused this principle (Ronjat 1913). In fact, it appears that more mixing does occur among children who hear both languages used freely and interchangeably by the same interlocutors (i.e. code switching) (Murrell 1966, Redlinger & Park's case 'Danny' 1980) and less in children who hear the languages separated by person and/or setting (Fantini 1978, Redlinger & Park's case 'Marcus').

It is difficult to ascertain the exact relationship between input and rate or type of mixing from the available research since descriptions of the language input conditions are either totally lacking (Padilla & Liebman 1975, Lindholm & Padilla 1978) or, at best, are general and impressionistic (Volterra & Taeschner 1978, Vihman 1982). In a study of parental language use in bilingual families, Goodz (1987) found that even parents 'firmly committed to maintaining a strict separation of language by parent, model linguistically-mixed utterances to their children', but are unaware of doing so. Thus, impressionistic reports are probably inaccurate. The problem is that some researchers purport to be studying bilingual development in families where the languages are used separately, and on this basis do not consider mixed input as a major contributor to the children's use of mixed utterances, although a number of researchers allude briefly to the possible importance of this factor (Burling et al 1978, Tabouret-Keller 1962, and Vihman & McLauglin 1982). Evidence that mixing by bilingual children can be traced in part or in whole to mixed input would weaken arguments that

mixing during early bilingual development necessarily reflects an underlying undifferentiated language system. Bilingual children with differentiated language systems may mix because the input conditions permit or call for mixing; we will see examples of this shortly.

What kind of evidence would be necessary to test for differentiated language systems? First of all, since one cannot examine the underlying representation of language directly, evidence for differentation would necessarily be based on functional separation of the languages, that is, how the languages are used. Moreover, data on language use would need to be collected in different language contexts in order to determine the relative functional distribution of elements from the respective languages. Finally, as noted earlier, children who mix during the early stages of bilingual development do so less with age as their lexical systems and presumably other linguistic subsystems expand making overextension and overgeneralization between languages less necessary. Therefore, it would be necessary to examine language use prior to this stage of development, that is, from the one-word stage on. Evidence of differential use of the two languages during the earliest stages of language development would be particularly convincing evidence in favour of differentiated systems.

In the absence of such ideal data, how plausible is the differentiated language systems hypothesis and what do existing data tell us? Differentiation of two languages during bilingual development minimally requires that children be able to discriminate perceptually between the spoken languages. Research on the perceptual abilities of infants suggests that they possess many, if not all, of the necessary prerequisites for speech perception (Jusczyk 1981) and that they are capable of fairly sophisticated perceptual discriminations. Jusczyk (1982) has commented that 'today, some researchers in the field . . . have been moved to comment that the most interesting kind of result would be to discover some aspect of speech perception that infants were incapable of' (p. 361).

Relevant to the present discussion, Trehub (1973) has found that infants of 6–17 weeks are able to differentiate phonetic contrasts in languages (Czech and Polish) that they have never been exposed to. Also, Mehler et al (1986) report that 4-day-old infants from French-speaking families were able to discriminate between French and Russian and that they showed a preference for French. That this was not simply a novelty effect is suggested by an earlier study by Mehler et al (1978) in which 4- to 6-week-old infants were found to discriminate between their mothers' voices and that of strangers but only if the speech was normally intonated; they were unable to make this discrimination when both voices were monotone. Thus, it would appear that it is the linguistic properties and qualities of speech, or at least their complex acoustic properties, that infants are sensitive to. The extant evidence then suggests that bilingual-to-be infants are capable of discriminating and differentiating between different spoken languages at the point in development when they begin to utter single words.

Although the available data are not entirely adequate to test unequivocally for differentiation, re-examination of a number of published language samples of interactions between children and their parents using the present methodological perspective reveals interesting findings. Three such samples will be examined briefly at this time (Murrell 1966, Volterra & Taeschner 1978, Redlinger & Park 1980). These interactions have been reproduced in Appendix A. Redlinger & Park report conversations between a German/Spanish bilingual boy, Marcus, and both his German-speaking father and Spanish-speaking mother (Appendix A1). Marcus was between 2;4.23 (years; months.days) and 2;5.20 and had an MLU of 2.21 at the time of the recording. German was used by the parents with one another; the father used only German with Marcus; and the mother used predominantly Spanish (70%); the family resided in Germany. It can be conjectured from the parents' reported language use that Marcus had learned more German than Spanish, and, indeed, German

predominated in both conversations. Of particular interest is Marcus's use of Spanish. He used four different Spanish lexical items with his Spanish-speaking mother and only two with his German-speaking father. These data could be interpreted as functional differentiation of his limited Spanish. The authors' interpretation was that 'Marcus appeared to have basically one lexical system consisting of words from both languages' (p. 340).

Volterra & Taeschner (Appendix A2) report a conversation between a German/Italian bilingual girl, Lisa, and her German-speaking mother along with three isolated utterances by Lisa to her mother. Lisa was 1;10 at the time of the recordings. With the exception of Lisa's use of 'la' (Italian for 'there'), all items used by Lisa could be German. The authors interpret Lisa's use of 'da' in the last utterance as mixing from Italian 'dare' (to give); an alternative interpretation is that it is the German 'da' (there) which Lisa had used previously.

Finally, Murrell reports conversations between a Swedish/Finnish/English trilingual child, Sandra, and the author and her mother (Appendix A3). According to the author 'At the nursery only Finnish was spoken. Her mother spoke mostly Swedish to her at home, while I spoke partly Swedish and partly English. Her mother and I spoke mostly English together' (p. 11). The recordings were made almost three months after the family moved to England when Sandra was between 2;3.25 and 2;4.1. Sandra's lexical usage with the author is predominantly in English, as initiated by the author. The only non-English lexical items used by Sandra are references in Finnish to a cat in a picture ('Kia') and responses in Swedish to utterances initiated by the author in Swedish. At one point, Sandra utters a word ('kekka') that the author interprets to be Swedish (to lick) but acknowledges that it might have been the corresponding English verb. As a result of this interpretation, the author responds in *Swedish* to the child's otherwise *English* string of lexical items. Sandra, in turn, responded in Swedish ('kikka'). The author then responds in Swedish (apparently intending to provide a corrected imitation of Sandra's previous Swedish utterance) and in English (apparently providing an English translation of his own previous utterance). Sandra then proceeds with a combination of English and Swedish. In short, most, and it could be argued all, of the child's Swedish utterances are made in response to Swedish modelled by the author; otherwise, the child used English. Contrary to evidencing linguistic confusion or lack of differentiation, this child appears to have used Swedish and English differentially within the same conversation with an interlocutor who switches back and forth, somewhat in confusion.

Analysis of Sandra's conversation with her mother yields a similar impression. In this case, Sandra uses predominantly Swedish except for three English content words (i.e. 'pull', 'bucket', and 'faggit'—the author's interpretation of the meaning of this word does not correspond with any meanings I solicited from British English speakers) and the demonstrative adjective 'that'. Lexical overextensions or mixings of this sort are probably not surprising given the fact that the family was living in England and English was commonly used between the parents and between the father and Sandra prior to moving to England.

Clearly, these transcripts cannot be interpreted unequivocally nor conclusively, but I would contend that they argue against the unitary language system hypothesis and in favour, albeit tentatively, of the differentiated language systems hypothesis. The present analysis differs from those of the authors', in part at least, because I have taken as the unit of analysis the entire conversation between the children and their respective interlocutors. The authors of these transcripts, and they are not unique, have typically used the individual utterance as the unit of analysis. As a result, they have not been able to ascertain the functional distribution of linguistic elements from each language. Consequently, their findings are limited and misleading.

The preceding analysis focussed on differentiation of language according to lexical distribution. One final piece of evidence which focusses on use of different syntactic features will be offered here in support of the differentiated language systems hypothesis. In a recent unpublished article, Meisel (1987) reports on the syntactic development of two French/German bilingual children. The children were observed between 1;0 to 4;0 years of age. Each parent claimed to use their respective native languages exclusively with their children. Meisel examined the children's use of word order sequences and verb inflections in French and German; these syntactic features were examined because they differ in mature forms of the target languages and in monolingual children's acquisition of the target forms. In brief, Meisel found that the bilingual children used different word orders in French and German as soon as they produced multiword utterances, and they correctly inflected verbs to agree with subjects according to the rules of each language as soon as they consistently filled the subject slot in their utterances.

SUMMARY

It is commonly thought that children learning two languages simultaneously during infancy go through a stage when they cannot differentiate between their two languages, a period of linguistic confusion. Language mixing in the same utterance/sentence or between sentences is a common language behaviour among linguistically mature adult bilinguals, phenomena referred to as code mixing and code switching, respectively. What is thought to distinguish bilingual children's mixing from adult mixing is the lack of systematicity or compliance to linguistic rules in the case of children. In fact, virtually all studies of infant bilinguals indicate that they do mix elements from their two languages, at least during the first two years or so. Children have been found to mix phonological, morphemic, lexical, and syntactic elements.

Most researchers have interpreted these results as evidence for an undifferentiated or unitary underlying language system. I have argued in this chapter that this interpretation is probably misguided. Both methodological and theoretical arguments have been presented against this interpretation and in favour of a conceptualization of infant bilingual development that is the same as monolingual development and, more particularly, during which bilingual children probably differentiate between their languages from the earliest, single word stage. Theoretically speaking, I have claimed that the language faculty, prior linguistic knowledge, and general cognitive abilities and knowledge of the world of children who are learning two languages simultaneously, are the same as those of children learning one language. Therefore, there are no reasons for supposing differences in bilingual versus monolingual development. Superficial differences would certainly be expected because bilingual children are learning two languages in contrast to monolinguals' one. The point is that no underlying differences in language acquisition would be expected. In support of this claim, instances when bilingual children have been found to mix lexical and syntactic elements from their two languages were interpreted in terms of processes that have been identified in first language acquisition.

I have also argued that the present research is methodologically insufficient to test the differentiated language systems hypothesis because: (1) it focusses on individual utterances and not discourse length speech (i.e.

conversations); (2) it fails to examine the relative functional distribution of linguistic elements in different language contexts; and (3) it has ignored the input conditions during which particular instances of mixing have been exhibited. A re-examination of three conversations between bilingual children and their caregivers using a more adequate methodological approach revealed results in support of language differentiation, in contrast to the respective authors' interpretations of the same exchanges as evidence for a unitary underlying system. An alternative hypothesis to account for much of the mixing that characterizes early stages of bilingual development was proposed. This hypothesis focusses on the occurrence of mixed input by mature language speakers in interaction with developing bilingual children. Accordingly, bilingual children may mix language elements in response to code mixing or switching by interlocutors and/or because models of mixed input indicate that differentiation of the languages is not necessary. Some evidence in support of this possibility was presented.

The general conclusion of this review is that bilingual development may differ from monolingual development in superficial ways, but that fundamentally they are the same. In particular, bilingual children use the same acquisitional strategies as monolingual children; they develop differentiated language systems from the beginning; and they are able to use their developing language systems differentially in contextually-sensitive ways.

APPENDIX

1. Redlinger & Park (1980, pp 340–341) (with permission of publisher)

a. *Marcus with German-speaking father*

F: Und was macht er hier? ('And what's he doing here?')

Ms: Haare putzen ('Hair cleaning')

F: Ja, er wäscht die Haare, und dann auch? ('Yes, he washes his hair, and then also?')

Ms: *Jabon!* ('Soap')

F: Bitte? ('What?')

Ms: *Jabón!* ('Soap')

F: Mit der Seife. Und was macht er denn hier? ('With the soap. And what is he doing then here?')

Ms: Putzen Zähne *con jabón*. ('Brushing teeth with soap')

b. Marcus with Spanish-speaking mother

M:	Qué hacen los niños? ('What are the children doing?')
Ms:	Müd. Die Kinder da müde. ('Tired. The children there tired.')
M:	Están cansados? No juegan los niños? ('Are they tired? Aren't the children playing?')
Ms:	Das *no juegan*. Arboles! ('That not playing. Trees!')
M:	Qué hay en los árboles? ('What are on the trees?')
Ms:	Manzanas. Hund schlafen. ('Apples. Dog sleeping.')

2. Volterra & Taeschner (1978, pp 315–316) (with permission of publisher)

Lisa with German-speaking mother

a.	L:	Miao miao
	M:	Wo ist miao? ('where is meow?')
	L:	*La* miao. ('there meow')
	M:	Wo is miao? ('where is meow?')
	L:	Da ist miao. ('there is meow.')

b. *L:* Daki Buch. ('thanks book') her mother had just given her a book

c. *L:* Daki. ('thanks') while giving the pencil to her mother

d. *L:* Mamma tita daki. ('Mommy pencil thanks') she wants her mother to give her the pencil

e. *L:* *Da* (authors interpret this as variant of Italian 'dare', to give; could be German 'da', there.) offering a sweet to her mother

3. (Murrell, 1966, pp 19–22) (with permission of publisher)

Sandra with father

Situation: looking at two pictures, the first (a) showing a woman with a cat, the second (b) showing the same cat, this time covered with milk, and a dog licking the milk off the cat's back.

a. F1 What else have you got there?
                That is, 'What other pictures have you got there?'

   S1 [ˌmami]
                See comment on S3.

   F2 Is that Mummy?

   S2 [ŋ ˈkʰi ŋˌɛə]
                [n]often preceded utterances at this stage (it did not apparently derive from Fin. *on* 'is' or Eng. *and*). See also S3 and b. S1. [kʰi] more commonly [ˈk(ʰ)i(ː)a]: Fin. *kissa* 'cat, puss', fs. *kissa* 'puss'. Cf. S3. [ŋˈɛə] Eng. *there*. Cf. b. S1.

   F3 Kia.

   S3 [ŋ ˈkʰia ˌmami]
                With [ˈkʰia] compare S2.
                This utterance meant 'Kia's mummy', i.e. 'the cat's owner'. The word *mummy* was still used to designate any older female in cases where a relationship was implied.

   F4 Pussy-cat.

b. S1 [ŋ ˈdɛə [ˈ . . .]ˈbɔββa . . . ˈkʰekka . . . ˈuːː ˈkʰia]
                [dɛə] Eng. *there* (Swed. *där*). Cf. a. S2. [ˈbɔββa] Eng. *bow-bow*, Swed. *vovve*. Cf. S3. [ˈkʰekka] Swed. *slicka* '(to) lick' (the Eng. word was less well-known than the Swed.). [uːː] was an exclamation of feigned shock and disapproval and real delight at seeing the cat covered with milk.

   F1 Vad gör han?
                Swed. 'What's he doing?' (I did not understand [ˈkʰekka] but assumed, partly because of the form [ˈbɔββa], that it was Swed. rather than Eng. she was speaking).

S2   ['ˋkikka]

                    Swed. *slicka* (the gemination and final [-a] suggest the Swed. word).

F2   ['kʰɪkä] . . . he's licking.

                    I may have thought she was using Eng. *kick*.

S3   [ˌʃikiŋ . . . ['ʋaɣʋa] ˋkikkan ˋkikin ['ʋaɣʋa] ˋkikin ['ʋaɣʋa ˋkikiŋ]

                    ['ʋaɣʋa] Swed. *vovve* 'bow-wow'; cf. S1. The diphthong now more closely resembles my
                    own (dialect-)equivalent of standard Brit.-Eng. /aʊ/; but cf. Fin. *hauva* 'bow-wow' and Fin.
                    vauva 'baby'. All four words were at first used indiscriminately for both 'dog' and 'baby'.

F3   Licking pussy-cat.

                    I repeat the verb and add the object.

S4   ['kiki bɔβɔa]

                    The final nasal is lost in ['kiki].
                    The diphthong in ['bɔβɔa] suggests the Eng. word. She is now excited, whereas in S3 she
                    was speaking more deliberately. She assumes I have contradicted her, that I mean it is
                    the cat that is doing the licking.

F4   Bow-wow licking pussy-cat.

                    I misunderstand her, too prematurely attributing to her a knowledge of Eng. syntax. Two-
                    item utterances were still maximal and the order arbitrary.

Sandra with Swedish-speaking mother

Situation: looking at two pictures, the first (c) showing a monkey pulling a girl's hair, the second (d) showing the girl with a bucket.

c. M1   Och vad är det?

                    Swed. 'And what's that?'

  S1   [ɑ:pa]

                    Swed. *apa* 'monkey'

  M2   Apa. Vad gör apan?

                    Swed. 'Monkey. And what's the monkey doing?'

  S2   [ˌpʋ ˌʃika ˋ˙ɪe]

                    Eng. *pull*, Swed. *flicka* 'girl' and Swed. *håret* 'the hair'. That is, 'he's pulling the girl's hair'.

  M3   Ja, han drar flickan i håret, så dum apa! Fy! dum apa.

                    Swed. 'Yes, he's pulling the girl's hair [lit. 'the girl in the hair'], what a naughty monkey!
                    Tut, tut! naughty monkey.'

  S3   ['ɛ: hɛ ɛ ˋkɔkkea]

                    Fin. *ei saa koskea* 'mustn't touch'

  M4   Ei saa koskea . . . 'ei ta kokia'.

                    Her mother repeats the sentence in its correct form and then in mimicry of a common
                    version of the child's.

  S4   [ˌei sa: ˋkɔkkia]

d. M1   Vad har flickan?

                    Swed. 'What's the girl got?'

  S1   [ˌem ˌen 'embala]

                    Swed. *ämbare* 'bucket'

  M2   Och vad har hon mera—i andra handen?

                    Swed. 'And what else has she got—in her other hand?'

  S2   [ˌbakit . . . 'dɑt ˌembala]

                    Eng. *bucket* and Eng. *that*. Both *bucket* and *ämbare* were used for both 'bucket' and
                    'spade', but here she seems to be making a distinction between *bucket* (= 'spade') and
                    ämbare (= 'bucket').

  M3   Det är *spade*.

                    Swed. 'That's "spade"'

  S3   [ˌpa:de]

  M4   Det där är *ämbare*.

                    Swed. '*That's* "bucket"'

  S4   ['embala . . . ˌfaggit]

                    The child repeats the Swed. word, then, after a pause, the Eng.

5

Language development in twins

K. Mogford

INTRODUCTION

There have been two main approaches to the study of language development in twins: the classical twin study and the comparison of language development in twins and single-tons. Both these approaches could be said to exploit a natural variation in human reproduction to help explain individual differences in language development. A third area of interest has been in twins who show a language impairment and a phenomenon that has come to be known as a 'secret language'. In this chapter evidence from studies of these three types will be examined and discussed to discover the insights that can be gained from the study of twins.

Approaches to the study of twins' language development

The first line of investigation has been followed sporadically over the last century. The classical twin study uses the opportunity that twins offer to study the relative contri-butions of genetic and environmental influ-ences to the development of human faculties. Galton is credited with the introduction of the classical twin study method during the last half of the nineteenth century. Despite subse-quent refinements in methodology, the logic of this design remains basically the same. It uses the genetic differences between mono-zygotic (identical) twins and dizygotic (fraternal) twins as the independent variable. In monozygotic twins the genetic constitution is the same for both members of the pair but in fraternal twins the genetic relationship is no more similar than for any two siblings of the same parents. Thus while the genetic relationship of the twins varies it is assumed that the environments in which they are reared will be equivalent. Each twin is assessed on some trait or ability and the degree of similarity between each pair is then calculated. When greater similarity in abilities is found between monozygotic twins than between dizygotic twins then the difference is attributed to genetic factors. By applying statistical formulae, for example see Falconer (1960) or Fuller & Thompson (1960), it is possible to arrive at an estimate of the degree to which inherited factors control the development of that trait or ability.

Considering the long preoccupation with the relative contribution of heredity and environment to language development, it is surprising that there have not been more studies of language development using this method, especially since the estimates of the contribution of genetic factors to language development that have been made vary considerably. There are many possible reasons why there has not been much enthusiasm for this approach in recent years. One major reason is the misgivings that have grown over the assumptions on which the classical twin study method is based. Various modifications in design have been devised to overcome some of the difficulties but many remain to be resolved. Elston & Blockage (1978) in an examination of the fundamental assumptions of the twin method concluded 'The twin method is based on many assumptions: some discredited, some untested, some untestable.' A particular problem in the study of language acquisition is that the twin method is based on the assumption that development in twins is essentially the same process as in singletons. Without this assumption it is not valid to generalize estimates of heritability made from the study of a sample of twins to the population of children as a whole. As will become apparent, the comparison of language development in twins and singletons suggests that there are both quantitative and qualitative differences in language development in twins and singletons.

Rather than investigating the influence of inherited factors, most recent research has come to examine twins in their own right, as a way of revealing the effects of the environmental experiences that may be considered unique to twins. Indeed twinship may be considered to provide the opportunity to look at a variation in socialization, the nature of which was not fully realized until comparatively recently 'The twin situation' has come to be recognized as one in which two infants with the same developmental needs share many experiences in the rearing process and develop patterns of interaction and relationships that are unlike those of singletons. They also share resources that are usually available to a single child. If some of these resources prove to be finite there will be a relative reduction in quantity for each individual child and this will be a potential source of disadvantage. Regarding twinship in this light dictates that the relevant comparison for study is that of twins and singletons. Initially the comparison of twins and singletons tended to underline the negative effects of twinship on the rate of development. More recent studies have looked for qualitative differences in development and for positive adaptations to the twin situation that may previously have been overlooked. This could have happened because the comparison of twins and singletons began by taking stages in the development of singletons' language as the starting point for comparison with twins. A new approach tries to predict aspects of language development which may be accelerated or which may develop in a different sequence as a result of the exceptional social circumstances in which twins develop.

Thus while classical twin studies have aimed to give estimates of the genetic contribution to language development, twin-singleton comparisons have the potential to identify aspects of the environment that can influence the rate and pattern of language development. In addition these studies indicate which aspects of language can vary with the social circumstances of child rearing.

Case studies have been the method chosen to study twins with delays or impairment of language. Twins provide an opportunity to evaluate methods of intervention. This method can use one twin for intervention and the co-twin as a control. The intervention and control treatments can then be reversed. A difficulty with this method is that altering the language system of one twin may well influence the language of the co-twin through their interaction.

The hazards of twinship

Before going on to review all three types of study it is necessary to consider some aspects of twinship that are essential to the interpretation of their findings. It is not only the rearing environment that is exceptional for twins. The sharing of developmental resources begins during gestation. Even a brief examination of the prenatal and perinatal experiences of twins shows that twins experience greater hazards than singletons. These hazards are more acute for monozygotic twins since around two thirds of them share not only the womb but the placenta and chorion as well, the remainder have separate chorions and placentas. Dizygotic twins always have separate chorions and placentas. Placentation in monozygotic twins depends on the stage at which the zygote, the fertilized egg, splits into two embryos (Corney 1975). When twins share a placenta the resulting intra-uterine competition is responsible for the finding that monozygotic twins show greater variation in intra-pair birthweights than dizygotic twins. However, dizygotic twins are also relatively at risk compared to singletons. In general, twin gestation periods are shorter and birthweights lower. There are a greater proportion of breech presentations at twin births. The greater risk to twins during this period is reflected in the perinatal death rate. It has been estimated that one in six twin concep-

tions lead to death for at least one member of the pair. The second born twin faces greater risks than the first (Farr 1975). Increased birth risks lead to a more unstable neonatal period compared with singletons (Hay & O'Brien 1981). Such a catalogue of increased risk factors suggests that there will also be a higher incidence of disabilities in twins that will include those with direct and indirect effects on language development. Accordingly, studies of language development in twins need to report clearly how samples selected for study were screened for disability and whether disabled children were excluded from the sample.

GENETIC INFLUENCES ON LANGUAGE DEVELOPMENT

The few studies that have addressed the issue of the relative influence of genetic factors on language ability in normally developing twins have each tended to study different aspects of language and used different methods of assessment. This may explain why estimates of the heritability of language vary widely between these studies. Lenneberg (1967) reviewed a number of studies of aspects of normal and disordered voice, speech and language development. He concluded that approximately 90% of identical twin pairs have a similar developmental history for speech and language compared to 40% of fraternal pairs. He attributed the greater similarity between identical twins to their shared genetic inheritance.

Since fraternal twins can be of opposite sex, two groups of fraternal twins are required for classical twin studies of language development. A design of this type was used by Koch (1966) and Mittler (1969). Koch studied the expressive language of twins by scoring errors in 400 consecutive utterances from a series of stories. There are problems with this method because lexical-semantic and syntactic errors were compounded and there may have been confusion of non-standard forms with developmentally immature forms. However, she did find that her identical pairs were more similar in the number and type of errors than her same-sex and opposite-sex fraternal twin pairs.

Mittler (1969) used the Illinois Test of Psycholinguistic Ability (ITPA) to measure the language skills of 30 identical twin pairs, 33 same-sex twin pairs and 37 opposite-sex fraternal twin pairs, with 100 singleton children as a control group. Mittler found that 56% of the total variance in the full scale ITPA scores was attributable to genetic factors. Mittler also found that different subscales gave different heritability estimates. Heritabilities were higher for the visual motor subtests and those not requiring speech than for those assessing auditory-vocal abilities.

Receptive grammatical development was studied by Munsinger & Douglass II (1976) who used a refinement of the twin study method to estimate language heritability. Their sample included 37 pairs of monozygotic twins, 37 same-sex dizygotic pairs, 11 siblings of monozygotic twins and 18 siblings of dizygotic twins. Language comprehension was measured using the Assessment of Children's Language Comprehension and the receptive section of the Northwestern Syntax Screening Test. Scores were corrected for age and nonverbal intelligence which was assessed on only one performance subtest of the WISC performance scale. Identical twin pair language scores were highly correlated (r = 0.831), while fraternal twin pairs were less closely related (r=0.436) and closely resembled the relationship between siblings (r = 0.492). Heritability of language ability was estimated using Falconer's (1960) method. They concluded that 80% of the variance in language development was due to inherited factors, but only around 10% to environmental factors. The remaining 10% of variance was attributed to error in measurement.

If we accept the assumptions and validity of the twin study method then these studies indicate that genetic factors have powerful control over the rate of language development, though nonverbal abilities have higher heritabilities. However, estimates of herita-

bility for language vary considerably and not all studies have tried to control or remove the contribution of intelligence from their estimates. The questions that have been asked in these studies have been fairly limited and so the answers obtained are of limited value. For example, rather than seeking to produce a global estimate for language ability it would be more interesting to know the comparative contributions of genetic and environmental factors to different facets of language development since it is probable that some aspects of language development are more likely to depend on environmental factors than others.

Lytton & Watts (1981) have come nearest to this kind of approach. They obtained a variety of measurements on a sample of twins at 2 and 9 years (17 monozygotic pairs, 29 dizygotic pairs and 44 singleton controls). At 2 years the assessments included the Peabody Picture Vocabulary Test and speech rate. At 9 years the children were given the Crichton Vocabulary Test, a spelling test and teachers' ratings for reading and speech maturity. This enabled the authors to compute heritability estimates for 2 and 9 years and to assess the stability of the genetic contribution over the 7 year period. They concluded that the ability to acquire vocabulary is heavily dependent on environmental factors and insignificantly on genetic factors. Spelling and reading both showed a significant genetic component. Speech measures at 2 and 9 years both showed significant genetic components and it was concluded that the genetic determination of speech appears to remain stable over the period studied providing one accepts the validity of comparing the two different measures used. Although the measures used were not ideal it would seem that this type of study can provide more valuable information than studies that treat language as a unitary skill.

However, it only makes sense to do this research if the assumptions on which the classical twin study method is based are considered valid. As was mentioned above, one such assumption is that language development in twins is essentially the same process as occurs in singletons. The remaining portion of this chapter is devoted to examining evidence that mostly undermines this assumption.

A COMPARISON OF THE LANGUAGE DEVELOPMENT OF TWINS AND SINGLETONS

Interest in language development in twins as compared with singletons began in the 1930s with two frequently cited studies. Day (1932) studied development from 2 to 5 years while Davis (1937) covered the period from 5;6 to 9;6 years. Rather than include their own control groups, both these studies used the data collected in a previous study of singletons by McCarthy (1930). Day (1932) and Davis (1937) both adopted McCarthy's language measurements in order to make meaningful comparisons. These included mean length of response, degree of grammatical complexity and measures of egocentric and socialized speech as defined by Piaget (1926). Day used 80 pairs of twins aged 2 to 5 years and found that the twins were markedly retarded in all aspects of language development when compared to McCarthy's singletons. The onset of speech was delayed with a mean of 25 months, sentence construction was relatively immature, vocabulary was reduced and expressive language was relatively impoverished in its conceptual content. Day concluded that the language inferiority shown by twins in comparison with singletons increased over the preschool period represented in her sample. Davis (1937) on the other hand, who extended the study of twins' language to $5\frac{1}{2}$, $6\frac{1}{2}$ and $9\frac{1}{2}$ years, found that as twins got older their language came closer to the development of singletons in relation to the length of utterance, though those twins raised in unfavourable environments remain delayed in language development up to the age of $9\frac{1}{2}$ years. Some aspects of twins' language development, particularly articulation and expressive vocabulary, remained delayed however.

The findings of these two studies have been broadly confirmed by most subsequent studies, particularly in regard to the rate of early development (e.g. Zazzo 1978). There has been some disagreement over the finer details such as the age of onset of speech in twins, but this is probably explained by the different criteria used to define onset. Lenneberg (1967), in a review of previously published studies, estimated that approximately 35% of identical twins and 40% of fraternal twins had normal onset of language. The remaining 65% of identical twins were equally delayed in onset as were 35% of fraternal twins. The remaining 25% of fraternal twins showed delay in one twin or an unequal delay in both.

The retardation of language development in twins has been confirmed in a number of subsequent studies using different methods of language appraisal. Mittler (1970) using ITPA and Peabody Picture Vocabulary (PPVT) at 4 years of age, found a systematic but relatively moderate delay of 6 months. He did not exclude any subjects from his sample because of handicap or speech retardation. Although Davis (1937) demonstrated that twins caught up with their singleton peers in some aspects of language development, once they reached school age, other authors have reported small deficiencies in language that persist into later childhood and adolescence (Zazzo 1960, Watts & Lytton 1981). If studies of academic achievement are used, then a delay in those areas that involve verbal abilities is evident (Fishbein 1978). There tends to be a higher incidence of slow readers in the twin population. Johnson et al (1984) found that success in reading could be predicted from earlier language development, at least in boys.

However, there are at least two studies of language development in multiple birth situations (Savic 1980, in twins, McCormick & Dewart 1986, in triplets) which indicate that under favourable social conditions early language delay is not inevitable. These two studies have looked at children in families with high levels of parental education and in relatively advantaged social positions. The children were not disadvantaged unduly either by low birthweight or other perinatal risk factors. These studies have collected detailed linguistic data, in a longitudinal design, in a few families. However, the studies that show a delay are of larger, less selected groups of twin pairs, are invariably cross-sectional and have relied exclusively on language tests or fairly gross measures of language development. In these non-selective studies, irrespective of the measures used and aspects of language studied, the finding of a significant but moderate early language delay in twins is consistent.

EXPLANATIONS FOR LANGUAGE DELAY IN TWINS

There are several possible explanations of language delay in twins. Firstly, language delay may be a consequence of increased perinatal risk factors. Since there is an increased incidence of frank handicap in twins (Farr 1975) it seems likely that there would be an increased incidence of developmental difficulties. Secondly, the birth of twins could produce a relative social disadvantage by increasing the family size and further stretching the families' resources for child rearing. Indeed these two factors are probably not entirely independent of one another. For although monozygotic twinning rates vary very little in all populations and seem to be a chance phenomenon, dizygotic twins are more frequently born to older mothers who have larger families (Nylander 1975). There sometimes appears to be a higher incidence of twins in lower social classes but this has been shown to be associated with the larger number of children born to women in lower social classes.

One way to look at the first of these suggested explanations is to argue that within the twin population those children subjected to the greatest hazards should show the greatest language delay. Since the second born twin is at greater risk of perinatal injury we would expect to find significant difference between first and second born twins in language development. Again, since perinatal risks for monozygotic twins are greater than for dizygotic twins we might expect to find a greater language delay for monozygotic than for dizygotic pairs. By the same logic, within the monozygotic twin population we would expect prenatal factors to affect monochorionic twins more than dichorionic twins. If this biological explanation is correct we would also expect to find that other aspects of development are affected, in particular physical growth and motor development.

One difficulty in examining this hypothesis is that it is often not made clear in twin studies if any measures were taken to exclude children with frank neurological impairment or if a decision was made to include them. If included, there would presumably be a higher incidence of low scores and greater variance in twin data.

Biological explanations of language delay

In fact, when we look at the development of twins in developmental terms, a general though mild delay has been found in most areas of development that reduces towards the end of the preschool period (Dales 1969, Kim 1969), though these findings are not totally consistent. Zazzo (1978) reports normal postural and motor development in a small sample of twins, 1 to 4 years of age, and claims that the twins were free from neurological deficit while still demonstrating the characteristic delay in language development. Growth, however, remains below average, reflected in norms for height and weight up to the age of 18 years (Mittler 1971), particularly in those children with low birthweights (Drillien 1958). However the largest and most systematically recorded delay is for language, followed by a mild delay in intellectual development (Zazzo 1960, Record et al 1970, Mittler 1971).

Various attempts have been made to assess the contribution of perinatal risk factors to language development and intelligence in twins. The conclusions are perhaps surprising. Lytton (1980) compared 2 to 3-year-old boy singletons with twins by observation of interaction with their parents in their own homes. He found that speech rates and speech development, as rated by observers, were lower for twins than for singletons. He found that monozygotic twins were inferior to dizygotic twins on vocabulary (PPVT) and rate of speech but these differences were smaller than twin-singleton differences. This suggested that increased birth risk might be to blame. When the birth histories and pregnancy records were examined for the twin pairs, the evidence pointed to greater risks for twins than singletons in general, though it must be said that the birth histories of the singleton controls were not examined. However, of the many indices of birth hazard examined for twins, only Apgar scores showed any systematic differences between monozygotic and dizygotic pairs. Lytton concluded that the speech differences between monozygotic and dizygotic twins in his sample could not be explained in terms of perinatal hazards. However, we could question this conclusion. The Apgar score is a measure of the state of the infant at birth and could be said to be of greater significance than some of the other hazard indices recorded.

The difference between monozygotic and dizygotic twins on language measures in Lytton's study could not be explained either by differences in mothers' education alone, or by social background or age. However, the difference was finally accounted for using a multiple regression analysis which established that a combination of factors including mothers' age and education were related to a number of biological risk factors. Mothers' education was negatively correlated with factors contributing to neonatal risk. The mothers of dizygotic twins tended to be older, better educated and to have experienced fewer difficulties at the birth of the twins which Lytton interpreted as the 'beneficial effects of a better social environment'. However, unless mothers of both twin types can be shown to have poorer education and greater social disadvantage than mothers of singletons, neonatal risk factors would not

appear to account for twin-singleton differences. Lytton states that 'Taking all the evidence together, it seems justifiable to conclude that the perinatal environment, potentially affecting children's neurological constitution, is a less important influence on the development of speech and language skills than is the postnatal environment provided by parents' (Lytton 1980).

Mittler (1970) also carefully examined the contribution of biological and social factors to language delay in twins. He examined a number of reproductive variables: abnormalities of pregnancy and delivery, birthweight, gestation period and birth sequence, to see if these would predict language development in the twin sample. Low birthweight showed only a weak association with ITPA scores. Length of gestation was the only reproductive variable to discriminate between twins with and without language delay. Of the developmental variables examined, only height at 4 years and age of first words showed any association with language development.

There have been no direct studies of language delay in monochorionic and dichorionic monozygotic twins, but in studies that have looked at the effects of sharing a placenta no differences have been found in intellectual development in early childhood, 18 months and 4 years (Welch et al 1978). However, studies at 7 years and on adults have found correlations with placentation (Melnick et al 1977, Rose et al 1981 respectively). Why perinatal hazards should be significantly associated with later rather than earlier development is not clear, though the findings may be just a consequence of the measures of intelligence that are used to assess intelligence at different ages.

In addition, a study by Record et al (1970) measured the intellectual development of twins, some of whom had been reared as singletons after the death of their twin sibling. Their findings showed that when twins were reared as singletons part of the small intellectual deficit found for twin pairs (5 IQ points) almost disappeared. The surviving twins were no different in birthweight from children reared as twins. This suggests that the sharing of the rearing environment does have a significant developmental influence.

These studies indicate a negligible effect of perinatal factors on language and intellectual development. While lower social class seems to be associated with increased birth hazard and a higher incidence of dizygotic twins, Mittler (1970) found that its effect on language development in twins was less marked than in singletons. Fishbein (1978) found this was also true in academic achievements. It cannot, however, be assumed that lower social class necessarily implies social disadvantage. Davis (1937) found on the other hand that social disadvantage tended to make language delays persist in middle childhood in twins, and Lytton found that in his sample social advantage tended to facilitate language development in dizygotic twins. Perhaps not too much should be made of social class differences in twins since recent studies of language acquisition in British (singleton) children that have used measures of spontaneous utterances, rather than test scores, have found small if any differences between singletons of different social classes (Wells 1985, Tizard & Hughes 1984). The relationship between the birth of twins, social class and disadvantage is a complex one and it is unlikely that any simple relationship exists between these factors and language development.

If the contribution of perinatal risk factors is only small and social class and disadvantage are difficult to disentangle then we need to look elsewhere for an explanation.

Intellectual retardation

Since rate of language acquisition can be predicted in part by intelligence, perhaps the slightly lower scores of twins in comparison with singletons on intellectual measures accounts for the language delay. However, it can quickly be seen that it is probable that the causal relationship runs in the opposite direction. Studies that measure verbal and performance abilities separately show that twins show most of their deficit on verbal

rather than performance scales (Koch 1966, Richon & Plee 1976 cited in Zazzo 1978). This indicates that it is the language delay that is mostly responsible for depressing intellectual ability.

The twin situation

The third possible cause of language delay is the twin situation itself. There are two forms of this explanation: each one places the emphasis on different aspects of the twin situation. The first version suggests that the close relationship between the twin couple reduces the need for verbal development and reduces opportunities and motivation to communicate. The second view is that adults have finite resources of time and attention for interaction with language learning infants. The division of those resources between two infants reduces the opportunities for each child. This is a similar argument to that used to explain the relative disadvantages for closely born siblings. This explanation seems more plausible when we consider a factor that has been shown in several studies at various stages of development to be correlated with advanced language development, i.e. adults' contingent response to the child's utterances. We can also think about the stress laid in studies of preverbal development on the adult's role in establishing structured exchanges in the context of which it is claimed language is acquired (see for example Ninio & Bruner 1978). The parent with a single child is described as monitoring the child's activity and line of regard so as to be able to respond contingently and meaningfully. This task is evidently made much more difficult when one adult has to do this with two infants at the same developmental stage. A possible source of language delay could result from difficulties in splitting attention, monitoring and comment between two infants whose selective attention is immature, consequently capricious and still at the mercy of extraneous stimuli. At this stage it may be especially crucial that the language models from which the infants learn are tailored precisely to individual need. In other words the initial source of language delay may be in sharing of adult interaction resources in infancy.

The main source of support for the first version of 'the twin situation' explanation which regards the close relationship as a source of language delay, comes from reports of secret language of twins. Zazzo (1960, 1978) calls this 'cryptophasia' and sees it as a stage that precedes the acquisition of socialized language in twins. This view derives from a psychoanalytic approach which suggested that twins have difficulty in establishing separate identities and egos and hence their need for interpersonal communication is reduced (Burlingham 1952). Communication of an intimate kind takes place only apparently within this self-sufficient relationship. In consequence there is a lack of interest in the communication systems of other individuals so that twins evolve their own system of communication, using one another as models. As a result, their speech is not intelligible to others. This suggests that twin language development is not only delayed but qualitatively different from development in single-born children.

TWIN/SINGLETON INTERACTION STUDIES

Whichever version of the last explanation is considered, proof of the hypothesis that it is the 'the twin situation' itself that is the source of language delay will emerge only from the study of twin-parent interaction. Indeed the most recent advances in understanding twin language development have come from comparing the interaction experience of twins and singletons (Lytton 1980, Savic 1980, Bornstein & Ruddy 1984, and Tomasello et al 1986).

Lytton (1980) in his previously mentioned study of twin boys (2 to 3 years), interacting with both parents, demonstrated that the amount of verbal interaction per twin was reduced in comparison with singletons. This observational study carried out in the home setting employed fairly crude measures of language used by the children and addressed to them. Speech rates were calculated for each child. The number of initiations and responses were also calculated for each participant. Together these measures demonstrated that each twin experienced fewer interactions with their parents than single children. Twin children initiated and responded less to parents than singletons, and the parents of twins initiated and responded less to each twin than parents did to each singleton. However, if rates of speaking to each twin could have been added together it would probably have been found that parents of twins were more active verbally than parents of singletons, but the way the data were collected meant that this was not possible. The outstanding factor, according to Lytton, was the degree to which parents failed to respond to twins. He concludes that since parents, especially mothers, were found to initiate and respond more than children, both with twins and singletons, it was parents who were chiefly responsible for the smaller amount of verbal communication recorded in parent-twin interaction.

However, since the study also found that twin language and speech were more immature than in singletons, an alternative explanation could be that parental initiation and responsiveness rates were influenced by their children's level of language development. It is likely that a child's rate of initiation increases with expressive language competence and parental initiation and responsiveness are related to this.

A different perspective on interaction between twins and parents arises from the detailed study of three twin pairs (15 months to 3 years of age) learning Serbo-Croatian (Savic 1980). This study showed that twins reared in favourable circumstances, when together with at least one adult, communicated more with the adult than with their fellow twin. Indeed Savic's twins were more likely to initiate discourse with adults than adults were to initiate discourse with them. Savic suggests that turn-taking in a triadic situation, which is more frequently experienced by twins than singletons, induces competition for a communication turn and so leads to modifications in utterance length and speed of speaking. She suggests that this may have given rise to the supposed inferiority of twins' language in comparison to singletons, especially when using MLU as a measure and comparing with singleton norms. She also suggests that twins are precocious in some discourse skills that are demanded more frequently in triadic than dyadic interaction.

Bornstein & Ruddy (1984) studied mother-child interaction in infancy. Their primary purpose was to explore abilities and experiences in infancy that would predict later cognitive functioning, including early language. They assessed two abilities that require little in the way of motor response: habituation and recognition memory. Their subjects were 20 4-month-old singletons and 11 pairs of twins who were all full-term at birth, normal and healthy. At 12 months they administered the Bayley scales of infant development and estimated the size of each infant's speaking vocabulary. At 4 months they found no difference between singletons and twins in their abilities. In singleton babies, their abilities at 4 months predicted performance on language measures at 12 months. In addition, some aspects of early language development were found to be partially predicted by mother-child interaction measures. In singletons, the frequency with which mothers encouraged attention to the environment predicted speaking vocabulary at 1 year. Surprisingly, frequency of mother's speech to the baby showed no significant predictive power. They were able to argue that it is maternal stimulation that predicts language development rather than maternal style reflecting the infant's vocal productivity. A multiple regression analysis showed that habituation rate and maternal attention behaviour together accounted for a significant proportion of the variance in speaking rates at 12 months.

The picture for the twins, however, was different. Although there were no differences

in the infants' abilities compared to singletons at 4 months, maternal behaviours were found to be different. Mothers of twins encouraged their babies to attend to the environment less than half as often as mothers of singletons. They also spoke less to them. At 12 months, twins used less than half as many words and performed less well on the Bayley scales. This suggests maternal behaviours rather than the initial abilities of twins account for early language differences. Bornstein & Ruddy point out that the effective factor may not be mothers' encouragement to attend per se, but some factor related to it like looking at picture books with their infants. Ninio & Bruner (1970) have suggested that this is a highly structured encounter which plays an important role in early language acquisition, and dialogues are only initiated during mutual visual attention to a book.

A recent study by Tomasello et al (1986) looked at an early period of language development (15 and 21 months). These workers were able to avoid the methodological difficulty of Lytton's (1980) study where there were no language matched controls for the twin subjects. Tomasello and colleagues compared the language learning environment of first-born singleton children with twins, matched on sex, age, maternal education and time spent with parents. At 15 and 21 months they took video recorded samples of interaction during play of the infants with their mothers in their own homes. The language measures were types and tokens of vocabulary and the number of turns per conversation. The language learning environment was assessed by measuring the frequency and type of maternal responses to each child's language as well as a number of measures of each mother's child-directed speech. Measures were also taken of the behaviour of all members of dyads and triads that led to episodes of joint attention. Although the Tomasello study did not include a perfect language-matched singleton control group, the design did allow the second sample of interaction in twins at 21 months to be compared with the first recording at 15 months in the singleton control group. At this stage the twins' language development was comparable to the earlier singleton language development on conversation but not on vocabulary measures. Maternal behaviours for the 21 month twin group could therefore be compared to the 21 month singleton group (a chronological age match) and with the 15 month singleton group (a rough language age match).

The results indicated that the language learning environments of twins and singletons differed and that these differences were not simply determined by the twins' level of language development. The differences in language learning environments were found for twins at 21 months in comparison with singletons at 15 and 21 months. The authors concluded that mothers have finite resources in terms of quantity and quality of their interactions with children and that the triadic nature of mother-twin interaction constrains the environment for each twin. Mothers of twins are as active as they are with singletons, but it is the division of their resources that is critical. Not only are some types of apparently critical resources reduced in quantity, but the coping strategies adopted by adults alter the quality of the interaction. The factors that are mainly implicated in the delay are behaviour that leads to joint attention and maternal responses to child speech that tend to extend the number of turns in a conversation. Tomasello emphasises that it is at this early stage that twin language development is especially vulnerable.

If the conclusions of Tomasello et al (1986) and Bornstein & Ruddy (1984) are correct, then there may be more substantial grounds for arguing for a relationship between the language learning environment in the pre-verbal and early verbal period and later language development. These studies also suggest that specific aspects of the language learning environment may be of greater significance at particular stages of development. This does not exclude the possibility that the attachment that develops between the twin pair could also negatively influence the development of language in twins.

QUALITATIVE DIFFERENCES IN THE LANGUAGE DEVELOPMENT OF TWINS

Secret language in twins

The second form of the environmental explanation of language inferiority in twins suggests that twin language development is not only delayed but also different in nature. This difference is attributed to 'the twin situation' in the sense that a specially close relationship is said to exist between each twin pair. The clearest statement of this view has been made by Zazzo (1960, 1978) who has identified a form of language, said to arise out of the close bond between twins, which he calls cryptophasia: literally secret language. Another term for a similar phenomenon that Luria noted in his case study of the twins Yura and Liosha G. is autonomous language (Luria & Yudovitch 1959). Zazzo suggests that cryptophasia allows the twin couple to be self-sufficient. The language is secret in the sense that it is unintelligible to others. Zazzo suggests that it is the early language of twins that is strange and archaic, making use of sounds, words and syntax that are not those of the language used to them by adults and other children. This special form of early language retards the onset of socialized language and Zazzo implies that it is a fairly common occurrence in twin language development. Mittler (1970) records that 47% of his sample of twins were reported by parents to have shown secret language, but it is not clear how this was defined by parents or identified by Mittler. The phenomenon was not more frequent among identical than non-identical twins, as might have been predicted. The proportion for same-sex fraternals was as high as 71%.

Luria & Yudovitch, while indicating that delayed speech and language was a characteristic of twins in general, did not imply in their report on Yura and Liosha that the autonomous speech system described for them was a more general characteristic of twins or the twin situation, although this inference is sometimes made. They particularly stress the unusual conditions that gave rise to this phenomenon, of which 'the twin situation' was only one factor. For example the twins were from a family where there was a history of phonological impairment in speech development and were the youngest children in a family of seven.

Evidence on the linguistic characteristics, existence or frequency of 'secret language' in twins is in short supply. There are no published systematic linguistic descriptions, for, although Luria's account is detailed and masterly for its time, it is not presented in a form that makes the linguistic features entirely clear. This makes it difficult to establish if he is describing something more than a very delayed but early form of language development seen also in some singletons. It may be that he is describing an early language system but one in which some aspects are exaggerated.

Because descriptions of the phenomenon are lacking, the precise nature of the claims made about this language remain unclear. It is also difficult to decide what precisely would constitute a 'secret language'. This term could mean an idiosyncratic form of communication used between twins but not to or in the presence of adults. Socialized language, developing later, would be used between adults and children but co-existing with the twins' first language. This would be a special case of bilingualism where the twin language is a novel first language and socialized (culturally transmitted) language would be a second language. This seems to match Luria's description of the language of Yura and Liosha G. Their language was also said to be inhibited in the presence of adults and therefore 'secret' in that sense. Another possible interpretation of a 'secret language' is that it is not a true language that can be analysed as a system on different levels, but a form of intimate verbal and nonverbal signals in which

meanings are shared by the twins by virtue of a shared developmental history in which their common experience of events and contexts in the past influences their understanding of shared experiences in the present. This is a special version of the intersubjectivity claimed for the preverbal period where meaning emerges from the recognition of shared and repeated exchanges (Newson & Newson 1975). Yet a third possibility is that twins' 'secret language' might be interpreted as a variant of native (culturally transmitted) language reserved for intimate communication, in which explicitness in both form and content are reduced and idiosyncratic forms are tolerated because of its restricted use. Which, if any, of these interpretations fits the case is not clear because of a lack of data.

In one of the best accounts, Luria claims that while at least 80–90% of Yura and Liosha's lexicon consisted of items derived from adult forms, 12% consisted of idiosyncratic items with broad meanings, often refined by the context, for which there were no adult equivalents. His description of the form of production of word structure and grammar seems to fit an early but essentially normal pattern of development described for singletons, both in phonology and word meaning as described by Clark (1973a). This interpretation is supported by Mittler (1971), Lytton (1980) and Savic (1980). Luria does make it clear that his twins were regarded as having a speech and language disorder from which their mother and maternal uncle also suffered. He does not suggest that autonomous language is a common characteristic of twin language development but that the problem of the delay was increased by the twin situation. However, the lack of intelligibility of twins' cryptophasia to other listeners is emphasized by Zazzo, though in contrasting cryptophasia with socialized speech he does suggest that the unintelligible form is restricted to monologues or intra-pair communication.

How twins communicate with one another in private is not known because there have been few detailed studies of communication between twins without adults present or actively involved in their interaction. Keenan (1974) recorded and studied early morning conversation and verbal play between one pair of male twins at 2;9 years. This study indicated that the boys were able to sustain two types of dialogue: one referential and one based on sound play. In both types of dialogue there was evidence that they were attending to each other's utterances during these exchanges. A very small proportion of the utterances (6.6%) were not addressed to their conversational partner, so monologues were rare. Although the sense of the reported dialogues is sometimes hard to penetrate, the sound play is clearly signalled as play by accompanying laughter and other paralinguistic signals, while the referential communication uses words and nursery rhymes clearly acquired from adults. Similar sequences have been recorded for singletons during 'crib' routines which often take place in semi-darkness, prior to sleep or on waking and so cannot be regarded as typical and purposeful communication. Where twins have been observed interacting with adults (Lytton 1980, Savic 1980, Tomasello et al 1986), the intra-pair communication has been found to be relatively low in frequency in relation to adult-child interaction. In these situations, twins have been observed to use speech that is more frequently directed (addressed), as opposed to undirected speech, in comparison with singletons (Savic 1980). There are no reports that the form or content of intra-twin communication was qualitatively different from interaction outside the twin pair, though there was no attempt to study this in a dyad with no adult participation. Savic (1980) on the other hand does report some exchanges that suggest that the twins she studied were able to correct each other over the form of their utterances, usually in the direction of more adult forms or precise meanings at a relatively early stage (15 months to 3 years of age). There is no evidence from these normally developing twins of unsocialized, private or idiosyncratic forms of language. However, the population of children with severe delay or

disorders of language development may offer different evidence.

Language impairment in twins

Our knowledge of language delay and impairment in twins has accumulated largely through case studies. In two recent case studies of twins referred for speech therapy during the preschool period (McLeod 1985, Briggs 1986) with supposedly secret language, the patterns of syntax and phonology from interactive data were analysed. In both cases twins willingly communicated with adults when studied, though in both cases the study began after a period of intervention. For each pair the same marginally intelligible patterns of communication were used when communicating with adults or between themselves. There was no obvious nonverbal code that was immediately available, though a detailed micro-analysis of nonverbal communication was not carried out. It was not possible to identify any 'autonomous' words either. Likely candidates could be explained by the simplifying processes in the children's very immature phonology, and word meanings were not especially overextended or diffuse. However, in both cases phonology was severely delayed and speech was unintelligible to all but the closest and most familiar communicators. Matheny & Bruggerman (1972) found that phonological development in a sample of 140 twin pairs was delayed compared to singletons, although birth order within the family and social class factors were demonstrated to account for some of this delay. It is likely that some of the cases reported to have a secret language reflect an immature phonology which is not recognized by parents or professionals without the ability to record and analyse the speech sound system in use by the twins.

In one 4-year-old opposite-sex fraternal twin pair studied by Briggs (1986), interaction between the twins during play was compared with interaction between each twin and another familiar but non-related peer. There was a little evidence to suggest a special style of interaction between the twin pair compared to other child interaction. MLUs in the twin-twin interaction were slightly lower than in the twin-peer interaction (Male twin : MLU 2.65 for twin-twin, 3.0 for twin-peer, Female twin: MLU 2.98 for twin-twin and 3.34 for twin-peer). The twins were more likely to respond verbally to a non-twin peer or teacher than to their co-twin. There was less directed speech when interacting with the co-twin and no examples of communicative breakdown. There were more examples of communicative break-down and requests for clarification in the male twin's interaction with a non-twin peer and with the adult teacher and the female twin and the adult teacher. There were differences between both kinds of child-child interaction and adult-child interaction, though this was mainly attributable to the adult teacher's ability and willingness to control, initiate and sustain discourse. This study suggests that a co-twin may not be a very demanding conver-sational partner. More studies of intra-pair interaction are required in both normal and disordered twins.

In case studies of language delay in twins, where the cause of delay is thought to be the twin situation, it is usually found that both twins are affected to some degree. A study by Haden & Penn (1985) reports a case where only the male twin in a non-identical opposite-sex twin pair showed a significant delay in syntax. The cause of this delay was thought to be the hospitalization and immobility conse-quent on a congenital foot deformity for which repeated orthopaedic surgery was required. Here, however, the relative imma-turity of language in the impaired twin was demonstrated to be maintained in interaction with the unimpaired twin. Some separation during a period of active therapeutic interven-tion served to restore more balance to the interaction.

This case study helps to emphasize that not all cases of language impairment in twins can be entirely explained by 'the twin situation'. However, because of the additional negative factors acting upon the language development of twins, it would be predicted that there

would be proportionally more twins than singletons with delayed or impaired language development. Indeed, a higher incidence of children requiring intervention for speech and language disabilities was reported in a study by Watts & Lytton (1981). Morley (1972), however, suggested this was not the case, but her sample was very small (10 twin pairs). She appeared to find no case where both twins suffered from a similar degree and type of speech and language disability. While it is apparent that a clinical sample is not composed only of twins where both twins show an overall language delay, it is true that such cases do arise (Luria & Yudovitch 1959, Douglass & Sutton 1978). Savic suggests that cases such as these arise when the environ-mental delay resulting from twinship is complicated by additional severe disadvan-taging factors.

Normal variation in language acquisition

Although the inferiority of twin language has been emphasized in studies that compare twins with singletons, and there is a probable higher incidence of language disabilities (Watts & Lytton 1981), this does not eliminate the possibility that twin language that is devel-oping normally may also be qualitatively different to singletons'. This will not always be evident if comparisons are made on the basis of measures derived from studies of language development in singletons. More detailed data collection and analysis is needed to reveal these qualitative differences. If these differences can be established, then it means that not all children need to develop by exactly the same route to language competence and opens up our understanding of the aspects of language that are free to vary as a consequence of developmental circumstances.

Savic (1980) claims to have found ways in which the language of three twin pairs acquiring Serbo-Croat differed from single-tons and she attributes these differences to adaptations to the twin situation. She argued that twins would have greater need for early command of person deixis: that is the ability to use linguistic markers (personal pronouns) to denote the speaker/listener role of persons referred to in an utterance. She found that these twins acquired the use of all forms of the first person pronoun more quickly than first-born singletons, although they started to acquire these forms later. She claims that 'Living as a pair, twins feel a strong need to find out quickly which language indicators mark their individual status in this pair'.

The fact that they start later is a reflection of the added complexity of the task for twins who in mastering personal deixis have to deal with terms used by adults to mark speaker, listener and the collective terms used to denote the twin pair. She also noted that the twins showed a particular competence in discourse somewhat earlier than in singletons. This was the ability to complete the utterance of their twin partner in a number of ways which suggested a syntactic ability in advance of the typical utterance length, and an ability to monitor dyadic exchanges between the adult with their co-twin, in which they were not participating, and to use discourse devices that allowed them to join in. Co-ordinating triadic discourse in a coherent way is a more demanding task than dyadic interaction since discourse turns do not simply alternate. Savic claims that twins, therefore, are more practised in this ability than singletons, although only a small proportion of communication in the twin situation was truely triadic. Because there have been few studies that have set out to look for these positive aspects of twin language development, or that have used methods suitable for uncovering these linguistic competences, there are few other examples of a similar kind. A study by Lavery (1985) included an examination of the development of personal pronouns in seven pairs of twins acquiring English between 20 and 41 months. Each pair was carefully matched with a singleton of similar age, mental ability and social background. The results failed to show any major differences between twins and singletons. Twins tended to use fewer personal pronouns and the data suggest delay rather than difference. However, Waterman & Shatz (1982) found that one pair of twins

invented a term 'gaga' to refer to the twin pair as a unit, and other forms and structures were used that reflected their twin status. A similar finding was reported by Malmstrom & Silva (1986) who found that a pair of identical twin girls, Kelda and Krista, developed conventional syntax and vocabulary but expressed their twin status in several distinctive ways between 2;0 and 3;9 years. One of these was the adoption of a double name to refer to themselves as a 'team' that they used with a single verb, e.g. 'Kelda, Kelda-Krista will call Mummy when Kelda-Krista is done' (2;10). They also used the single pronoun me to refer to themselves as a unit, e.g. 'Well, Mom, if you sit between me, then you can reach me better' (as Mom was about to sit beside one twin, avoiding the empty chair between the subjects. 3;9).

There are several points to be noted from Savic's study and the other studies in this section:

Firstly, methods and approaches that set out to discover inferiority may miss the positive aspects of linguistic ability adapted to exceptional circumstances, a lesson that can be profitably applied to children acquiring language in other exceptional circumstances.

Discourse skills may develop to meet the communication needs of the child in the social circumstances in which he interacts during child rearing. This may introduce sources of variation in rate and order of communication development.

The implications of these variations may be apparent in other aspects of language development such as as syntax and phonology.

This last point needs expanding in the light of what we know about language development in twins. Savic suggests, along with others, that the secret language or autonomous speech of twins is in effect an early form of communication development that persists or is reached at a much later time than usual in twins, particularly if they have had limited interaction with adults. She proposes that interaction with adults creates the motivation and opportunity for children to modify their system in the direction of adult forms. If this interaction does not occur then the system does not change. Interaction with the twin partner may in fact maintain the pattern since there will be fewer communication failures that act as a motivation to clarify. Savic makes the assumption that adults and children are equally free to interact in the twin situation. Although this may be potentially true, Lytton, for example, found that actually with singletons it was the adult (the mother) who made the most initiations between 2 and 3 years of age. Savic's assumption tends to discount the role given to the parent in the early stages of language development in which the discourse structure, the communicative intent and the shared attention to the environment are thought to be engineered by the adult communicator. As we have seen, however, in the early stages of language development, even in relatively advantaged twins, the amounts of such experience are reduced for each individual child because it is not possible to compensate for the presence of two infants at this particular stage of development. As the children become more autonomous, that is less reliant on adults to initiate and structure interchange, then the sharing of the adults' communicative resources for language learning may become easier. It is probably significant that in the case of Savic's twins, in all three homes there was an additional adult available to assist in child care tasks. Lytton (1980) quotes a study by Gosher Gottstein (1979) which showed that child care tasks reduced the amount of time available to parents of twins for interaction with each of their children. Help with routine child care tasks would therefore act as a positive advantage.

SUMMARY AND DISCUSSION

The study of twinship in its own right has proved to be more productive for our under-standing of environmental influences on language learning in childhood than for understanding the genetic influence on language acquisition. We may be justified in considering twins are at risk of delay in acquiring the language of the adult community from a number of biological and social factors. These risk factors all arise from the sharing of resources more normally available to a singleton. It would seem that there is an especially vulnerable period in twin language acquisition when the infant is dependent on adults' resources to manipulate attention and structure interaction on which it has been claimed for singletons that much subsequent language development is built. Nevertheless, the consequences of twinship are not inevitably negative and methods of study that are sensitive to differences as well as delay have suggested that some discourse skills may be relatively advanced. Finally we consider cases in which language development is regarded as so delayed and deviant as to be disordered, and examine the extent and nature of disordered development. There is some evidence to suggest that twin-twin interaction alone may not provide sufficient challenge to the child's language system to stimulate change. Reducing opportunities to interact with adults or other less familiar children may have negative effects, particularly on the phonological system. Delay in the early development of phonology may have given rise to the view that twins tend to develop a secret language. Similarity in the early sound systems of twins may be explained by similarity between singletons in early normal phonological development and by the possibility that twins may use one another as models. This tendency may be increased where adult-child interaction is reduced for any reason. In the state of current research this account of factors producing language impairment is necessarily speculative.

6

Intermittent conductive hearing loss and language development

S. K. Klein and I. Rapin

INTRODUCTION

This chapter reviews some of the many controversial issues concerning the effects of early fluctuating conductive hearing loss on the language and cognitive development of children. These issues have to do with assessment of the duration and severity of the hearing loss as well as of the severity and type of its consequences, and with the design of the studies employed to measure them. After several decades of effort, many uncertainties remain concerning the seemingly trivial problem caused by otitis media, by far the most prevalent cause for conductive hearing loss in small children. While one can safely predict that a study providing the last word on this topic has yet to be conducted, the goal of this chapter is to review the evidence.

Definitions

Otitis media in its various forms is one of the most common problems seen by pediatricians and otolaryngologists. Otitis media refers to an inflammation of the middle ear, an air-filled space that contains the ossicular chain, a series of three small bones connecting the tympanic membrane (ear drum) to the oval window of the inner ear (cochlea) (see Fig. 6.1). Sound waves induce vibrations of the tympanic membrane which separates the

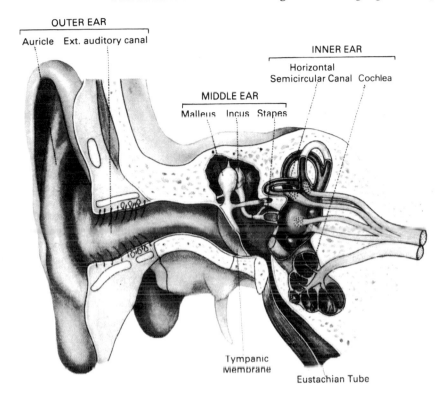

OUTER EAR
Auricle   Ext. auditory canal

INNER EAR
Horizontal
Semicircular Canal Cochlea

MIDDLE EAR
Malleus   Incus Stapes

Tympanic
Membrane

Eustachian Tube

Fig. 6.1 Schematic diagram of the right ear. (Reproduced from Ballantyne & Martin 1984.)

external auditory canal from the middle ear. The tympanic membrane and ossicles act as a mechanical transducer for transmitting sound from the low resistance air-filled external auditory canal to the hair cells that rest on the basilar membrane of the fluid-filled cochlea. The hair cells transform sound energy, which is mechanical, into electrical energy that stimulates the nerve cells of the inner ear which, in turn, transmit auditory information to the brain.

If there were no ossicular chain and sound were transmitted from air to fluid directly, more acoustic energy (loudness) would be needed to stimulate the nerve cells of the inner ear (Kelly 1985). This is exactly what occurs with middle ear effusion when eustachian tube obstruction and inflammation from bacterial or viral infection fills the middle ear with fluid. The middle ear communicates with the back of the nose through the eustachian tube which opens every time a person swallows or yawns, thus equalizing the pressure in the middle ear with atmospheric pressure. Whenever the eustachian tube does not open well because of a cold, enlarged adenoids, cleft or malformed palate, or chronic nasal obstruction from any cause, there is a tendency for air in the middle ear to be reabsorbed and for fluid to accumulate. This fluid provides an ideal culture medium for bacteria and it becomes easily infected by bacteria from the nose and pharynx. *Suppurative otitis media* refers to the presence of pus in the middle ear cavity. *Secretory* or *serous otitis media*, termed *'glue ear'* in the British literature (Black 1985), refers to a non-purulent effusion. Paparella et al (1985) suggest that the descriptors 'acute' and 'chronic' be used in a general sense to indicate the duration of middle ear effusion, not to indicate the exact number of days of illness. *Recurrent otitis* media refers to repeated (more than four) infections of the middle ear over a defined period of time, such as six months or one year (Scheidt & Kavanagh 1986). This condition should be distinguished from persistent middle ear effusion.

Hearing loss and otitis media

Middle ear effusion is the most common cause of transient conductive hearing loss (Bess 1983). Conductive hearing loss is defined as a decrease in perception of sound transmitted to the inner ear through air as compared with sound transmitted through bone (the skull) (Ruben et al 1985). The magnitude of the conductive hearing loss in otitis media with effusion averages about 26–30 dB, when measured by pure tone audiometry (Ruben et al 1985). Data from three studies suggest a spectrum of effects of otitis media on hearing in the speech sound frequency range: 7.7% of those affected have an average loss of 10 dB or less, 91.5% have a loss between 15 and 40 dB, and 0.8% have a loss of 50 dB or more (Cohen & Sade 1972, Bluestone et al 1973, Bluestone 1978). Testing over a range of high and low frequency tones shows that the configuration of the loss is relatively flat (Kokko 1974), that is the patient experiences the loss at all frequencies. Others report that the hearing loss fluctuates across frequencies, with the major loss in the low frequencies, and a window of preserved hearing at 2000 Hz (Northern & Downs 1984, Fria et al 1985).

Rarely, transient or permanent sensorineural hearing loss of some 15 dB for at least two frequencies results from recurrent episodes of otitis media with effusion. Paparella et al (1970) believe that middle ear infection causes inflammation of the round window membrane of the cochlea with apical spread and damage to the organ of Corti; others support this assertion (Arnold et al 1977, Moore & Best 1980, Munker 1981, Aviel & Ostfeld 1982). There are no known predictors of this rare sensorineural hearing loss, although Paparella and his colleagues suggest that, as in chin-chillas, a purulent middle ear effusion may be more likely than a serous one to result in sensorineural hearing loss.

Thus, middle ear effusion may affect hearing acuity in two ways: (1) it interferes with the mechanical transmission of sound to the organ of Corti, muffling hearing so that a greater volume of sound is needed for it to be heard; (2) it may also affect the organ of Corti by direct apical spread of toxins from the middle ear (Paparella et al 1984).

Since otitis media most often affects infants and toddlers, episodes of middle ear effusion may occur and recur while the children are learning language. The crucial question is whether the transient or permanent hearing loss experienced by children with chronic otitis media produces loss of critical auditory input in the speech-sound frequencies and distorts the sequence of normal language acquisition.

Detection of conductive hearing loss

Otoscopy

Middle ear inflammation and effusion can be documented by clinical examination with a pneumatic otoscope. With this instrument, the examiner can visualize the movement of the tympanic membrane through a small tube (speculum) placed in the external auditory canal. As air is introduced or aspirated through another part of the airtight speculum, the tympanic membrane moves in and out. In the presence of middle ear effusion, the mobility of the tympanic membrane is decreased and bulging or retraction of the tympanic membrane may be seen with the otoscope (Saunders & Meyerhoff 1980).

Impedance measurement

Reliance on clinical symptoms alone may fail to identify chronic otitis media (Downs 1985, Brooks 1985); Ferrer (1984) found that 18 of 25 children presenting for surgical management of middle ear effusion had had silent, chronic otitis media for two years or more. A number

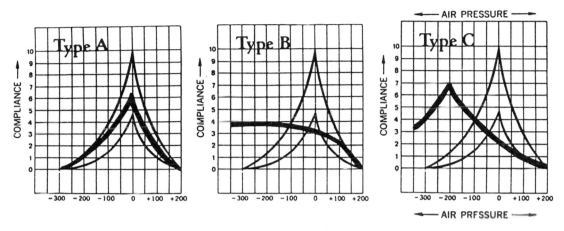

Fig. 6.2 Tympanograms based on Jerger's classification (Jerger 1970). See text for explanation. Bold line indicates compliance curve for each tympanographic profile; fine lines indicate range of normal compliance curve. (Adapted with permission from Northern & Downs 1984.)

of techniques have been devised to measure the resistance of the middle ear system in a more quantitative way. These are known as immittance or impedance measures, and they include tympanometry, static compliance measurement, the physical volume test (measurement of the volume of the ear canal), and acoustic reflex testing (measurement of threshold for reflex contraction of the tympanic membrane in response to loud sound) (for a complete discussion, see Northern & Downs 1984). Tympanometry is the most widely used of the impedance measurements. In tympanometry, air is insufflated into the sealed auditory canal and pushes the drum into the middle ear. When the air is slowly released and aspirated, the pressure change sucks the drum out slightly into the canal (Northern & Downs 1984). This procedure changes the tension of the ear drum; tension of the drum is measured by the amount of sound the drum reflects back when sound as well as air is introduced into the ear canal.

A pressure-volume curve can be drawn from these measurements. The normal tympanic membrane is most compliant (under the least tension) when the pressure on both sides of the tympanic membrane is equal (Jerger 'Type A' tympanogram, Fig. 6.2). In the presence of middle ear effusion, the tympanic membrane

becomes relatively noncompliant; the compliance curve is flattened because the tympanic membrane moves less in response to change in pressure in the external ear canal when the middle ear is filled with fluid (Jerger 'Type B' tympanogram, Fig. 6.2). Poor eustachian tube function may create pressure in the middle ear which is negative with respect to atmospheric pressure. In this case, compliance of the tympanic membrane may be normal, but the point of maximal compliance is shifted negatively (Jerger 'Type C' tympanogram, Fig. 2) (Jerger 1970, Northern & Downs 1984).

Tympanometry improves the accuracy with which otitis media is recognized and is useful for documenting persistent middle ear effusion following an acute episode (Shurin et al 1979). Tympanometry alone may not provide adequate screening for episodes of otitis media with effusion (Bess 1986). Dermody & Mackie (1983) performed tympanograms on 179 school-aged children showing that the incidence of middle ear effusion estimated from typanometry varies in a significant way depending on the pass/fail criterion chosen. Tos (1980) performed serial tympanograms on a group of children with an abnormal Type B tympanogram and found that their tympanograms improved spontaneously. Hallett (1982) showed that 45% of 553 children with recurrent otitis media required three tympanographic screenings for identification. These articles suggest that additional criteria such as pneumatic otoscopy should be used to diagnose recurrent otitis media.

Audiometry

Pure tone audiometry is a behavioural technique in which a subject indicates that he has perceived a sound at a specified frequency and loudness by hand raising or head turning toward the direction of the sound (Northern & Downs 1984). The sound stimulus can be delivered either through earphones as an air-conducted stimulus or by the vibration of a microphone held against the mastoid bone for a bone-conducted stimulus (Northern & Downs 1984). This technique estimates hearing threshold, the softest sound that the subject hears.

Behavioural audiometric testing can be extremely difficult in very young children, especially in the presence of a fluctuating hearing loss. *Auditory brainstem responses* are a particularly helpful means for estimating hearing threshold in the difficult-to-test child. A reproducible series of waves can be derived from computer-averaged EEG activity which is time-locked to an auditory stimulus (clicks or tones) (Picton et al 1986). The amplitude and latency of one of the waves (wave V) are measured in response to progressively softer stimuli so as to identify threshold of hearing (Picton et al 1986). Air and bone conducted thresholds can be estimated using this technique. However, even auditory brainstem response audiometry requires skill to detect small hearing losses in young children.

All these techniques have been used to define the risk of hearing loss, the presumed cause of language disturbance in recurrent otitis media (Downs 1985).

Incidence of otitis media

The first episode of otitis media often occurs in the first year of life. Casselbrant et al (1985) found a cumulative incidence of otitis media of between 53–61% in a population aged 2–6 years. In a Danish study, Lous (1987) found a 31% incidence in 7-year-olds examined monthly for 1 year. Howie et al (1975) reviewed the records of 488 children followed from birth in a pediatric practice and found that 240 children (49%) had their first episode of otitis media in the first year of life, with 296 (61%) identified by age 2.

A few of the more recent studies attempt to define the natural history of otitis media prospectively with impedance testing (mostly tympanometry) and otoscopy. Teele et al (1984) evaluated 205 children followed prospectively from birth to age 3 years, documenting the presence of middle ear effusion with otoscopy and occasional tympanometry (not applied consistently). Based on their own and others' (e.g. Shurin et al 1979) observations, Teele et al (1984) estimated that the median duration of middle ear effusion was 29 days, and used this estimate to calculate the number of days of middle ear effusion that each child in the study was likely to have experienced. Roberts et al (1986) documented the duration of middle ear effusion with daily otoscopy and tympanometry in 61 infants they followed from birth to 2 years in a residential day care setting. Their findings supported the estimate that the mean duration of an episode of middle ear effusion was 30 days. Each child had an average of six episodes of otitis media during these two years, wilh a range of 1–15 episodes; the total number of days a child had a middle ear effusion was 187 days on average, with a range of 8–931 days. Casselbrant et al (1985) substantiated these estimates with serial tympanometry in their prospective study of the incidence, prevalence and natural history of otitis media in preschool children. They also suggested that type C tympanograms with highly negative pressure in the middle ear predicted the occurrence of otitis media with effusion one month before its detection. Middle ear effusion may be present without overt symptomatology in many children.

Treatment

It is not surprising that treatment of recurrent

otitis media is controversial since the natural history of untreated otitis media is so variable. Management options must be selected taking into account the consequences of untreated disease (Gates et al 1985). The major consequences of untreated otitis media arise from middle ear infection; they include (1) chronic perforation and scarring of the tympanic membrane, causing changes in its elasticity; (2) accumulation of desquamated skin cells which may arise in the middle ear as a result of chronic inflammation or invade the middle ear from the external canal through a chronic perforation of the drum to form a ball of keratin (cholesteatoma) in the middle ear; (3) mastoiditis or spread of inflammation from the middle ear to the air filled mucosa-lined cavities of the adjacent mastoid bone. Mastoiditis often resulted in meningitis, brain abscess or cerebellar abscess in pre-antibiotic days (Northern & Downs 1984)

Since bacteria continue to be isolated from over half of the middle ear effusions which are aspirated (Bluestone 1982), antibiotic therapy plays a major role in the treatment of acute otitis media. Henderson et al (1982) found evidence of viral colonization or infection in approximately 30% of effusions, and suggested that, in addition to causing middle ear effusion, viral colonization or infection may facilitate the development of bacterial infection.

What is less clear is the role of antibiotic therapy vs various forms of surgical drainage for chronic purulent and nonpurulent middle ear effusion. Bluestone (1982) and others (Paradise 1980, Paradise & Rogers 1986) have recommended myringotomy (surgical puncture of the tympanic membrane to allow fluid not drained effectively through the obstructed eustachian tube to drain into the external auditory canal) and/or insertion of tympanostomy tubes or grommets in the myringotomy site (placement of a patent plastic flange in the surgical opening to prevent closure of the slit with healing) in cases of chronic or recurrent middle ear effusion. These procedures carry rare but important risks, including persistent perforation of the tympanic membrane, dislocation of the ossicles, severing of the facial nerve, and puncturing of the exposed jugular

bulb (Bluestone 1983). Gates (1983), citing the study of Brownlee et al (1969), projected a combined annual cost of approximately $1 billion for medical and surgical therapy for chronic middle ear effusion. Because of these high social and public costs, Black (1985) has called for re-examination of the indications of surgical treatment of otitis media. Gates et al (1985) have summarized possible multidisciplinary research approaches that would address these treatment controversies.

One crucial but unresolved issue in this debate is the extent to which intermittent conductive hearing loss can be held responsible for persistent language and educational problems in children. Clearly, if early surgical treatment can avert such problems, this may justify the high costs. However, the evidence on this point is far from conclusive.

IMPORTANCE OF AUDITORY INPUT FOR LANGUAGE ACQUISITION

The concept of the critical period

Critical periods are limited stages in brain maturation which must coincide with exposure to certain experiences; this results in seemingly effortless and rapid acquisition of new skills which are much harder to acquire or are not acquired at all at other stages. Other chapters in this book discuss how the nature and timing of experience affect language acquisition in children. The inter-relationship of degree, duration and timing of temporary hearing loss in a young child is the key issue in assessing the effect of recurrent otitis media on language acquisition. Whether critical periods exist for exposure to speech sounds and the acquisition of language remains an open question (Clopton 1980).

Animal studies

Support for the hypothesis of a critical period or periods in auditory development exists in the animal literature (for a review, see Ruben & Rapin 1980). Webster & Webster (1977) developed a model for studying the effects of auditory deprivation in CBA/J mice. In the first of several experiments, they simulated neonatal conductive hearing loss by removing the blastema of the external auditory canal of eight mice (operated group) at 3 days of age. Another group of eight mice (deprived group) were raised from age 3 days on by a silent mother in an environment designed to reduce ambient noise levels by 10 dB. Comparison of both the deprived and operated groups with a control group of eight mice showed that cell size was reduced in several brainstem auditory nuclei. No difference was found between the deprived and operated groups with respect to cell size reduction.

Webster & Webster (1979) used these findings to create a model of reversible auditory deprivation, which, in the light of the previous experiments, simulates reversible conductive hearing loss. Five 3-day-old mice were raised by a silent mother in the sound-attenuated chamber for the subsequent 42 days. At age 45 days, the mice returned to the regular animal colony. Webster & Webster used a more sensitive measurement of cell cross-sectional size, and showed that the auditory brainstem neurons of the reversibly-deprived mice were smaller when compared with controls.

Webster (1983a) studied another group of 4-day-old mice in which he removed only the left blastema of the external auditory canal. He found a decrease in the cross-sectional size of several nuclear groups of brainstem auditory neurons. Webster did not replicate Coleman & O'Connor's (1979) finding of a greater effect of a unilateral, versus a bilateral, lesion in reducing the size of large spherical cells of the ipsilateral cochlear nuclei. He concluded that the auditory neurons of the CBA/J mouse, which reach adult soma size at 12 days of age (Webster 1983b), shrink as the result of inadequate sound stimulation. Webster provides the strongest evidence to date for environmental modulation of the developing auditory system.

Critical beginnings of language acquisition in man; auditory perception studies

Studies of auditory experience during human development have added little information concerning the nature of critical periods. Many investigators have tested speech sound discrimination in young infants in order to assess the interaction of maturation and auditory experience. Most investigators agree that auditory comprehension precedes speech production in normal language development; the smallest amount of auditory input necessary for normal speech production is unknown (Ferguson & Yeni-Komshian 1980).

The speech sounds of a language, its phonology, are the building blocks of words and sentences (Menyuk 1979). The ability of a normal child to identify and discriminate among the meaningful speech sounds (phonemes) of a language has been the subject of a large body of research and has been reviewed eloquently by Skinner (1978) and Strange (1986). Menyuk (1979) emphasized that we do not know what effect alteration in early auditory input may have on discrimination of speech sounds and formant transitions (brief frequency changes in the acoustic energy bands that characterize consonants). Examination of the frequency distribution of common English speech sounds (Fig. 6.3) suggested to Downs (1985) and others that failure of children with recurrent otitis media to produce unvoiced frica-

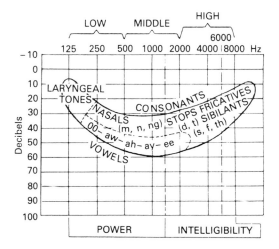

Fig. 6.3 The frequency components of English speech sounds. (Reproduced from Ballantyne and Martin 1984).

tives such as /s/, /ʃ/, /θ/ and /f/, implied that the children did not hear them clearly (Dobie & Berlin 1979). If children with otitis media fail to hear high frequency speech sounds such as the unvoiced fricatives, they miss the consonants which mark tense. possession, and number. These consonants also occur in key function words in English (e.g. shall, for, etc.) (Dobie & Berlin 1979, Downs 1985). Recent evidence suggests that preschool children are still learning how to discriminate among the voiceless fricatives (Phatate & Umano 1981, Wardrip-Fruin & Peach 1984). Accurate discrimination of other speech sounds such as /l/, /r/ and /w/ may occur even later in childhood (Fior 1972); the exact sequence of normal receptive language acquisition is still unknown (Ferguson & Yeni-Komshian 1980); it seems to vary considerably from child to child.

Suprasegmental auditory perception

In addition to jeopardizing the perception of speech segments, inconsistent auditory input may affect understanding of the prosody (intonation contours, stress, pitch) of speech and delay the concept of turn-taking in conversation (Menyuk 1979). Turn-taking requires that the child detect when a conversational partner has finished a turn, is asking a question, or giving a command—features that all depend on the detection of prosodic features of speech. Children with middle ear effusion may misunderstand both speech sounds and the prosodic messages of language because they have a hearing loss at all frequencies (Northern & Downs 1984). Insufficient data exist regarding the severity of the hearing loss which accompanies recurrent middle ear effusion, making it difficult to know precisely how auditory input is altered in affected children (Rapin 1979, Northern & Downs 1984, Jerger 1986).

Consequences of auditory deprivation in man: language acquisition in children with severe hearing loss

The severe deficits in spoken language acqui-

sition in the deaf are well-known and are reviewed in Chapter 7. Even unilateral hearing loss may affect language skills in children. Bess & Tharpe (1984) studied 25 of 60 children with a 45 dB unilateral hearing loss and a hearing threshold no poorer than 15 dB in the 'good' ear. Their criteria for selection of the subsample were not clear. Cognitive testing with the WISC-R showed that the IQs of the 25 children they selected did not differ significantly from controls, yet nearly a third of the 25 had failed one grade in school. These children also had difficulty with auditory localization on a specially designed test, and with recognition of nonsense syllables in noise, when compared with normally-hearing peers. Children with unilateral losses greater than 60 dB showed significant differences from children with milder losses on some tests of language ability including the Token Test and the Detroit Test of Learning Aptitudes.

Based on this evidence, many investigators have hypothesized that recurrent otitis media might perturb the normal sequence of language acquisition in young children.

METHODOLOGICAL ISSUES

Ventry (1980) and Paradise (1981) identified the major methodological problems which complicate the study of otitis media and language development: (1) experimenters have had various degrees of success in controlling their research design to minimize alternative explanations of results; (2) the ethics of human experimentation have prevented researchers from using a treatment/no treatment paradigm to study the effects of recurrent otitis media on language acquisition prospectively. The first point is a measure of internal validity; the second a measure of external validity (Ventry 1980).

Control of internal validity

A study controlled for *internal validity* minimizes the effect of treatment on interpretation of outcome and considers the power of alternative explanations for the results obtained

(Ventry 1980). This is difficult to achieve in a retrospective study, one which considers a group of individuals with a disease of interest (cases) and a group of individuals without that disease (controls) (Kudrajavcev & Schoenberg 1979), since subject selection is defined in an arbitrary way by design. Unwanted bias could affect such a study if, for example, children with clear-cut language disorders were more likely than other children to be referred for hospital treatment if otitis media were detected. Nevertheless, as Kudrajavcev & Schoenberg (1979) and Paradise (1981) have pointed out, retrospective studies are valuable in general and specifically for the study of the effect of otitis media on language development, since they have focussed the questions to be analyzed in more ambitious studies.

Paradise (1981) has summarized the three main questions that have emerged from retrospective studies concerning the effect of otitis media on language development. His first question 'Is there an association between early otitis media and later language delays?' has been brought into focus by *comparative* studies which assess language ability in children with conductive hearing loss versus children with normal hearing (Young & McConnell 1957, Wilcox & Tobin 1974, Needleman & Menyuk 1977, Zinkus et al 1978, Sak & Ruben 1981). These investigators all concluded that there is an association between early otitis media and later language delay. Their subject populations were small, usually including no more than 20 cases. Sak & Ruben (1981) used sibling controls; Zinkus et al (1978) used no controls. Young & McConnell (1957) did not define their cases as having conductive hearing loss per se; their subjects were 'hard of hearing'. Conclusions of positive association between early otitis media and later language problems were limited by problems of internal validity.

Paradise's second question 'If an association exists between early otitis media and later language delay—is it causal?' has been addressed by three types of studies:

1. *Comparative* studies examining auditory processing abilities and language skills in children with conductive hearing loss versus controls (Goetzinger et al 1964, Owrid 1970, Brandes & Ehinger 1981, Hoffman-Lawless et al 1981, Jerger et al 1983, Eimas & Clarkson 1986). Some of these studies have investigated ethnic groups known to have a high incidence of otitis media, e.g. Apache children (Fischler et al 1985), and Australian Aborigines (Lewis 1976). Other studies have concentrated on children considered at risk for developmental disorders because of perinatal problems (Thelin et al 1979).

2. *Correlative* studies of language-delayed children (defined in various ways) who are compared with control children without evidence of language delay with respect to a premorbid history of otitis media. Several populations have been studied, including learning disabled children (Masters & Marsh 1978, Freeman & Parkins 1979, Bennett et al 1980) and children with auditory processing deficits (Zinkus & Gottlieb 1980).

3. *Descriptive-longitudinal* studies looking at progress of language-delayed children with and without episodes of otitis media (e.g. Bishop & Edmundson 1986, Brookhouser & Goldgar 1987). Only Brookhouser & Goldgar have found an association between otitis media and later language delay using this design. These prospective longitudinal studies make stronger statements about the hypothesis tested since, as Kudrajavcev & Schoenberg (1978) point out, they are better able to define their population than retrospective studies. The absolute risk of developmental disability in children with a history of otitis media cannot be estimated with such studies, however, as subject selection is not random. With the exception of Brookhauser & Goldgar's (1987) study, none of the descriptive/longitudinal studies weigh predisposing risk factors (such as cleft palate) since, in fact, many of these factors are deliberately excluded in subject selection. Be that as it may, descriptive/longitudinal studies estimate the impact of otitis media on language development more closely than the smaller studies.

Control of external validity

Four groups of children have been followed

prospectively from birth for evaluation of the impact of recurrent otitis media on later language development: two groups of middle class children (Klein 1984, Teele et al 1984, Casselbrant et al 1985, Menyuk 1986) a group of children of lower socioeconomic status in a day care center (Roberts et al 1986), and a group of high risk premature infants of lower socioeconomic status (Wallace et al in press). In these prospective studies, a group of individuals is followed over time for the development of disease. Each group of investigators has tried to address Paradise's (1981) third question 'If early otitis media indeed results in later developmental impairments, are they permanent and irreversible?' These prospective designs attempt to maximize the *external validity* of the results, the extent to which the findings can be generalized. In the subsequent sections, we will evaluate the way in which these prospective and retrospective studies have assessed language acquisition in the setting of recurrent otitis media.

LANGUAGE DEVELOPMENT IN CHILDREN WITH RECURRENT OTITIS MEDIA

Receptive language

Auditory perception

In pilot work, Eimas & Clarkson (1986) measured the phonologic discrimination skills of eight children with a history of recurrent otitis media who were matched to controls with respect to age and IQ. They measured hearing levels and impedance at the time of testing. The affected children were less able than controls to discriminate between closely-related consonant-vowel (CV) syllables such as *da* and *ta* as the voice onset time (VOT) of the consonant (the time between release of the closed glottis and onset of vibration in the vocal cords) was shortened artificially. In addition, the children had greater difficulty assigning a given CV syllable to the category of *da* or *ta* when the VOT was varied. A slightly larger group of children (N = 11) with recurrent otitis could not discriminate between whole word stimuli (*bath*/*path*) manipulated

similarly with respect to VOT. The children's ability to make the speech-sound discrimination did not improve when the volume of the stimulus was increased. Eimas & Clarkson's findings suggest that recurrent middle ear effusion affects speech perception in a more permanent way than previously suspected, since the effects of abnormal auditory input (impaired phonologic discrimination) persist long after the episodes of otitis media have resolved. This may explain why auditory comprehension tests uncover subtle discrepancies between the performance of children with recurrent otitis media and controls.

Auditory comprehension skills have been examined in a number of studies of children with recurrent otitis media. Several studies have assessed performance on subtests of the Illinois Test of Psycholinguistic Abilities (Holm & Kunze 1969, Zinkus & Gottlieb 1980, Sak & Ruben 1981) or the Receptive-Expressive Emergent Language Scale (Brookhouser et al 1979, Thelin et al 1979, Brookhouser & Goldgar 1987) to assess receptive language ability. All these investigators found that children with a history of recurrent otitis media obtained below average scores. This is not surprising, since in one of these studies (Brookhouser et al 1979) the subjects were referred for language delay, and in another (Thelin et al 1979), the subjects were born from high-risk pregnancies. Other studies, using an expanded battery of central auditory processing measures, have not found any abnormalities (Lehmann et al 1979, Hoffman-Lawless et al 1981). In the best of these negative studies, Hoffman-Lawless et al (1981) supplemented the Goldman-Fristoe-Woodcock Auditory Skills Battery and the Auditory Sequential Memory Subtest of the Illinois Test of Psycholinguistic Abilities with filtered and speech-in-noise word repetition tests and a dichotic repetition test (Staggered Spondaic Word Test). In theory, this battery should cover the spectrum of auditory processing tasks. Norms for the Staggered Spondaic Word Test in this age group are unpublished. Hoffman-Lawless and colleagues comment that the failure of tests other than the filtered speech task, to detect a transient performance lag in children with otitis media may simply reflect the insensitivity of the battery itself. This is a reasonable conclusion.

Tests using whole word discrimination tasks may be more sensitive measures of auditory processing than tasks involving more complex but more redundant stimuli, such as sentences. Brandes & Ehinger (1971) maintain that otitis media does affect auditory processing, citing poor subject selection, inadequate audiologic testing and inappropriate statistical procedures as reasons for failure to detect this effect. They studied 15 children with a persistent conductive hearing loss of 20 dB or greater in the setting of a history of otitis media. The children with conductive hearing loss performed more poorly than controls only on the subtests of the Goldman-Fristoe-Woodcock Auditory Skills Battery which tested auditory perception of sound symbols. Jerger et al (1983) compared the performance of 25 children with a history of recurrent otitis media with that of controls who were asked to identify pictures named in quiet and then with a competing speech message. They found that the children with a history of otitis media had impaired performance when words were used as the competing speech message. However, when a sentence was used as the competing message, the children's performance equalled controls'. These results suggest that the added syntactic and semantic information provided by sentences may obscure a receptive deficit which is uncovered by the use of smaller speech units (words).

A few of the published prospective studies evaluated phonologic processing with a whole word measure. Teele et al (1984) found poorer phonologic comprehension as assessed by the Auditory Comprehension Quotient (ACQ) of the Preschool Language Scale in children who had experienced middle ear effusion during the first year of life. Bilateral middle ear effusion had a stronger correlation with low ACQ than unilateral effusion. Menyuk (1986) tested these 205 children at age 7 years with items from the Goldman-Fristoe and Goldman-Fristoe-Woodcock Tests to assess speech sound discrimination. She found significant differences between children with recurrent middle ear effusion compared with the controls on these tests of speech perception.

Semantics

Semantic skills, as tested with picture pointing tasks such as the Peabody Picture Vocabulary Test and the English Picture Vocabulary Test, have been normal in children with recurrent otitis media (Holm & Kunze 1969, Dalzell & Owrid 1976, Needleman & Menyuk 1977, Lehmann et al 1979, Jerger et al 1983). Brookhouser & Goldgar (1987) found that young children with otitis media improved their low scores over time on subtests exploring semantic relations, replicating the findings of Dalzell & Owrid (1976). Brookhouser & Goldgar linked this trend (as defined by the Peabody Picture Vocabulary Test and the Reynell Developmental Language Scales) to the hearing acuity of the better ear in 215 children with a history of early otitis media and conductive hearing loss. Children with unilateral losses greater than 15 dB scored better than those with bilateral hearing loss, and their 'language quotient' was directly related to hearing acuity in the better ear. Like Dalzell & Owrid's earlier study (1976), their study did not uncover a significant correlation between increasing severity of the unilateral loss and lower language quotients.

Prospective studies also suggest that semantic comprehension is normal in children with recurrent otitis media. Wallace et al (in press) found no difference in receptive language scores on the Sequenced Inventory of Communication Development in 15 high risk infants compared prospectively from birth with 12 controls. Though Teele et al (1984) found lower scores on the Peabody Picture Vocabulary Test in 3-year-olds with recurrent middle ear effusion, Menyuk (1986) found that their performance on this test at age 7 years no longer differed from controls.

Syntax

Few investigators have assessed syntactic

skills. Fischler et al (1985) used subtests of the Test of Language Development to evaluate Apache children, and found that the children with otitis media performed no differently than controls. These results must be interpreted with caution, however, in view of the cultural and language discrepancies between the test and normative populations. Bishop & Edmundson (1986) used several measures of syntactic function and found no differences between language-impaired children with a history of otitis media and those without such a history.

Menyuk (1986) analyzed spontaneous speech samples to study syntax. Children with a high frequency of recurrent middle ear effusions produced fewer sentences with prepositional phrases and used more co-ordinate sentences (simple sentences joined by 'and') than complex sentences with dependent clauses. These children showed no differences from controls in their comprehension of relations in complex sentences.

Expressive language

Many investigators have suggested that children with otitis media score lower than controls on tests which assess lexical and sentence production, such as the Sequenced Inventory of Communication Development, Receptive-Expressive Emergent Language Scale, Reynell Developmental Language Scales and Developmental Sentence Analysis (Needleman & Menyuk 1977, Brookhouser et al 1979, Brookhouser & Goldgar 1987, Menyuk 1986, Wallace et al in press). Most studies, including those with linguistic analysis of spontaneous language samples, have not uncovered any particular abnormalities characteristic of otitis media (Lehmann et al 1979, Brookhouser et al 1979, Bishop & Edmundson 1986, Brookhouser & Goldgar 1987).

A much larger study by Menyuk & Chase (reported in Menyuk 1986) refutes this. They demonstrated that children with recurrent middle ear effusion (defined as more than two episodes within a 7 year period) made more errors than controls in the production of morphologic markers. Menyuk & Chase's follow-up study of the 205 children initially reported at age 3 by Teele et al (1984) is the only study which suggests that early production errors may herald persistent linguistic errors uncovered by systematic tests of language skills in these children.

IQ tests

Some investigators have noted a depression of IQ scores in small groups of children with a remote history of otitis media as compared with controls (Sak & Ruben 1981). The effect of otitis media on IQ appears to be more pronounced in certain ethnic groups, such as Eskimo children (Kaplan et al 1973, Ling et al 1969). Some of the measures used to test these children may have been inappropriate, since norms for these populations are not available. Learning disabled children (Zinkus et al 1978, Zinkus & Gottlieb 1980) and high risk children with hyperbilirubinemia (Thelin et al 1979) also had lower IQ scores than normal controls in the setting of recurrent otitis media; however, a cause-effect relationship has only been suggested for learning disabled children (Masters & Marsh 1978, Freeman & Parkins 1979, Bennett et al 1980).

Prospective studies have failed to show that recurrent episodes of otitis media result in lower IQ scores (Teele et al 1984, Roberts et al 1986, Wallace et al in press). Roberts and her colleagues concluded that the effect of otitis media on language acquisition was minimal since the presence of otitis media with effusion did not affect IQ, the most important functional predictor of school performance. However, IQ testing may not be adequate to assess language skills. Wilson & Wilson (1977) gave an assortment of IQ tests to 59 children with developmental language delay diagnosed by other criteria. They found that the higher the auditory-verbal language content of the test, the more poorly the children performed. Wilson & Wilson concluded that the IQ score was difficult to interpret in the setting of language disturbance, since a child with weaknesses for a given skill tested within a 3 month interval could receive a standard score which differed by more than 3 standard deviations from the standard score of another test supposedly measuring the same cognitive abilities! Auditory processing disturbances are postulated in children with chronic otitis media, so that supplementation of orally-presented tests with other nonverbal measures would be reasonable for supporting the hypothesis suggested by the IQ scores.

Reading and spelling

Though Ling (1972) showed that reading skills in 38 hearing-impaired children lagged 15 months behind controls, other researchers found reading skills unaffected in children with recurrent otitis media compared to controls (Zinkus et al 1978, Zinkus & Gottlieb 1980, Brandes & Ehinger 1981), replicating the earlier study of Dalzell & Owrid (1976). Prospective studies confirm that children with a history of recurrent middle ear effusion have average academic attainments (Brooks 1986) and read normally. In the strongest of these studies, Lous & Fiellau-Nikolajsen (1984) identified 46 children with recurrent otitis media among a birth cohort of 509 children and followed them prospectively with tympanometry and other academic achievement measures. They found that only 6 of the 46 children scored below average on the Silent Reading Test; reading skills in the vast majority of children with recurrent otitis media were unaffected.

SUMMARY AND CONCLUSIONS

Over 50 studies of language performance in children with recurrent otitis media have been published, yet the cause-effect relationship between early recurrent otitis media and later cognitive and language impairment remains uncertain (Kavanagh 1986). This review shows that, although some large populations of children with otitis media have been identified and followed prospectively, problems in study design limit the applicability of the conclusions reached. Brookhouser & Goldgar's study (1987) is of particular interest because they tested all aspects of language systematically, and compared children with recurrent otitis media to a population of children with specific language disturbances. Brookhouser & Goldgar raised the interesting question of whether the combination of recurrent middle ear effusion with a developmental language disorder lowered verbal performance significantly more than a developmental language disorder alone (Ludlow 1980).

Most of the other studies of recurrent middle ear effusion and language acquisition concentrate on one area of speech and language but leave others unexplored. For example, Roberts et al (1986) identified episodes of otitis media by daily examination in a birth cohort. They established the number and duration of episodes of otitis media better than any of the other studies, but they never measured hearing levels, and their measures of language skills did not survey all levels of language. Menyuk (1986) found persistent phonologic and syntactic impairments in her follow-up study, but the practical significance of these abnormalities is unclear.

The importance and the effect of this common pediatric problem, recurrent otitis media with intermittent conductive hearing loss, for language acquisition in preschool children remains uncertain. Review of the literature suggests to us, as it has to many other investigators, that the effects of recurrent episodes of middle ear effusion on subsequent language acquisition are subtle if present at all. Recurrent middle ear effusion in early childhood may affect language skills transiently, but is probably of limited significance for children with normal and above average IQs and with a school and home environment conducive to learning. Whether this is also true of children growing up in suboptimal circumstances remains an open question. Only Wallace et al (in press) examine other factors such as mental deficiency and low socioeconomic status as independent variables; their subject sample is too small and too young to permit generalizations from their conclusions. We believe that these factors may potentiate the minimal effect of recurrent otitis media on language development (Rapin 1979, Sak & Ruben 1981). However, we suspect that in the absence of permanent hearing loss or other sensorimotor handicap, children with these additional risk factors will be unlikely to show significant impairment of language skills as a result of recurrent otitis media.

7

Oral language* acquisition in the prelinguistically deaf

K. Mogford

THE CONSEQUENCES OF A CONGENITAL HEARING IMPAIRMENT FOR LANGUAGE ACQUISITION

The effects of a congenital hearing loss on communication in the absence of any form of remediation are well known. To rescue children born deaf from isolation and muteness, amplification of sound and special educational programmes were introduced over a century ago in Britain and the U.S.A. Improvements in diagnosis, in efficiency and provision of hearing aids and in teaching methods mean that the outlook for children whose hearing is impaired before language is acquired is now regarded as comparatively optimistic providing that all the factors that help to overcome the handicap are favourable. These factors include early diagnosis, the prompt provision of suitable hearing aids and appropriate encouragement by family, school and community. The degree of hearing loss, intelligence and the presence or absence of additional handicaps are among the factors most influencing the outcome of remedial measures (Swisher 1976, Conrad 1979, Bench & Bamford 1979). Yet compared with most other disabilities described in this book, prelingual deafness still poses a

---

*This term is used to distinguish spoken language from sign language and refers not only to understanding and using speech but to reading and writing as well.

potentially devastating handicap in the acquisition of spoken language. The degree of language delay and disruption of communication for some individuals is still severe though short of mutism. Under less than optimal conditions spoken language is delayed in onset, slowly acquired and the ultimate linguistic achievements of severely and profoundly deaf persons differ in marked ways from hearing speakers.

It is not surprising that oral language development is delayed in the prelingually deaf because the difficulties presented to the child acquiring spoken language through lip-reading alone are immense. For those with severe or profound hearing loss amplification cannot replace the information lost through the hearing impairment, although the value of even minimal auditory information through residual hearing cannot be discounted. For the prelingually deaf child, speech recognition through lip-reading alone is an ability that appears to be slowly mastered (Mogford 1987). This is so even though visual processing of speech movements appears to play a part in speech acquisition in hearing infants (Dodd 1987b, Mills this volume). Lip-reading which does not have the advantage of concurrent auditory perceptual information, that is learned as an exclusively visual ability, does not permit the unambiguous discrimination of speech sounds. Also, as a visual ability lip-reading must share the unidirectional visual channel with other functions directly and indirectly related to communication. Thus lip-reading alone cannot replace the combined auditory and visual information through which language is normally acquired.

It has been argued that a better outcome would be possible if it were not the case that the provision of auditory information to the prelingually deaf infant is often too little and comes too late. Despite advances in detection methods, diagnosis still usually occurs some time after birth. A European study published in 1979 found that of 919 children born deaf in 1969 only 99 were diagnosed by 12 months and 407 were not diagnosed until after 3 years. By 3 years developmental changes have advanced in ways that preclude the normally inter-related aspects of human development unfolding in their natural sequence. By the time that remedial measures are introduced, differences in the way the prelingually deafened child interacts with the environment, construes and processes information may have occurred that change the developmental process in qualitative ways. These changes may have implications for the functional organization of the brain and auditory pathways. The fact remains that, although the ability to detect deafness and provide remedial measures has improved markedly in the last 40 years, the effects of a congenital hearing loss on spoken language development are still serious and pervasive. We see the effects not only in receptive language ability but also in expressive language forms, both spoken and written. Intelligibility of speech is impaired because of the inaccessibility of auditory models and monitoring control available through auditory feedback. Language structure and output is limited by the deaf speaker's knowledge of language, but also possibly by the need to maximize intelligibility.

The implications of deafness for language development are not all obvious from what appears to be simply a perceptual problem. While it is predictable that language development will be slow and imitation of speech sounds will prove difficult, it is less obvious that there will be difficulties in learning to read since there is no barrier to the perception of written symbols for the deaf. The frequently documented difficulty probably results from the dependence of literacy on pre-existing oral language. The language delay in the deaf interferes with the development of literacy because instruction in reading and writing typically begins when language development is rudimentary. The teaching of reading may also be impaired by communication difficulties with the teacher.

Terminology

In common with other disabled groups, the deaf experience negative expectations from the non-disabled community. Consequently, in recent years educators have stressed the achievements of the deaf, particularly in oral communication. Terminology has been changed to stress that a hearing loss is rarely total and that residual hearing is almost always available in some degree. The term 'hearing-impaired' is thus preferred to 'deaf' which is considered a negative term. However, some people with hearing impairments reject the negative connotation of 'deaf' as a meaning imposed by the hearing community: they view the label as a badge of positive identity. Mainly for ease of expression the terms deaf and hearing-impaired are used interchangeably here with no implications of degree of hearing loss. However, this chapter in the main is confined to consideration of the effect of severe and profound hearing impairments where individuals can make only minimal use of residual hearing. The degree of hearing loss of subjects in studies reviewed will be specified: mild, moderate, severe or profound. Unfortunately, there is little uniformity in the way that these labels are applied in the literature: therefore an indication will also be given of the average decibel loss. The terms describing the degree of hearing loss conventionally refer to a range of hearing loss as assessed on pure tone audiometry. The loss is usually expressed in decibels, for an individual's better ear, averaged across some of the speech frequencies (usually 500, 1000 and 2000 Hz). However, it should be remembered that this is a crude way of summarizing hearing loss that may disguise variations in perceptual profile and capacity of some significance. For example, it may disguise individuals with preserved hearing in lower frequencies but with a largely high frequency hearing loss. This would impair the perception of some fricative consonant sounds in particular. In addition the perception of speech through aided hearing cannot be predicted accurately from pure tone audiometry.

In this chapter studies of language development in the deaf are reviewed to explore the effects that a congenital hearing loss has upon oral language development. In Chapter 8 Bellugi et al consider the acquisition of sign language, which is regarded by many (e.g. Brennan 1975) as the natural first language of the deaf. In this century large amounts of information have been accumulated on both topics which is testimony to the intractable nature of the communication handicap. The review must therefore be selective, which poses a danger to objectivity and balance. However, it may help if the principles of selection are first made explicit.

Preoccupation with the severely and profoundly deaf will inevitably emphasize the extreme effects of the disability. In general terms those with less severe losses have less difficulty with language development but those difficulties are still of significance. Recent research reports statistically significant effects on language development for children with mild to moderate losses (Davis 1986, Bench & Bamford 1979), and even for those whose loss is confined to one ear. Some children were found to show language-related problems (reading, spelling and conceptual) in an educational context though not on standardized language tests (Klee & Davis-Dansky 1986, Culbertson & Gilbert 1986).

However, the clearest effects on spoken language are in those with severe and profound losses, although it is not possible to predict outcome entirely from degree of hearing loss. Several factors contribute to the linguistic success of the person with a prelingual hearing loss though all the factors are not yet known. To reduce self-fulfilling prophecies educators have continued to stress the levels of achievement of the more fortunate children with severe hearing losses since this helps to indicate what is possible. Studies of groups present an 'average truth' which can disguise the level of individual success. In this chapter the aim is to describe the nature of the effects of a prelinguistic hearing loss on spoken language development. This will mean referring to these average truths. While the success of individuals must not be forgotten, the less successful individuals also are disguised by the average truth. The aim of describing difficulties is to improve under-standing and find better methods of avoiding them. There is no intention to undermine the achievements of deaf people or their teachers.

The research reviewed has mainly taken place over the last 10–15 years. For previous research see reviews by Cooper & Rosenstein (1966), Swisher (1976). For a more extensive review of educational and developmental issues see Quigley & Kretschmer (1982) and Quigley & Paul (1984).

The causes of deafness

Most prelingual hearing losses are sensori-neural: that is they are caused by a lesion in the cochlea (the sensory receptor in the inner ear) or in the auditory pathways leading to the brain rather than in the mechanism that conducts sound impulses from the outer to the inner ear. There is currently no widely available, uncontroversial medical or surgical treatment for a sensorineural loss. The damage can result from a number of different factors that affect the development of the nervous system before, during and after birth. Different causes carry different probabilities of additional handicaps and different degrees and profiles of hearing loss. The incidence of severe deafness at birth is around 1 in 1000 births (Fraser 1971), though children can develop deafness due to disease and degener-ation before the onset of speech. Hence the term prelingual or prelinguistic is used instead of congenital.

The causes of sensorineural hearing loss can be broadly classified as follows:

1. Infection: e.g. prenatal rubella can also produce visual impairments, cerebral palsy, cardiac and mental impairments. The resulting loss is characteristically of similar degree across frequencies and bilateral but worse in one ear than the other. Mumps, measles and meningitis can cause hearing impairment after birth.
2. Trauma: this includes mechanical injury and perinatal hypoxia (Carrel 1977). Deaf-ness due to hypoxia is often in the high frequencies.
3. Maldevelopment: this occurs during prenatal development and is often inherited.
4. Prematurity: includes low birthweight infants who also have a higher incidence of neurological deficits.
5. Metabolic causes: inherited conditions associated with mental retardation may include hearing loss.
6. Toxic causes: drugs given to mothers (e.g. streptomycin and chloroquine) can cause profound hearing loss. Kernicterus: high levels of bilirubin in the infant's blood-stream can cause hearing loss. Modern treatments mean that this is now rare.
7. Genetic causes: in most cases there is no evidence of abnormality other than deaf-ness. It has been estimated that this accounts for 50% of congenital hearing loss (Fraser 1971). Many different modes of inheritance are involved. Some forms are of progressive onset after birth. (See Carrel 1977 for an extended account.)

There are two main implications of the causes of hearing loss. Firstly, in conditions due to pre- or perinatal damage there is a high possibility of additional handicaps which may go undetected, complicating the develop-mental picture. Secondly, the high incidence of genetic factors makes it likely that deaf chil-dren will be born to deaf parents. This has social and cultural implications that will be briefly examined.

Sociolinguistic and cultural factors

With two language forms available to the deaf, spoken and sign language, the various ways in which these two languages are acquired and used produce a complex sociolinguistic pattern. This pattern is influenced by attitudes towards language forms, the forms used in education and parental hearing status. Although this chapter is concerned with the acquisition of spoken language, the possible influence of a second (sign) language on the spoken form must be kept in mind. A brief account of language learning patterns is included to correct some common misapprehensions concerning the pattern of language acquisition and use.

The oral/aural approach to teaching language has dominated in Britain and the U.S.A for over a century. In 1971 Silverman estimated that around 82% of deaf children in the U.S.A acquired spoken language as a first language. Up to the beginning of the last decade the pattern in Britain was similar. Lewis (1968) found that signing was never used in 80–85% of primary schools and 67% of secondary schools for the deaf. Various forms of manual communication began to be introduced formally into classrooms during the last decade, though not all were sign language. A significant number of deaf people have always learned sign language as a first language. Where signing was acquired as a second language this often happened in the face of disapproval from teachers and flourished in informal situations outside the classroom. Sign language is now actively taught and promoted in Great Britain and the United States. This change of attitude to the language is reflected in the use of sign language in more formal and prestigious contexts.

Deaf children can be born to deaf or hearing parents, each of whom will have a preference for spoken or sign language depending on their own first language, social contacts, experiences in education and beliefs. Parental preference means that some deaf children learn sign language as a first language and others spoken language. Deaf children with a deaf parent constitute no more than 4–10% of the deaf population. The majority of the prelingually deaf are born to hearing parents. A deaf community exists with its own language and culture transmitted from one generation to the next. This creates a positive identity and attitude towards deafness and sign language. Where sign language is the first language, spoken language will be acquired virtually as a second language and this creates a bilingual situation (see Chs. 3 and 4). For children of hearing parents their first language will usually be spoken. Even if hearing parents choose sign language it will not be acquired in quite the same way as in children born to deaf parents. Hearing adults using sign language will usually use spoken language concurrently, and their mastery of sign language is likely to be incomplete and influenced by the structure of spoken language. Secondly, learning sign language will not begin until after the diagnosis of deafness so there will still be an initial delay in language acquisition. Even those deaf children whose first language is spoken will probably acquire some signing later in their lives. Thus there are no clear divisions between signers and speakers, nor is the first language mode entirely predictable from the parents' hearing status. Hartley (personal communication) found a variety of methods of communication adopted by deaf parents of 4-year-old deaf children in the U.K. The language experience of any individual may depend on a number of factors including parental preference, the philosophy of principal advisors and the availability of educational choice. Whatever the educational regime and form of primary language, every child will need to acquire literacy in conventional orthography and some degree of competence in spoken language is clearly desirable. The sociolinguistic picture in relation to sign language in Great Britain is described by Lawson (1981). For an account of the complexity of communication systems involving manual signs see Quigley & Kretschmer (1982).

Methodological factors

The sociocultural and educational background to deafness has a bearing on research methods. It is always important to specify details about the subjects used in studies of language development and their linguistic environment. Among other details that must be given are degree of hearing loss in full and unambiguous terms. Recent research has begun to realize the importance of better methods of assessing hearing for speech.

Although this chapter is concerned only with prelinguistic hearing loss, age of onset of deafness is important. A few months of hearing may make a difference to outcome.

Some studies use a late cut-off to define a prelinguistic group (2 or 3 years). Between 2 and 3 years old children acquire many linguistic fundamentals. Intelligence is an important factor in predicting success in language acquisition and should be reported. Cause of deafness should also be given because of the probability of additional handicaps with some causes. It is also important to check that care has been taken to ensure that the deaf children understand what is required in all tasks.

Issues in research

Research workers have been drawn to study the language acquisition process in prelingually deaf children for two main reasons. The first reason is the practical one: to understand the difficulties and nature of the process so as to be able to intervene more effectively. The second reason is that the study of language development in the deaf may shed light upon theoretical issues in language development in general.

Early studies of the language of the prelingually deaf were either descriptive or aimed to evaluate the level of language achieved at various stages in development (see Cooper & Rosenstein 1966, Swisher 1976). With improvements in detection, hearing aid provision and educational techniques it may be argued that the levels of competence described in these early research studies are no longer relevant. Advances in methods of studying language have brought about improved knowledge of language development in hearing children. With better comparative knowledge available, researchers became preoccupied with whether the development of language in prelingually deaf children was essentially similar in nature to the hearing child though delayed, or whether the process was qualitatively different. In retrospect this may appear another potentially barren controversy because it is difficult to resolve absolutely, and more interesting questions may be asked about language development in the prelingually deaf. However, this issue was thought to be of practical importance since if the process was essentially normal then it could be argued that what deaf children required was more and better versions of current intervention methods. If, however, the process was qualitatively different then remedial methods must take this into account. Interest in divergent patterns of language development was motivated, not only by controversy over educational methods but also because it would provide insight into the degree to which language acquisition could adjust to the exceptional circumstances of deafness. One feature of those exceptional circumstances is that a predominance of visual information is used in acquisition. Deafness also appeared to provide tests of certain hypotheses relating to language acquisition in general and to particular aspects or stages of development. For example, the congenitally deaf population can be considered to be deprived of sound stimulation during a critical period of development when processing capacities may be laid down. Research on animals (Ruben & Rapin 1980) has shown that early sensory deprivation can critically impair auditory processing abilities. The deaf, as a population in which the factors assumed to play a part in neurophysiological development can be studied, provide a test of a critical period hypothesis. Luria (1973) suggested that the functional organization of the brain develops differently if one sensory modality is absent. Support for this critical period hypothesis might be thought to come from research which showed a marked difference in prognosis between children with early and late diagnosis and provision of amplification.

Two hypotheses for which the deaf are thought to provide a test are mentioned in virtually every introductory text in language development. The first of these concerns the relationship between language and thought. It was once erroneously thought that the prelingually deaf provided a 'no language' condition for looking at this question. If thought of similar quality developed in the absence of language, then language and thought could be regarded as independent abilities, developing in parallel but not inter-dependent. However the deaf, whether acquiring spoken or sign language, are not without language though language development may be delayed. Once sign language had been recognized as a language of equal status with spoken languages, it was clear that being without speech did not preclude the development of language. Thus experiments that use the deaf as a no language comparison group lost their validity although not until some useful insights were gained in the pursuit of this debate (Furth 1966). There are still some more limited ways in which this problem can be addressed, for example by studying cognitive development in the often extended preverbal period in the deaf, but it is not possible to discuss this question in the detail it deserves in the space available here.

The second reference to language development in the deaf appearing regularly in textbooks concerns babbling. The deaf infant is used to elucidate the role of parental speech sounds in shaping infants' prespeech vocalizations and producing babbling. The theory, first attributed to Lenneberg, that babbling is an innately programmed stage of development which does not require an environment of speech sounds to elicit its production, can be tested in the deaf child as well as in the child of deaf parents in which speech sounds in the environment are reduced in quality and quantity. However, it has been claimed that auditory feedback and parental vocalizations play a necessary part in the maintenance of babbling, once emerged. This can be tested by seeing if babbling in deaf infants fades away or develops in quality after onset.

A further question that can be examined through studying the deaf is the relationship of oral language development to reading, since learning to read is difficult for the prelingually deaf despite the lack of perceptual problems it presents. The study of the deaf can help to unravel some of the linguistic components that are necessary for learning to read effectively and can also shed light on some practical questions. Can the deaf child learn language through reading at an early

stage of language development, or must some stages of linguistic ability be achieved before this is possible? This is a special version of the question which asks is it possible to acquire spoken language through a predominantly visual medium. This question is based on the idea that spoken language evolved for use and acquisition primarily through the audiovocal channel. It is organized to use the structure of temporally related units, whereas the visual channel is organized to deal with spatially related material (O'Connor & Hermelin 1983).

CHARACTERISTICS OF ORAL LANGUAGE DEVELOPMENT IN THE PRELINGUISTICALLY DEAF CHILD

Before examining specific aspects of linguistic development it may be helpful to indicate briefly the degree of delay experienced by prelingual deaf children during the acquisition process. For example, Gregory & Mogford (1981) studied eight children from 12–48 months, whose hearing losses were all diagnosed by 16 months of age, were all provided with hearing aids and whose parents were receiving guidance on oral language acqui-

Table 7.1 Ages (months) of stages in early language development, one, ten, 50, 100 words and two word combinations, for six* of eight hearing-impaired children in a study by Gregory & Mogford (1981), Mogford & Gregory (1982)

Children**	HL	1st	10	50	100	2WCombs
Dominic	45 dB	10 m	19 m	22 m	30 m	24 m
Jason	70 dB	13 m	17 m	24 m	26 m	21 m
Michael	83 dB	19 m	22 m	29 m	24 m	30 m
Paul	97 dB	15 m	22 m	28 m	33 m	28 m
Amanda	102 dB	19 m	30 m	38 m	43 m	43 m
Heather	107 dB	18 m	26 m	34 m	36 m	33 m
Mean	—	16 m	23 m	29 m	34 m	30 m
Hearing Group	—	11 m	12 m	19 m	22 m	—

*Two profoundly hearing-impaired children, Nigel and Zena, had fewer than 10 words or gestural equivalents at 4 years when the study terminated
**Names changed to preserve anonymity.

sition. Hearing losses ranged from moderate to profound and the children were broadly within the average range of ability. Table 7.1 shows the ages at which six children acquired 1, 10, 50 and 100 words and two word combinations compared with the mean for age-matched control groups. At 4 years the two most profoundly deaf children still had fewer than 10 words or gestural equivalents and are omitted from the table. At 4 years the Reynell Developmental Language Scales were administered. The range of results is shown in Table 7.2. These children can be regarded as relatively advantaged since their hearing losses were identified early and all families received consistent support and guidance.

At the other end of the educational process Conrad (1979) and Quigley et al (1977) studied reading ability at the school leaving stage. Conrad (1979) used the Wide Span Reading Test with 468 prelingually deaf 15–16 year olds leaving special education. The median reading age for the whole sample was 9 years. Success varied with hearing loss and intelligence. 50% of children with severe to profound losses (85 dB) failed to show any effective reading comprehension. Quigley et al (1977) studied 450 prelingually deaf students, 10–18 years, randomly selected from a variety of educational

programmes in the U.S.A, with hearing losses of 90 dB or greater and of average ability. They devised the Test of Syntactic Abilities to explore the deaf students' mastery of different syntactic structures and compared their achievements with those of 8-, 9- and 10-year-old hearing children. At 18 years none of the structures was as successfully mastered by the deaf as by the hearing children, but some progress was evident for the deaf throughout the adolescent period. These studies give a brief indication of the ultimate achievements of severely and profoundly deaf students. They agree with numerous previous studies that found delays of a similar order.

Preverbal development

Prelinguistic vocalization and babbling

For the reasons explained above babbling and prelinguistic vocal development have been a focus of interest in the hearing-impaired. Until recent advances in neonatal diagnosis it was difficult to identify deaf children before the onset of babbling, and discussions were based on a few studies concerning small numbers of infants. It must be noted too that, once diagnosed, amplification was provided and intervention implemented. In addition there are conceptual and methodological problems in the study of babbling which means that it is not always possible to relate the findings of different studies. Most of the received wisdom about babbling in the deaf can be traced to Lenneberg et al (1965) and Lenneberg (1967). Gilbert (1982) points out that the 1965 study involved only one deaf child, covered the first 3 months of life and concerned the infant crying and cooing only. Babbling does not normally develop in this period and no allowance was made for babbling in the coding categories reported. The study aimed to compare infants from homes with normal parental vocalizations with those homes where the parents were deaf. One of the children of deaf parents ultimately was found to be deaf. The study concluded that crying and cooing did not differ signifi-

Table 7.2 Scores on the Reynell Developmental Language Scales for the eight hearing-impaired children at 4 years showing available assessments of hearing losses

Children	HL	Comprehension scale A		Expression	
		Age	S.S.	Age	S.S.
Dominic	45 dB	3;4	−1.0	2;10	−1.8
Jason	70 dB	3;3	−1.1	3;9	−0.4
Michael	83 dB	2;7	−2.5	2;8	−2.2
Paul	97 dB	2;9	−2.2	2;8	−2.2
Amanda	102 dB	1;3	<−2.8	1;8	<−2.6
Heather	107 dB	2;9	−2.2	2;7	−2.5
Nigel	113 dB	0;11	<−2.8	0;11	<−2.9
Zena	+ +	No Score	−	No Score	−

+ + No audiogram available. Little or no response to sound or voice even with hearing aid: profoundly deaf. N.B. All children were assessed to be within or above average range on the Merrill-Palmer Scale of Mental Tests

cantly in quality, timing of onset or frequency in the two environments. Both vocal behaviours were considered to be maturationally determined and not contingent upon environmental auditory stimuli. No data on babbling were actually reported in this study or in Biological Foundations of Language (Lenneberg 1967). Mavilya (1972) indicated that deaf infants' vocalizations were not altered in character in the first 6 months of life. Maskerinec et al (1981), however, suggest that developmental differences can be detected in vocal activity as early as 6 weeks of age. Of five infants studied over the first 30 weeks of life, two were subsequently found to have bilateral hearing losses of different type and degree. For the hearing infants, one of whom lived with deaf parents, speech-like sounds increased and non-speech sounds decreased over the study period, but for the severely deaf child speech-like and non-speech sounds decreased with age. Data for the child with a bilateral conductive loss showed greater variability. Using the same methods the. authors re-analyzed Mavilya's data and found similar patterns. Mavilya reported canonical babbling at 6 months, but as Oller (1986) points out this is early even for hearing children. Using what he terms a meta-phonological approach, combining phonetic and acoustic descriptions, he has distinguished between marginal and canonical babbling. Marginal babbling is distinguished from canonical babbling on acoustic grounds: it lacks two features of canonical babbling (i.e. formant transitions of appropriate length and vowel resonance). It occurs in normal infants between 3–6 months and is the forerunner of canonical babbling. Oller (1986) reports marginal babbling for four severely-profoundly deaf infants but found that canonical babbling failed to occur in the first year. However, frequent glottal sequences that had some structural similarity to canonical babbling were noted, and Oller concludes that an auditory handicap may prevent the development of some properties of syllable sequences but that there are both similarities and differences in the vocalizations of deaf and hearing infants.

Stoel-Gammon & Otomo (1986) found qualitative and quantitative differences when comparing the consonant repertoires of 11 hearing-impaired and hearing infants from 4 months into the second year of life. Hearing-impaired infants' repertoires were smaller than the hearing infants' repertoires which increased with age. Babbling decreased with age in the hearing-impaired who produced fewer multisyllabic utterances with consonants. Smith (1982) compared the babbling of hearing-impaired infants from 3–15 months with normal and Down's Syndrome children, examining consonants for the place of articulation. Velar consonants dominated for all infants to 9 months, but alveolar/dental articulations dominated from 9–15 months for hearing and Down's syndrome infants with labials at an intermediate level throughout. Velars continued to dominate for the hearing-impaired until 15 months when labial sounds became dominant, remaining so until 3;6 years. Vowel development was similar in all three groups. It was concluded that similarities in babbling between all three groups were due to maturation and development of the oral cavity, but babbling in deaf children is influenced by visual information from 15 months when labial, visually accessible articulations start to predominate.

Vocal characteristics in deaf infants were noted by Lach et al (1970). Seven congenitally profoundly deaf infants, diagnosed between 11–32 months, joined an intervention programme to improve vocal quality. At the start none of the infants' vocalizations was judged to be normal and were limited in quality and quantity. Improvements were found after 12 months of intervention in the voice quality and phonetic inventory.

Do these more recent studies change the story that is repeated in many textbooks? They do not in that some early aspects of vocalization appear irrespective of the lack of auditory feedback and availability of human auditory-vocal models. However, there seems to be a gradual rather than sudden decline in vocalization, presumably due to lack of environmental stimulation and auditory feedback. What is the significance of the delay in canonical babbling and deviation in vocal quality and quantity for the deaf child? Although babbling is not used to communicate, as its speech-like characteristics are recognized and imitated by parents babbling becomes integrated into social situations. The nonspeech-like characteristics of deaf childrens' vocalizations and their relative infrequency may affect interaction. In the sample of deaf children studied longitudinally from 12–48 months in comparison with hearing children of the same chronological age, Gregory et al (1979) and Mogford & Gregory (1982) found that whilst mothers of hearing children commented on vocalizations, weaving them into a dialogue, mothers of the deaf children tended to ignore vocalizations or talk through them. Few of the deaf children's utterances had the speech-like characteristics of the hearing child's vocalizations at the same chronological age. Similar observations were made by Cheskin (1982). Thus lack of preverbal vocalizations to structure dialogue may further delay the emergence of language and verbal dialogue.

Interpersonal interaction and communication in the preverbal period

As a result of work on preverbal development in hearing children it was argued by Bruner (1975b) that preverbal communication was linked directly to the emergence of language. The nature of this link remains controversial. Continuity between preverbal and verbal development would be suggested if variations in preverbal development predicted differences in early verbal development. The study of populations where preverbal development is affected by disability is one source of such evidence.

Some of the abilities developed in the preverbal period, e.g. vocal imitation, relate very directly to the development of speech. Lack of hearing will clearly delay vocal imitation since this emerges from the mother's imitation of the child's vocalizations (Pawlby 1977) which the deaf child will be unable to hear,

especially if diagnosis is delayed. Other developments in the preverbal period are less immediately obviously related to language development. For example, the use of verbal reference initially takes the form of labels for objects, people and pictures in the immediate context. The ability to use labels presupposes the ability to establish some kind of mutual agreement between speaker and listener as to the objects and events distal to conversational partners to which these words refer. Shared visual attention to objects and events is established preverbally through pointing and mutual monitoring of gaze, and some vocal comment usually follows. The vocal aspect of an adult's communication will be inaccessible to the deaf infant, auditorily and visually, when looking at the object of the reference. Some evidence connecting difficulties with mutual visual attention to the development of verbal reference were reported by Gregory & Mogford (1981). Difficulties with developing joint visual attention in the preverbal period were associated with a lack of nominals in the early language of a sample of prelingually deaf children studied from 12–48 months. Curtiss et al (1979) also found that the function of labelling was delayed in preverbal communication of prelingually deaf children, although indicating locations was one of the most frequent and earliest developing semantic functions. They suggest that the dominance of the visual environment for the hearing-impaired infant tunes them into visual-spatial aspects of their environment and that preverbal communication may be used to signal meanings appropriate to the developmental stage. Thus some stages of semantic development are passed through while the deaf children are in the preverbal period and are not repeated in the early verbal period. However, it is difficult to see how labelling could take place preverbally without some representational communication system. In agreement with Curtiss et al (1979), Gregory & Mogford (1981) found that the greater cognitive maturity of the deaf children at the onset of language was reflected in early language in that more abstract qualities of size, colour and number appeared than in language-matched hearing children.

Phonology

The phonology of language can be considered in two parts: the segmental and the suprasegmental aspects. The segmental aspect refers to the contrastive sound system of speech (vowels and consonants), while the suprasegmental aspect includes intonation, stress and rhythm. Both aspects of phonology as realised in speech will be affected by difficulties with the control of voice quality. Voice quality and articulatory accuracy are phonetic aspects of speech. The difficulties experienced by the deaf in developing intelligible speech indicate that in hearing children the development of phonology and the phonetic accuracy of articulated segments are achieved primarily through auditory means, though visual perception of speech movements also plays some part in the acquisition of speech patterns in children with normal hearing and vision (Dodd 1987a, Mills 1987). It is the complementary nature of the distance senses that are involved in normal development, i.e. audition provides information where visual clues are minimal, and visual clues where auditory discrimination is difficult. However, it is considered that severely and profoundly deaf children acquire spoken language through the visual modality alone. As a result Dodd (1987a) regards the prelingually deaf as providing a test case of the degree to which the development of phonology is dependent on the auditory modality or whether the ability to control the phonology of a language is a more abstract ability that in exceptional circumstances can be developed independent of the auditory modality.

The development of phonology and articulation are undoubtedly disturbed by the auditory impairments of the prelingually deaf. Intelligibility of speech is frequently affected (Markides 1970, Jensema et al 1978). Conrad (1979) found that teachers rated 48% of 331 children leaving special schools as having speech that was very hard to understand or unintelligible. Markides in a study of 110 children in four special schools for the deaf and partially hearing reported that lay listeners found 64% of children either 'very difficult to follow' or 'unintelligible'. Poor intelligibility does not indicate the absence of an underlying system of meaningful contrasts realised in speech. Unintelligibility may be due to phonetic inaccuracy. The questions that need to be asked are: to what extent can phonological development proceed when auditory information is degraded if not totally absent? Can lip-read information replace the auditory channel as a means of acquiring segmental phonology? Can poor intelligibility be explained by unsystematic attempts to imitate speech or is there an underlying system of contrasts developing? Are suprasegmental features preserved and what contribution do they make to the perceived intelligibility of speech? Studies have been concerned with whether acquisition patterns resemble hearing children's or are different in nature. The degree of residual hearing may explain the large differences within the prelingually deaf population in their phonological development and speech intelligibility. However, the characteristics of residual hearing are not fully apparent from the assessments that average pure tone decibel loss across frequencies in the better ear. More analytical devices are now available to predict the usefulness of residual hearing for speech perception (Abberton et al 1986).

Early studies concentrated on consonant development. West & Weber (1973), Oller & Kelley (1974), Oller et al (1978) all demonstrated the use of phonemic contrasts and consistent phonological processes in single children with moderate and severe hearing losses. Oller et al (1978) reported that the phonology of a severely deaf 6-year-old resembled that of a younger normally hearing child. Processes reported were cluster reduction, final consonant deletion, voicing avoidance, velar plosive avoidance, fronting, stopping and only a normal proportion of 'strange processes'. Dodd (1976a) examined the consonant repertoires of 10 profoundly deaf children from 9–12 years. Although none of the repertoires were complete, she reported the missing consonants were those acquired late in hearing children. Two children had poor repertoires with only 12 and 15 of 24 English consonant phonemes present. The phonological processes present were found to be similar to those in hearing children's speech, although the influence of lip-read information was evident in some features. Dodd claimed that residual hearing played no part in the phonology of these profoundly deaf children as patterns could not be predicted from the hearing loss. This may not be so in less severely impaired children and when more sophisticated methods of auditory perception are used to relate hearing loss to speech patterns.

Although these studies considered only the segmental consonant system they partially explained that unintelligibility was due to an incomplete phonology. However, they reveal little about the rate and pattern of development although indicating the degree of delay in acquiring phonology. Preliminary reports are available of a study that illustrates some advantages of a longitudinal approach and examines phonetic and phonological development.

Abberton et al (1986) in a study of 12 children with hearing losses of 63–98 dB, attending an oral school in Britain, are recording progress four monthly from 7–14 years. Speech patterns can be related to pure-tone audiograms and 'more analytic speech-related measures of auditory ability'. The findings after 3 years agree with the previous studies in that these children show broadly similar patterns of phonology to normal development but with delay in the area of consonantal contrasts. Most children, though not all, have an adequate vowel system and use appropriate intonation patterns. However, there is persisting phonetic immaturity in all areas of speech production at the segmental and suprasegmental levels. Some of these immaturities persist into early adolescence and represent a gross delay. Abberton et al attribute the persistence of some processes to high frequency hearing loss. The patterns of

individual children are described in some detail and range from one child with the best pure tone audiogram whose speech showed occasional inaccuracies and a breathy voice quality through to a child with the most severe hearing loss who at the beginning of the study had extremely unintelligible speech. It was often impossible to segment and transcribe speech using conventional phonetic symbols. Her vowel system was poorly developed, there was abnormal speech rhythm, speech was hypernasal and there was difficulty in controlling vocal cord vibration. After 3 years the vowel system, intonation, voice quality and oral resonance all improved but the developing consonant system was still very immature but could be shown to be developing. Control of vocal quality proved difficult for all the children irrespective of hearing loss and this may also partially explain impaired intelligibility.

Questions concerning the phonology of the deaf go beyond those related directly to the perception and production of speech. There is evidence that some of the deaf can and do use their phonological abilities to perform mental operations. Evidence comes from several experimental studies that use tasks requiring the manipulation of a phonological code. The phonology of a language appears to play a central role in the development of short-term or working memory, in silent reading and spelling where grapheme-phoneme correspondence is employed. Certain meta-linguistic tasks, like the recognition of rhymes and homophones, also depend on phonological coding. These abilities have been explored by Dodd & Hermelin (1977) and Dodd (1987a) in children with severe and profound hearing losses. As a result of these investigations, Dodd concludes that the deaf can and do use a phonological system to do metalinguistic and linguistic tasks in a way that closely resembles that of normally hearing children. This can be demonstrated in children relying entirely on lip-reading and is thus an ability that is not totally dependent on hearing. Other investigators have found that not all the orally educated prelingually deaf have access to a phonological code. Conrad (1979) used a short-term memory task on his sample of school leavers and found variable degrees of ability to use internal speech which was affected by the degree of deafness but not entirely predicted by hearing loss. A few children with profound losses showed some ability to use a speech-based code in memory which was related to success in reading, lip-reading and speech intelligibility. The degree of subjects' success in using a speech-based code was also related to intelligence. Although it may be supposed that a negative correlation between degree of hearing loss and use of a speech-based code indicates a causal relationship, the nature and direction of the relationship between intelligence and internal phonological code is more questionable. It has been demonstrated that those who do not develop this code are at a disadvantage in the early stages of reading (Hanson et al 1984). Spelling skills, however, are amongst the better areas of linguistic development in the prelingually deaf and levels of performance comparable to or better than hearing children have been recorded (e.g. Gates & Chase 1926, Hoemann et al 1976). Dodd has suggested that these achievements result from the early and effective use of two spelling strategies: phoneme to grapheme correspondence rules and a visual graphemic strategy. The ability to use a phonemic strategy is dependent on the ability to develop an internal phonological code. Dodd (1980) demonstrated that deaf children can do this on the basis of lip-read information.

Thus the ability to use a phonological system to produce the spoken form of a language, to access meaning through the written form and for spelling new words, seems to be possible for some of even the deafest children. However, the ability is neither universal nor entirely predictable, though degree of hearing loss and intelligence are highly related to the ability. That a phonological system can be acquired and used by the most profoundly deaf suggests that it is an ability not entirely tied to the ability to hear. These findings do not necessarily conflict with reports of speech unintelligibility or poor reading achievements. Rather it suggests that while the chances of success are increased by the development of a phonological ability, it may not be sufficiently well developed early enough to guarantee speech intelligibility or reading success and that additional factors are involved in these achievements.

Syntax

Two previous research reviews (Cooper & Rosenstein 1966, Swisher 1976) point to the mid 1960s as marking a change in approach to language research, particularly in regard to syntax. Hitherto, studies had mostly been confined to written language and to assessment of reading ability because this eased the methodological problems of communication with the deaf. There were few studies of spoken language owing to the difficulty of transcribing and glossing the speech of the deaf. Many early studies used achievement tests which emphasized the severe language delay in the prelingually deaf but did not elucidate the nature of developing linguistic abilities. The methods used to study syntax were not sufficiently sophisticated to demonstrate the deaf child's knowledge of syntactic rules. Some distinctive qualities of deaf language were noted though. For example, Templin (1950) showed that although sentence length indicated a delay in written language development, the use of circumlocution to fill gaps in vocabulary distorted the measure. Myklebust (1960) and Simmons (1962) showed that there was a preponderance of so-called content words, nouns and verbs, whereas there were fewer 'function' words, conjunctions, verbal auxiliaries, prepositions and pronouns. Others described language as telegraphic. The written language of the deaf was found to have more 'errors' when matched against mature grammar (Myklebust 1960). The expressive language of the deaf was found to be lacking flexibility and was described as stereotyped and repetitious. The over-use of simple active declarative structures (subject-verb-object) was noted and, conversely, conjoined and complex sentences were found to be infrequent. Simmons (1962) reported that taught phrases were used repeatedly and certain word orders rigidly adhered to.

When methods were introduced that were similar to those used to study language development in the hearing child, researchers began to tackle the problems involved in studying spoken language that had previously been avoided. These advances increased insight into the development of syntax in the prelingually deaf.

Studies in the 1970s were concerned with asking whether oral language development in the prelingually deaf was simply delayed or deviant. The way in which deviance was defined varied with the methods of language assessment used and the aspect of syntax that was studied.

One approach used standardized language tests which assess different language structures with a known order of acquisition in the hearing child. The answer to the deviant/delay question depends on whether the hearing-impaired acquire structures in the same or a different order. A different order of acquisition is taken to indicate deviant development.

Presnell (1973), using the Northwestern Syntax Screening Test and Developmental Sentence Scoring (DSS), studied 47 moderately to profoundly prelingually deaf children (50–99 dB+), aged 5–13 years, attending schools using oral methods. Significant differences were found in the rate and order of development for verb constructions compared to hearing norms. Presnell concluded that language development deviated from the normal rate and pattern of acquisition. Chronological age and hearing loss were factors that significantly predicted performance, but the age at diagnosis and years of training showed only a weak association with syntactic development. It was suggested that the order of acquisition of structures might reflect the order in which structures were taught to the children and visual-auditory perceptual cues inherent in the language constructions.

Geers & Moog (1978) used an imitation task, the Carrow Elicited Language Inventory and the DSS, to study 52 severely and profoundly deaf children aged 4–15 years whose hearing losses ranged from 76–120 dB. Some children were integrated into mainstream schools while the remainder attended schools or units for the hearing-impaired. The results showed both a severe delay (over half the sample scoring below the 3 year level on DSS) and evidence of considerable improvement over the age range. The authors commented that the spontaneous language of the hearing-impaired differed from that of younger hearing children with similar scores. The hearing-impaired attempted more mature constructions but made many errors. The authors concluded that 'the language problem exhibited by deaf children may not be simply one of retarded language development'.

Davis (1977), in a study using The Test for the Auditory Comprehension of Language to assess receptive ability in two small samples of hearing-impaired children, one from an oral programme and one from a total communication programme, found all the children were significantly delayed compared with norms for hearing children. The oral deaf children made the most errors on some earlier developing constructions but fewer on later acquired structures, indicating a different order of acquisition.

Different methods of study produced different conclusions. Wilcox & Tobin (1974) examined 11 children of average ability with moderate losses (Mean 61 dB) on an imitation task. Sentences of equal syllable length were used over a range of constructions to assess the ability to imitate with and without picture prompts. Only 16% of the total responses were ungrammatical, and although the hearing-impaired were significantly poorer than hearing controls it was concluded that the difference was one of degree rather than of kind. Brown (1984) examined the deviance/delay issue in the acquisition of English morphology. Hearing and hearing-impaired children were matched by MLU. Although the deaf children were severely delayed in the acquisition of morphology, there was evidence that the morphemes acquired were appropriate to their overall stage of language development. Brown interprets this as evidence for the delay position. These studies, however, all used relatively small samples.

A large scale study was carried out by Bench & Bamford (1979) who used a more sophisticated approach to the delay/deviance question. Expressive speech samples were elicited through picture description for 263 children in oral education, ranging in age from 8–15 years. Although the majority of children had average pure-tone hearing losses between 40–85 dB, 76 children were included with losses greater than 85 dB. The nonverbal intelligence range (WISC) was IQ 64–150 (mean 103.4). The samples were analyzed using LARSP, a procedure that provides a profile of the grammatical structure of English at clause, phrase and word level over seven stages that correspond to normal stages of development from 1 to $4\frac{1}{2}$ years approximately (Crystal et al 1976). To study patterns for the whole group, individual profiles were averaged into a single profile and compared with that of a small sample of hearing children (10–15 years). The main differences between the profiles were a marked lack of entries at the word level (i.e. grammatical inflections) and to a slightly lesser extent at the phrase level for the hearing-impaired. Phrase and clause level entries were at a less advanced level and hence a shorter mean sentence length was found for the hearing-impaired. The overall profile was argued to be deviant in comparison with the hearing sample. This term, however, was carefully qualified because it was used in a distinctive way. Crystal et al (1976) use deviant to mean any utterance inadmissable in adult English patterns or not expected in normal child development. In fact, only a small number of utterances of this type were found. Bench & Bamford use deviant to mean an uneven distribution of frequency of structures within the three levels of analysis: word, phrase and clause levels. However, they also point out that the use of either meaning of deviant is problematical because of the diffi-

culty in deciding what would or would not be found in normal development. They point out that the mean profile shows far fewer advanced structures than the hearing profile and so in that sense is delayed, but this delay represents a lack of recursive features, complex sentences and sentence connectivity. They were unable to say if any deviant rules were used by the deaf to generate utterances, but examination of individual profiles suggested that this was probable.

The averaged profile may be thought to be unduly influenced by the data from the most handicapped children. However, when profiles for the 22 most profoundly deaf subjects were removed, no major differences were apparent in the pattern of the data. Measures were derived from the LARSP profiles that were related to major subject variables, namely degree of hearing loss, intelligence and age. These three factors were most strongly associated with language development, whereas age of onset of hearing loss, age of diagnosis and social class showed only a weak association. Although age was positively associated with language development the 14–15-year-old hearing-impaired group were less advanced than some 14–15-year-old hearing subjects of below average intelligence.

The most extensive study of syntax development has been carried out by Quigley in the U.S.A, using the written medium. Devising the Test of Syntactic Abilites (TSA), Quigley and associates studied 450 deaf pupils between 10–18 years from various schools in the U.S.A (Quigley et al 1977). The TSA explored in depth the comprehension of a variety of syntactic structures and allowed the abilites of hearing and hearing-impaired students to be compared. It was found that even when the deaf pupils understood the vocabulary and concepts involved they had difficulties in understanding the syntactic structures. Although the order of acquisition appeared broadly similar to the hearing children, there were some differences in the order of acquisition and the degree of delay was similar to previous reports. The 18-year-old hearing-impaired students were unable to perform at a level comparable with 10-year-old hearing controls. Moreover, in written language distinctive structures were identified that were not used by hearing students. When these were included as distractor items in the TSA the deaf students accepted these as grammatical. In addition, Quigley et al (1977) noted that in misunderstanding written sentences there was a tendency to treat all sentences as a subject-verb-object pattern. Thus a passive sentence such as 'The boy was helped by the girl' was read as 'The boy helped the girl': 'The boy who kissed the girl ran away' was read as 'The girl ran away'. From these and other examples it was deduced that the linear order of words dominated and deaf students were often unable to deal adequately with the hierarchical structures. Quigley and associates suggested that there were aspects of language development and functioning that were deviant and delayed.

So far the notion of deviance has been defined in a number of different ways. A study by Bishop (1983b) suggested that some of these definitions may be more revealing than others. Bishop's study also drew attention to the type of errors made by severely and profoundly deaf children in decoding English syntax and suggested that these are systematic and independent of the medium of communication.

Bishop investigated the ability of 79 deaf children (8–15 years) to comprehend English syntax through the Test for Reception of Grammar (TROG) presented in different modalities: spoken, written, and signed. The difficulty with assessing comprehension of spoken syntax is separating perceptual and vocabulary difficulties from those of grammatical competence. Presenting similar structures in different modalities allowed examination of the effect of modality upon performance, while pretesting of vocabulary allowed separation of these two elements in comprehension. The children in Bishop's sample were severely-profoundly prelingually deaf (hearing loss greater than 85 dB). Some attended oral schools where a sign system had been introduced which was designed to preserve English

word order, to signal inflections and other parts of speech used in grammatical constructions (Paget Gorman Sign System). Bishop compared the pattern of successful performance and errors in these hearing-impaired children with that of younger hearing children, over a range of grammatical contrasts tested using a multiple choice procedure with four examples for each contrast. Thus it was possible to compare the level of performance in different modalities, to look at deviance in terms of the order of contrasts acquired in different modalities and the nature and consistency of the errors. As expected, even those hearing-impaired children who recognized enough vocabulary on a pretest to perform the syntax test demonstrated low levels of competence on the spoken form and were below the mean of the 4-year-old hearing controls. Only 35% of those deaf children who took the written form performed as well as the hearing sample. The order of difficulty of contrasts was different between hearing and deaf children if the whole age range was examined. The order of difficulty was different between spoken and written forms for the deaf but not the hearing, but the order of difficulty was similar in written and signed forms for the deaf. Thus the oral presentation has an effect on comprehension in qualitative as well as quantitative ways, although written and signed modalities produced no significant differences. Looking at performance on spoken forms, order of acquisition reveals a pattern of delay rather than deviance. Analysis of patterns of errors, however, gives insights into how the children were processing sentences. Some errors on the spoken presentation were clearly due to failure to perceive words since they were passed in written presentation. However, on the written and signed forms erroneous choices of response were systematic and not random, suggesting particular strategies were used to decode structures. For example, for some children negatives were systematically interpreted as affirmative and passive as active sentences. Bishop also found evidence that order of mention and imposition of SVA structure onto embedded or recursive structures explained the errors made in comprehension. These strategies were not found among the hearing control group even though there have been reports of younger children dealing in similar ways with structures beyond their competence (Power & Quigley 1973), so Bishop suggested that the development of the understanding of grammatical contrasts is not simply delayed but involves different processing strategies.

Bishop (1983b) and Quigley & King (1981) have pointed out that these strategies are not exclusive to the deaf, being used by other groups with syntactic difficulties. These findings of different strategies in comprehension undermine the assumption that the language learning facility remains unaffected when lip-reading and residual hearing are used to overcome the perceptual barrier. Several explanations have been advanced to account for these findings.

Some comprehension strategies probably involve guesses at meaning with a heavy reliance on context and undoubtedly result from the difficulty of lip-reading. This, however, would be unlikely to account for the systematic errors noted by Bishop or for the fact that similar error patterns occurred in written and signed presentations. Another possible explanation is that these strategies result from learning language through the visual medium. It has been suggested that the visual medium leads to the coding of spatial information and interferes with the learning of patterns that rely primarily on temporal ordering (O'Connor & Hermelin 1983). This explanation is more difficult to sustain when similar processing strategies are found in those subjects with apparently intact hearing. Teaching strategies are sometimes blamed for language difficulties in the prelingually deaf (Presnell 1973). There are two forms of this argument. One maintains that the major fault is the simplistic model of language and language acquisition used in teaching (e.g. Wilbur 1977). The second view is that any attempts to teach language are mistaken (Presnell 1973). A further explanation is that grammatial

structures are influenced by the acquisition of sign language.

There have been no real critical tests of these explanations and it is unlikely that any one factor will explain all the observed difficulties. Difficulties at the morphological level have been attributed to the lack of stress and perceptual salience of these items (Bench & Bamford 1979). Reading difficulties have been attributed to premature instruction when language structures are delayed in comparison to the material of reading schemes (Quigley et al 1977). All these explanations assume that the development of syntax in the deaf is sufficiently deviant to warrant explanation. The deviant/delay debate is too simple for the complexity that the data presents and the two views of language development are not mutually exclusive.

Semantics

Relatively little attention has been given to the study of semantics in the language of the deaf. Early research was limited to the study of vocabulary which was found to be restricted and delayed (e.g. Templin 1950) and contained fewer abstract and more concrete nouns (e.g. Wells 1942). More recent research has challenged the conclusions of some of this work, although a coherent and systematic picture of the semantics of the prelingually deaf is not yet provided.

Standardized tests again provide one approach. Davis (1974) administered the Boehm Test of Basic Concepts to 24 hearing and hearing-impaired children between 6 and 8 years of age. The hearing-impaired group were moderately to severely deaf and all attended mainstream classes for some part of each day so were probably more successful than other samples studied. 75% of the hearing-impaired children scored at or below the 10th percentile on the norms. Although the children with milder hearing losses did significantly better, there was no difference in performance with age on this test. The most difficult concepts were those relating to time and quantity while spatial concepts were the most successful. The significance of the findings to the author was that mainstream teachers erroneously assume that the tested concepts are understood relatively early in a child's educational career. Davis also noted the patchiness of the children's response patterns.

Jarvella & Lubinsky (1975) investigated the understanding of terms concerned with temporal order of events (before, after, first, last). In six related experiments with 8-and II-year-old severely deaf children (mean loss 85.1 and 90.7 dB respectively) from oral schools, they found that the deaf children's performance resembled that of much younger hearing children. The deaf children responded to complex sentences as though the events being described occurred in the order mentioned and described events in a sequence of simple sentences which reflected the order of events.

Skarakis & Prutting (1977) studied the semantic functions and communicative intentions in the prelinguistic communication of four severely to profoundly deaf children of average ability (2;1 to 4;2 years) enrolled in an oral programme. Observation in a variety of interaction contexts revealed that the hearing-impaired exhibited the same semantic functions and communicative intentions as those previously identified in the communication of younger hearing children (Greenfield & Smith 1976). Although all the communicative intentions identified by Dore (1974) were found to occur with high frequency, those semantic functions which were used infrequently by hearing children or acquired late in the one-word stage were not always found in the data for the hearing-impaired. The results are interpreted as normal but delayed language development.

A way of examining the organization of the lexicon was devised by Anglin (1970). This technique involves sorting words into related groups and using a hierarchical cluster to represent the way in which words are related conceptually. The depth of the resulting hierarchy indicates the degree of abstractness within the organization. Anglin (1970) showed

that there is a progressively more abstract structure in the subjective lexicon of children as a function of age. This technique was used by Tweney et al (1975) to examine the organization of the lexicon of 63 hearing and 126 hearing-impaired adolescents, 16–18 years, using two sets of items. The first experiment involved common nouns and words referring to sounds (e.g. rustle, meow, roar), the second, words with high and low imagery. Contrary to prediction in the first study the performance between groups differed only for the words relating to sound, and in the second study the results for both groups were comparable in the depth of the hierarchy for both hearing-impaired and hearing adolescents. Tweney et al concluded that there are 'no qualitative differences · between the lexical structures of deaf and hearing persons except where difference in experience with lexical items is an important factor., Other investigators using different techniques have found differences in the semantic systems of deaf and hearing students (e.g. Cull & Hardy 1973).

It is sometimes suggested that the hearing-impaired experience difficulty with metaphorical aspects of language. Iran-Nejad et al (1981) studied deaf and hearing children aged from 9–17 years, matched on reading age. All 46 deaf subjects were profoundly prelingually deaf, of average ability and with no additional handicaps. Subjects were given brief stories to read and then asked to pick suitable titles from lists that varied in the degree of literalness: literal titles, similes and metaphors. Complex syntax was avoided as far as possible. No significant differences were found between hearing-impaired and hearing children in understanding the task or in idiomatic choices, although hearing-impaired subjects improved with practice indicating that the difficulty observed may be one of knowing when to interpret language non-literally.

Pragmatics

At first sight there is no reason to expect any differences in the range of uses of language or the intentions expressed by children with hearing difficulties compared to those with normal hearing, though problems in recognising the intentions of others and in acquiring linguistic devices to mark pragmatic functions seem probable. Because language structure is delayed it would be predicted that intentions will be marked by less sophisticated devices. In the early stages of development this appears to be so. Curtiss et al (1979) studied 12 children, 22–60 months, in an oral programme, with severe and profound hearing losses. From videotaped material from a variety of interaction contexts, they were able to demonstrate a wide range of pragmatic intentions expressed mainly through single words and by nonverbal means. In terms of the range of intentions expressed, the hearing-impaired children performed at a level appropriate for their age, and although verbal ability was delayed they were able to communicate though the amount of communication was less than hearing children.

Schirmer (1985) studied 20 3–5-year-old oral children with severe to profound hearing losses but no additional handicaps. The children were found to use the functional categories specified by Halliday (1975) at levels appropriate to their overall linguistic development but were delayed in comparison to the hearing children. Schirmer concludes that the deaf children were simply delayed in developing language functions. This is slightly at odds with Curtiss et al who suggested that similar intentions were expressed in a developmentally earlier form.

Wilbur (1977) suggested that some difficulties shown by hearing-impaired children with particular syntactic devices represent pragmatic rather than syntactic problems. She refers to the use of parts of speech that are governed by rules that operate across the boundary of single utterances in conversations or narratives, such as appropriate selection of the indefinite and definite articles to indicate new or previously mentioned referents. Correct usage must take into account the knowledge of the listener and the linguistic context in order that the intended

meaning is successfully communicated. Wilbur maintains that deaf students' difficulty is knowing when or how to use these devices. In language tests, at the sentence level these devices were used appropriately but in written narrative correct usage was considerably reduced. The difference in performance levels was attributed to pragmatic disabilities stemming from language instruction that concentrates on the single sentence.

Another aspect of pragmatic skill is the ability to use language effectively in conversations: responding appropriately to a partner's contributions and the ability to initiate and sustain conversational exchanges. However, the nature of a conversation depends partly on the conversational partner and the opportunities given for participation. This is particularly relevant in dialogues where one participant may exert control over the conversation by virtue of status or superior linguistic ability. Most studies of conversational skill in deaf children have used parent/child or teacher/child dyads. These studies also provide information about the language learning environment of the deaf child acquiring oral language.

At first, studies of conversational exchanges between mothers and deaf children focussed on mothers' characteristics. There were practical and theoretical reasons for this. The practical reason was the burden placed on mothers' speech in remedial programmes (Fry 1966, Gregory 1986). The theoretical reason was that the young deaf child provided a test of the factors controlling Motherese: the deaf child being delayed in language development provided a mismatch between linguistic and cognitive ability. Mothers' speech to deaf children was found to be limited in quantity and complexity compared to hearing children of similar age and ability. Thus the complexity of the language learning environment was reduced (Gregory et al 1979). Were the linguistic abilities of the child determining the level of the mother's speech? A study by Nienhuys et al (1985) compared dialogue between mothers and severely prelingually deaf (mean loss 70 dB) and hearing preschool children using a design that allowed comparison of children matched on chronological age and linguistic ability. Four groups of eight mother-child dyads were used, two hearing groups (2 and 5 years) and two hearing-impaired groups (2 and 5 years). Whereas at 2 years deaf children learning spoken language were preverbal, at 5 years their language development was roughly equivalent to 2-year-old hearing children. In all four groups mothers initiated much more than their children, although mothers of deaf children initiated more than mothers of age-matched hearing children but not more than mothers in the language level match. Mothers of the deaf children dominated interaction completely at 2 years when the infants had minimal verbal abilities. However, preverbal hearing infants can take an active part in preverbal exchanges so it is not clear if the very limited interaction found at 2 years was typical of preverbal hearing children. Curtiss et al (1979) found that the amount of interaction for their hearing-impaired sample was reduced in quantity. Interaction in the Nienhuys study had improved by 5 years and it was concluded that mothers adapt their language to the language levels rather than the cognitive levels of their children. However, there was evidence that the cognitive complexity level of mothers' utterances to deaf children was inappropriately reduced. The flow of dialogue was limited because deaf children gave more 'no responses' where the hearing children gave inadequate or ambiguous responses. Nienhuys suggests that dialogue develops along with linguistic ability. However, the study failed to discriminate between different types of controlling maternal utterances. Also the greater number of 'no responses' for the deaf suggests the nature of dialogue may well have been different. Mogford & Gregory (1982) found that conversations were shorter and fewer between mothers and their hearing-impaired infants in a picture-book situation. This was attributed mostly to the difficulty experienced by mothers in establishing and maintaining joint attention and reference.

Two studies of conversations between deaf pupils and their teachers investigated the effect of level of conversational control on dialogue. Wood et al (1982) and Wood & Wood (1984) studied interaction between orally educated deaf pupils and their teacher in a classroom conversation intended to give opportunities to relate experiences in a coherent way. It was established in the first study that the teachers typically exhibited high levels of control which negatively correlated with length of children's contributions and degree of initiative. The teachers used much questioning, probably to reduce difficulties in understanding the children. In a subsequent study three teachers, each with a pair of profoundly deaf children (5;6–11;9 yrs) of at least average (nonverbal) mental ability, systematically and deliberately manipulated conversational moves over a series of sessions. The children followed the teachers with systematic changes in mean length of turn and, where control of the conversation was relaxed, the deaf children showed more conversational initiative and longer contributions. The resulting conversations were not necessarily characterized by mutual understanding although the flow of ideas and communication were loosely linked to a shared topic, but the children did demonstrate awareness of the obligations that the teachers' moves placed upon them. A question would be followed by an answer, and a comment from a teacher by a free contribution to the discussion. The youngest children displayed little expertise in starting and developing conversations coherently. Difficulties were observed in establishing mutually relevant themes. Teachers had difficulty understanding the short ambiguous contributions from the children and dealing with misunderstandings without disrupting conversational flow. These two studies demonstrate the difficulties that deaf children experience in making themselves understood and in understanding, with competent adult conversationalists. However, there is much more to be learned about the development of conversational competence in deaf children.

From the studies reviewed we know only that linguistic development, speech intelligibility and speech comprehension affect the nature of conversations with deaf children. The conversational purpose, the relative linguistic and pragmatic competence of the conversational partners and the level of control that they exert must also be taken into account in the study of discourse skills in the oral deaf child.

RETURN TO THE ISSUES

Some of the questions which the study of language acquisition in the deaf have helped to elucidate have been discussed during the course of the review, but the issues previously outlined will now be re-examined.

In all areas of the linguistic development of oral deaf children the deviant/delay issue has been addressed, though the meaning of 'deviance' has been variously defined and studied. Most studies, whatever their methods and conclusions, suggest that this is an either/or question capable of resolution. It should be evident now that language is far too complex for this view to be sustained, and it is both possible and probable that delay and deviance characterize language development in the prelingually deaf. It is unlikely, given the dislocation between language and other aspects of development, that at least some meanings of the term deviance will not match the data or that there is no overlap in the process of acquisition with hearing children. What is not in doubt is that in the most profoundly handicapped the delay is severe and acquisition is slow. It could be argued that this changes the quality of development in significant ways. Language is taught or shaped whereas it is acquired in an active way by hearing children. Change in the system of the normally hearing child is rapid: attempts to produce acceptable utterances are matched with available models; erroneous forms are rapidly eliminated. The deaf child's errors must be more actively corrected and erroneous forms often persist. This suggests that the deaf child has a different experience of language acquisition: different insights and different attitudes as well as strategies that may develop to deal with the difficulties and demands experienced. The slow and laborious nature of the process and the level of ultimate achievement have led some authorities to question the wisdom of attempts to teach oral language as a first language (e.g. Brennan 1975).

Perhaps the process of oral language development is irreparably damaged because of early sound deprivation. Is there any evidence to support the sensitive period hypothesis? It would be predicted that unless the critical period was limited to a very early developmental 'window', age of diagnosis would prove to be an important predictive factor. However, studies that considered this variable found only weak associations with language development and other factors were more powerful predictors of success. Does the period of early sound deprivation have any significant effect? There is some evidence that it may have an effect on the development of cerebral dominance (Ashton & Beasley 1982, Marcotte & LaBarba 1985). However, the lack of cerebral dominance may be related to the etiology of deafness.

Although hearing loss seems to be the factor which most predicts the success of oral acquisition, Quigley & Paul (1984) point out 'somewhere along the continuum of hearing loss is a point where the hearing-impaired individual becomes linked to the world primarily by his eyes'. Can oral language be acquired through the visual medium? This is a difficult question to answer unequivocally. The answer is probably that it is possible to a certain extent and that some individuals are more able to do this than others, but the determining factors are unknown. However, the assumption that spoken language acquisition is entirely visual in all but a minority of the deaf may not be valid since some useful information may be available for bimodal speech perception which is of no use for speech perception in the auditory channel alone. The question is again rather simplistic. Language development is a complex process achieved through interaction with other speakers/listeners and in relation to other aspects of development. Once development begins to diverge from the norm the nature of the language learning process changes. The lack of auditory input in the preverbal period influences vocalization and interaction so that the language environment changes in character. There is evidence that it takes some time before the child uses the visual channel systematically for communication and language learning (Tait & Wood 1987). Later, speech intelligiblity influences the nature of dialogue. All these factors and many others may influence the way that language is acquired which means that the effect of the visual medium is difficult to disentangle from other factors affecting acquisition.

Can the deaf child learn language through reading? It appears that the difficulties with language comprehension are eased but not eradicated by written presentation. This is probably due to a number of factors including the role that a phonological code plays in learning to read. Prereading experience with picturebooks and stories appears to be difficult. Slow syntactic acquisition and limited vocabulary are additional reasons why reading development is slow. Language acquisition from reading will be difficult unless it is related to a context that a child understands.

Written language is by definition decontextualized, though linguistic context can be used providing the necessary level of linguistic ability has been developed. This then becomes a chicken and egg problem.

SUMMARY AND CONCLUSION

Although the deaf acquiring oral language appear to be a promising group to help provide answers to general questions about language acquisition, the results are rather disappointing when examined in more depth. In this chapter the results of research into language development in the profoundly and severely deaf have mainly emphasized the powerfully dominant role of audition in language development. Although the visual channel allows some compensation, the disruption to the process is evident in virtually every aspect of linguistic development. The review has also emphasized how different aspects and stages of development are inter-related and how deficits in acquiring language appear to build in layers upon one another. Given the difficulty of the process described it is all the more remarkable that a few individuals reach high linguistic levels in spite of severe disability.

8

The acquisition of syntax and space in young deaf signers

U. Bellugi, K. van Hoek,
D. Lillo-Martin and L. O'Grady

THE STRUCTURE OF A VISUOSPATIAL LANGUAGE

Deaf children who have been deprived of auditory experience and who rely on a sign language as their principal mode of communication provide a privileged testing ground for investigating the interplay between the development of a spatial language and its spatial cognitive underpinnings. The study of the acquisition of American Sign Language (ASL) in deaf children of deaf parents brings into focus some fundamental questions about the representation of language and the representation of space.

In research over the past decade, we have been specifying the ways in which the formal properties of languages are shaped by their modalities of expression, sifting properties peculiar to a particular language mode from more general properties common to all languages. American Sign Language exhibits formal structuring at the same levels as spoken languages and similar kinds of organizational principles (constrained systems of features, rules based on underlying forms, recursive grammatical processes). Yet our studies show that at all structural levels, the form of an utterance in a signed language is deeply influenced by the modality in which the language is cast (Bellugi 1980).

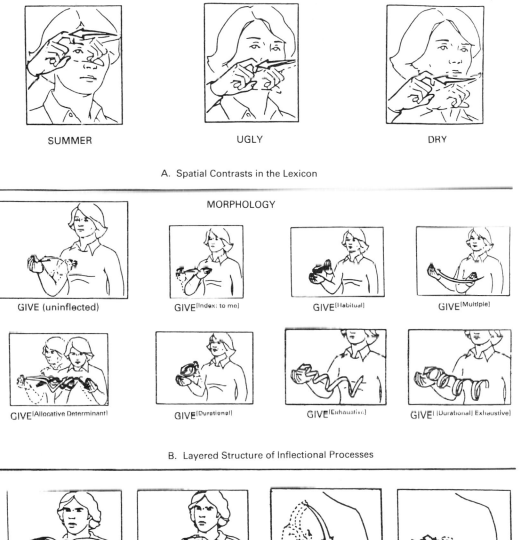

LEXICON

SUMMER   UGLY   DRY

A. Spatial Contrasts in the Lexicon

MORPHOLOGY

GIVE (uninflected)   GIVE[Index: to me]   GIVE[Habitual]   GIVE[Multiple]

GIVE[Allocative Determinant]   GIVE[Durational]   GIVE[Exhaustive]   GIVE[Durational] Exhaustive]

B. Layered Structure of Inflectional Processes

TELL-STORY   STORY   SIT-DOWN   CHAIR

C. Derivationally Related Pairs in ASL

Fig. 8.1 Linguistic contrasts in American Sign Language

American Sign Language has been forged into an autonomous language with its own internal mechanism for relating visual form with meaning. ASL has evolved linguistic mechanisms that are not derived from those of English (or any spoken language), thus offering a new perspective on the determinants of language form (Klima & Bellugi 1979, Bellugi et al 1987a). ASL shares underlying principles of organization with spoken languages, but the realization of those principles occurs in formal devices arising out of the very different possibilities of the visual-gestural mode (Bellugi in press). We consider briefly the structure of ASL at different linguistic levels—the layered structure of phonology, three-dimensional morphology and the spatially organized syntax.

'Phonology' without sound

Research on the structure of lexical signs has shown that, like the words of spoken languages, signs are fractionated into sublexical elements. The elements that distinguish signs (handshapes, movements, places of articulation) are in contrasting spatial arrangements and co-occur throughout the sign. For example, the signs SUMMER, UGLY and DRY[1] are made with the same handshape and movement at three different spatial locations (shown in Figure 8.1A, top).

Vertically arrayed morphology

The grammatical mechanisms of ASL exploit elaborately the spatial medium and the possibility of simultaneous and multidimensional articulation. Like spoken languages, ASL has developed grammatical markers that serve as inflectional and derivational morphemes; these are regular changes in form across syntactic classes of lexical items associated with systematic changes in meaning. Some sample inflections on the single sign GIVE are shown in Figure 8.1B (middle), including inflections for person, number, distributional aspect, temporal aspect, e.g. conveying the meanings 'give to me,' 'give regularly,' 'give to them,' 'give to certain ones at different times,' 'give over time,' 'give to each,' 'give over time to each in turn.' Figure 8.1C shows sample derivationally related pairs of signs in ASL: verbs and their formationally related noun pairs, distinguished only by subtle features of movement. In ASL, families of sign forms are related via an underlying stem: the forms share a handshape, a location and a local movement shape. Inflectional and derivational processes represent the interaction of the stem with other features of movement in space (dynamics of movement, manner of movement, directions of movement, spatial array and the like) all *layered* with the sign stem.

Spatially organized syntax

Languages have different ways of marking grammatical relations among their lexical items. In English, it is primarily the *order* of the lexical items that marks the basic grammatical relations among verbs and their arguments; in other languages, it is the morphology of case marking or verb agreement that signals these relations. ASL, by contrast, specifies relations among signs primarily through the manipulation of sign forms in *space*. Thus in sign language, space itself bears linguistic meaning. The most striking and distinctive use of space in ASL is in its role in syntax and discourse, especially in nominal assignment, pronominal reference, verb agreement, anaphoric reference and the referential spatial framework for discourse. Nominals introduced into ASL discourse may be assigned to specific points in a plane of signing space. In signed discourse, pointing again to a specific locus clearly 'refers back' to a previously mentioned nominal, even with many other signs intervening. The ASL system of verb agreement, like its pronominal system, is also in essence spatialized. Verb signs for a large class of verbs move between the abstract loci in signing space, bearing obligatory markers for person (and number) via spatial indices, thereby specifying subject and object of the verb, as shown in Figure 8.2A. This spatialized

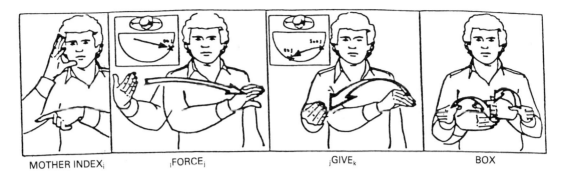

MOTHER INDEX$_i$ $_i$FORCE$_j$ $_j$GIVE$_k$ BOX

A

"Mother$_i$ forced him$_j$ to give him$_k$ the box."

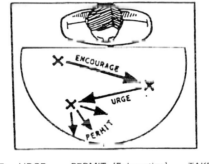

John ENCOURAGE$_i$ $_i$URGE$_j$ $_j$PERMIT$_k$ [Exhaustive]   TAKE-UP   CLASS

"John encouraged him$_i$ to urge her$_j$ to permit each of them$_k$ to take up the class."

B

Fig. 8.2 Syntactic spatial mechanisms in ASL. (A) A spatially organized sentence in ASL showing nominal establishment and verb agreement. (B) Spatial reference diagram for multiclausal sentence

system thus allows explicit reference through pronominals and agreement markers to multiple, distinct, third-person referents. The same signs in the same order, but with a reversal in direction of the verb's movement, indicate a reversal of grammatical relations. Furthermore, sentences with signs in different temporal orders can still have the same meaning, since grammatical relations are signified spatially. Co-referential nominals are indexed to the same locus point, as is evident in complex embedded sentences, such as shown in Figure 8.2B. Different spaces may be used to contrast events, to indicate reference to time preceding the utterance, or to express hypotheticals and counterfactuals. This pervasive use of space for referential indexing, verb agreement, coreference and grammatical relations is clearly a unique property of visual-gestural systems.

American Sign Language is thus markedly different in surface form from English, and from spoken languages in general. The inflectional and derivational devices of ASL, for example, make structured use of space and movement, nesting the basic sign stem in spatial patterns and complex dynamic contours of movement. ASL is in fact unique in its use of space at all levels of linguistic organization. Other signed languages examined to date suggest that these characteristics turn out to be general characteristics of primary signed languages (Volterra 1981, Fok et al in press).

ASL is also different from spoken languages in the extent and degree of congruence between meaning and form. ASL signs for basic level objects, for example, themselves are sometimes globally iconic, their form resembling some aspect of what they denote. At the morphological and syntactic levels also, there is often some congruence (motivatedness) between form and meaning. Spoken languages are not without such direct clues to meaning (reduplication processes, e.g. 'very, very', and ideophones provide direct methods of reflecting meaning through form), but in sign languages such transparency may be more pervasive. ASL thus bears striking traces of its representational origins, but at the same time is fully grammaticized. It is important to note that ASL and British Sign Language are totally independent and unrelated sign languages, as recent research on British Sign Language demonstrates (e.g. Deuchar 1983).

Given these differences, the task that the deaf child faces in learning sign language may be radically different from that faced by the hearing child for spoken language. For one thing, the mapping between meaning and form is more direct than in spoken language, and this might offer the child a more direct route into sign language at all levels. There are also differences in the channels used for production and perception of signed and spoken languages. The change in transmission system (from the ear to the eye, from the vocal apparatus to the hands) might be expected to have a profound influence on acquisition. An additional, important question is the effect, if any, of the spatial and iconic aspects of ASL on the course of acquisition. In a language where the articulators are directly observable and, moreover, manipulable, the language learning situation takes on a different character. What effects do these special characteristics of a language in a visual modality have on the course of the acquisition process?

We have studied the acquisition of sign language by deaf children of deaf parents using a variety of techniques: videotapes of mother-child interactions in the home, elici-tation of narratives, and specialized tests of language development. The children are all learning ASL as a first, primary language from deaf parents as their primary mode of communication. We have undertaken longitudinal studies of ten children between the ages of 1 year and 8 years, and have now charted the course of the acquisition of particular grammatical domains (e.g. pronominal reference, verb agreement, inflectional processes, derivational processes). We have also conducted cross-sectional studies with deaf children of deaf parents between the ages of 1 and 10 years old, and have developed formal tests for each of the grammatical processes we have found in ASL (for phonological, lexical, inflectional, derivational, and compounding processes as well as syntax; Lillo-Martin et al 1985a). These tests have been standardized with young deaf adults and are being used with deaf children of deaf parents as well as other groups. Several doctoral theses that had their origins in intensive examination of the deaf children of deaf parents in our acquisition studies—including Petitto (1983a), Launer (1982), Supalla (1982), Meier (1982), Loew (1982, 1983) and Lillo-Martin (1986)—are based on the same group of subjects. In this chapter, we highlight acquisition of some aspects of ASL which might be expected to lead to a different course of acquisition from spoken language.

THE ACQUISITION OF SPATIALIZED MORPHOLOGY

Pronominal reference in a spatial language

The system of personal pronouns in ASL affords a dramatic example of the unexpected similarities between the acquisition of spoken and signed languages, despite striking differences in the form of the two types of language (Bellugi & Klima 1982, Petitto 1983a, 1983b). Deixis in spoken languages is considered a verbal surrogate for pointing. In ASL, however, deixis *is* pointing. The pronominal signs in ASL are, in fact, the same as pointing gestures that hearing people use to supplement their words nonverbally. This transparency of meaning could be expected to lead to ease of acquisition of such forms by young deaf children learning ASL as compared with spoken languages.

The problems children have in learning terms that 'shift' with speaker and addressee (such as *I* and *you*) are well known and well documented for spoken languages (Clark 1978). Some, though not all, children temporarily 'reverse' the meanings of the pronouns, using *you* to refer to themselves, and using *I* and *me* to refer to the addressee. The hearing child's problems with the shifting nature of such arbitrary strings of sounds as *you* and *me* is readily understandable. In hearing children, problems with such deictic pronominal terms involving shifting reference are usually resolved by the age of 2;6 to 3;0. In contrast, we fully expected that, because of their transparent nature, the learning of the sign equivalents of pronominal reference in ASL would be early and error-free ('trivial' is the way we expressed it). In ASL, the pronoun signs are exactly the same as the pointing gestures we would use to indicate self and addressee. Given such obvious gestures, directness of reference would seem inescapable. However, to our surprise, we found that deaf signing children made errors in pronominal reference exactly analogous to those made by hearing children learning English.

Laura Petitto was the first to study this important aspect of the acquisition of ASL in depth. Her involvement in the study of pronominal references surfaced very naturally; one day a deaf mother and child (age 1;11) were visiting our lab, and the child began signing YOU where she clearly meant herself. Her mother, embarrassed, signed 'NO, NO, (YOU) MEAN (YOU)' taking the child's hand and making the pointing sign directly and forcibly on the child herself. In a language where the 'speech organs' are directly visible and manipulable, the form of mother to child correction is remarkably direct; yet astonishingly, the mother's corrections at this period had no effect whatever on the child's productions, and the child continued

to walk around the lab blithely pointing *incorrectly* for reference to herself and others. Thus the child was patently ignoring the transparency of the pointing gesture.

Petitto found that deaf children display precisely the same progression, at the same ages, as do hearing children learning pronominal reference systems in spoken languages. Her results provide dramatic evidence of the transition from gesture to sign. It is a transition marked, first, by the emergence of a form used as a pointing gesture; then its absence over a period of several months; and finally the re-emergence of the same form as a pronominal sign that is integrated into a linguistic system but marked by some systematic errors. Importantly, the errors and their resolution occur exactly on target with those observed in children learning spoken languages, at the same ages. It appears to make little difference, then, whether pronominal terms are symbolized by arbitrary streams of sound segments, as in spoken language, or by pointing signs which are indistinguishable in form from pointing gestures, as in sign language. These studies provide evidence for *discontinuity* in the transition from prelinguistic gesture to linguistic system, even when the form of the two are identical and share a single channel of expression. This is one form of evidence that the transition from gesture to sign requires a reorganization of the child's linguistic knowledge, and suggests 'that the structure of a gesture *as a linguistic unit*, rather than the iconicity of its form, determines the course of acquisition.'

Spatial verb agreement

How do children acquire a morphological system which is grammaticized, but which nevertheless displays a large amount of iconicity? Does the iconicity of ASL signs or grammatical processes give children a special way into language learning? Does iconicity have a pronounced facilitative effect on the mastery of the verb agreement system? Since the origins of such processes are so obviously direct, the child might well begin via the mimetic basis of signs or inflectional processes.

Richard Meier in our laboratory has examined the acquisition of verb agreement in ASL (1981, 1982). If the iconic properties of ASL signs are accessible to 2- and 3-year-old first-language learners, the iconicity of agreeing verbs should be highly accessible. The effects of such iconicity could be expected to appear in the acquisition of verb agreement. Meier develops three models which make specific predictions about what agreeing forms the children will acquire early and what error types they will produce. Two of the models make predictions based on iconicity: the first based on the relative similarities of agreement forms to mimed gestures, the second based on their relation to an analogic use of space with verbs of movement and transference. The third model makes predictions based on morphological complexity—a model which has been found to predict the course of the acquisition of inflectional systems in spoken language (Slobin 1985). Meier's analysis of the acquisition of verb agreement in deaf children of deaf parents ranging in age from 1;6 to 3;9 (coupled with an experimental study of a group of such children) reveals that verb agreement is acquired by children within a narrow age range. In one child, for example, verb agreement begins at 2;0 and is complete by 3;0; at that point the child is consistently providing correctly agreeing verbs across samples. We describe two periods in the children's acquisition of their first inflection:

1. Signing children around age 2 do not make use of the inflectional apparatus of ASL—including verb agreement—during the two and three sign stage. (The same phenomenon has been observed by Fischer (1973) and Newport & Ashbrook (1977)). Even when young children imitate adults' signing, their imitations tend not to preserve featural markings of the morphologically complex forms of parental utterances. For conveying a notion such as 'you give me,' 2-year-old children, rather than using the required agreeing form, which would be highly iconic, instead sign the verb GIVE in its uninflected form which resembles the mimed act of its opposite (i.e.

'I give you') and sometimes add the separate pronoun signs as well. Children thus use uninflected forms in contexts where the agreeing form is required, even when the agreeing form would be more iconic than the uninflected form. The child does not enter the agreement system by exploiting the mimetic potential available within a visual-gestural language.

2. Between the ages of 2 and 3, the deaf children in our study begin to produce forms inflected for verb agreement in contexts in which the referent is present in the discourse setting. By around 3, across deaf children, verb agreement with present referents is mastered in required contexts, and consistently used. The forms that children use and the errors that they make en route to mastering the system support a morphological model of acquisition, rather than either an iconic model based on mimed actions or one based on an analogy with spatial displacement.

Just as do children learning spoken languages, deaf children learning ASL as a first language produce a variety of overgeneralizations, as the children begin producing inflected forms in earnest. Children provide agreeing forms for verbs which cannot be marked for agreement in the adult language, such as SPELL, SAY, and LIKE. These forms are not mimetic or spatial analogic. The child inflects the verb SPELL for object (*SPELL[X:'to me'], although SPELL is not an agreeing verb. The child intending to sign 'I say to you' inflects *SAY[X:'to you'], which is not permitted in the adult language. The verb LIKE is over-marked for object — *LIKE[X: 'to it'], meaning 'I like that.' Deaf children's overgeneralizations are shown in Figure 8.3. Furthermore children extend verbs like DRINK and EAT to agree with the subject, when in fact these verbs are not indexible in the verb agreement system. These errors are morphological over-regularizations, entirely analogous to English-speaking children's provision of *goed* and *holded* for past tense.

During this period, there are also errors in which the movement of the verb form is toward the wrong argument. For example,

*SPELL[X: 'to me']/SPELL   *SAY[X: 'to you']/SAY

*LIKE[X: 'to it']/LIKE

Fig. 8.3 Overgeneralizations of verb inflections by young deaf children of deaf parents

children inflect the verb GIVE toward the object to be given (e.g. *GIVE[X:'to plate'] HIM), for the intended meaning of 'Give the plate to him,' instead of toward the recipient (GIVE[X:'to him']). These forms are both ungrammatical and counter-iconic but they are, nonetheless, consistent with a morphological model; it is one of the grammatical arguments of the verb that is being marked but simply the wrong argument.

Thus the weight of the evidence supports a morphological analysis on the part of the signing child, and indicates strongly that the child does not make use of the iconic potential provided by the visuospatial mode to enter the grammatical system. Rather, he begins with uninflected signs, and then systematically analyzes the morphologically complex forms, as well as analyzing which verbs do and do not undergo agreement, what arguments are marked, and whether the markers are optional or obligatory, etc. All of these aspects are worked out by signing children by approximately age 3, at which time the ASL system for marking verb agreement is stabilized and mastered, comparable to the emergence of aspects of inflectional morphology in spoken languages, despite the differences in form.

Derivational morphology

Like other languages, ASL marks morphological distinctions between lexical categories, and has a set of regular morphological operations for deriving new lexical items. For example, there is a consistent formal relationship between verbs and their formally related deverbal nouns (e.g. SCISSORS and CUT;

CAR and DRIVE), as first described by Supalla & Newport (1978). The members of such a pair share handshape, place of articulation and movement shape, but the noun form is regularly differentiated from the verb form by frequency and manner of movement: while the verbs show a variety of movement characteristics, the related nouns are always *repeated*, *small*, and *restrained* in manner (illustrated in Fig. 8.1C).

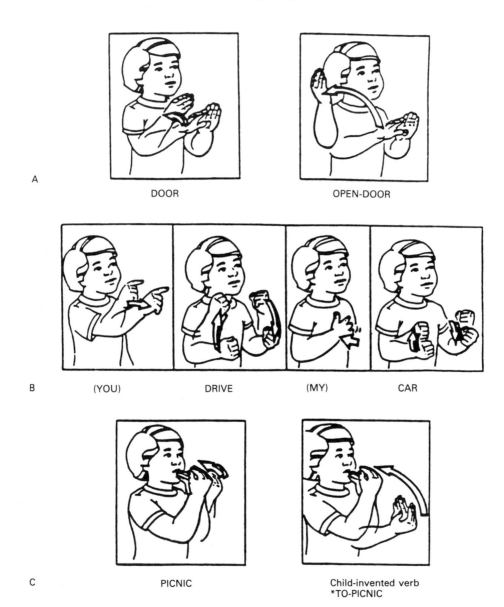

A DOOR   OPEN-DOOR

B (YOU)   DRIVE   (MY)   CAR

C PICNIC   Child-invented verb
*TO-PICNIC

Fig. 8.4 Acquisition of derivational relationship between noun and verb. Child's correct instances (A and B) and over-extension (C).

Launer in our laboratory studied the acquisition of the morphological distinction between nouns and verbs and found the following pattern of development of this subtle distinction in movement features. She found that deaf children younger than 2 are acquiring lexical items but not morphologically marking related noun and verb forms. By ages 2 and 3, the children sporadically mark nouns and verbs with appropriate features, but do not do so systematically, often providing noncanonical or idiosyncratic markings. Children aged 4 and 5 mark full morphological distinctions between nouns and verbs quite systematically, and even make overextensions of the formal markings to unpaired forms and to lexical innovations.

Figure 8.4A shows the child signing the noun DOOR and the verb OPEN-DOOR with the appropriate morphological markings. A child of 3;6 invented a story in which she had an imaginary car that she did not want to drive. 'Here's the key,' she signed to her mother, handing her an imaginary key: 'YOU DRIVE MY CAR' (see Figure 8.4B). The child used the single root of DRIVE and CAR but differentiated the two forms by their full morphological markers. The most striking evidence that children have analyzed out morphological marking from across sign forms differentiating noun and verb classes is that they extended these markings to new instances in a variety of ways. 4-year-old children invented signs and provided the appropriate morphological markers, as in invented signs for LAMB, TYPEWRITER-KEYS, BUILD-HOUSE. One child extended the ASL noun sign PICNIC, which does not have a related verb, and using an appropriate verb marker, signed something like 'to have a picnic' (see Fig. 8.4C). By age 5, most nouns and verbs are marked with appropriate featural distinctions.

We suggest that, despite obvious differences in surface structure and modality, the course of the acquisition of ASL morphology is remarkably similar to that for spoken languages (cf Slobin 1985). We now turn to the acquisition of a domain in which the use of space and spatialized linguistic mechanisms is most apparent: the level of syntax and discourse.

THE ACQUISITION OF SPATIALLY ORGANIZED SYNTAX AND DISCOURSE

Languages have different ways of indicating relations of reference and co-reference: ASL specifies co-reference relations primarily through the manipulation of loci in space. In this section, we discuss the acquisition of the syntactic and discourse-level uses of space: the establishment and maintenance of referential loci, and their use in verb agreement and co-reference relations. As an illustration of the complexities involved in a spatially organized syntactic system, consider a brief account of the use of spatial loci for referential indexing, co-reference, for verb agreement, and the fixed and shifting spatial framework underlying sentences and discourse. Nominals introduced into ASL discourse may be assigned to arbitrary reference points in a horizontal plane of signing space. In signed discourse, pointing again to a specific locus clearly 'refers back' to a previously established nominal, even with many other signs intervening. *Co-referential* nominals must be indexed to the same locus point, both within and across sentences. This *spatial indexing* in ASL allows explicit co-reference and may reduce ambiguity. Further, since verb signs move between such points in specifying grammatical relations, the ASL system of *verb agreement* is also essentially spatialized; classes of verbs are inflected for person-number agreement via spatial indices. Because verb agreement may be given spatially, sentences whose signs are made in different temporal orders can still have the same meaning. Overall, then, in *function* this system is like grammatical devices in spoken languages (Lillo-Martin, in press). However, in its *form*—marking connections between spatial points—spatially organized syntax in ASL bears the clear imprint of the mode in which the language developed (Bellugi & Klima 1982, Padden 1983).

The 'Paint' Story

Fig. 8.5A Pictures from story booklet without words for syntax and discourse study

NOMINAL ESTABLISHMENT COMPREHENSION

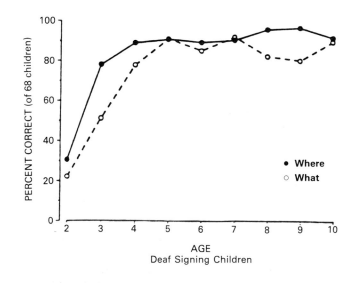

Fig. 8.5B Results of the nominal establishment comprehension test

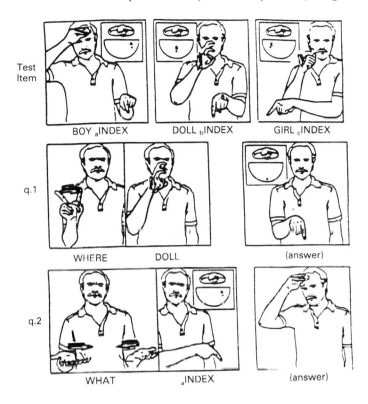

Test Item

BOY aINDEX   DOLL bINDEX   GIRL cINDEX

q.1

WHERE   DOLL   (answer)

q.2

WHAT   aINDEX   (answer)

Fig. 8.5C Sample items from nominal establishment test

In a series of studies, the spatially organized syntax has been broken down into component parts to investigate the young child's production and comprehension of separate aspects of linguistic structure (Lillo-Martin et al 1985b). We report here on the production and comprehension of nominal establishment and the integration of verb agreement with the spatial reference system. To elicit aspects of spatially organized syntax story booklets were designed, containing pictures but no words. One such story is illustrated in Figure 8.5A.

The ASL data to be considered here come from partially longitudinal studies of 23 deaf children with deaf parents. The children range in age from 1;7 to 8;11, and are learning ASL as a first language. Most of the children were videotaped for two to four sessions, with a deaf research assistant conducting conver-

sation entirely in ASL. For the narrative elicitation tasks, the child was shown each page one at a time and asked to sign what was happening in that picture. After each book was finished the child was then asked to tell the whole story again. The data discussed here come from both of the tellings.

Nominal establishment

Nominal establisment—the mechanism by which a noun or noun phrase is associated with a spatial locus in a specific horizontal plane of signing space—is central to ASL's spatialized syntax. Examining the children's narratives for examples of nominal establishment we found that the youngest age at which a child establishes a nominal and uses it for reference (in this case, for verb agreement) was 4;11. This is congruent with the findings from a number of researchers, as reported in Newport & Meier (1986), that explicit nominal establishment appears at approximately 4;6–4;9. Other children through age 5;6 used verb agreement without otherwise explicitly establishing referential loci. By age 6, referential loci were correctly established and maintained in narratives.

In light of the production findings, we next investigated the child's comprehension of spatial locus establishment and verb agreement. We explore the possibility that the young signing child may understand that nominals may be abstractly associated with arbitrary points in space, even when he is not producing such spatial mechanisms regularly in his ongoing signing. This question was examined with 68 deaf children of deaf parents between the ages of 1 and 10, using a formal language test devised to examine in particular the association of nominals with spatial loci.

The Nominal Establishment Test examines perception, comprehension and memory for spatial loci associated with specific nominals. In the test, nominals are assigned to arbitrary loci in the horizontal plane of signing space that serves for definite reference. Two kinds of questions are asked: (a) where a certain nominal has been established (to which the child answers by pointing to a specific locus); and (b) what nominal has been established at a certain locus (to which the child answers by signing the nominal). Two and three nominals are used in different parts of the test. In associating loci with their nominal referents, this test assesses a key aspect of co-reference structure in ASL syntax and discourse, and has been used with deaf children, with deaf adults of different language background, and with left and right brain-lesioned deaf signers (Poizner et al 1987). Figure 8.5 (B and C) present sample test items and results with 68 deaf children of deaf parents.

When we attempted to test 1- and 2-year-old deaf children, they were quite unable to deal with the test. When the deaf experimenter signed 'Where's the doll?' (after previously associating an arbitrary locus with the sign DOLL), these young children looked around the room as if looking for an actual doll; one ran to her bedroom to take one out. When asked 'What is at point X?' (an arbitrary point in space previously associated with the sign BOY), the children seem nonplussed. Thus 1-year-olds and most 2-year-olds fail the test; but importantly, already by the age of 3, deaf children perform well on the task, even with two and three nominal assignments to abstract points in a plane of signing space (Lillo-Martin, et al 1985b). This is despite the fact that such nominal establishment to spatial loci is not reported in deaf children's signing before the age of 4½ (e.g. Loew 1983). Such results suggest that the deaf child by the age of 3 does understand that in this language a nominal can be associated with an arbitrary point in abstract space; furthermore he is adept at processing this aspect of the language structure, and can handle two and three nominals at a time at different spatial loci with ease and facility. We have since found that young deaf children can also process the spatial syntax of the language in sentences involving minimal pairs, distinguished only by different spatial endpoints of the verb for subject and object marking (Lillo-Martin et al 1985b).

Integration of verb agreement with spatial reference

As discussed, verb agreement morphology is acquired and correctly used by age 3;6. However, verb agreement by that age is used only in contexts in which the referents are actually present. Correct use of verb agreement in ASL spatial syntax is dependent upon the establishment of spatial referential loci. Thus even once agreement morphology has been acquired, integrating it with the spatial reference system represents an additional level of complexity.

We examined the children's use of verb agreement with spatial referential loci, and found the following progression: the youngest children, approximately through age 2;6, use

A. Use of Sign Order

B. Incorrect Attempt at Spatial Reference

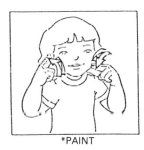

C. Morphological Innovation

D. Correct Spatial Reference

Fig. 8.6 Deaf children's acquisition of spatial syntax

only single signs to describe each picture, and single signs are used for telling the whole story. In the 2- to 3-year range, several-sign combinations are used, but without the establishment or use of referential loci. Instead of using the spatially organized syntax, the children use uninflected verbs along with word order to indicate reference (Fig. 8.6A). This strategy continues to be used through age 4. In most cases the use of uninflected verb signs and reliance on word order is not grammatical adult ASL, although it is understandable.

As the children bring together the systems of verb agreement and spatial reference, they make errors which provide intriguing clues to their understanding of ASL's spatialized syntax. At around age 4, a number of children used verb forms which are not used in adult ASL, but which nevertheless appeared similar in principle to inflected verb forms in the adult language. Rather than establishing and using spatial referential loci, the children contrasted the right and left sides of the face and head, articulating verbs on one side for one referent and on the other side for the other referent (Fig. 8.6B). They also used both sides of the face for a two-handed reciprocal form (illustrated in Fig. 8.6C). The children appear to have acquired the principle of spatial contrast, and are giving it a novel realization (van Hoek et al in press). Sometime after 5, the children begin to establish referential loci and to use verb agreement utilizing these loci (Fig. 8.6D). By age 6, the children consistently use verb agreement appropriately. Referential loci are correctly established and maintained.

As with our study of nominal establishment, we separately assessed the children's comprehension of verb agreement as an indicator of reference. In one test, the children were asked to act out, using toy figurines, the action signed by the experimenter. The test involved verbs which take two arguments (subject and object). These tests were given to 51 children from the ages of 2 to 8 who are deaf children of deaf parents.

For the test of verb agreement comprehension, a score of approximately 80% correct

was reached by age 5. Thus we find that, despite the complexity of the task—comprehending and remembering spatial loci for referents, as well as processing verb agreement using these loci—deaf signing children evidence good comprehension of the verb agreement system by age 5.

To summarize, the deaf child's knowledge of the linguistic use of space in ASL must include information on the differentiation of signing space, explicit establishment of nominals at discrete spatial loci, consistent spatial identity of loci, and contrastive use of established loci in sentences and across sentences in discourse, in long distance dependencies. Despite these complexities, deaf signing children are able to comprehend the major components of the syntax (nominal establishment, verb agreement) by age 3;6. The integration of these subsystems into a fully productive system takes somewhat longer, but appears to be complete by age 6. Before the children have complete mastery of the spatialized syntactic system, they make use of other referential devices which are available to them, such as word order and the innovative use of the principles of spatial contrast.

THE SEPARATION BETWEEN SPATIAL COGNITION AND SPATIAL LANGUAGE

In other studies (Bellugi et al in press) we have presented the results of deaf, signing children's performances on a selected battery of visuospatial tests measuring spatial construction, perception and organization. Emerging from these studies is a picture of deaf, signing children's spatial abilities which is at least comparable to that of hearing children and, indeed, strongly enhanced for some aspects of spatial cognition. These results provide intriguing clues to the effect of linguistic experience on the development of spatial cognition.

In a separate series of studies, we are investigating the effects of unilateral brain lesions of the left and the right hemisphere in deaf

VISUAL SPATIAL TASK: Block Design

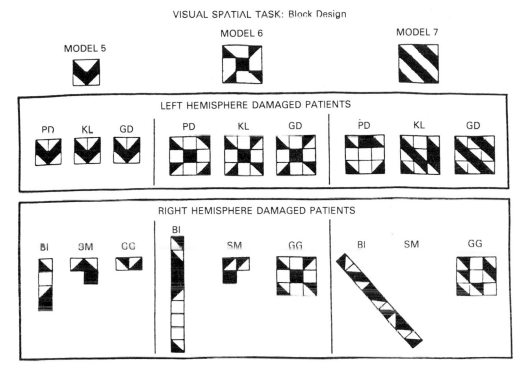

(Note impaired performance of Right Hemisphere Damaged signers)

ASL LANGUAGE TASK: The Sign Equivalent of Rhyme

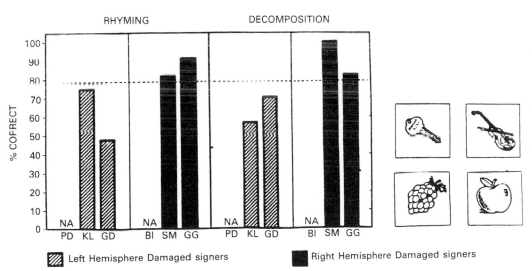

(Note impaired performance of Left Hemisphere Damaged signers)

Fig. 8.7 (A) *Block Design Task*: the subject must construct a pattern from 4 or 9 cubes to match the models shown. (B) *ASL Language Task*: A sample from the rhyming test is illustrated. The correct answer is 'key' and 'apple', since signs for these items share all major formational parameters but one

signers. Since ASL displays the complex linguistic structure found in spoken languages, but conveys much of its structure by manipulating spatial relations, it exhibits properties for which each of the hemispheres of hearing people show a different predominant function (see Ch. 13). The study of brain-damaged deaf signers offers a particularly revealing vantage point for understanding the organization of the brain for language and spatial cognitive functions in deaf signers (Poizner et al 1987).

We found that on nonlanguage spatial tasks, there were clear-cut differences in performance between left hemisphere damaged signers and right hemisphere damaged signers across a range of tasks. In spatial tasks, the right hemisphere damaged signers were severely impaired; they tended to show severe spatial disorganization, were unable to indicate perspective, and neglected the left side of space, reflecting the classic visuospatial impairments seen in hearing patients with right hemisphere damage (Fig. 8.7, top). These nonlanguage data suggest that the right hemisphere in deaf signers develops cerebral specialization for nonlanguage visuospatial functions. On linguistic tasks and in analyses of ongoing signing, the two groups of patients were also markedly different. The signers with right hemisphere damage were not aphasic. They exhibited fluent, grammatical, virtually error-free signing, with good range of grammatical forms, no agrammatism, and no signing deficits (Fig. 8.7, bottom). This preserved signing existed in the face of marked deficits in the processing of nonlanguage spatial relations. The signers with left hemisphere damage, in great contrast, were not impaired in nonlanguage visuospatial tasks, but were very impaired in language functions. They showed distinct sign aphasias; one left hemisphere damaged signer even had impairment of spatially organized syntax. These data show that in deaf adult signers, it is the left hemisphere that is dominant for sign language, even though processing sign language involves processing spatial relations at all linguistic levels (Poizner et al 1987).

Language and spatial representation are attributes for which the two cerebral hemispheres in hearing people show different specializations, and we have extended this finding to deaf signing adults as well. The use of the two hands in sign language may provide clues to hemispheric specialization that one cannot obtain from speech, since in sign language, the hands themselves are the language articulators. The development of hand dominance in very young deaf signers affords a unique opportunity for marking the onset of cerebral specialization. Indeed our preliminary studies suggest that hand dominance for sign language appears very early in some deaf children (perhaps as early as the first signs) and is much stronger than hand preference for nonlanguage activities in the same young children (Bellugi et al 1986, Vaid et al 1984). In these ways, then, the study of the acquisition process in sign language may provide additional clues to the biological foundations of language.

SUMMARY OF ACQUISITION OF GRAMMAR AND SPACE

Here we have examined some of the grammatical systems mastered by the deaf signing child learning ASL as a natural language from deaf parents who sign among themselves as a primary mode of communication. Because of the transparency of ASL forms, one might expect that these would be systems profoundly influenced by iconicity. What we found, instead, was that their transparency at all levels appears to have little or no effect on acquisition. Indeed Meier (1982) has argued that the young child may not be disposed to make use of the transparency of forms. Rather than focussing on iconicity, the deaf child analyzes morphological components of the linguistic system presented to him. The fact that the articulators in sign language are visible and manipulable could plausibly be thought to provide a special route to learning: mothers do occasionally mould and shape young children's hands in signing. Our evidence suggests, however, that even this is steadfastly and systematically ignored by the signing child who firmly holds his ground, continuing his incorrect analysis and resulting errors, until he arrives at his own reorganization of his language system. The evidence demonstrates that, just as the structure of ASL exhibits the same formal patterning as spoken languages, the course of acquisition of grammatical processes in ASL is remarkably like that for spoken languages. These findings thus dramatically underscore that the biological substrate for the human capacity for creating and acquiring linguistic system is modality independent.

ACKNOWLEDGEMENTS

This research was supported in part by National Institutes of Health grants #NS15175, #NS19096 and #HD13249; and the John D. and Catherine MacArthur Foundation Research Network. Illustrations were drawn by Frank A. Paul, copyright Ursula Bellugi, The Salk Institute. We thank Edward S. Klima, and Howard Poizner for helpful comments on this chapter and the research on which it is based. Many researchers took part in the acquisition studies and in our lively discussions in sign language including Maureen O'Grady, James Tucker, Patricia Richey, Dennis Schemenauer, Leslie Jamison, Patricia Launer, Ted Supalla, Elissa Newport, Richard Meier, Ruth Loew and Laura Petitto among others. We are very grateful to Dr Henry Klopping and the staff of the California School for the Deaf in Fremont, California, as well as to the deaf children and their parents for their spirited participation in these studies.

FOOTNOTES

1 We use the following notation in this chapter:

SIGN =	Words in capital letters represent English labels (glosses) for ASL signs. The gloss represents the meaning of the unmarked, unmodulated, basic form of a sign out of context.
SIGN[X:] =	A form that has undergone indexical change. The form or meaning may be specified, as in INFORM [X:1 to 2] or INFORM [X:'I to you'].
SIGN[N:M] =	A form that has undergone inflection for number and distributional aspect or for temporal aspect, focus, or degree.
SIGN[D:] =	A form that has undergone a derivational process.
*SIGN =	An asterisk preceding a sign form indicates that it is ungrammatical within adult ASL.

9

Visual handicap

A. Mills

INTRODUCTION

Research on the language of blind children has focussed relatively seldom on theoretical questions in language acquisition. The main body of information which is available on language acquisition in blind children stems from research carried out by practitioners in the field[1]. In this work on language the main concern has been the locating of areas where blind children have difficulty and subsequently attempting to find solutions. In the more theoretically oriented work the general aim has been to describe the role of vision in the language acquisition process of 'normal' children by determining those areas in which differences between sighted and blind children emerge. From such work it is also possible then to describe the alternative routes by which blind children acquire language. In recent years more work has been carried out with this general theoretical perspective, but it is not new.

In this chapter I shall first discuss the general theoretical questions to which data from blind children relate and the methodological problems which affect interpretation of the data. I shall subsequently consider the traditional areas of language acquisition individually and present the data available on blind children. In conclusion I shall return to

1. see Gill 1983, 1987, for a register of all ongoing research on visual handicap

the theoretical questions and consider the relevance of the data to these general issues.

THEORETICAL ISSUES

Language and experience

In language and philosophy the case of the blind person has been of interest for several centuries, most prominently in the school of British empiricism. For philosophers such as John Locke experience is an essential prerequisite for language learning; concepts which are primarily visual cannot be learned by the blind person and therefore the language labels for these concepts are for the blind person meaningless. Within an empiricist theoretical framework blind children must necessarily acquire language differently from sighted children, since their experience of the world is different. This topic was the subject of a recent book by Barbara Landau and Leila Gleitman (Landau & Gleitman 1985) and will be discussed below.

Language and cognition

The data from blind children have also been drawn into the debate on the relation between cognitive development and language acquisition. If language acquisition is seen as closely related to and dependent on cognitive development, any factor influencing cognitive development will therefore affect language. In the theory of Piaget, for example, it is claimed that such a close relation exists. Jean Piaget argued this point with Noam Chomsky in 1980 (Piatelli-Palmarini 1980) with Chomsky taking an opposed standpoint.

Chomsky maintained that there are only indirect links between cognitive development and language acquisition, so that handicaps affecting cognitive development will not necessarily influence language:

> I don't know if anyone has investigated this, but my own prediction is that it would turn out that there is no relation whatsoever, or at best the most marginal

relation, between even extreme defects that would make it virtually impossible for a child to develop and do all the things that Piaget was discussing, and his acquisition of language (Piatelli-Palmarini 1980, p. 171).

He later related the debate to blind children specifically, claiming that blind children are not delayed or deviant in their language acquisition in support of his argument. The findings to be reported below will indicate that this latter claim is somewhat exaggerated but the question of the relationship between language and cognition remains an interesting issue.

In order to investigate the relationship between language and cognition, it is clearly necessary to have information on the cognitive development of blind children. The literature here is too extensive to discuss (e.g. Cromer 1973, Hall 1979, Ochaita et al 1986, and Warren 1977 for a review). What is infrequent, however, is work which carefully traces the development of cognition and language in the same children. In the study of blind children this has to my knowledge not been done.

Partial models of language development

The theoretical questions discussed above are very broad issues in the area of language acquisition. Data from blind children also are significant in considering partial models of acquisition, that is in examining restricted areas of acquisition such as the acquisition of the sound system.

It may not be so obvious that blindness could affect the development of language. It is only when the, usually implicit, role of vision is considered in these models that the lack of vision may seem to be a problem. In learning the sound system, for example, do blind children have a more difficult task because they cannot see the lips articulating the sound? A great deal of nonverbal interaction is based on visually-perceived behaviour such as smiling or gestures and this interaction is viewed as an essential precursor of language development; what nonverbal communication systems do blind children use and how do these affect their early interaction patterns? Much recent literature has claimed that the kind of language spoken to children is different from that spoken to adults and the features of this language affect the development of language; do adults speaking to blind children speak differently and what effects do these differences have? These more particular questions will be discussed in detail in the following sections. A final section will deal with language disorders that occur disproportionately in the blind population in order to reflect on the role of blindness in causing a disorder.

Methodological problems

It was stated above that work on blind children which has focussed on primarily theoretical issues has had the general goal of describing the role of vision in language development. Ideally this description is made on the basis of a comparison of sighted and blind children, all other things being equal. It is, however, rarely the case that all other things are equal, and I will summarize the areas in which the main problems for such a comparison arise.

First, there are many degrees of visual handicap varying through 'no light perception', 'minimal light perception', 'perception of contours' to, for example, 'extreme short-sightedness'; the definition of 'blind' is a legal question which is formulated differently in different countries. In addition it is often very difficult to diagnose visual acuity in young children with any degree of accuracy.

Age at onset of blindness can clearly vary, and the influence of even a few months of visual experience must not be underestimated; surprisingly, early blindness is not always a disadvantage (Warren et al 1973, Birns 1986). Whatever the effect of age at onset may be, it becomes very difficult to make comparisons between blind children when this is a variable.

An even more critical problem is the frequent occurrence of blindness with another handicap; the figures for North America have been placed between 50% and over 90% in a study by Jan et al (1977). There are many causes of visual handicap, and it is often difficult to diagnose precisely the cause of the visual problem. In many cases it is not clear whether the children have a concomitant handicap; if such cases are excluded, the group size becomes even smaller; if they are included, the reliability of any comparison is jeopardized.

For the purposes of comparison with sighted children, in order to determine the role of vision, the ideal subjects should be children who are congenitally blind, with no or minimal light perception, and who have no other handicap. Such subjects are very difficult to find, which means that studies are either based on very small numbers of children, mainly case studies (see Mulford 1987 for a review), or include so many variables that the results are difficult to interpret. This will be referred to in the studies presented below where it is relevant to their interpretation.

PREVERBAL COMMUNICATION

A considerable amount of research in general language acquisition has concentrated on showing the links between preverbal and verbal communication (for example Bates et al 1977, Bruner 1978a, Bates 1979). Several studies have also been carried out on this period of development in blind children and in general have reinforced the finding with sighted children that successful interaction in the preverbal period is an important factor in determining the onset of language.

Sighted infants and the adults interacting with them monitor the gaze of the partner in order to establish a mutual focus of attention (Collis & Schaffer 1975). In very young infants the adults make most use of the direction of gaze of the infant to choose a topic for interaction. Clearly this use of vision is absent in blind infants and the direction of gaze cannot be interpreted by the adult as indicating focus of attention. There also exists a range of gestures important in early interaction which are visually directed, for example reaching for an object, pointing to an object or showing it to the adult. These gestures are missing in blind infants so that their communicative intentions are often difficult to follow.

Adults interacting with blind infants have to learn to pick up on other signals which indicate direction of attention and communicative intent. Failure to do so seems to be related to failure to develop normal communication and language. Fraiberg in an early study in 1974 and in the longitudinal study of ten visually-handicapped children (Fraiberg 1977) stressed the importance of parents reacting sensitively to their children's communicative attempts. Subsequent work has supported that conclusion. Als et al (1980) followed the development of one child whose parents were quick to pick up the information she was trying to communicate; her development in the first year was good in comparison with many blind infants.

The studies by Urwin (1978), Dunlea (1982) and Rowland (1983) all report cases in which the development was not so successful. Rowland investigated three preverbal blind infants and found, as did the other investigators, that affective states were most successfully communicated by the infants to the adults. They were also able to express a desire for the repetition of a play routine through behaviours that the parents learned to interpret, such as crying, the articulation of sounds which were interpreted as expressing pleasure, and certain hand movements. All the children had difficulty in determining the topic of interaction by directing the attention of the adult to an object not directly involved. Rowland also found that the infants did not respond with vocalizations in the same pattern as sighted infants; rather the blind infants produced fewer vocalizations during and after the adult's vocalizations compared with

sighted infants. They were strikingly silent after the adult's turn and tended to vocalize when alone. Rowland interprets this as follows: 'Listening may be so critical to the interpretation of the distal environment that it would be maladaptive for the blind infant to clutter the auditory environment with her own vocalizations' (Rowland 1983, p. 127).

Two of the children studied by Rowland were considerably more delayed in their language development than the third. The mothers of these two children did not respond as frequently to the vocalizations of their child as did the mother of the third infant. This suggests that it is essential for successful language development that the adult embed the child's vocalizations into a communicative routine.

Emotional problems related to abnormal interaction patterns have been reported in the literature (Kastein & Gillman 1976, Adelson 1983), although it is difficult to sort out what is cause and effect. It would not seem as though this kind of emotional disturbance causes more or different language problems in the case of blind children than in any other group.

In conclusion it appears that vision is an important factor in the establishment of early communicative patterns. Blind children have particular problems in developing such patterns unless the interacting adults are particularly sensitive to their less obvious communicative signals. Further research is still needed in this area to explore the role of vision in more detail, particularly the use of vision by the adult. For this purpose it is useful to consider interacting dyads in which the adult is blind. Collis & Bryant (1981) found that in general the social interaction pattern was little affected by a parent's blindness but they remarked that they had paid too little attention to language. Work being carried out at the University of Stockholm is concentrating on this aspect (Brumark personal communication, Hellspong personal communication, Junefelt personal communication) and will add a new dimension to our understanding of the importance of vision in this context.

SOUND PERCEPTION AND PRODUCTION

Babbling

The onset of babbling appears from most studies to be the same as in sighted children, that is between 6 and 7 months (e.g. Burlingham 1961, Haspiel 1965, Warren 1977). One case is reported of a child failing to babble before he was one year old (Wills 1979). Fraiberg (1977, pp. 109–110) judged the general amount of vocalization from the 10 children she studied to be less than in sighted children, but this was not quantified. Rowland's suggestion that blind infants tend to be more silent in interaction because of attending to the adult's vocalizations may explain Fraiberg's observation.

Since babbling appears to begin at the same time for both sighted and blind infants, it would appear that observation of the talking face is not crucial for this activity to be triggered.

Burlingham (1961, pp. 134–5) reports from the observation of a group of infants that babbling continued for a longer period than in sighted infants. This went together with an observed delay in the acquisition of the first words. Since Burlingham was working within a psychoanalytic framework, her explanation for the extended period of babbling also falls within the framework, namely it being due to the mouth pleasure derived from the the motor activity of articulation rather than being related to the development of communication which would lead on to first words. However, Burlingham does not specify her group size, and the data on the acquisition of the first words are so mixed that it would not seem warranted to state that babbling is generally extended.

Sound perception

There are, as far I know, no studies on sound perception in young blind children. It might be expected that auditory discrimination would be more refined in blind children, at least in older children, because they have to rely on auditory cues to a far greater extent than sighted children. Only two studies report a less well-developed auditory perception, and this not in all blind children (Lux 1933, Elstner 1955). An audiometric study of 38 blind children between the ages of 7 and 16 years (Semzowa 1961) showed no difference in their perceptual skills. One study showed blind children aged 5 to 7 years to be superior to their sighted peers in identifying mispronounced words in a story context (Lucas 1984). One consonant was altered to form a nonsense word. No details are given of the range of consonants used and the pattern of correct identification, so that it is impossible to interpret this result further. It would be relevant to have further research carried out on the development of auditory discrimination skills, especially in young blind children, in order to be able to relate these skills to the production of speech sounds, which does develop differently.

Speech production

A considerable number of studies have investigated the production of speech sounds in blind children; an even greater number of authors have referred to the effect of not being able to see the articulatory movements on blind children's speech without having a clear basis for the remarks (for example, Wundt 1898). The earlier studies that were carried out produced contradictory results which are often difficult to interpret for methodological reasons (Mills 1987).

Göllecz (1972) completed a study based on electromyographic and sonographic data of articulations from 13- to 14-year-old children. He found far less lip movement in the articulation of vowels by the blind children but minimal deviations in the acoustic properties. This appears to be due to a compensatory restriction of the oral resonance chamber: an alternative route to the same acoustic result.

The only data on speech sound production in young blind children comes from a study of three blind infants learning German (Mills 1983, 1987; Mills et al 1983). These three children were compared with three comparable sighted children in the age range 1;0 to 2;1 and with a MLU range of 1.0 to 1.6. An analysis was carried out of the word-initial consonants produced by the children in spontaneous speech collected over the period of investigation. For the purposes of the analysis the German consonant inventory was divided into two groups: those sounds with highly visible articulatory movements (labials and labio-dentals e.g. /b/, /m/, /f/) and those sounds with scarcely visible articulatory movements (alveolars, palatals, velars and glottals e.g /t/, /j/, /k/, /x/, /h/). The division into these two groups was based on a study with German adults (see Mills & Thiem 1980).

The study showed that in their production of target sounds which have a visible articulation the visually-handicapped children made more errors than the sighted children: 41% compared with 21%. The difference between the two groups in their production of target sounds with non-visible articulation was not significant, which shows that blind children do not have a general delay in sound acquisition. The sighted children were significantly better at producing the sounds with visible articulation than the sounds with the non-visible articulation: 79% compared with 49%. There was no significant difference between the two groups of sounds for the blind children. The visible information about articulation clearly gives the sighted child an advantage in production.

An analysis of the sounds substituted in the errors made shows that sighted children rarely substitute a sound from the other visual category; for example they rarely produce /n/ instead of /m/, but rather another labial. Blind children make such cross-category substitutions much more frequently: 34% compared with only 10% in the sighted children. These findings have been supported by subsequent work, e.g. Dodd (1983), and Wilson quoted in Mulford (in press).

It is also evident from an analysis of the vocabulary of the children studied that the blind children attempted far fewer words including a sound with a visible articulation than the sighted children. This finding was confirmed by an analysis carried out on the early lexicons of nine English-speaking children (Mulford 1987). As Mulford points out, it has been previously observed that front-articulated consonants are predominant in the early lexicon but the explanations have been based on the distributional bias in languages (Vihman et al 1985) or on physiological factors (Smith 1987). The evidence from blind children indicates that these explanations are not correct since they would apply to blind children equally. Rather the visible articulatory movements must be recognized as important to the learning of accurate production and incorporated in any model of speech production and its acquisition. Secondly the findings confirm the view that the child actively selects the vocabulary to be produced on the basis of the acquired accuracy, although it is not possible to decide if the sighted child actively prefers frontal consonants or if the visually-handicapped child actively avoids them.

Although visually-impaired children clearly follow a different and slightly slower path in their early phonological acquisition, it is not the case that a disordered phonology will necessarily result. None of the children in the Mills study, who were followed up to the age of 2;6, showed any sign of such problems. Details of later phonological acquisition are not available but some blind children seem to have sound systems equivalent to those of sighted children by the age of 5 years. Several studies have, however, reported a higher incidence of articulation problems in visually-impaired children (e.g. Miner 1963, LeZak & Starbuck 1964, Elstner 1983), which suggests that the lack of visual information from the articulation may be a compounding factor which leads to a disorder, but not the sole cause.

THE FIRST WORDS

Onset

In order to compare blind and sighted children, various criteria have been used to match for stage of language development, making it difficult to relate one study to another. These include age of acquisition of the first word, of the first two words, of the first ten words or the first 50 words.

However, several studies of blind children report a delay of several months in the onset of the first two words (Norris et al 1957, Burlingham 1961, Omwake & Solnit 1961, Elonen & Zwarensteyn 1964, Fraiberg 1977, Reynell 1978). These studies were of groups of children, and in the latter two studies mentioned it is possible to see that there are blind children whose language is within the normal limits, although the mean for the group shows a delay.

Mulford (in press) analyzed the data from 14 more recent case studies and found that the acquisition of the first word for these children did not show any major delay: the youngest being nine months and the mean age for the group 14.7 months. The children did not show any delay in the acquisition of the other lexical milestones either.

Mulford suggests that the reason for this discrepancy in findings can be explained by the change in the cause of blindness which has taken place in the last twenty-five years. Retro-lental fibroplasia used to be a frequent cause of infant blindness due to the administration of too much oxygen to premature babies. The delayed onset of language may, therefore, have been due to a general developmental delay related· to prematurity or to a general impairment of the central nervous system caused by the excess of oxygen. Mulford also mentions the methodological problems that were discussed in an earlier section and suggests that the more detailed case studies she analyzed will give a more accurate picture. Again blindness alone cannot necessarily be said to be responsible for a language onset delay.

Lexical structure

On the basis of her analysis of the first 50 words in sighted children, Nelson (1973) showed an inter-relation between lexical categories in early vocabulary which can be used for the purposes of comparison with other groups. Nelson divided the early words into different types such as General Nominals, Action Words or Modifiers, and in her study indicated the frequency of items in the different categories. Several researchers have examined early lexicon in blind children (Bigelow 1981, 1982, Dunlea 1982, Landau 1983, Andersen et al 1984), but their conclusions have been different, as discussed in detail in a review article by Mulford (1987).

To summarize: the categories set up by Nelson are represented comparably in the lexicon of blind children but certain differences can be observed within the categories. So, for example, within the category of General Nominals blind children have fewer terms for animals but more terms for household items. This seems related to the differences between the usual experiences of blind and sighted children. Blind children's experience of animals is restricted to the few kinds of animals in the environment and to toy animals, whereas sighted children have access to pictorial representation of animals through books or television and therefore to a far greater range of animals. There does not seem to be anything problematic about these differences however.

Nelson (1973) also classified the sighted children she studied into two types according to the structure of their early vocabulary. Referential children have a large number of General Nominals, Specific Nominals and Action words with few Function words; expressive children have fewer General Nominals and more multiword phrases. The dichotomy would not seem to be particularly helpful in characterizing blind children: blind children would seem to be like expressive children in that they have few General Nominals (see Urwin 1978), but on the other hand they seem more like referential children in the other features (see Mulford in press). A more detailed description of early lexicon could, however, bring out those factors which are typical for the learning situation of the visually-handicapped child.

One point on which the researchers disagree is the frequent occurrence of under-extension of word meaning in blind children and a corresponding lack of overextension. That is, blind children will more frequently use a term to refer to one specific object only, rather than generalizing it to a class of objects. For example one child in my observation group would say *bear* for a particular toy bear, but not for any other furry bear; Bigelow (1982) has other examples. Visually-impaired children seldom incorrectly overgeneralize a term to other objects on the basis of some common property (Dunlea 1982), whereas sighted children at the early stage of lexical acquisition are prone to do this (Nelson 1973). Where overextension did take place in blind children, it was based, not unexpectedly, on features perceptible mainly in the haptic-kinaesthetic mode.

The researchers do not so much disagree that a difference exists here between sighted and blind children but on its significance. Andersen et al (1984) argue, on the basis of observing no sorting play in the blind children, that: 'the absence of visual input has a detrimental effect on category formation, a cognitive difference that leads to a language difference, since categorization schemata are thought to underlie lexical extension' (p. 655). Landau & Gleitman (1985) on the other hand consider the underextension and lack of overextension as unimportant for language acquisition since they reject a position in which such a close link is made between the development of cognition and language. This is an area in which more data are required on the cognitive development and language of both sighted and blind children before a clearer answer can be given.

MORPHOLOGY AND SYNTAX

As with language onset, there is conflicting evidence on the question of any delay in the area of morphology and syntactic structure. Where delay is observed, this may well be linked to factors other than lack of vision.

There are no indications of any major deviations in these areas in visually-handicapped children, whether younger (Landau & Gleitman 1985) or older (Maxfield 1936). Where problems are noted (Elstner 1983), a multiple handicap is frequently involved.

In one aspect of syntax Landau & Gleitman (1985) recorded a significant delay in the three blind children that they investigated. All three children were slow to acquire the verbal auxiliary in English, although no major delay was seen with any other construction. Landau & Gleitman (p. 48–49) found that this delay was immediately related to the structure of the maternal input which contained fewer instances of the verbal auxiliary. This was the case because the adults were using more imperative forms, containing no verbal auxiliaries, and fewer declarative and questions which do contain auxiliaries. The more frequent use of imperatives was due to the situation between the adult and blind infant in which the adult more frequently tells the child what to do or how to do it.

This complex chain of causes has been found also to apply to sighted infants (Newport et al 1977) and raises the important question of input as a factor in acquisition. Here the influence of the structure of the input is to delay the acquisition of a part of speech but there is no indication that the children suffer any permanent damage from this delay. In other languages the prolonged use of imperatives may have no major effect, or conversely it may cause more far-reaching impairment in syntactic acquisition. In German, for example, the use of imperatives is related to a non-adult positioning of the verb (Mills 1985, pp. 158–162). Thus structures of the type *Hände waschen* 'wash your hands!' are common in input and children produce utterances such as *Andreas Hände waschen* with the verb *waschen* in final position, whereas the adult form puts the verb in second position. The positioning of the verb at the end also impedes the acquisition of verb morphology (Clahsen 1986). The role of input would therefore seem to be language-related, but it could be nevertheless profound for speakers of some languages; this question will be discussed further below.

SEMANTIC DEVELOPMENT

Verbalism

Cutsforth (1932, 1951) introduced a term 'verbalism' which has unfortunately become strongly associated with the language of blind children. By verbalism is meant the use of language without the back-up of concrete experience. This is a very loose definition which has been criticized by Dokecki (1966). Functionally it has been interpreted as the ability to define the meaning of a word without being able to identify the object to which the word refers (Harley 1963, Demott 1972, Civelli 1983). Even in this form it is clear that the concept is ill-defined and applies to many aspects of language in sighted individuals—take the word *neutron* as an example.

Cutsforth applied the term to the language of the blind because they use words involving vision; this use he felt to be 'loose' and 'meaningless' and should be fought against in educational practice. This view presupposes an extremely close link between language and experience and has been argued against at length by Landau & Gleitman (1985) from a theoretical standpoint. Their work has also shown that terms involving vision are not meaningless for blind children (Landau 1983, Landau & Gleitman 1985).

Von Tetzchner & Martinsen (1980) suggest that 'verbalisms' are due to lack of visual cues rather than to lack of visual experience. In their study sighted children, when blindfolded, also produced a higher number of 'verbalisms' than when they used vision; that is they were more often unable to recognize an object but able to define the meaning of the word. Where blind children are unable to identify familiar objects tactually but can define the names for the objects (Demott

1972), the implications for educational practice would seem to be to improve tactual recognition skills and enrich experience rather than to restrict language.

Use of sighted terms

Landau & Gleitman (1985) investigated the use of some of the verbs of vision in one blind child, Kelli. They found that Kelli used and interpreted the verbs *see* and *look* as if they meant 'haptically be aware of' and 'haptically explore' respectively, indicating that the terms have distinctive meaning for her and reflecting her awareness of the difference in agentivity between the two verbs. They also show that Kelli was aware of different features when the verbs were used with a sighted person as agent; for example at age 4;8 Kelli knew that sighted adults could not see an object that was behind a barrier, although they could have felt it.

Landau & Gleitman's conclusion is that blind children will interpret the visual verbs in terms of the modality next dominant which is the haptic modality. On the basis of personal observation of blind children I would argue that it is not correct to say that the haptic modality is always the next dominant: I have observed blind children using the verb *see* with the meaning of 'to hear'; their use seems to be dependent on the situation. There is possibly individual variation in the hierarchy of modalities.

On the basis of Kelli's performance with the visual verbs and her use of some colour terms, they argue that the acquisition of lexical concepts is not deficient in blind children. Through an analysis of the situational context they want to show that Kelli could not deduce the meanings of the visual verbs as distinct from other verbs from environmental context alone. They argue that the syntactic contexts in which terms are used provide the most probable basis for their acquisition, along with innate categories of lexical concepts. Certainly Landau & Gleitman have shown that lack of vision does not necessarily mean deficient acquisition; but the language of blind children is clearly *different* in this area since, for example, they use the visual terms far less frequently (McGinnis 1981).

Deictic terms

Mulford (1981) investigated the acquisition of deictic terms, personal and spatial, in three blind children, comparing these with sighted children. In an experimental situation the blind children showed a delay in their acquisition of spatial deictic terms, i.e. *this, that, here* and *there*, compared with the sighted children; the blind children were still making errors at 6 years. In their spontaneous language these terms were also more rare and used without clarifying gestures (see also McGinnis 1981). Like the sighted children they learned personal deixis (personal pronouns) before spatial deixis. The blind children seem to be learning the proximal terms (this, here) before the distal terms (that, there), whereas the sighted children at this age do not show any clear order. Mulford explains these findings in terms of a delay in the acquisition of the underlying cognitive concept of space. This assumes, of course, a close relationship between cognition and language acquisition.

Locational terms

Bigelow & Bryan (1982) investigated the acquisition of *in, on* and *under* in blind children and noted that the children were able to place an object in relationship to themselves more quickly than two objects in relation to one another. This prompted a study of sighted children where the same sequence was observed. Clark (1973a) had previously established that familiarity of a relationship between objects, such as a cup being usually *on* a saucer, influences the order of acquisition. Relating an object to self is stronger than this factor however.

A current research project by the author is investigating the acquisition of locational terms, which are often mastered late by blind children. The goal is to assess how the two factors mentioned above interact with one

another and with a third factor: the orientation of the object. The interpretation of prepositions such as *in front of* is determined by the nature of the object; if an object has features which characterize a front surface, then the preposition means 'before this surface' as opposed to the interpretation 'before the speaker'. It is necessary to know about these fronting features (see Cox 1986 on sighted children) in order to interpret the prepositions correctly. The recognition of fronting features and the change of reference point according to the object appear to be particularly difficult for blind children.

Personal pronouns

In order to use and understand pronouns correctly the child must be aware, amongst other things, of the change in perspective necessary according to speaker at any one time. So, for example, when an adult says *you*, the child is referred to, but when the child uses the same form, the adult is referred to. In English the child must also master the singular/plural distinction, and gender for the third person singular forms, but languages are different in these respects.

Several researchers have noted that blind children appear delayed in their acquisition of the first person pronoun *I*. Fraiberg & Adelson (1973) explained this through a delayed learning of a self-concept. They argue that evidence for a delayed self-concept should be seen in the later development of symbolic play. Even assuming that this is correct, a connection between the two should also be evident in sighted children which it is not. Secondly, if self-reference is delayed, it would also be expected that blind children are later in their use of proper names in this function. This delay is not apparent; in fact blind children continue to use proper names for self-reference where the first person pronoun would be more appropriate (Mulford 1981).

Mulford suggests that the explanation of a delay, where it occurs in a blind child, lies rather in the problem of determining shifting roles for which the sighted child can use visual information. These shifting roles may also be related to a spatial concept, as Love-land (1984) has argued from evidence from sighted children. The development of the spatial concept does appear to be later in blind children.

Another possible explanation is the high frequency of proper names used in place of first and second person pronouns in adults' speech to blind children. Where this is continued for a long time, in the input to both sighted and blind children, the acquisition of the pronouns seems to be delayed. This explanation has some support from cross-linguistic evidence: in languages in which this 'simplification' of using proper names does not occur, for example Kaluli (Schieffelin 1985, p. 555), children do not have problems with the shifting roles.

Gender errors have also been reported as being more common in blind children, still occurring between 5 and 6 years, whereas sighted English children usually use gender correctly by the time they are 4 years (Mills 1986). Through her detailed analysis of the data from blind children, Mulford was able to relate these errors to problems in determining the sex of the referent, which is difficult in the absence of visual cues.

INTERACTION AND LANGUAGE FUNCTION

Requests

Urwin's (1978) study of three blind children indicates that the requests expressed in early language are mainly those related to self, that is requests for a repeated play activity etc., rather than requests for objects. Requests for objects began around the age of 20 months. Urwin sees this as a continuation of the pre-linguistic pattern of communication with language first taking up those functions already present.

Dunlea (1982) reports the predominant category of requests as being requests for objects, but her observations continue into a later period of development in her children. This indicates that blind children develop new

functions for language, once language emerges, much in the same way as sighted children do. This in turn has important consequences for interaction, with the adult's role changing to fit the child's growing ability to determine the topic of discourse (Urwin 1983).

Attention-getting

As part of structuring discourse it is necessary to obtain the attention of the listener and to direct the attention of the listener to the topic of discourse. Sighted children achieve these ends by nonverbal means, using eye-contact, and directing gaze to the topic of discourse where appropriate. This is not possible for blind children. Younger blind children use various alternative methods of obtaining and directing attention such as touching, calling of the addressee's name (Mulford 1983). The constraints on their use are learned slowly; so, for example, younger blind children will behave in a socially inappropriate way by pinching the person they wish to talk to or be unsuccessful in attracting the attention of the desired listener, because they cannot assess the chances of the listener hearing them. There is a danger here that the blind child can become discouraged in initiating discourse. For blind children and adults, language takes on many additional functions in this area, and so has additional importance for successful discourse.

The use of questions

One of the means of entering into conversation and getting attention is to ask a question. A study by Erin (1986) of 12 blind and 12 visually-impaired children between 4 and 10 years has shown that the blind children asked more questions than the sighted (see also Maxfield 1936). The older sighted children showed a decline in the number of WH-questions which was not observed in the older blind children. Erin suggests that the greater use of questions relates also to the use of language for the acquisition of knowledge which is essential for the blind person, particularly in social and mobility situations.

Workman (1986) observed that where an adult deliberately communicated information about the social environment, that is told the children, for example, who was present and what they were doing, there was a higher incidence of peer-peer interaction involving young preschool blind children, compared with a situation in which the adult did not make such information explicit. This implies that adults interacting with young blind children need to provide this information at the same time as encouraging children to ask questions so as to obtain the information themselves.

In the five children McGinnis (1981) observed aged 3 to 5 years, questions were also used frequently to effect a change of topic. Topic changes were also more frequent in general than in sighted children. This may be because blind children cannot use eye-contact to determine whether the listener is still attending.

Social interaction

Although it has been noted that younger blind children do not verbalize as frequently as sighted children of the same age, studies of older blind children (aged 4 to 9 years) show a greater amount of verbalization compared with sighted children (Olson 1983, Schwartz 1983). This appears to be related to the function of maintaining the interaction, which sighted children could achieve by eye-contact and visual nonverbal behaviour. Many of the aspects discussed in this section relate to differences which still hold for the blind adult. This point will be returned to below.

LANGUAGE INPUT

There has been a considerable amount of research with sighted children on the features of the input speech they receive, that is in what ways speech addressed to children is different from speech addressed to adults and the effect these differences can have on the development of language (Snow 1986). The discussion of this issue in the literature takes place within a general theoretical debate as to whether input can affect language development in any way; those supporting a nativist approach such as Noam Chomsky argue, of course, that it is irrelevant. The possible influence of adults' speech has been mentioned in some areas already discussed, for example in connection with personal pronouns. In this section, therefore, only research that has focussed on the structure of input to blind children will be reviewed.

Imperatives have been noted to be more frequent in speech to blind children than in speech to young sighted children of a comparable age (Kekelis & Andersen 1984, Landau & Gleitman 1985). A high frequency of imperatives is a characteristic of input to sighted children who are at an early stage in their language development. Kekelis & Andersen interpret their finding with blind children as indicating that language input changes at a slower rate for blind children compared with sighted children, leading to a slower rate of language development. Landau & Gleitman interpret their result as significant only in causing a delay in the acquisition of the verbal auxiliary.

Kekelis & Andersen recorded fewer attributions and descriptions in the language input to young blind children (16 to 22 months), with a greater incidence of labels. They were surprised at this finding because they had hypothesized that blind children would need more verbal information about the environment in order to categorize experience than sighted children. Research with sighted children indicates that adults wait for an indication from the child that an object is interesting. Kekelis & Andersen suggest that adults interacting with blind children have difficulties in knowing when the child is interested in an object and when the child has understood a description. The blind children's own language also contains more labels than that of sighted children, which suggests a delay in the development of language functions. Kekelis & Andersen interpret this finding as a result of the adults' input.

Adults talking to blind children up to the age of 3 years also tend to initiate the topics more than adults talking to sighted children (Urwin 1978, Kekelis & Andersen 1984). In the latter study almost 50% of the topics were not related to a context which the child could perceive. This makes it difficult for the child to interpret the language. For blind children of this age topics are more frequently child-centred than for sighted children. As mentioned earlier, the children themselves also initiate more child-centred topics than sighted children. Kekelis & Andersen see a delay here in the development of environment-focussed language related to the structure of the input.

Establishing a causal link between input and children's acquisition is still methodologically problematic. In the case of input to blind children there certainly appear to be differences, but the effects of these differences are not clear. Much more research is needed in this area.

NON-VERBAL BEHAVIOUR

As mentioned earlier, the pattern of non-verbal behaviour can affect language behaviour, as for example when blind children use language to attract the listener's attention whereas sighted children use nonverbal means. This section will therefore review what is known of the nonverbal behaviour of blind children.

Many researchers have reported a reduced repertoire of nonverbal behaviour in blind children as well as a muted quality in facial expression (see Warren 1977, pp. 166–170 for a review). Fraiberg (1977) related the lack of eye-contact and reduced amount of smiling in blind infants to problems in establishing a mother-child bond, which would then affect subsequent interaction involving language.

The only study of nonverbal behaviour in older blind children as it relates to language was carried out by Parke et al (1980). They compared 30 blind children (aged 5 to 15 years) with 30 sighted children in a standard-ized conversational situation. They reported far less use of the head nod from the blind children, although it was appropriate when used. This suggests that a different pattern of turn-taking control exists in blind children but it has yet to be described. The blind children smiled on similar occasions to the sighted children but they smiled for far longer. Parke et al suggest that this could be due to a desire to express friendliness or due to nervousness felt in a stressful situation. Eyebrow-raising was generally similar in blind children, although some children raised their eyebrows inappropriately, that is at a point not related to communication in the conversation. This appeared to be an involuntary movement. It is not clear whether these movements were interpreted by the conversational partner in any way. There is considerable scope here for research into the patterning of turn-taking in older blind children, which would certainly show different methods of regulation.

LANGUAGE OF THE BLIND ADULT

In recent years a considerable amount of research has accumulated on the language of blind children, although large gaps still exist in our knowledge. However, there is practically no research on the language of blind adults. This is highly relevant to the study of acquisition, since it cannot be assumed that the end-state of acquisition for the blind child is the same in every instance as for the sighted child (see Garman 1983).

Landau & Gleitman (1985) examined the definitions of visual terms in one blind adult and found no difference compared to sighted adults. Clearly it is necessary to study a larger group of adults, but in this area the problem of variation in sighted adults would probably make comparison difficult.

Kemp's (1981) review of social psychological aspects of blindness indicates that blind adults' language is different in some ways. From my own personal observation, blind adults appear to use language for functions which sighted adults do not need it for: for example, to continue social interaction, to establish mutual reference, and to control turn-taking. This gives the frequent impression that they 'talk a lot'. It is essential that detailed work be carried out on the language of blind adults to give the acquisition data a perspective.

LANGUAGE PROBLEMS IN BLIND CHILDREN

Echolalia

Inappropriate repetition of words or phrases has been noted by several researchers on blind children. This echolalia which is frequent in autistic children is one of the characteristics which has suggested a relationship between autistic children and the visually-impaired (Keeler 1958, Fay 1973).

In a recent paper Prizant (1984) reviews the literature and suggests that echolalia occurs in blind children more frequently than in sighted children for several reasons: first, there exists a variation in acquisition styles in which some children learn 'chunks' of language without analysing them (Peters 1983). Second, some blind children may have a delay in their comprehension of language but a more sophisticated rote memory. Third, lack of vision can cause difficulty in segmenting contextual events which in turn causes problems in segmenting the related language. Fourthly, the structure of input may favour an imitation. Forthcoming work (Prizant & Booziotis in prep., Lansky personal communication) aims to describe these factors in more detail.

Language retardation

Although frequent reference has been made in the preceding sections to a delay in acquisition in blind children, from the research conducted to date there is no evidence that blindness alone will necessarily cause language retardation in the clinical sense. It does, however, appear to be a serious compounding factor when it occurs with another handicap (Elstner 1983). In order to complete the coverage of the effects of visual handicap, the research with the blind multiply-handicapped child will be summarized.

It might be expected from the work which has shown a link between the development of mobility and language (Sibinga & Friedman 1971) that the blind physically-handicapped child would have severe language problems. However the one study known to the author, Egland's (1955) investigation of blind cerebral palsied children, did not reveal any major language problems.

As mentioned above, autistic characteristics are often cited in descriptions of the language of blind children. Some research has shown a high incidence of autism in children with retrolental fibroplasia (Chase 1972). It is not clear from the studies to date that blindness increases the language problems connected with autism; no study has actually tried to demonstrate that. One problem involved in such a study would be finding a clear working definition of autism in order to separate the two groups definitively.

Mental handicap has severe delaying effects on language acquisition which are increased in the presence of blindness (Elonen & Zwarensteyn 1964, Rogow 1972, Mori & Olive 1978). Elonen & Zwarensteyn suggest that some of the language problems are due to overprotection on the part of the parents, since they do not force the child to use language, but this can apply to any handicapped child. The presence of the two handicaps would seem to be the most important factor.

SUMMARY AND CONCLUSIONS

Blind children are clearly different in some aspects of their language development, for example in their acquisition of phonology, in the patterns of interaction in infancy, in the structure of the early lexicon. Some of these differences involve a delay compared with sighted children, others an alternative path. In some areas it is not clear where the endpoint of development lies, since there is not enough information about the competence of the blind adult; therefore it is difficult to evaluate the child's acquisition. Nevertheless the data we have show how flexible the language learning process can be and require our models of acquisition to be general enough to include these alternatives.

At this point in time there is not enough evidence from blind children to prove any of the theoretical issues discussed above, that is how experience determines language learning, to what extent language is steered by cognitive development, and whether input is a central factor in acquisition or only peripheral.

In discussing the relationship between language and experience, Landau & Gleitman (1985) argue from the data of Kelli that they cannot show that experience alone suffices as a basis for language acquisition, therefore it does not and we must assume innate principles. Although the analysis Landau & Gleitman carried out are extensive, the possible ways of describing experience are manifold, if not infinite, so that it is difficult to see how this issue can be proven. Certainly similar work needs to be carried out with sighted children to explore the experiential basis of language further.

In the areas of language and cognition and language and input, not enough work has been done with visually-handicapped, or with sighted, children to demonstrate a close causal relationship (see Atkinson 1982 for a discussion of the problems here). Even if there is agreement on the differences found between blind and sighted children, they are interpreted quite differently. Interpretations tend to follow a given theoretical standpoint rather than being seen as arguments for or against a point of view. Research would be more productive if this stopped being the case.

The delays or differences which have been found and are associated with blind children do not inevitably lead to any ultimate language handicap; there are blind children who develop language successfully, albeit by an alternative route. It is therefore clear that lack of vision is not *necessarily* the cause of a serious language problem. However, blindness can compound with other factors, most seriously with another handicap, to produce difficulties in acquisition. It is therefore essential to understand the role of vision to be able to create a more favourable environment for the language learning process.

10

Down's syndrome

J. A. Rondal

GENERAL FEATURES OF DOWN'S SYNDROME

Most authorities credit John Langdon Down (1866) with the first comprehensive description of a disorder he called mongoloid idiocy or *mongolism*. Influenced by Haeckel's recapitulation theory, Down thought that many symptoms present in the one idiotic subject he studied were typical of the Mongol ethnic group. This group was then considered to be at the lowest level of mankind together with blacks and women. Such views have of course been totally discredited, and the term Down's syndrome is now preferred over the racially perjorative label 'mongolism'. The chromosomic origin of Down's syndrome was established in 1961 (Lejeune et al 1959). Approximately one in 800 live newborns is diagnosed as suffering from Down's syndrome (Hook 1981). The condition represents about one third of the moderately to severely retarded population. The general prevalence of the disorder (not talking of the risk at birth which remains approximately the same) continues to mount because medical science can better ensure the survival of the high-risk Down's syndrome infant. About 20% die in the first two years of various defects, mostly present at birth, but the survivors live around 40 or 50 years. Conventional opinion is that Down's syndrome occurs in a ratio of about 60 males to 40 females (Gibson 1981).

Subtypes

Three subtypes of chromosome anomaly have been distinguished in Down's syndrome: (1) standard trisomy 21 (presence of three chromosomes 21 instead of two in all body cells) accounting for approximately 95% of cases; (2) translocations (identical to regular trisomy 21 in terms of the spread of extra-chromosomic material in the body cells but not in terms of the causal mechanisms involved) accounting for 4% of cases; and (3) mosaicisms (in which certain types of cells contain the extra chromosome but the remainder have the normal number of chromosomes) accounting for 1% of cases. It has not been clearly demonstrated that subtype of chromosome anomaly is a predictable source of variability in Down's syndrome, although the research on this topic to date has not considered language development.

Course of development

Developmental variability is an important characteristic of Down's syndrome. This is worth mentioning because there is a tendency in the public and sometimes also among educators to deal with people with Down's syndrome according to a set of stereotypes. Most babies with this syndrome present with muscular hypotonia, a function both of cerebellar immaturity and factors relating to skeletal-circulatory systems (Benda 1960), but this varies in degree. The primitive reflexes (palmar and planting grasp, Moro, automatic stepping, etc.; see Cowie 1970) are usually weak and prolonged over time, but there are exceptions. The median onset of walking unsupported is 24 months with a range from 14 to 66 months (Share & French 1974). The median age for the ability to draw or imitate a circle is 48 months with a range from 31 to 67 months (Share & French 1974), as compared with a median of 24 months for a normally-developing child. Most children with Down's syndrome start to talk between 2½ and 4 years, but a few produce word-like sequences of sounds as early as 18 months.

The literature on Down's syndrome is replete with confusing statistics on speech and language problems. Not taking into consideration older studies, one may mention Buddenhagen's assertion (1971) that after 5 years of age 10% of institutionalized children with Down's syndrome are fundamentally mute, and Johnson & Abelson's report (1969) that 81% of individuals with Down's syndrome are unable to communicate with others understandably. Schlanger & Gottsleben (1957) found 95% of their speaking Down's syndrome group had articulation problems, 45% stuttered and many presented voice disorders. A later survey by Blanchard (1964) produced similar results. Preus (1972) reported stuttering in 34% of his sample. Cabanas (1954), on the other hand, found cluttering symptoms but no active stuttering in his sample of Down's syndrome children. Other studies have obtained slightly and sometimes markedly different results (see Gibson 1981 for a review). The contradictions are partly a function of the considerable variability in speech and language within the syndrome and of sampling differences (age, sex, life in institutions or in families, hearing losses, etc.). Although often mentioned, the language variability in Down's syndrome has not been investigated systematically. It has been observed in group studies that variance often tends to increase as the subjects grow older (see Rondal 1978, Rondal et al 1980, Rondal & Lambert 1983). But besides preliminary observations of this kind nothing is known about the types of variation, the exact range of variation, and its possible causes.

NONLINGUISTIC DEFICIENCIES IN DOWN'S SYNDROME

Given the number and severity of the factors that militate against them, it is suprising that individuals with Down's syndrome develop language at all. Should we need another proof of the robustness of language development in the face of biological and psychological hazards, Down's syndrome subjects amply supply this proof. The list of their language-relevant intrinsic deficiencies seems almost limitless.

Mechanical problems in speech

Benda (1949) and Buddenhagen (1971) have detailed several of the peripheral pathological factors associated with defective speech in Down's syndrome. They include an under-sized mouth cavity, a protruding tongue, a larynx often located too high in the neck with a thickening of fibrotic mucosa, an edematous tongue that does not groove properly for the distinction between sounds like $/\int/$ and $/s/$ and is impaired in its motility, hypotonia of the speech muscles, including the tongue, lips, soft palate and respiratory muscles. Other authorities mention broad lips with irregular-ities in the shape including lateral inversions of the lower lip (Oster 1953), palatal anomalies (Spitzer et al 1961), fissured tongue (Blanchard 1964), excessive salivation, flabbiness of tongue and an undersized jaw (Strazzulla 1953), defective teeth (Kraus et al 1968), flat-tened nose, under-development of sinuses and nasal passages (Spitzer et al 1961), enlarged tonsils and adenoids, frequent respiratory infections, including inflammation of the pharynx, laryngitis and bronchitis producing coughing, hoarseness and reduced breathing capacity.

Voice quality deviations, such as breathi-ness and roughness, have been described (Montague & Hollien 1973, 1974). There is still disagreement concerning voice fundamental frequency in Down's syndrome. Some reports (e.g. Weinberg & Zlatin 1970) suggest a higher fundamental frequency in preschool children with the standard trisomy variety of the syndrome. Other reports find no difference when control is exercised for factors like 'purity' of karyotype, verbal task (spontaneous versus elicited speech), and degree of close-ness in matching control subjects (see Montague & Hollien 1974).

Sensory deficits

Other organic factors influencing communi-cation include auditory and visual defects. Hearing loss is unusually common in Down's syndrome, even compared to other categories of mental retardation. In Rigrodsky et al's report (1961), hearing impairment was said to affect 60% of the Down's syndrome sample. The loss was mainly in the mild to moderate range with half perceptive, half 'mixed' and conductive impairment. Other studies report lower rates of hearing loss and a predomi-nance of conductive losses over perceptive or mixed ones (e.g. Clausen 1968, Colton 1973). A major cause of hearing impairment in this population is otitis media (Balkany 1980), but there are also otologic abnormalities associ-ated with the syndrome such as malformations of the middle ear ossicles and shortened cochlear spirals. Differences in brainstem neural structures including reduced weight and incomplete myelination may also affect transmission of the auditory signal along the VIIIth cranial nerve (Crome & Stern 1967).

Ocular defects that impair visual function in Down's syndrome include strabismus, myopia, nystagmus and lens opacities (MacGillivray 1968). Watering eyes, conjunctivitis and respir-atory infections may also appreciably reduce visual efficiency.

Cognitive factors

Goddard (1916) claimed that the ultimate mental capacity of a Down's syndrome indi-vidual was almost always that of a 4-year-old normal child. Subsequent research has confirmed that a mental age of 4 to 5 years is the realistic upper limit of mental growth for the majority of individuals with Down's syndrome. 12 to 15 years of age seems to be the time when intellectual maturation is complete.

Among the usually cited cognitive limi-tations and deficits of Down's syndrome indi-viduals are short attention span, slow reaction time, deficiency in auditory-vocal processing, limitation of short-term memory (varying with different aspects of sensory information), reduced perceptual discrimination and gener-alization capability, a deficiency of symboliztion facility (particularly with non-concrete symbols) and some inherent inability to adopt an abstract attitude (O'Connor & Hermelin 1961, 1963).

Arousal-motivational variables

Several authors (e.g. Wesner 1972) have hypothesized that arousal states are generally deficient in Down's syndrome, and that they cannot be sustained without special environmental inducements. Depressed arousal and low reactivity may lead to a failure of sensory perception in some situations. The hypothesis that low arousal may adversely affect mental development in Down's syndrome remains speculative, but provides an interesting adjunct to explanations purely in terms of cognitive processes (Zigler 1966, Gibson 1981).

LANGUAGE ACQUISITION

A number of mechanical, cognitive and arousal-motivational variables combine to render psychological development and learning difficult for individuals with Down's syndrome, particularly in speech and language areas. These factors have been presented separately in the preceding section, but there is little doubt that they interact in various ways, although the precise mechanisms are not yet understood. Three additional general characteristics of development in Down's syndrome should be mentioned. The first two are a progressive improvement of (a) muscle tone hypotonia and (b) sensory efficiency in later years. Unfortunately, as these improvements take place, they are counteracted by an acceleration in central neuropathological processes.

In order to appreciate the negative effects of Down's syndrome on speech and language it is necessary to describe the acquisition process in more detail. In what follows, data collected over the last 20 years are briefly summarized according to five categories: phonetics and phonology, lexicon, semantic structures, morpho-syntax and pragmatics.

Phonetics and phonology

Investigators have attempted to classify those types of sounds heard in babbling in terms of the sound system of the mother's language. Such studies have found similar results in Down's syndrome and nonretarded infants. Similar developmental sequences and timing appear to hold for the two groups of children. Front and central vowels like $/i/$, $/ə/$, $/a/$, appear first, then back vowels like $/ɑ/$, $/ɔ/,/ʊ/$. For the stop-like sounds, up to approximately 6 months, velar sounds like $/k/$ and $/g/$ tend to dominate. Velars then decrease in frequency of production and alveolar stops $/t/$, $/d/$ and nasal $/n/$ become dominant. Labial stops $/p/$, $/b/$ and nasal $/m/$ remain intermediate in frequency throughout the first 12 months. Reduplicated babbling begins around 8 months (range 6–10 months) in normally developing as well as in Down's syndrome infants (Smith 1977).

Phonological development is slow and difficult in Down's syndrome for a number of reasons, but the overall sequence appears to parallel the development in normal children (e.g. Menn 1985). Vowels, semivowels, nasal and stop consonants are produced and mastered first. Fricatives $/f/$, $/θ/$, $/s/$, $/ʃ/$, $/v/$, $/ð/$, $/z/$, and $/ʒ/$ are more difficult to articulate and take much longer to be fully mastered (if they are). Intelligibility of speech remains low in most individuals with Down's syndrome (Ryan 1975, Rondal 1978). The errors they make, however, appear to be of the same type as those observed in the phonological development of nonretarded children, mainly, feature changes, cluster reductions, and assimilations (Smith 1977). Dodd (1976b), however, has argued that Down's syndrome children have different problems with phonology from other severely subnormal children, attributing this to a disorder in motor planning (see Frith & Frith 1974 on this point).

It used to be considered that tongue size was a contributing factor to the speech problems of Down's syndrome people (Zisk & Bialer 1967). However, a recent pre- and post-operative evaluation by Parsons et al (1987) of

18 children with Down's syndrome suggests that tongue-reduction surgery has no effect on the articulation of sounds.

Lexicon

The onset of meaningful speech (one-word utterances) is delayed by approximately twelve months in Down's syndrome (first words usually around 24 months) (Fisher et al 1964, Share 1975). At this time the proportion of identifiable meaningful speech in the vocal productions of most Down's syndrome children is lower than 5% (Smith 1977). This figure slowly increases with age up to around 4 years when more meaningful productions can be recorded. At corresponding mental ages, Down's syndrome and normal children seem to be able to define, understand and use a similar number of words (Mein & O'Connor 1960, Bartel et al 1973). Word-association tasks also yield similar results for Down's syndrome and mental-age matched normal children (Sersen et al 1970). Also see Rondal (1975) for a review of this literature.

Semantic structures

When they begin to combine two and three words within the same utterance (usually around 4 to 5 years of age), children with Down's syndrome appear to express the same range of relational meanings as are reported in studies of normal language acquisition (e.g. Brown 1973). Examples of semantic relations expressed are *notice* or *existence, disappearance, recurrence, attribution, possession, location, agent-action, action-patient,* and finally *agent-action-patient* (Rondal 1978, Layton & Sharifi 1979). Down's syndrome children also appear to correctly understand the same set of relational meanings when they are expressed in the speech addressed to them (Duchan & Erickson 1976).

Morphology and syntax

The grammatical organization of the verbal productions of individuals with Down's syndrome remains deficient despite some progress being made with increasing age as indicated by the progressive lengthening of mean length of utterance (MLU : a reliable and valid index of early productive grammatical organization, see Rondal et al 1987). Table 10.1 summarizes MLU data obtained by Rondal and collaborators through spontaneous speech analyses in free-play and free-conversation conditions. These data appear to show that grammatical complexity continues to increase beyond adolescence in Down's syndrome.

However, several remarks are in order regarding the data in Table 10.1. Firstly, they are cross-sectional data used to address a longitudinal problem and are therefore

Table 10.1 MLU in morphemes from spontaneous speech in dyadic free-play and conversation conditions for Down's syndrome and nonretarded (NR) subjects

source	N subjs	age Down's		NR		MLU Down's		NR		upper bound[1] Down's	NR
		mean	(s. d.)	mean	(s. d.)	mean	(s. d.)	mean	(s.d.)	mean	mean
Rondal (1978)	14	4;1	(0;9)	1;11	(0;2)	1.26	(0.23)	1.27	(0.22)	2.86	3.57
	14	6;6	(2;1)	2;3	(0;2)	1.94	(0.19)	1.96	(0.21)	6.14	6.29
	14	9;9	(1;9)	2;6	(0;3)	2.87	(0.14)	2.88	(0.19)	11.00	10.57
Rondal et al (1980)	19	11;6	(1;8)			3.40	(0.95)				
Rondal & Lambert (1983)	12	26;6	(4;5)			5.98	(2.62)				

[1]number of morphemes in longest utterance

subject to criticism. Secondly, Rondal's study (1978) was conducted with American-English speaking children, Rondal et al's study (1980) and Rondal & Lambert's study (1983) had French-speaking Belgian subjects. No metric exists at this time for relating MLU computed on different languages (even for such lexically and grammatically close languages as English and French). Thirdly, the MLU data from the American-speaking children were obtained through free-play interactive sessions at home with the mothers. The MLU data in the two French studies were obtained in dyadic free-conversation situations between the retarded adolescent or adult and a familiar nonretarded adult either at school (for the adolescents) or in an occupational facility (for the adults). Fourthly, as indicated in Table, 10.1, the adult data exhibit such large interindividual variability that the mean MLU may be misleading as a summary index for this group of subjects. It is possible that the differences in the MLU data in three studies reflect only dissimilarities between the studies and high interindividual variability. However, the hypothesis of a moderate but steady MLU growth between early adolescence and adulthood in at least some Down's syndrome individuals cannot be ruled out. Longitudinal research is needed to clarify this question. It might prove Lenneberg's contention wrong (see Lenneberg 1967, and Lenneberg et al 1962) that Down's syndrome subjects inevitably reach a plateau in language development after puberty. See Rondal (1985a) for a discussion of Lenneberg's hypothesis as it is applied to mentally handicapped subjects.

Whether or not the hypothesis of MLU growth with increasing age is warranted, the spontaneous combinatorial language of Down's syndrome individuals remains largely telegraphic. It is characterized by a reduced use of the so-called function words (prepositions, auxiliaries, copula, pronouns, conjunctions). When third person pronouns are used, for instance, the lack of mastery over cohesive discourse devices like anaphora may render the referring expression somewhat opaque to the conversational partner (for instance, 'He

took the ball and then the other guy came, he said something; he was angry, you know'). Such a state of affairs often persists into the adult years, as conversational data gathered by Rondal & Lambert (1983) with French-speaking Down's syndrome adults living in the community indicate. Only half of the utterances recorded in this study were sentences. When the verb was expressed, it had the correct inflection only half of the time. The tense most often used was the present indicative followed by the past (perfect), even in clearly narrative contexts. On the whole there was less than one article per utterance (mean proportion per utterance = 0.44), and slightly over one inflection marking gender or number in two utterances (mean proportion per utterance = 0.56).

Pragmatics

Although limited in form, the language of Down's syndrome individuals is not devoid of communicative value as the analysis by Rondal & Lambert (1983) further demonstrates. Conversational topics are dealt with in such a way as to allow for the necessary continuity in the exchange between interlocutors. The major illocutionary types of sentences allowed by the grammar are used (i.e. declaratives, imperatives and questions).

Younger Down's syndrome subjects already make use of a variety of illocutionary devices in relating verbally to the interlocutor as shown in the data supplied in Table 10.2. These data were obtained in free-play interactions at home with the mothers. In such situations, mothers (of retarded as well as of normally developing children) are known to lead the interaction, asking questions and giving orders much more often than the children.

Strictly speaking the classification in Table 10.2 uses grammatical as well as illocutionary criteria. The three subtypes of questions shown in Table 10.2 have approximately the same illocutionary force (i.e. requesting information from the interlocutor as opposed to giving orders or to expressing declarations).

Table 10.2 Classification of utterances by normal and retarded children at three MLU levels in verbal exchanges with their mothers

	Down's syndrome (aged 3 to 12 years)			nonretarded (aged 20 to 32 months)		
MLU range	1.00–1.50	1.75–2.25	2.50–3.00	1.00–1.50	1.75–2.25	2.50–3.00
% full sentences	10	23	42	7	26	44
utterance type:						
% declarative	2	14	31	4	18	28
% imperative	2	3	5	2	4	7
% yes/no question by intonation	0	0	1	1	1	2
% reversed yes/no question	0	0	0	0	0	1
% WH-questions	5	5	4	0	2	5

They differ, however, in the grammatical way used to express the illocutionary force to the interlocutor. Intonation yes-no questions are those yes-no questions formulated in a declarative form but with a raising intonation (e.g. *You had breakfast?*). Reversed yes-no questions signal their question status by reversing the usual subject verb order in the sentence (e.g. *Have you had breakfast?*). WH-questions contain interrogative words (e.g. *when, where,* who, etc.) specifying the type of information that is requested from the interlocutor (e.g. *Who did you have breakfast with?*).

COGNITIVE BASIS FOR LANGUAGE ACQUISITION

From what precedes, keeping in mind the interindividual variability within the syndrome, one could propose a general summary of language in Down's syndrome including the following major points:
1. Problems with speech production (voice problems, hypotonia, phonological feature changes, cluster reductions, phoneme assimilation)
2. Lexicon reduced but correctly used and understood
3. Short telegraphic utterances with limited morpho-syntactical elaboration
4. Language informative and not devoid of illocutionary force.
We must consider these achievements in face of the numerous and severe deficiencies identified in the general description of the syndrome, and particularly in view of the drastic cognitive limitations known to affect people with Down's syndrome. The most obvious conclusion is that the mechanical problems listed do not prevent functional speech even if they delay and limit development to a serious extent. Quite obviously too, the cognitive limitations of Down's syndrome do not prevent a modest but real language development. We need to go beyond such obvious relationships and try to relate more specific aspects of language and cognition. Relevant to our discussion is Gibson's (1966, 1981) psychometric account of the relationship between mental age and chronological age in Down's syndrome. Examining a large number of data and plotting the relation of chronological age to mental age for all cases, Gibson arrives at a schematic representation of the staging of mental growth for the syndrome. He distinguishes three mental-age growth periods followed by a plateau for the first two and by a gradual decline for the third. Plateau one is reached between 4 and 6 years of age. It is located at a mental-age level of approximately 18 months. Plateau two is reached between 8 and 11 years of age and corresponds to a mental age of approximately 30 months. Lastly, plateau three (not attained by all individuals) is reached between 12 and 17 years of age. It corresponds to a mental age of approximately 48 months.

Using Rondal's data (1978) as reference points (see Table 10.1), it can be suggested that at a mental age of around 30 months, children with Down's syndrome have achieved a level of language development corresponding approximately to MLU 3.00 (i.e. the dividing line between revised Brown's stages III and early IV, see Miller & Chapman 1981). They appear to develop language in accordance with what would be predicted from general cognitive capability as assessed by the mental age index. Their language characteristics parallel rather well the characteristics of normal children's language at the same mental age. This correspondence can be considered as supportive of a cognitive explanation of the general process of language acquisition (see Bohannon 1985, for example, for a recent exposition of the basic tenets of this position). One central assumption of this theory is that basic linguistic developments must derive from general changes in (non-linguistic) cognition (Bates & Snyder in press). The sequence of cognitive development may be viewed as determining the sequence of language development. Consequently, at no point could language development be ahead of relevant cognitive development. Such a conception, it should be noted, can have true explanatory status only to the extent that the cognitive prerequisites for linguistic development are independently identified and proven to be causally involved. Over the years, a number of cognitive factors (several of them related to the Piagetian approach in cognitive development) have been postulated as being necessary conditions for general linguistic acquisitions. But none so far has been proven to be so. A world of correlational evidence exists on this point but the usual limitations of this type of data as indicators of causal relationships are well known.

A good case in point in the mental retardation literature is the study by Kahn (1975). He showed that retarded children at Piaget's sensorimotor intellectual stages 5 and 6 significantly increased their productive lexical repertoire and started combining words within the same utterance. From this, the hypothesis was made that sensorimotor stages 5 and 6 are prerequisites for early combinatorial language development. This is possible. No causal relation has been documented so far, however. As Curtiss (1981b) and others (e.g. Newport et al 1977) have pointed out, age-related correlations and co-developments frequently occur. The growth of collar and other bones in children is positively correlated over age with the size of their vocabularies and MLU. Such co-occurring developments are rarely assumed to be causally related. In the case of Piaget's sensorimotor stages 5 and 6, and combinatorial language development, several alternative hypotheses could be considered, and they should be until a clear causal relation is worked out.

Thus, in the language acquisition of mentally retarded children as well as in that of normally developing children, the broad assertion that cognitive development determines language development remains virtually untested at this time. Of interest, however, is the fact that very little data has been found to clearly contradict the cognitive hypothesis (Bates & Snyder in press) (but see Ch. 11). Our above analysis of the MLU data in Down's syndrome and normal children also supports the cognitive expectations.

DELAY-DIFFERENCE ISSUE REVISITED

A question often asked is whether language development in mentally handicapped subjects is literally delayed or whether it is truly different from language development in nonretarded children. This question was first dealt with by Yoder & Miller (1972). From their review of the literature up to that time, they concluded that the 'delay answer' was likely to be the correct one. As will be shown, Yoder and Miller's conclusion now seems questionable. I will further argue that the delay hypothesis may be responsible for the limited success encountered by current remedial language programs.

According to the delay point of view, mentally retarded individuals developing language pass through the same sequence of stages and substages as those observed in nonretarded children. The only difference is that their linguistic development takes more time and eventually it is not complete. In other words, language in mentally deficient subjects is comparable to language in younger normal children. The variation between retarded and normal language development is only quantitative. In contrast, the difference point of view states that language acquisition in mentally retarded individuals does not follow the same developmental path as in nonretarded subjects. The variation between retarded and nonretarded subjects is truly a qualitative one. Conceptual and methodological problems render the interpretation of the data gathered on the delay-difference issue difficult.

Conceptually, there is no neat opposition between the delay and difference positions as defined in the literature. Any development may be delayed and different at the same time or delayed because different, or different because delayed. Language is not a unitary phenomenon. Some aspects of the acquisition of the linguistic system could conceivably be described as being delayed in the sense defined above, whereas other aspects might be more appropriately thought of as exemplifying differences with respect to normal development. Let us take a simplified example. Suppose a 10-year-old child with Down's syndrome is at a 2-year-old level for speech articulation, 3-year-old-level for lexicon and semantic development, 3-year-old-level for syntax, and 4-year-old-level for pragmatics. Each one general component of his language could be said to be delayed. On the whole, however, this child would not be comparable to any younger normal one. His linguistic system would be truly different.

The delay-difference issue presents a number of problems. First, the delay position predicts that language development in the retarded will come to a stop before reaching normal adult levels. No study to date has set criteria for distinguishing between incomplete and different developments. We may be unable in practice to specify whether some of the differences observed between normal and retarded children in language development should be interpreted as evidence for a difference position or if they attest to an arrested development at an earlier but normal stage. Second, a proper answer (if possible) to the delay-difference question should be based on longitudinal data. The studies that have addressed the issue up to now are all cross-sectional (see Rondal 1985b, for a review and discussion of this literature). Third, the delay-difference issue really bears on processes of language development and not so much or not at all on language products. Conceivably, products of language acquisition can be explained by a number of candidate processes or interactions of processes. The literature on language development in mentally handicapped children mainly refers to products. This is no surprise for, at the present time, the processes responsible for first language acquisition in the normal child are little understood, alas for the retarded. Fourth, the literature on the delay-difference issue, and more generally the literature on language acquisition in the retarded child, tend to adopt the simple-minded view that there is one single way to language mastery. Recent emphasis on individual differences in early lexical development and word combinations in the normal child (e.g. Goldfield & Snow 1985) makes this assumption somewhat incautious. If there are several routes or sub-routes equally conducive to language acquisition, this certainly will make it more difficult to define delays and/or differences in the language acquisition of retarded children.

Methodologically, several problems exist that hinder the interpretation of the empirical data gathered in comparing language of mentally retarded and nonretarded individuals. Three types of matching procedures have been used:

Matching on the basis of chronological age

Studies using a chronological age match usually reveal large gaps between retarded and normal children. These studies cannot answer the delay-difference question except where the data obtained with the retarded can also be compared with corresponding data from younger normal children.

Matching on the basis of mental age

Matching children for mental age should guarantee that they function cognitively at similar levels. This assumption has been questioned. It has been argued (e.g. Baumeister 1967) that as there is no one-to-one correspondence between IQ scores and the response patterns to the test items, the same mental age can be obtained in various ways. This is certainly true but does not mean that mental-age matched children will not function cognitively at close or corresponding levels.

Matching for level of language development

Another strategy is to match normal and retarded children for linguistic level (for example, using mean length of utterance— MLU—as the criterion variable) and look at other characteristics of the language used. If the language produced by the retarded and the normal children matched on one aspect of language can be characterized in the same way, this is considered to be supportive of a delay position. A particular feature of this procedure is that both the criterion and the dependent variables pertain to the linguistic domain. On the negative side, it is not clear which and how many comparisons within the linguistic domain should be performed in order to be reasonably sure that the organization sustaining the language function in the retarded and the normal children is or is not similar.

The research data relevant to the delay-difference question have been reviewed by Rondal (1985b), and will not be summarized here. Suffice it to say that in several general respects basic aspects of language development in mentally retarded (including Down's syndrome) children seem to proceed according to what is known of language development in

normal children. Babbling and phonological development proceed in the expected general order. Lexical development, early morpho-syntactic development and basic pragmatic acquisition also proceed according to the sequences known in normal children. However, when one takes a more in-depth look into the matter, numerous differences appear between retarded and mental age or language-level-matched normal children that no longer allow for a simple delay interpretation. In other words, the more general and abstract the categories of analysis, the more the retarded child looks like a younger normal one in terms of linguistic evolution. More specific analytical patterns, however, will distinguish the retarded from the nonretarded child.

Further, a recent study by Leifer & Lewis (1984) using a multiple-matching procedure demonstrates the existence of asynchronies in the acquisition of various components of the language system in retarded children. These authors have compared retarded and non-retarded children's verbal and nonverbal behaviours in response to questions by the mother. The subjects formed three groups. The first group included nonretarded children aged 18 to 23 months who were at the one-word stage. The second group consisted of retarded children (including Down's syndrome children) matched with the nonretarded group for chronological age. These children were not producing language yet. The third group included retarded children matched with the nonretarded group for MLU. These retarded children were around 4 years old. The children's responses were coded as appropriate or inappropriate according to whether or not they successfully matched the pragmatic intent of mothers' questions. Type-token ratio and number of intelligible lexical productions were also computed from children's responses. Retarded children showed immature response performance by comparison with chronological age-matched nonretarded peers. When matched for language level, however, retarded children demonstrated significantly greater response abilities than nonretarded children on all question types. No significant differences were found in the vocabulary measures for the nonretarded and the retarded children at the same MLU level. Leifer & Lewis' data (1984) indicate that the synchrony of syntactic and lexical developments, on the one hand, and the acquisition of conversational skills (question-answer abilities), on the other hand, may vary in retarded and nonretarded children.

The situation may even be more damaging for a strict delay position when individual patterns in retarded children are taken into account. Miller et al (1981) analyzed clinical data gathered on mentally retarded children including Down's syndrome children up to 7 years. They assessed cognitive functioning with Uzgiris-Hunt's version of Piaget's sensori-motor tasks as well as other Piagetian tasks involving preoperational intellectual functioning. Syntactic comprehension was assessed through tasks requiring compliance with instructions, answers to WH-questions and the Miller-Yoder test of grammatical comprehension. The Peabody Picture Vocabulary test was also administered. Free-speech samples were analyzed to assess production level (MLU, frequency of use of various morpho-syntactic structures). Each language characteristic (syntactic comprehension, semantic comprehension, morpho-syntactic production) was judged to be either consistent with, advanced or delayed relative to each child's cognitive level. Comparative data were available from a large group of normally developing children. Three frequent patterns emerged: (1) a production-only-delayed pattern (24% of the retarded versus 2.5% of the nonretarded subjects) in which both syntax and vocabulary comprehension were within expected range but production was delayed relative to expectation based on cognitive level; (2) a delayed-comprehension-and-production pattern (17% of the retarded children and no nonretarded children) in which all language measures were delayed relative to cognitive level; (3) a 'flat pattern' in which all three linguistic dimensions were within the expected range for cognitive level. 36% of the retarded children and most of the

nonretarded children fell into this category. A few additional and less frequent patterns accounted for the remaining subjects in the sample. As confirmed by Miller et al's study (1981), mentally retarded children are heterogeneous with respect to the development of language skills. The existence of several patterns of relation between cognitive level and aspects of language functioning seems to rule out the view of language acquisition in the retarded as a slower version of normal development.

The emerging picture is complex. It is becoming increasingly clear that the delay position, while not being false, captures only the most trivial aspects of the developmental language problem in the retarded child including the Down's syndrome child. Language acquisition in the retarded is not a slow-motion picture of the same development in normal children. Differences exist in several aspects of language as the acquisition process unfolds in retarded and nonretarded children. In view of the above, it should be suggested that the delay-difference framework is not appropriate for characterizing language development in the retarded. A strict delay-difference dichotomy may even be misleading.

Research should be intensified on those aspects of language development in the retarded child that differ most from the normal course. Homogeneous samples of retarded children should be used. Down's syndrome children, and even etiological subtypes of Down's syndrome children, could prove interesting for this purpose. Research should also switch from a concentration on language products to an emphasis on processes.

Intervention and stimulation programs developed over the last twenty years for Down's syndrome and other mentally retarded children have met with mixed success (see Gibson 1981, and Cunningham 1986 for recent reviews and evaluations). Among the various aspects of psychological development treated in these programs, language is regularly found to give fairly unimpressive results. It might be possible of course that language development in many Down's syndrome individuals simply cannot be improved in any significant way beyond spontaneous evolution.

But it is also possible that as most of our intervention tools and strategies were not designed to address the differential aspects of language acquisition in the retarded (these not being recognized or not being known), they are not as efficient as they could have been (see Rondal in press, for a further discussion of this point). It may be time for a change of strategy.

SUMMARY AND CONCLUSIONS

Down's syndrome individuals present numerous intrinsic deficiencies that seriously complicate the process of language acquisition. But they do develop some functional language, testifying to the robustness of basic language acquisition. The amount of language that is acquired by Down's syndrome subjects is in general proportion to their cognitive capabilities. In the present state of knowledge, it could be said that language development in Down's syndrome is compatible with the hypothesis of a gradual unfolding of linguistic propensities allowed by spared cognitive capabilities. Certainly, despite many drastic limitations, most children with Down's syndrome acquire some basic language that corresponds to the fundamental grammatical organization of their native language. Preliminary analysis of interindividual variability in the language of Down's syndrome children indicates that this variability is indeed larger than that existing in normally developing children at corresponding levels of language development. This variability does increase

from childhood to adulthood although comparative data with normal subjects are not available for the adult age range. Although there are important interindividual differences in Down's syndrome, it is nevertheless possible to specify language characteristics holding true for the syndrome. Additional work has to be conducted in order to establish to what extent such a description would be specific for Down's syndrome in comparison with other etiological categories of moderate and severe mental retardation and whether the etiological subtypes of Down's syndrome correspond to specific subsyndromic sets of language characteristics. My hunch is that a search for subsyndromic language characteristics is not likely to succeed. What exists in all probability is a series of language dimensions along which children vary in accordance with their degree of deficiency in a number of nonlinguistic aspects, with only limited convergence within etiological subtypes.

The usual answer to the delay-difference issue so far has been 'delay'. While not being overtly false, as basic language in Down's syndrome seems to develop according to normal sequences, the delay answer is not appropriate and can be misleading if taken literally. Recent and more analytical work uncovers an increasing number of differences between normal and Down's syndrome patterns of language development, particularly beyond early language production. Abandoning the delay-difference dichotomy in favour of analyzing developmental facts for their own sake may be more productive for furthering research in the language acquisition process of mentally retarded children and for designing more efficient and hard-nosed language remediation programs.

11

Dissociation between language and cognitive functions in Williams syndrome

U. Bellugi, S. Marks, A. Bihrle and H. Sabo

INTRODUCTION

The general objective of our research is to understand the brain mechanisms that underlie language and cognition. Mental retardation has been generally considered as representing a uniform impairment in all domains of cognitive functioning. Williams syndrome, a rare metabolic disorder, appears to be a dramatic exception to this broad generalization. Our pilot studies suggest that this intriguing disorder results in a form of mental retardation characterized by a rare fractionation of higher cortical functions: linguistic functioning is selectively preserved in the face of severe cognitive deficits. These studies of Williams syndrome should provide new insight into the relationships between domains of higher cortical functioning and their underlying neural substrate.

It is well known that specific language deficits can exist without an accompanying cognitive deficit. However, the opposite finding in which language outstrips other cognitive deficits is rarely documented. According to Piaget, language develops at the end of the sensorimotor period and directly reflects emerging symbolic abilities. Even stronger versions of such a stance suggest that certain cognitive underpinnings are, in fact, prerequisites to language development. Children who show a facility with linguistic structure despite a lack of hypothetically associated cognitive substrates have been hard to find. Curtiss and Yamada (1981) reported on one such case, noting that the difficulty of finding such children may be influenced by the fact that because fluency in speech is not generally associated with mental retardation, these children tend to be labelled as emotionally or behaviourally rather than cognitively deficient.

We report here on not one child or isolated cases but on a group of adolescent subjects with Williams syndrome whose knowledge of linguistic structure appears almost to outstrip other cognitive abilities. Our research suggests that this disorder may differentially affect language and cognitive development in highly specific ways. The children appear to be functioning as a group at the preoperational stage of cognitive development in terms of their drawing, copying, nesting, seriation, conservation and classificatory skills. Yet their mastery of linguistic structure exceeds what would be predicted in light of their depressed level of cognitive functioning. These cases represent striking divergencies from normal development, and provide a rare opportunity to investigate the interrelationship and separability of language and other aspects of mental development in the normal child. Furthermore, in the long run, these studies may provide important clues to brain and behaviour relationships.

Pathology of Williams syndrome

Williams syndrome was identified following a clinical study by J. C. P. Williams and his colleagues who described four patients with supravalvular aortic stenosis (a narrowing of the aorta) in association with mental retardation and a peculiar facial appearance (Williams et al 1961). In 1963, Black & Bonham-Carter associated the characteristic facial appearance of these children with 'Infantile hypercalcemia' (as the syndrome is known in Great Britain). A recent study has shown that

Williams syndrome subjects have abnormalities in both calcium and calcitonin metabolism (Culler et al 1985), providing an endocrine marker for the syndrome. Clinical features of Williams syndrome include a failure to thrive in the first year of life, mental retardation, supravalvular aortic stenosis and an 'elfin-like' facial appearance consisting of a stellate (star-like) pattern in the iris, medial eyebrow flare (eyebrow hair growth pattern toward nose), depressed nasal bridge with anteverted nares (upturned nose), and thick lips with an open mouth posture (Jones & Smith 1975). In addition, the children are said to share certain personality characteristics and are described as friendly, outgoing, and loquacious (Bennett et al 1978).

Previous studies of Williams syndrome

Studies of the behavioural characteristics of Williams syndrome children are only recently beginning to appear. In one of the earliest papers, Von Armin & Engel (1964) provided case studies of four patients with Williams syndrome, summarizing the salient psychological features as 'as unusual command of language combined with an unexpectedly polite, open, and gentle manner.' Other recent papers include Arnold & Yule (1985), Bennett et al (1978), Kataria et al (1984), Meyerson & Frank (1987) and Udwin et al (1986); these reports present conflicting results regarding patterns of abilities and disabilities.

Our current program with Williams syndrome children is designed to provide a complete neuropsychological profile associated with the syndrome in studies ranging from neuropsychological to neurobiological. We include behavioural studies (language and other cognitive abilities), a neurological evaluation, sensory and motor studies, studies of brain functioning (using electrophysiological techniques), studies of brain structure (using Magnetic Resonance Imaging), and studies of the neurobiological basis of the syndrome (using techniques from molecular biology). In this chapter we report on the language and cognitive functions of the first three adolescent children studied with respect to the separation of linguistic abilities and other cognitive functions that appears to be characteristic of the neuropsychological make-up of older Williams syndrome individuals. The intensive study of subjects with Williams syndrome may in the long run provide a remarkable opportunity to clarify the connections and interdependencies between language and other cognitive functions.

We began our investigation of Williams syndrome with three adolescents—Van (age 11), Crystal (age 15) and Ben (age 16)—chosen because they had already attained major language and motor milestones. The children had been diagnosed by dysmorphologists as having Williams syndrome based on the criteria described by Jones & Smith (1975), and were enrolled in special education classes for the mentally retarded. Their full-scale IQ scores on traditional intelligence tests (e.g. the Wechsler Intelligence Test for Children—Revised) were: Van, 50; Crystal, 49; and Ben, 54.

The Williams syndrome children are mentally retarded, as defined by the American Association of Mental Deficiency: 'Mental retardation refers to significantly subaverage general intellectual functioning existing concurrently with deficits in adaptive behaviour, and manifested during the development period.' The Williams syndrome children's deficits in adaptive behaviour are pervasive and their inability to lead independent lives as adults attests to this disability. Even as adolescents they require constant supervision; they are in classrooms for the mentally retarded, they have difficulty dressing themselves, remembering routines, handling money, and in functioning independently in life, quite unlike their normal younger siblings.

COGNITIVE FUNCTIONING

Although the specific cognitive mechanisms underlying language acquisition remain unknown, one model of language acquisition asserts that language reflects cognitive growth as viewed from a Piagetian framework. In order to test the hypothesis that components of language functioning are achieved in Williams syndrome in the absence of the purported cognitive underpinnings, we selected tests that are critical determinants of a child's placement in either the sensorimotor, preoperational, or concrete operational stage of cognitive development as outlined in Piagetian theory. The three adolescent Williams syndrome children in our studies are still functioning at some phase within the preoperational stage of cognitive development. They were uniformly unable to perform tasks reflecting the attainment of concrete operations, skills which are easily mastered by normal children by the ages of 7 to 8 years. We present here illustrations of two specific cognitive abilities (seriation and conservation) that are each purported to underlie a particular aspect of linguistic functioning.

Seriation

Our task, adapted from Piaget & Inhelder (1959) and Inhelder & Piaget (1964), consists of two conditions. The subject is shown a line drawing of bottles arranged from smallest to largest, then presented with eight rods of different lengths and told to 'put them in order, just like the bottles.' The child's task is to arrange the rods from smallest to largest. If successful, the child is then asked to insert two additional rods where they belong in the array. The Williams syndrome children were unable to seriate or insert. They arranged the rods in a somewhat random array, focussing on only two sticks at a time. The seriation task is particularly important to our line of research because various authors (e.g. Shaffer & Ehri 1980) have proposed a specific relationship between seriation and certain language milestones—specifically, the comprehension of comparative and equative relational expressions.

Conservation

The attainment of concrete operations is

generally equated with success on various tasks of conservation—which means that the child recognizes that certain properties, such as substance, weight, volume, or number, remain unchanged in the face of certain perceptual transformations. The ability to manipulate internal representations, the hallmark of the concrete operational stage, is the critical foundation for all higher level cognitive abilities and has important ramifications for adaptive functioning in the real world. Further, it has been proposed that conservation, particularly reversibility and transitivity, is an important prerequisite to the development of specific linguistic structures, including the comprehension and production of passives (Beilin 1975) and the acquisition of comparative constructions (Sinclair-deZwart 1967). In order to examine whether the children have achieved the Piagetian concept of conservation we administered The Concept Assessment Kit (Goldschmid & Bentler 1968). In this task, the children are required to make judgments regarding conservation in the following domains: two-dimensional space; number, substance, continuous quantity, and discontinuous quantity; and weight. Although conservation is attained by most 7- and 8-year-old children easily, the Williams syndrome children, regardless of age, are uniformly unable to deal with any aspect of this task.

The children demonstrated deviant performance in a number of cognitive realms. In separate studies, we focussed on spatial cognition because this is one aspect of cognition that is the polar opposite of language, both in terms of the processing operations that are brought into play and in terms of one of the most basic divisions in the functional operations of the brain. Particularly interesting were the peaks and valleys of abilities seen in the three Williams syndrome subjects on visuospatial tasks. On tasks of drawing, spatial orientation, spatial transformations, spatial arrangements, and scores of all three children were uniformly depressed. In a task that involved copying geometric figures, the adolescent Williams syndrome children scored at the level of normal 5-year-olds. In general,

the children were able to handle straight lines and circles, but were unable to represent any of the more complex shapes. On a task requiring the arrangement of blocks in a specific design (the Block Design subtest of the WISC-R), in which the items are arranged in increasing difficulty, the children were unable to pass even the first, simplest item. Furthermore, the children show topographic disorientation, spatial memory deficits and visuoconstructive impairments. And yet in a task that assessed the capacity to recognize and discriminate unfamiliar faces in different orientations (Benton et al 1978), the three Williams syndrome children were surprisingly quick and accurate, scoring above their mental ages and in the normal range for adults (Bellugi et al in press). We hypothesize that this unusual pattern of peaks and valleys—visuospatial deficit but sparing of abilities to recognize and discriminate unfamiliar faces—may turn out to be a signature part of the unique profile of Williams syndrome.

DISSOCIATION BETWEEN LANGUAGE AND VISUOSPATIAL FUNCTIONS

Our preliminary research with a few Williams syndrome subjects points to a profile in which striking dissociations exist between expressive language and spatial cognitive functions (Bellugi et al in press). Examples of the children's impaired drawing skills can be seen in Figure 11.1. We asked each child to draw an elephant and a bicycle freehand. The examiner added labels to the drawings based on the children's remarks as they drew. The examiner noted that each child verbalized before and during the task, as if 'talking themselves through the drawing.' In the drawings, parts of a bicycle are represented and labelled (i.e. wheels, handlebars, pedals, seat, basket, wheel protectors, crankcase and chain), and the children could explain the parts as well as label them ('It has wheel protectors like this and that; the wheel protectors are against dirt and rust')—but note the lack of integration of parts; for example, the chain is stretched out

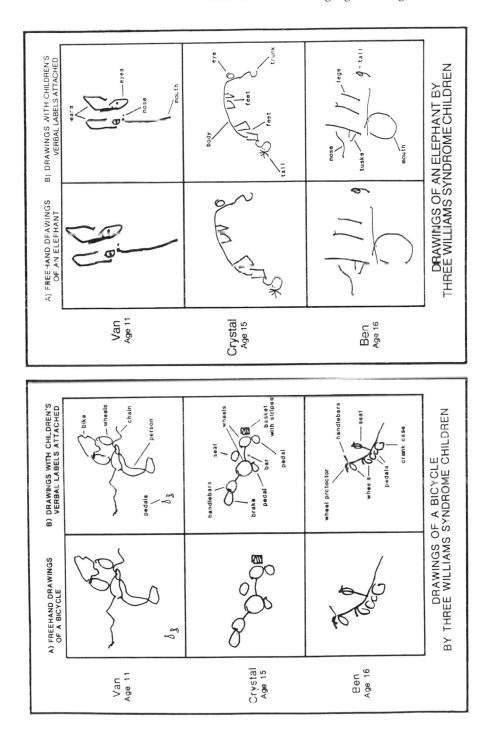

Fig. 11.1 Drawings of an elephant and a bicycle

below the wheels in Van's drawing, and the pedals are floating below the 'person.'

The examples of the children talking while drawing demonstrate the dissociation between language and visuospatial skills. The children would often name the various parts of the model and draw them as they named them, one next to the other; the drawings consist of separate parts that show no integration into functional objects. From our studies it seems that the children's difficulties in drawing (whether from a model or without one) are not motor in nature, but rather derive from visuospatial deficits. It is interesting, therefore, to note that they use their relative strengths in language to mediate in this visuospatial task.

LANGUAGE FUNCTIONING IN WILLIAMS SYNDROME CHILDREN

In contrast to the Williams syndrome children's low level of cognitive and visuospatial functioning, the children demonstrate impressive lexical semantic abilities, complex expressive morphology and syntax, and good metalinguistic skills. Although their language abilities are not at chronological age levels, their scores on formal tests of language are higher than performance on nonlanguage cognitive tasks. This relative sparing of language in the face of other cognitive impairments is unusual (the more typical pattern is the reverse), and is particularly impressive considering the reportedly delayed onset of language development (Von Armin & Engel 1964). The dissociation between language and nonlinguistic cognitive capacities is quite dramatic and is consistently found across the children tested.

Spontaneous language

Samples of the children's spontaneous utterances were obtained from a number of tasks. The children were asked biographical questions about home, family and pets, with probes designed to elicit complete sentences and a variety of linguistic structures. In addition, they were asked to describe familiar routines such as getting dressed, going to the store or going to the zoo. Finally, the children were shown story books made up of pictures without written text and were asked to tell (and, later, retell) the stories to the examiner. All sessions were videotaped and transcribed for linguistic coding and analysis.

The Williams syndrome children are so loquacious, social and interactive that the amount of spontaneous language elicited in a test session is considerable. They interact in the conversation rather than passively respond to questions. The children contribute almost to a fault, keeping up more than their share of the conversation. For example, in administering specific tests (e.g. the Vocabulary subtest of the WISC-R), the examiner has been unable to write the children's responses directly onto the score sheets because of the amount of language produced by the children to define a word.

Unusual vocabulary and phrases

One facet of the Williams syndrome children's language ability is the use of unusual vocabulary. This vocabulary is surprising because it is above the level one might expect from children of equivalent mental ages, and this is confirmed by formal language tests. We have noted appropriate use of such low frequency words as 'surrender, sauté, nontoxic, commentator, and brochure.' When questioned about the meaning of those words, the children provide appropriate responses such as 'I wish I could surrender. That means I give up.' 'It's nontoxic. That means it is not dangerous.' 'I wouldn't want to wrestle. I would like to commentate it. It means that . . . like all the sportscasters do . . . they tell who's doing what.' This ability to define words used spontaneously in discourse shows that the children's language is not merely echoic.

Crystal's expressive language, as seen in following examples, does not reveal her impaired level of cognitive functioning. In all cases, these statements were contextually appropriate.

Examiner: 'May I borrow your watch?'

Crystal: 'My watch is always available for service.'

Crystal: 'I like the word "lady" better than "woman."'

Examiner: 'Why do you?'

Crystal: 'Because it is appropriate to say "ladies."'

Crystal: 'It's a rabbit fur. It's comfortable inside, It's soft and the outside is pretty. When I got it I said "Look out world; here comes Crystal in a fur coat."'

Co-occurring with marked cognitive deficits, the children's expressive language is complex and generally grammatically correct: an island of sparing of language capacites in the face of general mental retardation. The older Williams syndrome children's mastery of the linguistic system despite severe cognitive deficits appears remarkable. In relating the experience of having a Magnetic Resonance Image of her brain, for example, a Williams syndrome girl who is 17 years old and has an IQ of 50, described the experience to her father as follows:

> There is a huge magnetic machine. It took a picture inside the brain. You could talk but not move your head because that would ruin the whole thing and they would have to start all over again. After it's all done they show you your brain on a computer and they see how large it is. And the machine on the other side of the room takes pictures from the computer. They can take pictures instantly. Oh, and it was very exciting!

Average sentence length in morphemes

One superficial measure of language complexity is in mean length of utterance (MLU) in morphemes. Studies of Down's syndrome children may provide an important contrast with Williams syndrome. Gleitman (1983) reported a study of the language abilities of three adolescents with Down's syndrome. These children had mental functions at about the level of 6-year-old children, and language functions (assessed by a variety of standard psycholinguistic instruments) at approximately the level of $2\frac{1}{2}$-year-old normal controls. Their MLU was between 3.0 and 3.5, a level usually achieved by normal children between the ages of 2 and 3 (see also Ch. 10). In contrast, we calculated the mean sentence length in morphemes of 100 consecutive utterances during a storytelling task for the three Williams syndrome adolescents and obtained values of 8.6 for Van, 13.1 for Crystal, and 10.0 for Ben. This suggests a crucial difference between Williams syndrome and Down's syndrome with respect to language functions.

Preserved inflectional morphology and syntax

The older Williams syndrome children's expressive language is complex in terms of morphological and syntactic structures including full passives, embedded relative clauses, a range of conditionals and multiple embeddings. The children's sentences are complex and the syntax correct, although there are occasional 'errors' of overgeneralization of morphology and pronoun usage. Despite these occasional weaknesses, it is interesting that the children spontaneously use specific linguistic structures (such as full reversible passives) in the absence of their purported cognitive prerequisites or concomitants. The children are able to use a wide variety of synactic structures productively and appropriately. Complex structures in the spontaneous speech of the Williams syndrome children are abundant, as the following examples suggest:

a. *Van*:
Isn't she going to come over here and talk with us?
When I got up the next morning, I talked but couldn't say anything so my mom had to rush me to the hospital.

Maybe you could ask your son if I could have one of your posters.

b. *Crystal*:
The dog was chased by the bees.
Then before they climbed over, they saw baby frogs.
If you gave him a bone he would roll over.
It was a good movie for children to see because it has action and it has comedy and it has lots of different things in there.

c. *Ben*:
After it stopped hurting, I was told I could go to school again and do whatever I feel like doing.
If it got really infected they would have taken my toe off.
They had to give me ether so I wouldn't feel the pain.

As the examples illustrate, the children demonstrate proper use of grammatical inflections, tense and aspect markers, passives, conditionals and the full range of the complex grammatical structures of English. Expressive language in these older Williams syndrome children characteristically exhibits grammatical well-formedness, even when there is grammatical complexity.

Formal language testing

The children were tested across a range of formal language tests designed to assess their skills in the areas of lexical semantics, morphology and syntax, as well as metalinguistics. Many of the tests were standardized with normative data; others were devised by us to evaluate the children's use or comprehension of specific linguistic structures.

Lexical semantics

Numerous investigators, testing a variety of mentally retarded groups, have reported that vocabulary size and complexity parallel normal mental age-matched individuals. In fact, in Down's syndrome, the most common cause of mental retardation, verbal abilities are actually lower than one may expect for mental age (Fowler in press). In sharp contrast to this pattern, the mental retardation that accompanies Williams syndrome results in vocabulary scores (both receptive and expressive) that are above mental age. Three aspects of lexical organization in Williams syndrome were assessed: vocabulary, definitions, and verbal fluency or lexical access skills.

Vocabulary

In order to assess receptive vocabulary we administered the Peabody Picture Vocabulary Test-Revised. On this test, subjects are asked to point to the picture, from an array of four, that corresponds to a word spoken by the examiner. The test, which contains 175 items, has norms for ages $2\frac{1}{2}$ through 40. Van obtained a raw score of 100, which converts to an age-equivalent score of 9;0 years. Crystal's raw score of 105 converts to an age-equivalent score of 9;8 years, and Ben's raw score of 118 converts to an age-equivalent score of 11;7 years. Following are examples of items correctly identified by each child:

Van: peninsula, slumbering, husk, solemn, dissecting, hoisting

Crystal: canine, archaeologist, fragment, arctic, pod, cubical, gnawing

Ben: cornea, spherical, abrasive, syringe, tranquil.

Figure 11.2 shows the children's age-equivalent scores on this test.

Definitions

The ability to focus on and define the attributes of words or objects gives us a clue as to the structure of the feature analysis of a subject's environment. On the Oral Vocabulary subtest of the Test of Language Development, the subject is required to give oral definitions for 20 common English words. The responses are scored for accuracy and

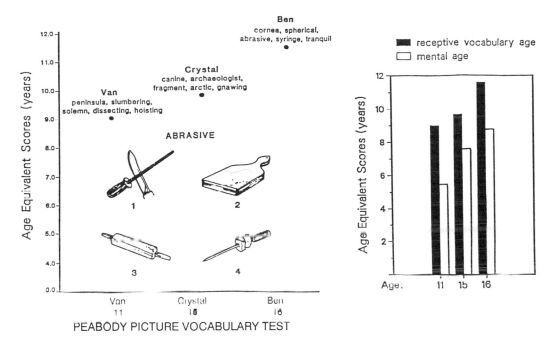

Fig. 11.2 Excellent lexical-semantic skills in Williams syndrome children

completeness. Either a precise definition or superordinate category or two descriptive characteristics are required for the subject to receive full credit. Van and Crystal both obtained age-equivalent scores of 9;5, while Ben received a score of 8;4. Although the children performed below the mean for their ages and frequently did not include the most salient features of the word being defined, their definitions tended to be lengthy and descriptive. They often used the words correctly in context or were able to produce associations to the target word in the form of somewhat tangential anecdotes. For example, when asked 'What does *poor* mean?', Crystal said, 'Means they are hungry; they don't have any money; they are dying from exposure.' Following are examples of each child's response when asked for the meaning of *sad*:

Van: 'Sad is when someone dies; someone is hurt, like when you cry.'

Crystal: 'Sad means that someone hurts your feelings, or when someone starts crying.'

Ben: 'When you lost somebody that you love and care about. It means something happens to you like your grandmother died or some part of your family or your cousin.'

Fluency

The extent to which names of objects can be accessed automatically can also provide information about the semantic capabilities of the children and the organization of the mental lexicon. We administered the Clinical Evaluation of Language Functions-Subtest 9: Producing Word Associations. In separate trials, the subjects were asked to name as many food and then animal names as they could within 60 seconds. The subtest can be scored quantitatively (i.e. by observing total number of new words recalled) or qualitatively (i.e. by investigating the number of subclasses within each semantic class and the number of shifts between them). The subjects received the following grade-level scores: Van, 3rd-4th grade; Crystal, 8th–9th grade; and Ben, 5th grade. Note that Crystal's performance on this task was at the level of her chronological age. It is apparent that the Williams syndrome children had no difficulty accessing numerous members of a given semantic category; however, the words they generate are not just basic items. The following examples are surprising in that the children provide not general subclasses of items but rather very specific and in some cases rare and nonprototypical animals.

Van: Sea lion, zebra, hippopotamus, lizard, beaver, kangaroo, chihuahua, crocodile, tiger, owl, turtle, reptile, frog, giraffe

Crystal: Koala bear, antelope, moose, anteater, lion, tiger, rat, bear, giraffe, elephant

Ben: Buffalo, leopard, sabretooth tiger, condor, vulture, turtle, bear, snake, giraffe, lion, bull, dog, cat, tiger

This ability to generate numerous members of a semantic category is demonstrated in spontaneous speech as well.

Crystal: I love fish. I eat fish shishkebob and swordfish, or sea bass or a couple of different kinds like shrimp or like shrimp shishkebob with butter or something like that. I love fish.

Examiner: Crystal was telling me about all the languages she knows.

Crystal: Belgian, Swedish, Spanish, Japanese, and Chinese.

Mother: I haven't heard that you know all of those. How do you say something in Chinese?

Crystal: Chow Mein!

Examiner: What kinds of foods do you like to eat?

Van: Spare ribs, chicken, rice, eggs, carrots, beans, taffy.

Examiner: What else?

Van: Carrots, and how do you call it. . . papaya.

The Williams syndrome subjects demonstrated superior lexical semantic skills in light of their cognitive deficits. One of the most striking features of their spontaneous conversation is their use of unusual and adult-like vocabulary items in what appear to be appropriate ways. Upon further probing, the children demonstrate that their language use is clearly not simply echoic nor is it merely formulaic; they are often able to explain the words used in their own and other's speech. We are currently engaged in studies of the unusual semantic organization in Williams syndrome.

Morphology and syntax

Grammatical comprehension

We assessed the children's abilities in this area by administering several tests that measured their ability to comprehend specific grammatical structures. The Test for Reception of Grammar (TROG) consists of 80 items in which the subject is required to select from an array of four pictures the one that corresponds to a sentence spoken by the examiner. Items on the test are divided into blocks of four; each block tests comprehension of a particular contrast, such as passives, relative clauses and complex negation. A sample item from the TROG, showing a reversible passive sentence, and scores for the three Williams syndrome children are presented in Figure 11.3. Age-equivalent scores were at mental age levels for all three children. However, item analysis of failed blocks indicated that the children often passed three of the four grammatical items tested within that block.

The Clinical Evaluation of Language Functions-Subtest 1: Processing Word and Sentence Structure was designed to assess the child's ability to comprehend selected word and sentence structures. The subtest contains 26 items that probe several syntactic structures

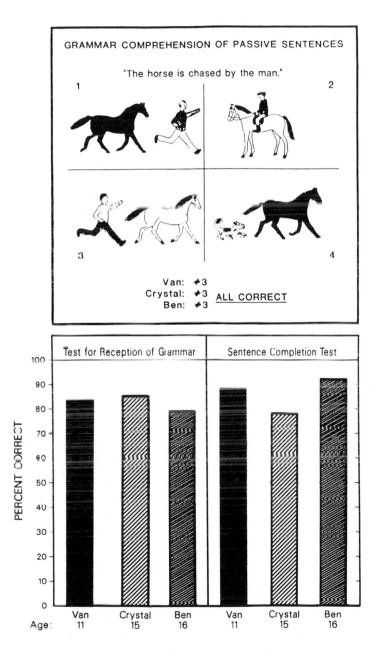

Fig. 11.3 Grammatical abilities in children with Williams syndrome

and forms: prepositional phrases, pronouns, verb tense, noun plurals, possessives, noun phrase modification, explicit negation, passives, wh-interrogatives, and relative clauses. Crystal and Van achieved scores of 81% and 87%, respectively. These converted to an age equivalent of 12;2 years and a grade-level score of 7th grade, which was Van's grade placement at the time of testing. Ben's score of 66% correct (age-equivalent of 7;1 years) is still good relative to his performance on visuospatial and cognitive tasks.

The Test of Language Development—Subtest 3: Grammatic Understanding, an additional measure of receptive language, requires the subjects to choose the correct picture, from a set of three, that corresponds to a sentence spoken by the examiner. This test examines structures such as verb tense and aspect, adverbial clauses, passive structures with agent deleted and embedded within relative clauses, and multiple transformations within one sentence. Again, the children performed well on this task: Van obtained a score of 80% correct, corresponding to an age-equivalent score of 8;4; Crystal obtained 96% correct, age-equivalent > 9;4; and Ben, 72% correct, age-equivalent 7;3.

In order to assess features of aspectual information and implication, we administered the Sentence Completion test (adapted from Bellugi 1968). On this test, subjects are given a set of 44 incomplete sentences. The subjects are to provide appropriate completions when provided with a picture stimulus. The sentence frames and pictures constrain the choices sufficiently so that only a small number of responses are appropriate. For example, 'The mouse has a tail but the frog . . . (doesn't);' 'If this butterfly didn't have wings, it . . . (couldn't fly).' The test requires attention to both the syntactic and semantic structure of the phrase provided. Items were scored as being either appropriate or inappropriate and error type was noted.

All three children performed well on this test (see Fig. 11.3). Van scored at 88%, Crystal at 78%, and Ben at 92%. The error analysis reveals that the majority of errors were at the phrasal level, and as such can be considered semantic/syntactic errors. Errors included the following: absence or incorrect use of grammatical markers such as failure to use the possessive marker or incorrect tense markings, incorrect choice of lexical items, predominantly incorrect pronoun usage, and incorrect interpretation at the phrasal level.

On all of these measures, the children consistently demonstrate comprehension of linguistic structures that have been linked to particular cognitive skills—skills that these children have not mastered. For example, all the children comprehended affirmative and negative comparative and equative relational expressions, which purportedly require the ability to seriate (Shaffer & Ehri 1980). As noted earlier, the children also comprehended and used full reversible passives appropriately, although none of them were able to conserve on Piagetian tasks. These preserved linguistic abilities in the face of significantly impaired cognitive capacities is important. Such findings suggest that linguistic functions can occur separate from cognitive functions.

METALINGUISTICS

Judgments of grammaticality

The ability to detect and correct linguistic anomalies requires awareness of the constraints that determine syntactic well-formedness as well as semantic appropriateness. Although the Williams syndrome children spontaneously produce largely error-free grammatical sentences in discourse, the ability to reflect on grammatical structure requires greater resources. In order to investigate this metalinguistic ability, we adapted a technique used by Linebarger et al (1983), requiring subjects to detect and correct grammatically incorrect sentences. The sentences were ungrammatical due to violations of strict subcategorization features, phrase structure rule violations and errors in reflexive pronoun usage (violations in number, gender, and/or person).

Linebarger et al suggested that the ability to detect errors in syntactic structure requires the subject to first construct correct syntactic representations of sentences. The authors found that their aphasic subjects display a remarkable sensitivity to structural information as demonstrated by their performance on the grammaticality judgment task. In our version of the task, the Williams syndrome subjects were not only able to detect ungrammatical sentences, but were able to correctly change the sentences to more acceptable forms. In this way, the subjects demonstrate a sophisticated awareness of the constraints that determine syntactic well-formedess. When the children erred, they typically made errors involving reflexive pronouns. Examples of sentence correction items follow:

> *Examiner*: The log swam lazily away.
>
> *Crystal*: Logs cannot do that. Logs *float* lazily in water.
>
> *Examiner*: He flutted up the book.
>
> *Crystal*: He fluffed up the *pillow*.
>
> *Examiner*: She slept the baby.
>
> *Crystal*: She slept in bed. She slept *with* the baby.

In addition, when given semantically anomalous sentences or sentences violating transformational rules (e.g. subject-auxiliary inversion), the children usually converted them to plausible English sentences.

> *Examiner*: The picture that painted the person was very kind.
>
> *Van*: The picture that was painted by the man was very kind.
>
> *Examiner*: Were delivered the flowers by the messenger?
>
> *Van*: Were the flowers delivered by the messenger.

The Williams syndrome children studied so far show some ability to handle metalinguistic tasks such as grammaticality judgements, and they make self corrections as well, suggesting that their linguistic abilities involve awareness and manipulation of grammatical structure.

CONCLUSIONS

Williams syndrome is a metabolic disorder

that has hitherto been little explored. Jones & Smith (1975) described the physical and medical characteristics associated with the syndrome, specifying the facial features and heart defects. Our studies with three Williams syndrome children suggest that they may also share a highly consistent neuropsychological profile that is discontinuous from normal and not characteristic of other syndromes (impaired general cognitive functioning, unusual peaks and valleys of abilities in spatial cognition, preserved linguistic abilities).

Cases of selective impairment in development are rare, since mental retardation generally results in similar depression of cognitive functions across domains. The Williams syndrome disorder results in an uneven profile of cognitive abilities: linguistic performance far outstrips other cognitive domains and often appears *decoupled* from purported cognitive prerequisites. Co occurring with marked cognitive deficits, the children's expressive language is complex and often grammatically correct—an island of sparing of linguistic capacities, presenting a challenge to important theoretical models of the relationship between language and cognition. These studies of Williams syndrome promise in the long run to provide insight into the relationship between domains of higher cortical functioning and their underlying neural substrate.

ACKNOWLEDGMENTS

This research was supported in part by the National Institutes of Health, grants #NS 15175, #HD 13249, and #P50 NS22343; the March of Dimes, grants #12-169 and #1-1017; and the John D. and Catherine MacArthur Foundation Research Network. We are very grateful to the children and parents who have taken part in our studies of Williams syndrome. In particular, we thank the Williams Syndrome Association and the families for their spirited participation in these studies.

12

Infantile autism

W. H. Fay

In his book *Thought and Language* the famous Russian psychologist Vygotsky (1962) wrote: 'To understand another's speech, it is not sufficient to understand his words—we must understand his thought. But even that is not enough—we must also know its motivation' (p. 157). After years of struggle some higher functioning autistic individuals understand words. Fewer still learn to appreciate the thought behind their interlocuter's utterance. But knowing the motivation of a remark remains elusive for most, if not all. Consequently, human communication as we have come to know it with all of its social implications remains beyond the autistic individual's grasp.

In this chapter we shall address the nature of the syndrome of infantile autism from a verbal developmental perspective. A brief history and description of the syndrome is followed by a more detailed account of its peculiar verbal manifestations. Finally, the belated and prolonged nature of autistic language development provides insights which help elucidate some features of the acquisition process in children, autistic or not.

THE SYNDROME

Autism is a severely incapacitating lifelong developmental disability that typically appears during the first three years of life. The syndrome was first recognized and described by child psychiatrist Leo Kanner (1943). What he termed *early infantile autism* was, in his original assessments, the earliest manifestation of childhood schizophrenia with extreme autistic aloneness from the start. These children showed profound withdrawal, preservation of sameness, skilful and even affectionate relations to objects, an intelligent and pensive physiognomy and either mutism or the kind of language not suitable for communication. He observed that the children typically displayed excellent rote memory.

Among the designated language symptoms were echolalia (the immediate repetition of a word or word group just spoken by another person: 'How old are you?'/'Old are you?') and delayed echolalia (the repetition of stored utterances in new and often inappropriate contexts). Delayed echolalia may be with communicative intent (as when a child says 'Do you have to go potty?' to indicate a desire to do so) or without apparent intent. Other symptoms include the so-called pronominal reversals (the child's use of second and third person forms as self-reference) and the absence of the concept of 'yes'. Extreme literalness (the picture is *near* the wall, not *on* the wall) and metaphoric language in which the utterance appears to have no reference or a strictly private reference also were noted by Kanner.

Initially Kanner believed that the syndrome was the product of a parent type (cold, intellectual, ego-oriented, driving and ambitious). Subsequent research, however, has proven otherwise. After reviewing recent family research McAdoo & DeMyer (1977) concluded that, as a group, parents of autistic children (1) displayed no more signs of mental or emotional illness than parents whose children have 'organic' disorders with or without psychosis; (2) do not have extreme personality traits such as coldness, obsessiveness, social anxiety, or rage; and (3) are not deficient in infant and child care skills.

Kanner erred also in his original belief that most autistic children were of normal intelligence. He apparently based this belief on their intelligent physiognomies and generally

good performance on such tasks as the Seguin formboard. Their generalized poor functioning was attributed to a secondary consequence of their failure to make relationships. 'Kanner's belief that autistic children must have *good cognitive potential*,' noted Lorna Wing (1976), 'has perhaps given rise to more difficulties than all the other abstractions put together' (p. 17). Although they often do achieve relatively normal Block Design and Digit Span scores (Lockyer & Rutter 1970), overall IQ scores present a different picture. In a large follow-up study of intelligence estimates from standardized tests De Myer et al (1974) examined 135 autistic children (mean age 5½ years) at initial evaluation and 70 of these same children 6 years later. In the preschool years about 74% had a general IQ below 52 and only 2.6% had an IQ above 85. While performance IQs were higher than verbal IQs, nevertheless 78% of autistic children had performance IQs below 68. It was concluded that the intelligence of autistic children can be measured reliably and validly, that the IQ has good predictive power, that most autistic children have subnormal intelligence, and that in only a few children does the verbal IQ reach normal levels—no matter how intense the treatment and education.

Another characteristic of the syndrome which Kanner and succeeding observers have noted among some patients has been termed developmental discontinuity. Here, islets of often remarkable skill or talent are seen against a general background of disproportionately poor performances. (The term 'Idiot savant' has been used frequently to describe individuals of low intellect who possess an extraordinary talent or skill). Perhaps the most common feature observed is remarkable long-term retention usually manifested in memory list reiterations. Recitations of names of musical compositions, lists of animal names, the roster of presidents, city bus routes, road signs, and a variety of television commercials are but a few of the favoured topics. Long-term storage might also include situational pairings revived months or years subsequently. For example, Caparulo & Cohen

(1977) cited the case of James who, upon meeting strangers, mechanically introduced himself without establishing eye contact. He then rushed on to ask the person's birthday, anniversary, and social security number—often appearing not to pause long enough to get answers. Years later, upon encountering the person again, he was able to recite back these facts!

More notable examples of this isolated precocity include art, musical talent and hyperlexia. Probably the most famous autistic artist is Nadia (Selfe 1977) who displayed extraordinary drawing ability at a very early age. Ironically, Nadia's talent seemed to diminish as she acquired greater language functioning in her school years. An adult, Jack Dewey, has perfect pitch, has composed classical musical selections, and is a self-employed piano tuner. He recalls, nevertheless, being constantly re-referred for hearing tests during his school years (Fay & Schuler 1980). Whitehouse & Harris (1984) studied 20 autistic boys with precocious ability in word recognition (hyperlexia), frequently self-taught. The most striking feature of the group was the compulsion to decode written material without comprehension. The authors suggested hyperlexic children might constitute a separate subgroup of autistic children.

Early interpretations of these interesting behaviours were based largely on psychoanalytic theory and the notion that the behaviours were wilful and socially aggressive. Thus, resolution of the basic disorder of autistic aloneness was thought to be the key to ameliorating the unusual behaviours and symptoms. Extremes in this line of thought can be illustrated in this account of pronominal reversals and avoidance as interpreted by Bettelheim (1967), who, incidentally, is one of the few latterday advocates of the earlier ego-based analyses and treatment approaches. He views the pronominal difficulties as the result of a confusion of personal identity and its consequential psychic defence mechanisms. Regarding pronominal reversals, for example, Bettelheim writes 'It is not easy to talk constantly in opposites, to do quite well in getting across what is wanted, and never make the *mistake* of using pronouns correctly' (p. 243). Bettelheim viewed list memorizations similarly. 'Far from indicating that the child can only memorize but does not understand the complex functions of language,' he wrote, 'it suggests to me that the children understand them very well indeed' (p. 429). But, as we shall see subsequently, pronominal errors are not vindictive and list recitals are seldom semantically valid.

Although the psychopathic etiology and ego-oriented therapy dominated the literature well into the 1960s, an early (and generally overlooked) counter position is worthy of note. The work is 'resurrected' here because of the remarkable correspondence it bears to conclusions evident in the literature of today. Scheerer et al (1945) compared Kanner's description of autistic language and that of a case of 'idiot savant'. In both instances they interpreted the major deficiency as an impairment of abstract capacity. They wondered whether the fact that the children did not grasp the meaning of language in the normal way might not be the key to their heightened responsiveness to, and their tenaciously obsessive reproduction of, sound patterns. They regarded the problem as the result of a concrete level of thinking in which the child cannot detach the words from their experienced 'belongingness' in the actual situation and reverse this belonging in terms of a relational symbol. The autistic child and the idiot savant, they suggested, have done all that they could with language: repeat it rather than understand it.

Three events of the mid-1960s combined to change the focus of the syndrome from one of psychosis and psychotherapy to cognition/language disorders and behavioural therapy. One such event was the publication of Rimland's (1964) *Infantile Autism* which theorized that the autistic child suffers from an inability to relate present sensations to past experience. Rimland contended that the afflicted child cannot perceive himself as an organized and unitary entity. What earlier was presumed to be part of the affective component of the disorder was reassessed by Rimland to be the consequence of the child's inability to associate the biological rewards given by the mother with the social relationships in which they were presented. He postulated a malfunctioning of the brainstem reticular formation.

A second milestone of the 1960s was the publication by Lovaas et al (1966) revealing elicitation of speech in mute autistic children through the use of operant learning techniques. This 'break through', coupled with the results of follow-up studies (Eisenberg 1956) indicating a poor prognosis for children not having useful speech by age 5, tended to increase professional focus on verbal symptoms and their potential for treatment.

The third, and probably most important, event of the decade was the dramatic increase in systematic group studies of these children and their behaviours. Crucial to our present understanding of the syndrome were early group studies of language function (Wolff & Chess 1965), psychological experiments contrasting autistic children with control groups having other disorders (Hermelin & O'Connor 1970), and the comparative studies of Wing (1969, 1971). Also of inestimable value were the extensive large-group follow-up studies carried out in England (Rutter et al 1967, Rutter & Lockyer 1967, Lockyer & Rutter 1969, 1970) and in the U.S.A. (DeMyer et al 1973).

An important contribution of the present decade has been the reclassification of infantile autism as one category under the rubric of pervasive developmental disorders in the new DSM-III: *Diagnostic and Statistical Manual of Mental Disorders* (American Psychiatric Association 1980). Much terminological and diagnostic confusion of the past has been eliminated by this reclassification (e.g. the separation of infantile autism from schizophrenia). The definition of the syndrome of autism has also been revised and refined on clinical and research bases (Ritvo & Freeman

1977). Following is a condensed version of the revised definition employed by the American Psychiatric Association and the National Society for Autistic Adults and Children:

> The syndrome of autism is a developmental disability which is defined and diagnosed behaviourally. Signs and symptoms appear before 30 months of age and include disturbances of (1) developmental rates and/or sequences (delays, arrests, or regressions), (2) responses to sensory stimuli (over- or under-reactions), (3) speech, language and cognitive capacities and (4) capacities to relate to people, events, and objects. The syndrome is caused by an underlying physical dysfunction within the brain, the exact nature of which remains unknown. It occurs four or five times per 10 000 births and is four to five times more common in males. Studies of families with autistic individuals have failed to identify unique features. Although autistic persons live a normal life span, the syndrome is severely incapacitating.

It has become increasingly clear in recent years that the autistic individual is indeed unique. As Levinson & Osterwell (1984) point out, the clinician's question 'Is this child autistic?' does not arise for every mentally retarded, language disordered and socially deficient youngster who presents for diagnosis. Rather, Kanner's autism has come to be looked upon in the wider context of the triad or interaction of cognitive, linguistic and social development (Wing & Gould 1978, Fay & Schuler 1980, Wing 1981). 'The child with the triad,' wrote Wing, 'is strange and puzzling to other people because, whatever his level of speech and practical abilities, he lacks the whole complex pattern of action and response that makes human beings recognizable and important to each other' (p. 40). Wing submits that although much of this pattern is learned and varies among cultures, evidence is accumulating that the essential basis is present in the normal child from birth.

CHARACTERISTICS OF AUTISTIC COMMUNICATION

Mutism

Mutism is generally associated with deafness, profound retardation or some variation of elective mutism or wilful silence. None of these can explain autistic muteness, although deafness is a frequent early suspect. Approximately 80% of the autistic children in the Bartak & Rutter (1976) study were thought to be deaf at one time. Not uncommonly parents will consider deafness even when faced with the contradictory evidence of frequent displays of signs of intolerance to noises such as vacuum cleaners or other environmental sounds. Apparent nonrecognition of speech is an almost universal report and, undoubtedly, the reason to suspect the child's hearing.

About 65% of the autistic children who were mute at age 5 in the study by De Meyer et al (1973) were still mute when re-evaluated several years later. The number of children who fail to acquire speech varies from study to study according to sampling techniques, but it is clear that the mute or nearly mute represent a sizeable proportion of total individuals regarded as autistic.

Increased attention is now being given to the widely recognized fact that these children are not only mute (or severely delayed in speech onset), but have also demonstrated virtually no evidence of preverbal communicative intent through gestures or bodily expressions (Ricks & Wing 1975, Fay & Schuler 1980). Thus, the focus of the problem has widened to concerns for communication rather than simply oral output.

Autistic mutism was thought originally to be a deliberate withholding of speech and a systematic storing of verbal information during the silent period (Kanner 1943, Bettelheim 1967). And there remains evidence that some of these children do find speech objectionable. For example, a child who became very interested in a phonograph and record playing avoided the portions of the record which had human voices (Ritvo & Provence 1953). Whether such avoidances are primary to the pathology or secondary to efforts of society to invoke performance in the absence of the ability to perform cannot be easily determined and may, indeed, vary from child to child. In any event, many mute autistic children cannot be made to talk even with extremely persistent efforts. Lovaas (1977) reported on one patient who required 90 000 trials to obtain two simple word approximations. Hingtgen & Churchill (1969) found 'little improvement' in a child who received 600 hours of silence-breaking effort.

Such efforts, as well as the frequently limited progress of many mutes once the silence has been broken, explains—in part at least—a shift toward non-oral intervention strategies. These efforts, primarily signing or some variation of total communication, have yielded some successes beyond what could be obtained orally (see Schuler & Baldwin 1981, for a review). Nevertheless, the reader is once again reminded that autistic individuals can be differentiated from most others with language handicaps by the fact that they have difficulty with *all forms of communication*, not vocal alone.

Although some autistic children show good progress once speech has begun, prognosis is highly variable. One adult in his twenties had a history of but 4 single-word productions. Jeremy, an 8-year-old studied by Layton & Baker (1981) produced 302 utterances over $1\frac{1}{2}$ years. This compares with the progress of four normal children who had a total of 24 711 spontaneous utterances over a 6-week period (Bloom et al 1975).

Not uncommonly the initial utterances will be fully intelligible words or phrases that have never been tutored. Early case studies reported such first utterances as 'You go there', 'Put the foot in the bed', 'Beethoven', 'American flag', 'Chocolate', and 'Want to go home'. It is easy to see in retrospect why such adult-like utterances after mutism served the notion of 'verbal storage' and encouraged the mistaken belief that complex, non-infantile language had finally emerged from years of silence.

In the study by Bartak & Rutter (1976) the first words by their higher IQ subgroup occurred at a mean age of 2;6. First phrases for this group came at a mean age of 4;8. For the lower IQ subgroup first words were at 4;7 and phrases at 6;5. Some children have a history of having begun speaking normally (or presumably normally) and then at an age of 16 to 22 months have lost their entire speaking repertoire.

Because silence isolates individuals, prolonged or permanent mutism exacerbates the autistic aloneness which characterizes the syndrome. While communication alone cannot resolve the problems of the autistic person, it makes it easier to address them.

Echolalia

An estimated 75% of all autistic children who develop communicative speech have been reported to go through an echolalic phase (Rutter 1974, Ricks & Wing 1975). Echolalia is generally defined as the meaningless repetition of a word or word group just spoken by another person. If it is a single word it is generally the final word spoken by the interlocutor. With increments in the echoer's short-term auditory memory span the echo reaction expands from the final word(s) spoken toward the beginning of the triggering utterance.

Although autistic children are the greatest practitioners of echolalia in both quantity and fidelity, the behaviour may also be observed in normally developing children and in a variety of mental afflictions of young and old. It is reported in mental deficiency, developmental aphasia, transcortical aphasia, congenital blindness, clouded levels of consciousness, catatonic schizophrenia, senile dementia, and de la Tourette syndrome. See Schuler (1979) for a comprehensive review of the multiple pathologic manifestations.

Developmentally, some normal children

become quite proficient echoers whereas others are never heard parroting aloud. In any event, it is a passing phase in normal children. Nakanishi & Owada (1973) noted echoic utterances developing along with vocabulary up to approximately 2 to $2\frac{1}{2}$ years of age. After this age normal echoing gradually disappeared and was followed by a further growth of vocabulary. Zipf (1949) found that after 29 months of age echolalia is no longer a statistically significant component of the child's verbal output.

Slower children, however, may continue the behaviour to an older age. Fay (1966, 1967a) followed 24 non-autistic echolalic 3-year-olds to 4 years of age. At 36 months the mean percentage of echoic utterances on a standardized interview was 40.9; at 48 months the percentage was but 6.1 on the same protocol. In a subsequent study (Fay & Butler 1968), these 3-year-olds showed significantly poorer performance than IQ-matched controls on measures of verbal expression, verbal comprehension and object naming, but did not differ on measures of articulation. Among the investigators' conclusions was that this asymmetrical language status is evidence of the developmental nonconvergence of two independent systems: an audiomotor system and a deficient syntactic-semantic system.

Some authorities (e.g. J Brown 1975, Simon 1975) view echolalia as strictly pathological, yet its abatement in normal children and those with delayed language development suggests that it is a reflex-like phenomenon which may lack inhibition but is otherwise not indicative of physiological pathology (Fay & Coleman 1977). The effects of the pathology are to be seen in the maldevelopment or retarded development of language—not of speech. Whereas normal children ascend developmentally to more symbolic forms of behaviour, the autistic child reaches a plateau at a level of persistent repetition. On a hypothetical echoic continuum developing from the more automatic repetition to the less automatic, and more contextually appropriate production which characterizes growth toward abatement in most children, the typical autistic child would seem to have gained audiovocal competence but very little else. It could be argued that the child's excessive echoic output is 'pathological', but if all one can do with speech is repeat it, then a more accurate assessment would be the maladaption of an otherwise nonpathological process.

So why do they do it? What is the gain? Why bother when the communicative potential with the interlocutor is nil and even destructive to rapport? Stengel (1947, 1964) concluded from his clinical observations of multiple manifestations of the behaviour that all instances of echolalia reflect difficulty in communication because of impairment or lack of understanding coupled with an attempt at overcoming this difficulty through identification with the interlocutor. The term *identification* is a Freudian expression referring to the assimilation of one ego to another one, as a result of which the first ego behaves like the second in certain respects, imitates it and in a sense takes it up into itself (Freud 1965, p. 63).

Because so many children with autism echo so much and do so generally for extended developmental periods they are particularly good subjects for behavioural analysis. One school of thought is that echolalia is an abnormal behaviour to be eradicated and replaced by more appropriate linguistic target behaviour (e.g. Risley & Wolf 1967, Coleman & Stedman 1974, Freeman et al 1975, Lovaas 1977, Schreibman & Carr 1978). Another approach is that echolalia may represent an important intermediary step in the acquisition of better communicative skills and, as suggested by Stengel (1947, 1964), reflects the child's attempt to maintain social interaction in the face of severe communicative disorder (Fay 1973, Philips & Dyer 1977, Shapiro 1977, Schuler 1979).

This second school of thought has received considerable investigative support. Baltaxe & Simmons (1977) did a discourse analysis of the bedtime echolalic soliloquies (self-echo and delayed echolalia) of a 7-year-old autistic girl. They reached the conclusion that the autistic child may use verbal play with echolalic patterns as a language learning strategy. The echolalic patterns tended to be partially broken down and then resynthesized with similar chunklike units originating from other echolalic patterns. Baltaxe and Simmons concluded that the major acquisition strategy of autistic children may be the reverse of that of normal children and may be one of gradual breakdown of larger echolalic patterns into smaller, more useable chunks. In normal development the strategy is one of a gradual building up of linguistic patterns from smaller to target units.

In a similar vein Prizant (1983a) has developed an intriguing theory of gestalt language and gestalt processing in autism. Based on Peters' (1977) proposals about individual differences in the units that form the building blocks of language acquisition, Prizant has linked interactive deficits as well as other language peculiarities in the autistic population to a gestalt mode as opposed to an analytic approach. Prizant suggests that success with many nonlanguage and nonsocial tasks may be accomplished through the use of such a wholistic processing approach in which events are stored as whole unanalyzed units rather than analyzed selectively according to prior experience. He argued that the use of this type of wholistic processing style would not be conducive to analyzing and understanding the shifting rules of social interactive language use across different social contexts.

Prizant & Duchan (1981) studied four young, echolalic, autistic children over an 8-month period and discovered seven functions of immediate echolalia for the children. Videotaped analyses of verbal and nonverbal features revealed that immediate echolalia served specific communicative as well as cognitive functions and often occurred when the children demonstrated comprehension of the model utterance. In these primarily echolalic individuals, repetition appeared to be used as either a turn filler, a processing aid, a means of behavioural self-regulation, a rehearsal strategy, or as a vehicle for expressing communicative intentions such as affirmation.

Another verbal behaviour, delayed echolalia, has been defined as unrestructured old forms used in new situations (Shapiro 1977). Although Kanner (1943) regarded it as a form of echolalia, there is considerable evidence that it is a somewhat different phenomenon, at least with respect to neurophysiology and triggering circumstances. A delay of minutes and more would seem to involve other physiological mechanisms than the postulated audiovocal reflex previously discussed (see Fay & Schuler 1980, Ch. 3). Moreover, delayed echolalia seems to be more commonly associated with psychotic illnesses than with other language disorders or normally developing language, although the latter may have an analogue in what Baldwin (1895) described as 'persistent imitation'. Baker et al (1976) reported delayed echolalia in mean percentages of 5.2 of the total utterances of their autistic children, but only 0.1 for their comparison group, diagnosed as receptive aphasic.

There have been many attempts to categorize different types of delayed echolalia. From anecdotal evidence Dyer & Hadden (1981) discussed six functional categories of delayed echolalia: stereotypic, negativistic, egocentric, time-lag, transferred and mitigated. Wolff & Chess (1965) proposed two categories. *noncommunicative repetition* (purposeless) and *communicative repetition*, which is used for communication even though it consists of the exact phrases a child has heard others use.

A study by Prizant & Rydell (1984) has been the only systematic analysis of delayed echoes in naturalistic interactions with familiar people. Fourteen functional categories of delayed echolalia were derived from videotape analysis of linguistic, extralinguistic and paralinguistic features. Delayed echolalia was found to vary among individuals as well as along the dimensions of interactiveness, comprehension of the utterance spoken, and relevance to linguistic or situational context. They found

that communicative intent may or may not underlie the production of delayed echolalia. Although acknowledging the problems of inferring communicative intent, the investigators noted that when there is behavioural evidence that an utterance is used to achieve a particular result, it can be concluded that the utterance is part of an intentional communicative act.

Another variation of echolalia was noted by Pick (1924) who introduced the concept of mitigated echolalia to define the slightly modified echoic responses observed in the speech of some of his adult aphasic patients. Stengel (1947) noted two characteristic modifications: (a) introducing the first person singular into the repeated sentence, ('Did you sleep well?' . . . 'Did I sleep well?') or (b) appending an intelligent response to an echoed question or order. ('How old are you, Bobby?' . . . 'How old are you, Bobby? Twelve'). Fay (1967b) tabulated 331 samples from 40 echolalic (non-autistic) children. Three major types were classified as pronominal reciprocation, echoic segment preceded or followed by utterance, and a third grouping of miscellaneous combinations. In this writer's experience mitigation is rare among autistic children but nevertheless important. In a later study Fay & Butler (1968) found that mitigated echoers had higher verbal performances than the pure echoers and significantly higher mean IQs. Thus evidence of mitigation in an echolalic child can be interpreted as a positive linguistic sign.

It is noteworthy that some congenitally blind children demonstrate a form of echolalia remarkably similar to that of the autistic echoer (Fay 1973). See Chapter 9, 'Visual handicap' (this volume) for additional discussion of this and related similarities.

Pronominal reversals and avoidance

When Kanner (1943, 1946) first described the syndrome of autism he regarded confusion of pronouns with reversal of 'I/me' and 'you', as 'typical, almost pathognomic' of the condition.

He considered the pronominal difficulty as the incidental by-product of echolalia. 'Personal pronouns are repeated just as heard', he wrote, 'with no change to suit the altered situation' (1943, p. 244). Subsequent psychoanalytic observers saw the absence of *I* and other pronominal confusions as avoidance and as problems in self-differentiation (e.g. Despert 1946, Mahler et al 1959).

Research has verified Kanner's original explanation (Fay 1971, Bartak & Rutter 1974). Bartak & Rutter exposed spontaneously echolalic autistic children who had never used the pronoun *I* to short sentences containing several pronouns in all positions in a 3-word utterance. There was no tendency for children to avoid the repetition of *I*, once sentence position was controlled. A number of children echoed the final word of the sentence while others repeated the whole sentence. Research on short-term memory shows that the retention of the end of an input stimulus depends on different memory mechanisms from those used for retention of the beginning of the stimulus (Clark 1977). Typically, final items are reproduced first (as in echoic reproduction). According to Clark, retention of the beginning depends on rehearsal, and children will be unable to rehearse stimuli with which they are not already familiar.

To imitate or rehearse a pronoun is of course not tantamount to using it symbolically. The development of personal pronouns by normal children has been extensively investigated and is beyond the scope of the present paper. Nevertheless, it is of interest that an understanding of the use of words to specify objects or persons is believed to develop from pointing and showing gestures (Bruner 1975a, Bates 1976b, R. Clark 1977). Bruner describes *indicating* as the gestural, postural and idiosyncratic procedures for bringing a partner's attention to an object or action or state. Initially, what is mastered at a very young age by normal children is a procedure for homing in on the adult's attentional focus. This, according to Bruner, develops into a mutual attentional system between caregiver and child, which is a prerequisite for the development of reference in language.

With their early autistic aloneness and typical gaze aversion autistic children would seem to be poorly equipped to develop a mutual attentional system and the subsequent linguistic devices, including personal pronouns to denote reference and speaker/listener relationships. As a consequence, pronouns have little if any meaning. Parenthetically, Paul (1987) has theorized that failure in establishing joint attentional routines such as described by Bruner (1975a) may have far more extensive results. She suggests that a disorder of joint attention in which children had either no desire or no means of achieving such a status may be the whole basis of the language deficit.

Yes/no answers

Another linguistic abnormality noted by Kanner (1943, 1946) was the absence of the 'yes' concept and its corollary, affirmation by repetition (e.g. 'Do you want a cookie?'/'wanta cookie'). There is considerable evidence that the grammatical demands of appropriate affirmation and negation overwhelm the autistic individual (Fay 1982). It is generally agreed that verbal 'yes' and 'no' responses develop from head gestures (Spitz 1957, Eibl-Eibesfeldt 1972). Studies of normal children reveal that early on they have an incomplete knowledge of how to deal with adult yes/no questions. They learn that a response is required to an adult probe through an appreciation of the rising intonation contour at the end of the question. Many children answer affirmatively, even in an absence of comprehension, because of such clues as pleasant facial expression and general body language. Some children respond through affirmation by repetition. Ultimately, the child learns not only to decode the adult's grammar but also to appreciate pragmatically the prober's intent. For example, the intent of the question 'Do you have a hobby?' goes beyond the desire for a simple affirmative. Then the respondent must learn how to apply language to meet the functional demands of the question, i.e. make a statement about a statement based upon an appreciation of the meaning and a value judgment about the subject of the probe.

If you cannot tune in to the relevance of pitch changes or sense the body language of the prober or understand the grammar and meaning and intent of the question, it probably matters little what your response may be. Repetition is one option. Higher functioning autistic individuals can employ it as a signal of affirmation. Clinicians can program a child to say 'yes', 'no', or 'I don't know' (Garber & David 1975, Schreibman and Carr 1978). But the words can have little value to speaker or listener without comprehension.

LINGUISTIC ANALYSIS OF AUTISTIC LANGUAGE

'It is clear that man is born to talk, innately provided both with the capacity and with the motivation, almost a need, to learn, at least in the case of the native language' (Hebb et al 1971, p. 213). And in this desire for communication we witness the first expressions of social life (Jakobson 1968) What can we say about the plight of the autistic child and this urge to communicate and socialize? Clearly, something has gone awry in the verbal development of these youngsters. But because their verbal development is belated and slow in unfolding we are afforded a far more extensive 'look' than in the acquisition stages of normal children and of most other language disordered patients.

Many autistic children never gain speech. Others spend a prolonged period in a stage in which echolalia is the predominant form of speaking. Let us consider the linguistics of autistic language once it emerges.

Phonology

Most observers of autistic individuals will recognize peculiarities of their vocal output regardless of the context of the message. Even as infants they come across as different even if the differences are difficult to pinpoint. Ricks (1975) studied parents' identification of the meaning of prelinguistic vocalizations of autistic children. These studies revealed that unlike parents of normal children, parents of autistic children were easily able to identify recordings of their own children's vocalizations.

These peculiarities no doubt vary with age and linguistic skills, but tend to persist into adulthood. Kanner's (1971) follow-up report of Barbara, one of his original subjects, described her at age 36 as parroting with a little girl's voice, while humming certain melodies in a bizarre, monotonous manner.

Monotony is probably the most frequent designation of autistic vocal delivery. Other adjectives include 'bird-like,' 'mechanical,' 'hollow,' 'dull,' 'wooden,' and 'arrhythmic.' Idiosyncrasies in vocal quality including hoarseness, harshness, and hypernasality have been described (Pronovost et al 1966) as well as hyponasality. Loudness variables include seemingly inappropriately high levels as well as low.

Of perhaps most importance are the deviations subsumed under the classification of prosody, which include intonation, rhythm and stress. Receptive appreciation of such features is believed critical to a number of language functions. For example, Baltaxe (1984) noted that perception of prosodic information assists the listener in segmenting the flow of speech by contouring words. Syntactically, prosodic features help differentiate among sentence types through different intonational patterns ('Jimmy IS missing' versus Jimmy is MISSing'). Lexically, prosodic features aid in differentiating grammatical categories. They also serve a number of pragmatic functions. Thus deficiencies in the appreciation of what might seem to be insignificant characteristics, could negatively affect a wide variety of grammatical and cognitive functions essential for the rapid and efficient coding and decoding of utterances.

When Eisenberg (1956) re-examined Kanner's original eleven cases, he noted a precocity of phonological development in the eight children who developed speech. Subsequent studies have noted immature phonology, but have generally failed to uncover any significant developmental deviations peculiar to the syndrome (Bartolucci et al 1976, Boucher 1976). Some observers, it is important to note, have contrasted the somewhat higher quality of phonology in echolalia with the poorer quality in spontaneous speech (Pronovost et al 1966, Ricks & Wing 1975). There appears to be general agreement, in summary, that the autistic child's phonological development stands in favourable contrast to his or her other linguistic and communicative abilities.

Grammar

Few studies have provided accounts of the grammatical development of autistic children. Baltaxe & Simmons (1981) suggest that a reason for this paucity in both syntactic and semantic investigations may be the inherent difficulty in differentiating between freely generated speech and delayed echolalic utterances.

Bartolucci & Albers (1974) found significant differences in the use of past tense markers by autistic children when compared to mentally retarded and normal children. In a subsequent study (Bartolucci et al 1980) autistic, mentally retarded and normal children, matched for mental age, were compared for their corrrect use of morpheme rules. When compared to studies of morpheme development among young normal children (DeVilliers & DeVilliers 1973) the autistic group showed a significant degree of internal concordance in their use of these rules, but they omitted morphemes significantly more frequently than the normal group. Differences between the autistic and mentally retarded children were not significant. Howlin (1984) obtained similar results in a replication of Bartolucci et al (1980) with a group of 16 autistic children.

Pierce & Bartolucci (1977) used Lee's Developmental Sentence Scoring system with spontaneous speech samples from 10 autistic, mentally retarded and normal children matched for mental age. The autistic group was significantly less advanced in their syntactic skills than the normal controls, but differences between the autistic and retarded subjects were not significant. Tager-Flusberg (1981a) concludes that syntactic development in autistic children is similar to that of normal children but proceeds at a slower pace and is related to developmental level.

Semantics

Semantic development of speaking autistic children has been addressed only recently. Shapiro & Kapit (1978) examined the semantic concept of negation in a group of six autistic children (mean age 9;3) using a production/imitation/comprehension paradigm developed by Fraser et al (1963). Twelve pairs of contrasting cards were designed by the authors to elicit negative responses. They used Fraser's procedure in questioning with the following expansions. Four cards each were planned to evoke three semantic categories: *nonexistence* employed one card with an object present and a contrasting card which omitted the object, e.g. a box with shoes and a second card with the box alone. The second type of card was designed to elicit a response of a *denial of a proposition*. For example, a boy is in bed on one card and present in the second, but not in bed. The third type is a representation of *rejecting* feelings. For example, a card represents a dog with a bone in its mouth and its tail wagging. Its pair involves a dog turning away from the bone. The 12 pairs of cards were presented to the subject, who was asked to say 'what is the difference between the pictures' he saw. This is the *production* task. The examiner then asked which card represented the negative of the pair in the same grammatical form used in the imitative task, and the child was requested to point to the card so designated. This is the *comprehension* task. The examiner then asked the subject to repeat the negative statement, following his words exactly. This was done in increasing syntactic complexity as the cards were presented. This is the *imitative* task. All groups studied showed better comprehension than either imitation or production. But the autistic subjects imitated significantly better than they produced negatives. Nonautistic 3-year-olds, on the other hand, showed better performances in their productions than in their imitations.

Sentence comprehension and strategy use were investigated by Tager-Flusberg (1981b) in two experiments. 18 autistic subjects were compared with 30 normal 3-and 4-year olds, matched on the Peabody Picture Vocabulary Test and Raven's Coloured Progressive Matrices. In the first experiment the children's use of comprehension strategies with active and passive sentences was tested using an act-out procedure. As the experimenter spoke, 'The girl touches the truck,' she acted it out with the relevant toy and then instructed the child to 'Do as I say.' The child's task was to select the two relevant toys and act out the sentence (girl touches truck or truck is touched by the girl). The autistic group's overall comprehension was lower than that of the normal controls. Although they used a word-order strategy, they did not generally use a probable-event strategy, as determined by adult judges prior to the experiment. These findings were confirmed in the second experiment in which the same procedure with anomalous three-word items were used (girl touch boy; boy touch girl; girl boy touch; boy girl touch, touch girl boy, touch boy girl). The results were interpreted as evidence that in autism there is a semantic-cognitive deficit in the use of conceptual knowledge about relational aspects of the environment. (For additional data and elaboration of this theoretical position see Tager-Flusberg 1986.)

Pragmatics

Observations of autistic individuals clearly demonstrate that communicative effectiveness does not depend solely on competence in morphology, syntax, and semantics, but also includes such social skills as initiating a discourse, responding to different interlocuters, handling of topics, considering presup-positions of different listeners and emitting and responding to subtle turn-taking cues. All of these behaviours may be subsumed under the linguistic classification: pragmatics (Bernard-Opitz 1982). Deficient linguistic pragmatics permeates every aspect of the verbal development of autistic children. From extended mutism, echolalia, and abnormal prosody on up to fully developed language the effects of this deficit are evident. For example, one high functioning adult described his pragmatic dilemma as follows:

> I do not know what subjects to talk about with different people. I have commented that certain girls are sexy, because I have heard guys say this about girls. Once I told a bank teller to her face that she was sexy, and that was probably not the right thing to say. But I heard guys talking dirty to each other and I told them this was not right, and they got angry with me. I have learned that it is normal for guys to talk this way to each other, but I still do not think it is normal to do it around girls. Yet, sometimes I do hear guys say fresh things to girls and the girls don't get mad at them. But they do with me (Dewey & Everard 1975).

Pragmatics has received increased attention in recent years as a focus of research (e.g. Bernard-Opitz 1982, McCaleb & Prizant 1985). It provides a framework for analyzing material previously communicable only anecdotally. The subject has also provided a new perspective for integrating the multiple communication problem of the syndrome. Journal issues devoted almost entirely to the subject have been edited by Duchan (1982) and by Prizant (1983b). An improved appreciation of both normal and deviant pragmatics should ultimately benefit the subjects and their families as well as the professionals who serve them.

Closely allied with pragmatics is the question of how the autistic individual regards others. This is a social-cognitive issue recently addressed by Baron-Cohen et al (1985, 1986).

These researchers are addressing the question of what, specifically, is cognitively unique about these children. They note that although the majority of autistic children are mentally retarded with symptoms attributed to that fact, this in itself cannot be a sufficient explanation for their social impairments. For example, some autistic children have IQs in the normal range and many mentally retarded non-autistic children, such as Down's syndrome, are socially competent relative to their mental age. They employed a new model of meta-representational capacity to predict a cognitive deficit which would explain a crucial component of the social impairment in childhood autism (Baron-Cohen et al 1985).

Their experiment made use of a puppet play paradigm and compared performances of 20 autistic children with 14 Down's syndrome and 27 clinically normal preschool children. The autistic group's mean IQ was 82 whereas the Down's group's mean was 64. Two dolls, Sally and Anne, were the protagonists. Sally placed a marble into her basket. Then she left the scene, and the marble was transferred by Anne and hidden in her box. Then, when Sally returned, the experimenter asked the critical Belief Question: 'Where will Sally look for her marble?' If the children point to the previous location of the marble, they pass the question by appreciating the doll's now false belief. But if they point to the marble's current location, then they fail the question by not taking into account the doll's belief. Two control questions, if answered correctly, confirmed the conclusions: 'Where is the marble really?' and 'Where was the marble in the beginning?' The three questions were considered different in conceptual complexity but similar in psycholinguistic complexity.

Results for the Down's syndrome and normal subjects showed pass rates on the Belief Question of 85% and 86% respectively. By contrast, 80% of the autistic children failed the Belief Question, a highly significant difference. The 16 autistic children who failed

pointed to the real location of the marble. Every child correctly answered the control questions, but the autistic children answered the Belief Question in a distinctly different way from the others. Even though the mental age of the autistic children was higher than the Down's syndrome group, they alone failed to impute beliefs to others. The investigators concluded that this dysfunction, this lack of a 'theory of mind', is independent of mental retardation and specific to autism. Clearly, such a dysfunction would be incompatible with good pragmatic performances.

CONCLUSION

Every aspect of speech, language and communication, with the possible exception of phonology, seems to be negatively affected in autistic individuals. The problems are cognitive, linguistic and social. There is not only a delay in development of these skills, but deviant development as well. Additional clinical and experimental experience increases our understanding of the syndrome and offers the potential for improved treatment methods. But not surprisingly, many complex questions remain unanswered and many approaches to treatment remain unexplored.

In the meantime these fascinating individuals have provided vastly improved insights into language development, normal and otherwise. Or, as John Wing (1976) expressed it so well:

> Autistic children do have a fascination which lies partly in the feeling that somewhere there must be a key which will unlock hidden treasure. The skilled searcher will indeed find treasure . . . but the currency will be everday and human, not fairy gold. In return for our attention, these children may give us the key to human language, which is the key to humanity itself (p. 14).

13

Language development after focal brain damage

D. Bishop

CAUSES OF BRAIN DAMAGE

The human brain at birth consists of around a hundred billion nerve cells, or neurons, plus a large number of glial cells which support and nourish the neurons. For most parts of the body, as cells die they are replaced by division of the remaining cells. This is not the case for the central nervous system. We are born with our full complement of neurons, and cannot grow new ones if these are destroyed by disease or injury.

Brain damage may arise from physical trauma, from tumours which compress the brain or which invade cerebral tissue, from disruption of the blood supply due to blockage or bursting of an artery, or from infections, poisons or ionizing radiation. The effects may range from a localized, focal lesion of a small brain area, as with a gunshot wound, to diffuse damage of the whole brain, as may occur with cranial irradiation. Our concern here is with the effects of focal brain damage, but it must be recognized that there is no clear-cut boundary between focal and diffuse lesions. For instance, traumatic head injury produces obvious contusion and laceration at the point of impact, but damage may also be sustained at the opposite pole, and there may be tearing of nerve fibres far from the site of trauma.

The frequency of the various causes of brain damage varies with age. The brain is particularly vulnerable around the time of birth, when there is a risk both of traumatic injury and of interruption of the oxygen supply (asphyxia). Premature babies are at particular risk, as they seem less well able than full-term infants to respond physiologically to changes in blood pressure. If regional cerebral blood flow is too high, there will be ruptured blood vessels and haemorrhage; if too low, insufficient oxygenation and death of brain cells (Pape & Wigglesworth 1979).

Infectious diseases such as measles and whooping cough used to account for a relatively high proportion of cases of postnatal brain damage in young children. In modern medical practice, however, neurological complications of these diseases are seldom seen. Strokes can occur in childhood, although they are rarer than in adults (Shillito 1964, Menkes 1974). Brain tumours in children are much commoner in the posterior fossa than in the cerebral hemispheres, and, therefore, the brain damage that is associated with them is diffuse (caused by hydrocephalus) rather than focal. Traumatic head injury, as a result of a fall or road traffic accident, is the commonest cause of acquired brain damage in children, especially in boys (Rutter et al 1983).

CONSEQUENCES OF FOCAL BRAIN LESIONS IN ADULTS

Language and the left hemisphere

Studies of brain-damaged adults have taught us a great deal about which areas of the brain are important for language. As long ago as 1863, Broca observed that some patients had difficulty in producing articulate speech despite having adequate motor control of the articulatory apparatus and good understanding. On the basis of post-mortem studies he reported that this clinical picture was reliably associated with lesions of a specific area of the frontal lobe, now known as 'Broca's area' (see Fig. 13.1). In 1865 he confirmed what he had originally suspected, namely that it was specifically lesions of the third frontal convolution of the *left* hemisphere that were

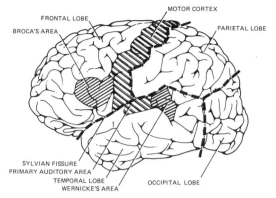

Fig. 13.1 Side view of left cerebral hemisphere

implicated in what he referred to as 'aphemia', now known as 'Broca's aphasia'.

This is not the only way in which language can be disrupted. Some patients have fluent, grammatically complex speech, but their utterances are empty of content, and they have difficulty in understanding what others say to them. Words may be substituted for one another, so that, e.g. the patient says 'table' for 'chair'. This is termed a semantic (or literal or verbal) paraphasia. Although the patient has no difficulty in articulating sounds, words may be mispronounced so that, e.g. 'alligator' is produced as 'allibaker'. This is a phonemic paraphasia. The patient may produce totally meaningless strings of sounds (neologisms). Fluent but largely incomprehensible speech is referred to as jargon. Wernicke (1874) associated this pattern of language disorder with more posterior lesions of the left cerebral hemisphere (Fig. 13.1).

During this century, research on acquired aphasia has proliferated. Most studies have been concerned with two main issues: the linguistic characterization of aphasia, and the relationship between the lesion location and type of aphasia. The original observations of Broca and Wernicke have been broadly confirmed, and many research studies continue to categorize patients as 'Broca's or Wernicke's' aphasics. It is clear, however, that the linguistic distinction between these categories is far more complicated than the traditional contrast which was made between 'expressive' and 'receptive' aphasia. For instance, Broca's aphasics can be shown to have comprehension problems when grammatically complex materials are used, and their language problems typically involve written as well as spoken language (see review by Saffran 1982). Also, many patients do not fit into either category, and additional subtypes of aphasia have been proposed. Furthermore, whilst there is a relationship between aphasic symptomatology and location of lesion, this is less straightforward than was originally thought (Kertesz 1983, Damasio & Geschwind 1984).

Although there is much to be learned about the relationship between location of lesion and aphasia type, there is no doubt that in the vast majority of cases aphasia arises from damage to the left cerebral hemisphere. Thus although the two sides of the brain appear on superficial inspection to be physically equal, they are functionally different.

The terms *language lateralization* and *cerebral dominance* refer to the tendency for language to be mediated predominantly by one side of the brain.

There are occasional exceptions to the general rule that the left hemisphere controls language. The likelihood of aphasia after right-hemisphere lesions is related to hand preference. Although aphasia in left-handers, as in right-handers, is usually the result of a left-hemisphere lesion, the probability of aphasia after a right-hemisphere lesion is much higher in left-handers than in right-handers (Alekoumbides 1978).

Role of the right hemisphere

For many years, the assumption was that the left hemisphere was the important 'dominant' hemisphere, with the right hemisphere playing a minor, subservient role. The term 'cerebral dominance' reflects this view. However, from the 1940s onwards there came increasing recognition that the right hemisphere played an important part in mediating nonverbal, visuospatial functions (Brain 1941, Paterson & Zangwill 1944, McFie et al 1950).

Evidence is now accumulating that the right hemisphere has an important role in some verbal as well as nonverbal functions. Although the left hemisphere is unquestionably specialized for phonological and syntactic processing, the right hemisphere appears to play a part in semantic and pragmatic aspects of language (Perecman 1983, Foldi et al 1983, Millar & Whitaker 1983).

CONSEQUENCES OF LATERALIZED LESIONS ACQUIRED BEFORE 1 YEAR OF AGE

Given the association between left-hemisphere lesions and aphasia in adults, we might expect to find that left-hemisphere damage early in life would preclude language development, but this is not so.

In his original writings on localization of language functions, Broca (1865) described a woman in whom post-mortem examination revealed that substantial areas of the left hemisphere, including 'Broca's area', had simply failed to develop. Although of low intelligence, this patient spoke quite adequately. Subsequent workers, including Freud (1897), commented on the lack of association between side of brain lesion and language disturbances in children with *hemiplegia*. The neural pathways concerned with movement control cross on their route from cortex to spine, so the motor centres on the left side of the brain control the right side of the body and vice versa. The observation of paralysis of one side of the body, i.e. a hemiplegia, can thus be regarded as evidence of damage to motor cortex on the opposite side of the brain. The phenomenon remarked upon by Freud and subsequent neurologists was the rarity of persistent language disturbances in children with congenital right hemiplegia (and hence left hemisphere damage). These clinical observations have since been confirmed by a number of psychological studies of hemiplegic children. For children whose brain damage is acquired at birth or in the first one or two years of life, there is no difference between those with left- or right-sided brain damage in verbal IQ or in other measures of linguistic skill such as reading ability (Basser 1962, Reed & Reitan 1969). Although a relative delay in starting to talk has been reported in children with early left-sided as compared to right-sided brain lesions (Annett 1973), most studies find no difference (Hood & Perlstein 1955, Crothers & Paine 1959, Basser 1962). Some hemiplegic children fail to develop language, but these are usually children of low general intelligence, and as likely to be left hemiplegics (with right-hemisphere damage) as right hemiplegics (Kastein & Hendin 1951).

One might wonder whether the low rate of language disturbances after left-hemisphere lesions in children reflects differences in the location and extent of cerebral lesions at different ages: perhaps the diseases that cause brain damage in children are less likely to involve the traditional speech areas than diseases of adulthood. We now have evidence that this cannot be a satisfactory explanation for adult-child differences. The main source of evidence comes from patients in whom the entire cerebral cortex of one hemisphere has been removed to treat intractable seizures. Typically the brain disease is present at birth or acquired in the first year of life, although the surgery may not be carried out until several years later. This procedure, traditionally called *hemispherectomy*, but more accurately termed *hemidecortication* (since only cerebral cortex is removed), can abolish seizures and result in considerable improvement in quality of life for patients with infantile hemiplegia. One might anticipate that removal of half of the cerebral cortex would result in profound mental handicap, and severe aphasia if the left hemisphere is removed, but this proves not to be the case. Undoubtedly, these patients do tend to have lower than average levels of intelligence, but this is the case preoperatively, and is not something that is caused by hemidecortication. The operation remains controversial, but this is because of the medical risks rather than because of adverse effects on intellectual function (Goodman 1986).

One of the earliest studies to draw attention to the importance of hemidecortication for our understanding of the biological basis of language development was by Basser (1962). He reported results from a series of 102 patients with infantile hemiplegia, including 17 cases of left hemidecortication and 18 cases of right hemidecortication. Although several hemidecorticate patients used only simple language, this seemed to be a general consequence of mental retardation, and was unrelated to side of removal. In 12 cases with left-hemisphere removal before the onset of speech, 6 children began to speak at the normal age, and only two cases had not started to speak by 4 years. Later studies of patients undergoing hemidecortication for infantile hemiplegia confirmed Basser's findings of lack of aphasia and no effect of side of removal on Verbal or Performance IQ (see reviews by Wilson 1970, Smith 1972).

These studies of hemidecorticate patients provide clear confirmation of the view, first proposed by Broca (1865), that language will develop in the right hemisphere if the left hemisphere is damaged early in life. Rasmussen & Milner (1977) specified in more detail the conditions under which right-hemisphere language develops. They studied 371 patients with intractable epilepsy who were candidates for surgery for removal of diseased brain tissue, usually from one temporal lobe. In such cases, it is crucial to ensure that functionally important areas of brain are not removed. Fortunately, it is possible to determine cerebral dominance prior to surgery. A technique developed by Wada involves injecting sodium Amytal into the vascular system of one side of the brain. This causes a transient inactivation of the injected side, so that all functions controlled by that side of the brain are disrupted for about 5 to 10 minutes. One can contrast the effects of injection of the left and right hemispheres, and identify patients where, atypically, language is disrupted after right-hemisphere injection. Rasmussen & Milner found a strong association between right-hemisphere language representation and left-hemisphere damage acquired early in life.

Furthermore, they discovered that lesion site played an important role. Provided that the traditional language areas were spared, even extensive early lesions of the left hemisphere did not result in right-hemisphere language representation. However, lesions that encroached upon Broca's area or Wernicke's area were likely to bring about a functional reorganization of the brain, with right-hemisphere specialization for language.

CONSEQUENCES OF LATERALIZED LESIONS ACQUIRED IN CHILDHOOD

We may contrast the consequences of left-hemisphere lesions acquired very early in life, which do not selectively impair language development, with those acquired in adulthood, which frequently cause aphasia. This raises the question of what happens if a lesion is acquired in childhood, after the child has started to talk, but before language acquisition is complete.

Studies carried out prior to 1978 were in broad agreement that aphasia did occur after left-hemisphere lesions in children, but that it differed from adult aphasia in two important respects. First, the prognosis was considerably better than that found for adult aphasia, with many children making full and rapid recovery. Second, aphasic symptoms in children usually followed a distinctive pattern rather different from adult aphasia. More recent studies have modified some of these conclusions.

Prognosis

Basser's (1962) study included 30 patients where hemiplegia was acquired after language had developed. 20 cases (13 with left and 7 with right-sided lesions) developed a language disturbance, but recovery occurred in all cases. Basser did not give detailed accounts of language status in his patients, many of whom were of low IQ, so we cannot tell how complete recovery was.

Byers & McLean (1962) studied 12 children who acquired aphasia in association with

hemiplegia at the age of 3 to 15 years, usually as a consequence of left-hemisphere vascular malformation or thrombosis. No test results relevant to language or scholastic attainments were given, but it was stated that all of the children recovered normal language, although other intellectual functions remained impaired in several cases. Alajouanine & Lhermitte (1965) reported a high rate of recovery (75% with normal or near normal language after a year or more) in a group of 32 children with aphasia due to left-hemisphere lesions. Similarly high rates of recovery were reported in studies by Collignon et al (1968) and Assal & Campiche (1973).

Lenneberg (1967) combined results from 8 personal cases with 17 published case reports and noted that, in general, the younger the child, the better the prognosis. Aphasia due to a unilateral lesion acquired before 10 years of age would usually recover completely, whilst post-pubertal brain damage usually left some permanent residue of aphasia. He used the biological concept of 'critical period' to account for this finding. A critical period is a biologically-determined period of development during which an individual has particular sensitivities, response propensities, or learning potentials, which are not found later in maturation. According to Lenneberg, puberty marks the end of a critical period for language learning in humans.

It is worth noting that while aphasic symptoms usually resolve after focal brain damage in children, virtually every study reviewed so far noted persisting academic and intellectual problems. Alajouanine & Lhermitte (1965) found that although the majority of children were no longer clinically aphasic at follow-up, *none* of them made normal progress at school. They had difficulty learning lessons, particularly those involving languages, and seemed unable to acquire new knowledge. Woods & Carey (1979) looked at the process of recovery from childhood aphasia using tests of language comprehension and expression. Their study of 27 patients with unilateral left-hemisphere lesions included 16 who had incurred their lesion after one year of age. Some of these patients had never been aphasic, and these children were not impaired on any language measures at follow-up. However, children who had apparently recovered from a pre-existing aphasia were impaired on all language measures. This result could not be explained in terms of general intellectual retardation in the previously aphasic children, as their IQ scores were very similar to those who had never been aphasic. Evidently the language assessments used in this study were picking up residual verbal impairments after apparent recovery from childhood aphasia.

Recent studies have also called into question the relationship between age at onset and outcome of aphasia in children (Woods & Teuber 1978, Hecaen 1983). However, the evidence is hard to evaluate, mainly because the numbers of patients in any one age group are usually very small. Also, where studies include children with bilateral brain damage, one would not *expect* to find any relationship between age and outcome (Assal & Campiche (1973), van Dongen & Loonen (1977), van Hout et al (1985)). Bilateral lesions will presumably preclude right-hemisphere language developing, and so have a poor prognosis whatever the age of the child. Nor would one expect a straightforward inverse relationship between age at onset and outcome in children with acquired epileptic aphasia (Landau-Kleffner syndrome). Children with this syndrome typically have no signs of focal damage but do have evidence of electroencephalographic abnormalities, often bilateral. Inclusion of such cases in series of children with acquired aphasia is likely to cloud the issue when considering age at onset relative to outcome, as the relationship goes counter to prediction in this syndrome, with the worst outcome the earlier the onset (Bishop 1985a). If consideration is restricted to children with unilateral lesions, it does seem to be broadly true that the probability of persisting aphasic impairment is raised for children aged 10 years or more at time of injury, but this is not a particularly strong relationship, and one does find cases of poor outcome in younger chil-

dren, and good recovery in older ones. Perhaps, rather than talking of a critical period, which implies a clear-cut boundary, we should think in terms of a gradual diminution in the capacity of recovery of verbal functions after left-hemisphere damage from the first year of life up until adolescence. In any case, it is evident that many factors other than age play a role in determining prognosis, and it would be wrong to assume, for example, that just because a child was aged under 10 years, complete and rapid recovery would ensue.

A few studies have looked at other factors relating to prognosis of acquired aphasia in children. Van Hout et al suggested that location and extent of lesion were important, and they confirmed that aphasia due to bilateral lesions has a particularly poor prognosis. Van Dongen & Loonen (1977) noted a positive relationship between severity of aphasic symptoms at onset and subsequent outcome, with initial level of comprehension being a good prognostic factor. However, there are counter-examples. Van Dongen et al (1985) described two children with initial severe comprehension problems but good outcome. It seems that for the present, our understanding of factors relating to outcome of acquired aphasia is too limited to allow confident predictions about likely outcome in individual children. Furthermore, we know nothing about the extent to which the prognosis of acquired childhood aphasia can be influenced by specific therapeutic and educational measures. We need larger-scale studies using objective measures of language function to disentangle the influences of etiology, lesion location, severity of initial symptoms, age at onset and experience of therapy.

A study by Vargha-Khadem et al (1985) has made a start in addressing some of these issues. They looked at language outcome in hemiplegic children. Like Woods & Carey (1979), they found evidence of verbal impairment (on both the Token Test and Object Naming) in children with left-hemisphere lesions, especially those acquired after 5 years of age, even though only one case was judged aphasic at time of testing. Extent of lesion did not appear to be an important determinant of language status. Their sample was too small, however, to look for relationships between age at onset and outcome in children whose lesions were acquired after language had developed, and they did not have data on initial language status of this subgroup.

Symptoms

Guttman (1942) suggested that aphasia in children tended to be overlooked because, unlike adults, children tended not to complain about their language difficulties and obvious symptoms such as word-finding problems were less apparent. He described 16 cases of acquired aphasia in children seen in a neurosurgical unit, and noted that all cases aged under 10 years and some older children were characterized by extreme reticence or mutism. Recovery was usually rapid, and as children recovered they went through a stage of dysarthria and telegrammatic speech.

A number of subsequent studies reported data in good agreement with Guttman. Alajouanine & Lhermitte (1965) studied 32 children aged from 6 to 15 years with acquired aphasia due to left-hemisphere lesions, and commented on the striking reduction of expressive language, to the extent that spontaneous speech was nearly nil. Although dysarthria was also common, this was not seen as responsible for the reticence. When children could be induced to speak, it was found that their syntax was simplified rather than erroneous, and it was felt that to this extent the children differed from agrammatic adults. Writing was invariably more severely disturbed than oral language and reading. Alajouanine & Lhermitte also commented on the rarity of certain aphasic symptoms that are relatively common in adult aphasia. They never observed jargon in children, even if the temporal lobe was affected, and only 7 of the 32 children produced phonemic paraphasias. Receptive language disorders were found in 10 cases, but were marked in only four.

A similar picture was found in studies by Assal & Campiche (1973), Collignon et al (1968) and Hecaen (1976, 1977). Mutism was the predominant symptom, and paraphasias and jargon were rare or nonexistent. The frequency of comprehension problems varied from study to study, perhaps reflecting differences in methods of assessment. Assal & Campiche found that comprehension problems were rare, although when they did occur they were associated with poor prognosis, whilst Hecaen reported that comprehension problems were not uncommon in the early stages of recovery, but usually resolved rapidly. All studies noted that problems with written language often persisted, even after spoken language had apparently fully recovered.

All these early accounts agreed that one did not encounter Wernicke's aphasia in children. However, Woods & Teuber, in their 1978 study of childhood aphasia, remarked that although the typical clinical picture was one of nonfluent aphasia, other forms of aphasia could occur. One of their patients, aged 5 years at onset, had a severe receptive aphasia with expressive jargon. Van Hout et al (1985) produced further instances of fluent aphasias in children. They studied a sample of 16 children aged from 2 to 13 years, selected on the basis of their having an acquired aphasia. (It should be noted that some of these children had bilateral brain damage.) It was reported that the youngest children had mutism and speech regression, and the oldest displayed features of Broca's aphasia, but the remaining 11 children, aged from 4 to 10 years, had more unusual symptoms that did not correspond to those traditionally thought characteristic of childhood aphasia. Both phonemic and literal paraphasias were common in their sample, and two children produced neologistic jargon. Although for the majority of children paraphasias disappeared in the course of recovery within two months or less, they persisted, although at a lower level, over several months in three children. Van Hout et al consider various explanations for the discrepancies between their findings and those of other workers. They note that differences in selection criteria for patients, and the relatively short interval they used between onset and assessment, might account for some of the discrepancies. However, they point out that paraphasias were seldom remarked in some studies that seemed broadly comparable in terms of subject selection. They suggested, therefore, that the assessment techniques they used might explain the differences. Many studies do not use standardized tests but rely solely on clinical medical examination to detect aphasia. Van Hout et al suggest that in many aphasic children positive symptoms may be masked because of their reluctance to speak. They conclude that when children are given ample encouragement to respond in a formal testing situation their symptoms may become far more obvious.

Van Dongen et al (1985) confirm the conclusions of van Hout et al, reporting that out of 27 children with acquired aphasia referred to their department over a four year period, four had fluent aphasia with comprehension problems (as assessed by the Token Test). Three of these children are described in detail. All had left-hemisphere lesions involving Wernicke's area. Further cases of aphasic children producing paraphasias, neologisms and fluent aphasia have recently been reported by Visch-Brink & van de Sandt-Koenderman (1984) and van Hout & Lyon (1986).

Hecaen (1983), however, observed no cases of logorrhea or jargon in his series of 25 aphasic children, despite including 10 cases with temporal lesions. Further, only one of these 10 children produced paraphasias. He suggested that lesion location and etiology were important determinants of aphasic symptoms in children, but the relationships he reported did not agree very well with other studies. For instance, he found that anterior lesions were associated with more severe disturbances (including receptive language impairment) than were temporal lesions.

Clearly, it is very hard to make any generalizations about the typical clinical picture in childhood aphasia. Although differences in subject selection may account for some of the variability between studies, much remains unexplained. For further progress to be made, we must have more studies using objective assessments of language function. The need for this is particularly urgent because so many of the symptoms reported in children consist of reduction or simplification of language, rather than frank abnormalities. These symptoms are likely to be missed on clinical examination, as are all but the most severe receptive problems.

EXPLANATIONS FOR ADULT-CHILD DIFFERENCES

Differences in outcome more apparent than real?

The most striking demonstration of different recovery in children and adults is found in cases of hemidecortication (see review by Smith 1972). St James-Roberts (1981) has argued that the difference in outcome of hemidecortication in adults and children could be due not to *age* at injury but to other factors, especially recovery period. We are impressed, he argues, with the apparent lack of impact on language function when hemidecortication is carried out for infantile hemiplegia, but how can we know that a similar good outcome would not be found if a similar procedure were carried out in an adult who was then able to recover over many years? We do not know the answer because neurosurgeons would only consider hemidecortication for disease acquired in adulthood as a drastic life-saving measure. The typical pathology is a malignant tumour which is likely to invade the other hemisphere and which significantly reduces life expectancy so that one cannot observe recovery over a prolonged period. St James-Roberts pointed out that a man who underwent left hemidecortication in adulthood for glioma showed some recovery of language functions, especially receptive language, even though his expressive language remained severely aphasic (Smith 1972). Ten months after surgery he scored well within normal limits on a test of receptive vocabulary, the Peabody Picture Vocabulary Test.

Could total recovery of language functions occur after left hemidecortication in adulthood? The only way of excluding this logical possibility would be by performing such an operation on a person who had no progressive disease and an intact right hemisphere. As this is not an ethically acceptable procedure, we cannot know the answer. However, this does not seem very plausible when we consider that much less drastic left-hemisphere lesions in previously healthy adults frequently cause severe aphasia with very limited recovery over periods of many years (Sarno 1980). In order to accept St James-Roberts' position we would have to maintain that the total removal of left-sided cerebral cortex in an adult has less severe consequences than more restricted left-hemisphere lesions.

Perhaps the strongest argument against the position adopted by St James-Roberts comes from the study, described above, by Rasmussen & Milner (1977), which used the Wada test to investigate cerebral lateralization. They found that for 92 left-handed patients with left-hemisphere lesions acquired before 6 years of age (usually in the perinatal period) 72% had atypical (bilateral or right-hemisphere) language representation. In contrast, atypical language representation was found in only 36 out of 122 (30%) other left-handed patients. Rasmussen & Milner concluded that injuries to the left hemisphere occurring after the age of 5 years rarely changed the laterality of language representation at maturity. In other words, the processes mediating recovery are structurally different for early and late-acquired lesions.

Initial bilaterality of language representation

In his classic text 'Biological Foundations of Language', Lenneberg (1967) put forward a unified theory to explain the different consequences of unilateral lesions early and later in life. He proposed that cortical control of language is initially bilateral, but then gradually lateralizes, usually to the left hemisphere, as the child matures. In early childhood, while there is still bilateral involvement in verbal processes, language can develop in the corresponding area of the right hemisphere if the left hemisphere is damaged. Hence the relatively good recovery from acquired aphasia in children. The theory predicts that since the right hemisphere is still playing a part in language function early in life, *right* hemisphere lesions in young children should result in aphasia, though this should resolve rapidly. Only in the case of bilateral lesions, or left-hemisphere lesions in older children with established cerebral dominance, should persistent aphasia be observed. Lenneberg produced evidence supporting this prediction, but more recently this has been challenged. A major source of evidence was the study by Basser (1962), in which it was found that 7 out of 15 children who acquired *right*-hemisphere lesions after the onset of speech developed aphasia. This was a lower rate of aphasia than was found after comparable left-hemisphere lesions, but was appreciably higher than one would have predicted from studies of aphasia acquired in adulthood.

However, in their study of language function in children with unilateral brain lesions, Woods & Teuber (1978) found that only 4 out of 31 children with right-hemisphere lesions became aphasic. There thus seemed to be a puzzling drop in the frequency of right-hemisphere aphasia in children from nearly 50% in Basser's report to 12% in this study. Woods & Teuber suggested a possible explanation: earlier series of patients included several cases with neurological complications of bacterial infections. Such infections may well affect both sides of the brain, even if symptoms are apparently unilateral. If a child who really has a bilateral lesion is classified as a case of right-hemisphere lesion, this will give a spuriously high estimate of the incidence of aphasia with right-hemisphere lesions. The introduction of antibiotics dramatically reduced neurological complications of childhood infectious diseases, so contemporary series of patients are less subject to such error.

Satz & Bullard-Bates (1981) and Carter et al

(1982) attempted to quantify the incidence of bilateral and right-hemisphere language representation in adults and children. The problem for anyone attempting this exercise is that aphasia in children is sufficiently rare that cases from many different centres must be combined to obtain a sample including even a small number of children of different ages. Reliance on reports from the literature is dangerous, as there may be a tendency to highlight unusual cases, and not to report negative data (e.g. lack of aphasia after a lateralized lesion). Furthermore, all too often, crucial information is missing. Carter et al made the best they could of the existing literature, discarding numerous studies because of various inadequacies in the data. As well as noting the need to exclude possible cases of bilateral damage, they argued that the apparently high rate of aphasia after right-hemisphere lesions in children failed to take into account the fact that many of the children in the early studies were not right-handed. We know that atypical cerebral dominance is associated with hand preference. Therefore, they argued, we should take into account hand preference before comparing the rates of aphasia in children and adults. It was found that in children acquiring lesions below 5 years of age, the frequency of aphasia after right-hemisphere lesions *was* significantly raised compared to estimates from the adult population, even after excluding cases with possible bilateral involvement. However, when cases with unclear hand preference were excluded, then the figure was similar to that found in adults.

This argument, however, is on a shaky foundation. Hand preference is something that develops as the child matures, becoming clearly established as fine motor skills are mastered. Young children are far more random and unskilled in their manual behaviour than older children and adults, and we find that the proportion of children who are regarded as 'mixed handed', i.e. without a clear hand preference, declines with age (Bishop 1983c). Zangwill (1962) has explicitly related the gradual development of hand pref-

erence to the lateralization of cerebral dominance, arguing that as the left hemisphere's predominance for language develops, there is a concomitant trend for right-handedness to emerge in most children. If establishment of hand preference *is* an index of cerebral lateralization, then by restricting consideration only to right-handers we will exclude exactly those cases whose language is not yet fully lateralized. How is this problem to be overcome? The answer would seem to be that we should *not* restrict consideration to right-handers, but rather consider the whole population when comparing rates of aphasia in adults and children.

Because of the numerous sources of potential error in post hoc analyses of published data, it may be wisest to conclude that the case for a raised incidence of aphasia after right-hemisphere damage in young children is not proven. If there is a true increase in aphasia after right-hemisphere lesions in children, this seems only to apply to those under 5 years. Should we therefore accept Lenneberg's view that both hemispheres are initially implicated in language, but revise our estimate of the time course of right-hemisphere involvement down to 5 years of age, as proposed by Krashen (1973)?

There are problems even for this modified version of Lenneberg's theory. Reviews by Kinsbourne & Hiscock (1977), Seron (1981) and Witelson (1985) query the assumption that recovery from focal brain damage has anything to do with progressive lateralization of language functions. They draw attention to studies that use techniques such as dichotic listening or evoked responses to assess cerebral lateralization in normal subjects, which provide evidence for cerebral lateralization well before 5 years of age. Also there is now good evidence that there are physical differences in size and shape between the two cerebral hemispheres, not only in infancy but even in fetal brains. If we accept that these structural asymmetries are related to functional asymmetry, then we may conclude that cerebral specialization is present before birth. According to Witelson, we are misled into thinking that cerebral specialization increases with age, because manifestations of that specialization become more obvious as cognitive development proceeds. Thus it is much more difficult to demonstrate cerebral specialization in babies, who cannot speak and can carry out only a very limited range of language-related tasks, than it is in an older child, where we can look for evidence of lateral differences in a wide range of behaviours.

If cerebral specialization is established even before birth, why should early right-hemisphere lesions produce aphasia? One solution is to argue, as Satz & Bullard-Bates (1981) have done, that the apparent increase in right-hemisphere aphasia in young children is an artefact of biased subject selection. There is, however, reason to question this conclusion, especially as it concerns children under 5 years of age, in which case we are left with a puzzle to be explained.

Seron (1981) has suggested a possible resolution. He notes that there is evidence that in adults the right hemisphere is involved in certain aspects of verbal comprehension, and it may be important in the pragmatic functions of language. While the grammatical skills mediated by the left hemisphere are still underdeveloped, the relative importance of these right-hemisphere skills in determining overall verbal competence may be quite large. If the child has not yet mastered many aspects of grammar, a lesion of the left hemisphere may not produce a dramatic change in verbal functioning. However, once grammatical skills are well developed, a left-hemisphere lesion would produce a much more obvious change in verbal behaviour. Thus, according to Seron, there is no change in what the right hemisphere does: in both adults and young children it is involved in aspects of semantic and pragmatic functions, whilst the left-hemisphere is important for syntax and phonology. What changes with age is the relative level of development of these functions. This is an interesting explanation which leads to the prediction that, if one used appropriate tests, it should be possible to demonstrate lexical comprehension and pragmatic disorders in older children after *right*-hemisphere lesions, even though these children would not be overtly aphasic. A further prediction is that where aphasia is observed after unilateral right-hemisphere lesions in young children, this should be different in kind from aphasia associated with left-hemisphere lesions. Detailed linguistic accounts of preschool children with acquired aphasia are virtually nonexistent, so we cannot as yet test this prediction.

Explanation in terms of general plasticity of the immature nervous system

It could be argued that Lenneberg's notion of a diminishing role of the right hemisphere in language acquisition is in any case unnecessary. Early studies using experimental brain lesions in animals found that as a general rule there was better outcome after brain damage in infancy as compared to damage later in life (Kennard 1936). Can we not explain differences in language outcome for adults and children in terms of the same general rule?

The problem is that the 'Kennard principle', as it has come to be known, is an oversimplification. It is not true that recovery of function is always better after an early lesion than after a later one. There is considerable variability from one function to another (Goldman 1976, Rudel 1978). As Teuber & Rudel (1962) showed in a study of brain-damaged children, there is a complex interaction between age at injury and function. Some functions are more impaired by early than by late lesions, others are more impaired by late lesions, for other functions age at injury is immaterial. Furthermore, brain damage may have delayed effects, so that deficits become increasingly apparent with age. The Kennard principle is not an explanation but a description which is valid only for certain functions.

For a long time it was thought that the Kennard principle reflected an underlying neurophysiological difference between mature and immature brains. Although brain cells, once destroyed, cannot be regenerated, immature neurons adjacent to damaged tissue are capable of forming new interconnections (collateral sprouting), and it was originally thought that this occurred only in immature brains. However, this cannot be the explanation. Not only has collateral sprouting of neurons been found in mature animals (Lynch & Gall 1979): it has also been demonstrated that ability of neurons in a given area to sprout has little relationship to functional recovery possible after lesions of that area (Goldman 1976).

Degree of right-hemisphere specialization as a factor limiting recovery

Even though there may be little relationship between neuronal maturity and collateral sprouting, and between collateral sprouting and functional recovery, there is some evidence for a relationship between neuronal maturity and functional recovery. Bishop (1981) related data on age of myelination, from Conel's (1939–1967) series of neuropathological studies, to degree of functional impairment after hemidecortication for infantile hemiplegia. Myelination refers to the formation of a sheath of a fatty substance called myelin around neural processes. This has the effect of speeding neural transmission, and is regarded as one index of neurological maturity. On the whole, Conel's data were consistent with prediction. Thus, within motor cortex, the earliest area to myelinate is that controlling the arm, followed by the hand, leg, and much later, the face area. Reports of motor deficits in hemidecorticate patients (Ignelzi & Bucy 1968, Wilson 1970) find least impairment for the face, moderate impairment of the leg, severe impairment of the hand, and virtually no use of the arm. Language is consistent with this pattern: areas of the brain that mediate language become myelinated much later than those controlling motor functions, and language impairment after early brain damage is far less evident than motor impairment. Thus a case can be made for arguing that long-term recovery of a particular function is inversely related to the age at

which areas normally controlling that function mature. However, the evidence used to support this argument is indirect, and not always consistent (striate cortex does not fit the general pattern), so this should be regarded as a hypothesis in need of more direct test rather than a proven fact.

Let us suppose for the moment, however, that there is a relationship between neurological maturity and recovery of function, so that the more mature an area, the more limited the ultimate functional recovery. If it is not ability to sprout which changes with maturity, and which limits functional recovery, what then might it be? In order for new neural connections to be formed it is not only necessary for new neural processes to grow from the damaged region: they must be able to find their way to suitable sites and form new connections there. This may not be possible if undamaged areas of the brain which have the potential for mediating recovery by forming new connections are already committed to other functions. Recovery of language function can be interpreted as a special instance of this general rule (Penfield 1965, Goldman 1972). The degree to which the *right* hemisphere is already committed to other functions would be what limits the potential for language development.

Landsell (1969) reported data that fit this interpretation. He studied a group of epileptic patients who were known, on the basis of the Wada test, to have right-hemisphere language. He found that although there was no relation between overall IQ and age at injury, ultimate verbal proficiency was directly related to age at which right-hemisphere language development was initiated: the earlier the injury, the higher the verbal skill and the lower the nonverbal skills. This result can be explained by arguing that the potential for adequate right-hemisphere language depends on the extent to which visuospatial functions are already established in that hemisphere. With early lesions, verbal functions take priority, so patients are left with a relative visuospatial deficit. With later lesions, visuospatial functions are already established in the right hemisphere, so there will be limited potential for development of verbal functions.

Is it possible that the opposite could occur, with early right-hemisphere damage causing visuospatial skills to become established in the left hemisphere, blocking development of verbal skills? Goldman (1972) suggested that in humans the association areas of the left hemisphere develop before those in the right hemisphere. If this is so, then recovery of language function after a left-hemisphere lesion in infancy or childhood would be more complete than recovery of visuospatial ability after a comparable right-hemisphere insult, since the intact right hemisphere in the former case would be less mature, and hence less 'committed' than the intact left hemisphere in the latter case. Compatible data have been reported in three studies of children with lateralized brain damage. In each study it was found that whilst right hemisphere damage produced a significant deficit in performance IQ relative to verbal IQ, comparable left-hemisphere lesions resulted in a much more even pattern of abilities, with similar (usually low) levels of verbal and performance IQ (Rudel et al 1974, Woods 1980, Riva & Cazzaniga 1986).

Woods (1983) has succinctly summed up current thinking on the effects of brain damage on language development. He notes that there is no question about the right hemisphere's ability to mediate language if the left is damaged early in life. What is in question is the notion that the right hemisphere is initially implicated in normal language acquisition. Current thinking has shifted so that rather than postulating a diminishing role of the right hemisphere in language development, the focus is on the right hemisphere's increasing differentiation and irreversible specialization for functions other than language.

RIGHT HEMISPHERE LANGUAGE CAPACITY: COMPLETE OR LIMITED?

Studies reviewed so far suggest that, provided a lateralized lesion is acquired early in life, it makes no difference to language development whether it is the right or left hemisphere which is involved. In other words, at birth, the left and right hemispheres have equal potential (or, to use current jargon, are *equipotential*) for language development. Unilateral lesions of either hemisphere are likely to depress general intelligence, but do not, apparently, result in selective verbal deficits.

This conclusion is based predominantly on studies that measured language functioning with verbal IQ tests. Dennis & Kohn (1976) questioned whether Verbal IQ was an adequate measure of language status. Verbal intelligence tests measure such skills as ability to define words, reason, and give factual information, but do not demand any syntactic sophistication from the testee. A child may obtain an average Verbal IQ despite using very simple and immature grammatical constructions. Dennis & Kohn argued that tests designed to assess specific aspects of language function can give very different results.

Studies contesting the notion of equipotentiality

Dennis & Kohn compared the performance of five left- and four right-hemidecorticate patients on a new syntactic comprehension test, the Active-Passive-Negative test. In this test, the patient is presented with two pictures which correspond to contrasting SVO sentences, such as 'the boy pushes the girl' vs 'the girl pushes the boy'. Using these simple materials, one can test comprehension of positive and negative sentences in active and passive voice. For instance, in a passive negative item, the subject would be asked to select the picture corresponding to: 'the boy is not pushed by the girl'. Dennis & Kohn argued that if there was true equipotentiality, then there should be no difference between patients with a single right hemisphere and those with a single left hemisphere in their ability to do this test.

What they found was that although the two groups did not differ in verbal IQ, the left-hemidecorticate group performed more poorly than the right-hemidecorticate group on this syntactic test. They concluded that the two hemispheres are *not* equipotential at birth: although the right hemisphere can mediate language, its ability to do so is more limited than that of the left hemisphere, and linguistic deficits can be found if suitable tests are used.

Since publication of this seminal paper, several further studies, mostly supporting this conclusion, have appeared, and a casual glance at the literature suggests that the evidence against equipotentiality is overwhelming. However, careful scrutiny of the published evidence leads to scepticism, because of numerous methodological problems.

Methodological problems of studies concerned with equipotentiality

It is inevitable that any study concerned with hemidecorticate patients will be restricted to a small sample size. It is not inevitable, however, that there should be no normal control group included in such studies, yet this is often the case.

One could argue that a normal control group is not necessary in these studies. Suppose we had found that left-hemidecorticate patients did more poorly than a normal control group on the Active-Passive-Negative test. Most people would say that was not a very interesting result. Performance on a test like this is likely to be affected by a host of general factors as well as specific syntactic skills, and brain damage tends to affect all aspects of functioning. To demonstrate that patients with left-hemisphere damage do poorly relative to people with no brain damage is relatively uninformative, as this could just be a consequence of neurological patients being less motivated, more anxious, less attentive, more easily tired or discouraged, or of lower general intelligence.

It is therefore seen as much more sensible to contrast patients with left-hemidecortication and those with right-hemidecortication. General impairments affecting test performance should apply to both groups. If they differ on a particular linguistic test then it seems reasonable to attribute this to a specific linguistic impairment associated with left-hemisphere removal.

Despite these arguments, there are very good reasons for collecting normal control data. First, it enables one to quantify just how defective performance of a brain-damaged group is relative to the spread of scores in the normal population. Second, it allows for the possibility that individuals with left-sided damage may *not* be impaired relative to a control group on a language test. Suppose we have only five left-hemidecorticate patients and four right-hemidecorticate patients, as in the Dennis & Kohn study, and we found no difference in their scores on a linguistic test, we could place little confidence in this result, because the numbers are so small. If, however, we were to find that both groups were unimpaired relative to a large normal control group, we could place much more confidence in this negative finding, which would support the equipotentiality position.

The use of control data becomes particularly important when, as is the case in this field samples of brain-damaged patients are not only small but also have a wide spread of age and ability. The sample tested by Dennis & Kohn, for instance, ranged in age from 8 to 28 years, with verbal IQs ranging from 78 to 96. Within any group, then, we can expect substantial variability in test scores, which may result in spurious group differences, or, alternatively, may mask genuine differences between groups.

Variability related to age can be controlled for by using standardized scores based on age-appropriate norms. This is, in effect, what happens with an IQ test. The raw test scores corresponding to an IQ of 100 will be higher for a 10-year-old than for an 6-year-old, but both results mean the same thing, i.e. that the score is average for a child of that age. Most studies contrasting the effects of left- and right-sided lesions fail to control for age effects and rely on raw scores, which makes interpretation difficult when there is a wide age range.

Bishop (1983d) argued that lack of control data gave a misleading picture in the study by Dennis & Kohn (1976). Of two left-hemidecorticate patients who did particularly poorly on the Active-Passive-Negative test, one was 8 years old and the other had a full scale IQ below 80. Bishop gave the Active-Passive-Negative test to control young people of normal and dull-normal intelligence and found that overall performance of this control group did not differ significantly from that of either of the hemidecorticate groups studied by Dennis and Kohn. It seemed that poor performance on this test might have more to do with age and IQ rather than being a specific problem associated with development of language in the right hemisphere. This conclusion is supported by a study of two French-speaking patients who had undergone left hemidecortication for infantile hemiplegia (Leleux & Lebrun 1981). Neither patient had any difficulty with the Active-Passive-Negative test.

Subsequent papers by Dennis and her coworkers drew sweeping conclusions from even smaller numbers of hemidecorticate patients, and not only did not include normal control data, but ignored existing normative data. Dennis & Whitaker (1976) presented raw data from three children, two with left hemidecortication and one with right hemidecortication, on the ITPA and the Token Test. Sample size is obviously too small for meaningful statistical analysis, but the authors note that on some of the tests the two patients with left hemidecortication appear to obtain relatively low scores. If, however, we use standardization data to take age into account and to transform scores into standard scores, the evidence for a selective linguistic deficit in those with left-sided removals is unimpressive (Bishop 1983d).

Bishop (1988) reviewed eight studies concerned with the equipotentiality hypothesis that were published between 1980 and 1986 (Kohn 1980, Leleux & Lebrun 1981, Dennis et al 1981, Rankin et al 1981, Vargha-Khadem et al 1985, Aram et al 1985, Aram et al 1986, Lovett et al 1986), seven of which

claimed to support Dennis & Kohn's conclusion that there are subtle linguistic impairments associated with early left-hemisphere lesions. Bishop found that only one study, that by Vargha-Khadem et al (1985), provided anything like convincing evidence of a linguistic impairment associated with early left-hemisphere damage. This study reported impaired performance on the Token Test in children with left-hemisphere lesions acquired around the time of birth, compared to children with right-hemisphere lesions. The study included a normal control group, and used sample sizes large enough to allow statistical analysis of results. Unfortunately, even here raw scores were used rather than age-adjusted standard scores when comparing groups spanning a wide age range (6 to 17 years). To complicate interpretation yet further, the deficit in the Token Test found by Vargha Khadem et al is discrepant with other studies finding normal levels of performance on this test in individuals with early left-hemisphere lesions. These include the studies by Woods & Carey (1979) and Leleux & Lebrun (1981), as well as a study of patients with right-hemisphere language by Kohn (1980).

There are three possible explanations for these discrepant findings.

1. It may be that there is a genuine disadvantage for the right hemisphere as compared to the left hemisphere in terms of ultimate linguistic competence that can be achieved, but that this effect is small relative to the substantial variability in linguistic skill within any group of patients. If so, then one would need large groups of patients, preferably all of similar age, to demonstrate the effect, and this poses practical problems.

2. Differences between studies may arise because of variation in the age at which patients are assessed. As Smith (1972, 1981) pointed out, the consequences of a lesion are not static but evolve with time.

It may be that ultimate linguistic competence of the right hemisphere is as good as the left, but that functional reorganization of the brain takes time, so that language development is delayed. If this were so, then it would be easier to demonstrate differences between groups for subjects tested in childhood rather than in adulthood.

3. The final possibility is that at birth the left and right hemispheres do have equal potential for language development, and that where left-right differences in verbal outcome are reported for patients with unilateral lesions, these are artefacts. There are two important sources of potential error in this area. First, studies may inadvertently include subjects with bilateral brain damage. Smith (1981) noted the substantial variations in intellectual capacities of hemidecorticate patients, and suggested that this may be related to extent of unsuspected preoperative damage to the residual hemisphere. He noted that many hemidecorticate patients (82% of those in his series) had sensorimotor impairments on the non-hemiplegic side, indicating damage to the remaining hemisphere. Strauss & Verity (1983) make a similar point. It is therefore vital that investigators provide what evidence they can to support claims that the patients under study have strictly unilateral brain damage. Ideally one would want to see quantitative evidence of normal sensorimotor function on the non-hemiplegic side, plus negative findings for the unaffected hemisphere from CT scan and electroencephalography. Most studies give inadequate detail of the criteria they used to determine unilaterality of lesion.

The other potential source of error is easier to guard against. This is the use of raw test scores across wide age bands. When considering why verbal IQ tests fail to differentiate left- and right-hemisphere groups, whilst other language tests appear to do so, it is argued that this has to do with the verbal functions measured by different tests. The true explanation may prove to be far less interesting: IQ test data are invariably transformed to standard scores independent of age and are thus not subject to the sorts of bias that can arise when raw test scores are used.

It is premature to conclude, as many have done, that the right hemisphere has some inherent limitation in the degree of linguistic sophistication it can achieve. This remains a possibility, but is far from proven. There are several cases of individuals with known right-hemisphere language representation who perform at a normal or above average level on tests measuring understanding of complex grammatical constructions. No language test has yet been discovered that invariably demonstrates impairment in individuals with right-hemisphere language.

OVERVIEW

The work reviewed in this chapter demonstrates the robustness of the young brain when affected by unilateral lesions. Language development is compatible with removal of the left cerebral cortex, provided the brain damage necessitating this operation is sustained very early in life. Damage to the left hemisphere after the child has started to speak can result in aphasia, but recovery is the rule, especially for children under 10 years of age.

Nevertheless, it would be wrong to give too optimistic a picture of recovery from focal brain damage in children. One thing that recent research demonstrates is the importance of objective assessment of language functions in brain-damaged children. Early studies of acquired aphasia based accounts of recovery purely on clinical examination, concluding that recovery had occurred provided the child did not have obvious aphasic symptoms such as paraphasias, anomia or agrammatical sentence structure. Studies using standardized tests have revealed persisting verbal deficiencies in many children long after such obvious aphasic features have resolved. Educational failure and problems with acquiring written language are common after left-hemisphere damage acquired in childhood. We should not be misled into thinking that the young brain is so resilient as to be able to recover fully from acquired aphasia, and we need to develop remedial approaches to help children overcome the verbal limitations that may persist after obvious aphasic symptoms have resolved.

Anyone attempting to assimilate the literature on acquired aphasia in children soon becomes frustrated at the paucity of data and the lack of detail given with many of the published cases. We are still a long way from understanding the complex interactions between age at injury, nature, location and extent of brain damage, aphasic symptoms and prognosis. Given the rarity of acquired aphasia in children, it is unlikely that progress will be made unless researchers start to co-operate in multi-centre studies. In this field small numbers of subjects are inevitable, but poor measurement of language function is not. It is to be hoped that future studies will increasingly supplement clinical observation with objective and standardized measures.

This chapter has concentrated on the importance of studying focal brain damage as a means of gaining a better theoretical under-standing of localization of function and plas-ticity in the developing nervous system. It should not be thought, however, that the study of children with focal brain damage is a topic only of esoteric interest to academics in ivory towers. Research in this area has tremendous practical implications. If we can develop assessment procedures which are sensitive to the acquired language problems experienced by children, these can be used to monitor the progress of children with brain disease, including those undergoing neuro-surgery. If we understand, and can measure, those aspects of language which are affected, it becomes possible to devise appropriate therapeutic procedures, and to assess their efficacy. We may indeed find that therapeutic techniques developed for this purpose have a broader application to children with more widespread brain damage.

14

Language development in children with abnormal structure or function of the speech apparatus

D. Bishop

INTRODUCTION

Why study language development in children who have physical difficulty in speaking? One reason is that these children can provide a vital test case for several psycholinguistic theories by enabling us to see how far mastery of spoken and written language can develop passively in a child whose ability to produce speech is limited or nonexistent. The other reason is practical. We need to know how physical difficulties in speaking affect language learning so that children can be offered appropriate education. For example, is it safe to assume that a child who cannot speak can be taught to read and write using traditional methods? Is it perhaps inappropriate to use a phonic approach, where the correspondences between letters and sounds are stressed, in teaching reading to a child who is unable to produce distinctive forms of speech sounds?

This chapter will first review physical conditions which can impair speech production in children. Five theoretical questions relevant to such children will then be considered in the light of current research. Finally, the practical implications of research findings for treatment and education of these children will be discussed. The emphasis will be not on the

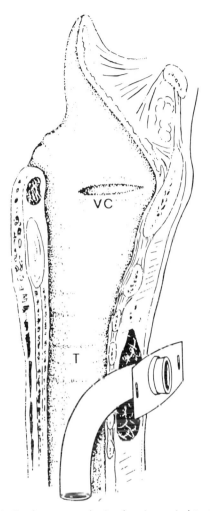

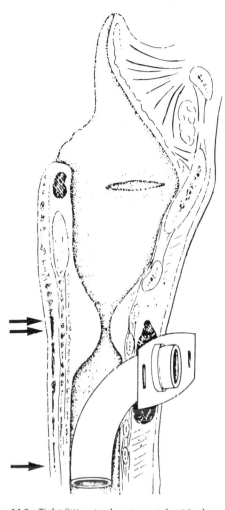

Fig. 14.1 Tracheostomy tube in place in cervical trachea (T). Note relationship to vocal cords (VC). (Reproduced with permission from Simon et al 1981.)

Fig. 14.2 Tight-fitting tracheostomy tube (single arrow) or constriction of the trachea (double arrows) can impede flow of air across the vocal cords. (Reproduced with permission from Simon et al 1981.)

nature and rehabilitation of speech impairment itself, but rather on the impact of speech impairment on overall language develoment.

PHYSICAL CAUSES OF SPEECH IMPAIRMENT IN CHILDREN

Surgical disruption of phonation: long-term tracheostomy

Tracheostomy is a surgical procedure which is carried out to provide an airway when some condition interferes with normal breathing. A vertical slit is created in the front of the neck allowing insertion of a tube (cannula) into the trachea. Air can then pass directly through the tracheostomy to the trachea and lungs. If the tracheostomy tube fits snugly inside the trachea, or if the trachea is blocked above the cannula, no expired air will pass through the larynx, and the child will be unable to vocalize (see Fig. 14.1 and 14.2).

However, in cases where the cannula is

more loosely fitting or has an opening made in it, it may be possible to vocalize despite the tracheostomy, since some air will pass over the vocal cords. Unlike the other conditions considered in this section, tracheostomy is reversible, although the tracheostomy tube may be kept in place for months or years in cases of chronic disease. Long-term tracheostomy is a vital life-saving procedure in infants born with total blockage or severe narrowing of the windpipe, either because of congenital malformation, or because of tumour or injury. It has also become an increasingly common procedure for very small premature infants who require long-term mechanical ventilation.

The medical problems that lead to tracheostomy are frequently associated with neurological damage and intellectual retardation. Singer et al (1985) note that as well as a high rate of mortality and significant medical complications, there is an increased risk of poor physical growth secondary to feeding difficulties, and poor parent- child attachment caused by prolonged or repeated hospitalization.

Structural abnormalities of the speech apparatus

Cleft palate, which may occur in isolation or in combination with cleft lip, is a fairly common congenital abnormality affecting the speech apparatus, occurring in approximately 1.36 per 1000 live births. Cleft palate may occur as part of a syndrome, or in various forms as an isolated condition without other symptoms. Nonsyndromic cleft palate tends to run in families, but the occurrence of the condition cannot be accounted for in terms of a single major gene (Sparks 1984). In normal embryological development, the upper lip and palate are formed by the 12th week of pregnancy, when processes surrounding the primary oral cavity grow and unite to form the mouth and nose, with development of the hard and soft palates dividing the mouth from the nose. Cleft lip and/or palate arise when there is a failure of these processes to unite, or a breakdown in their union (Morley 1970).

Most clefts are surgically repaired before the child starts to talk, and many children subsequently learn to speak without difficulty. However, despite early surgery, the incidence of articulatory abnormalities is considerably higher for children with cleft lip and/or palate than for the normal population. Speech problems arise because of poor control of the velopharyngeal mechanism. Air escapes into the nasal cavities, so the child is unable to generate adequate air pressure in the oral cavity to make many consonant sounds, and vowel sounds have a characteristic nasal quality. The child may make compensatory substitutions, so that, for example, a glottal stop is produced for intervocalic /t/ and /d/. This may be interpreted as an attempt to produce an articulatory gesture at a level where the airstream can be controlled (i.e. the larynx) before it escapes through the nose (Peterson-Falzone 1982a). There is considerable variability in articulatory proficiency, types of phonetic distortion, and intelligibility in children with cleft palate (Moll 1968). It has recently been recognized that the velopharyngeal anomalies of cleft palate impair the normal function of the Eustachian tube, resulting in unremitting conductive hearing loss unless ventilating tubes are inserted in the middle ear. There is some evidence that this hearing loss affects phonological development in these children (Hubbard et al 1985).

For accounts of other, rarer, conditions affecting the structure of the speech apparatus see Peterson-Falzone (1982a, 1982b) and Sparks (1984).

Neuromotor impairment: dysarthria/anarthria

Dysarthria is defined as motor speech impairment resulting from lesions of the central or peripheral nervous system (Noll 1982). Dysarthric children are able to talk, but their production of speech sounds is slow and distorted, often making them highly unintelligible. The most extreme case where the child is totally unable to speak is known as *anarthria*.

Cerebral palsy is the commonest cause of

dysarthria and anarthria in children. Cerebral palsy is a general term for motor impairment caused by nonprogressive brain pathology which is present from birth or acquired early in childhood. A wide range of severity and type of motor deficit is included under this heading: some cerebral palsied children may have normal speech and only mild motor impairment in one limb, whilst others may be severely impaired in all four limbs and be totally anarthric. The motor development of cerebral palsied children will be influenced by the degree of sensory loss, as well as by the extent of involvement of areas of the brain directly implicated in formulating motor programs and sending commands to muscles. For instance, in learning to speak one must be aware of the relative positions of the articulators. If, as is often the case in brain-damaged children, there is impairment of the sensation of touch, and poor awareness of muscle and joint movement and position, then motor learning will be affected.

Where motor impairment is widespread, it can be a challenging task to establish a means of communication with an anarthric or highly unintelligible child. Before the microcomputer revolution, such children were often limited to indicating 'yes' or 'no' by some motor response (e.g. blinking), or by eye-pointing at one item from an array. Nowadays, most children can have a switching system designed for them so that even if they are only able to make one voluntary movement reliably this can be used to control a cursor on a microcomputer screen to select items from a menu. If the child cannot hold a pencil, it may be possible to use a modified typewriter or computer to write, although this is usually slow and laborious. For children who cannot read, symbol systems such as Blissymbolics (Archer 1977) can be presented on the computer screen.

Limited mobility may mean that the child does not experience situations at home and school which are commonplace for an able-bodied child. The need for transport between home and school and within the school can result in effective curtailment of the school day. Rate of absenteeism is high in cerebral palsied children because of hospital admission for orthopaedic surgery, and because respiratory infections can be serious if the motor impairment limits the ability to cough. The nature of the curriculum and speed of progress through it may be constrained by the physical limitations of pupils. Experience of producing written work is usually much reduced compared to a non-handicapped child.

Furthermore, the neurological damage that causes dysarthria or anarthria often results in some degree of intellectual impairment (Nielsen 1966).

Since each of these factors alone is likely to have an impact on language development, one must be cautious in assuming that a language deficit in a dysarthric child is necessarily the result of the speech impairment The standard of comparison should not be the non-handicapped population, but rather a control group which is as closely matched as possible on intellectual and physical status, and school experience.

Although dysarthria is usually associated with other motor problems, there are exceptions. A rare disease which selectively impairs motor control of the face is Moebius syndrome, also known as congenital facial diplegia or congenital suprabulbar paresis (Worster-Drought 1956). Children with this syndrome have partial or total paralysis of one or both sides of the face with involvement of the cranial nerves VI (abducent) and VII (facial). Cranial nerve VII supplies many of the muscles involved in articulation, facial expression and feeding (see Fig. 14.3).

Dribbling is usually a persistent problem in children with Moebius syndrome, and in some cases the child is unable to modify facial expression. The resulting 'blank look' can give a misleading impression of low intelligence.

The underlying cause of this condition remains obscure, and it is unclear whether a disease of the muscles leads to inhibited development of the nuclei of cranial nerves VI and VII, or vice versa (Meyerson & Foushee 1978). The degree of paralysis may be mild or

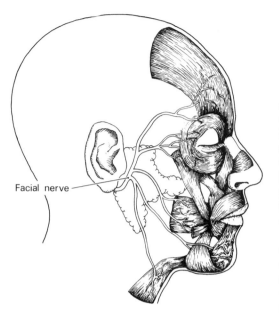

Fig. 14.3 Facial muscles innervated by cranial nerve VII

severe, and other cranial nerves in addition to VI and VII may be involved.

THEORETICAL QUESTIONS PERTINENT TO PHYSICAL SPEECH DISORDERS

Q1. How important is babbling?

The role of babbling in language development has been hotly debated. Opinions range from those who maintain that babbling is a fairly purposeless activity engaged in before the child is mature enough to speak, to the view that babbling is a vital stage of language development during which the child learns to relate particular articulatory gestures with acoustic characteristics. Some proponents of the latter view have further proposed that the period of life when babbling is most prominent, from 3 to 12 months of age, is a 'sensitive period':

> Delay or other abnormalities that appear or remain in this period would seem to have extremely serious consequences in terms of building in the fundamental

speech movement routines that are later refined in the overall co-ordination of the speech mechanism. (Netsell 1981; pp. 139–140)

One way of approaching this question is to consider how phonology develops in children who are prevented from babbling because of long-term tracheostomy in infancy and early childhood. What happens when a tracheostomy is repaired in a young child who has been tracheostomized very early in life for a period of many months? Can the child skip the babbling stage and go straight to a level of speech production appropriate for his or her age? How is the child's mastery of phonology affected by this deprivation of the opportunity to relate articulation to acoustic consequences? Can phonological development recover completely or are there persisting impairments resulting from this early experience? Lenneberg (1967) gave a brief account of a 14-month-old child who had been tracheostomized for 6 months. One day after the tube had been removed (decannulation), the child produced the babbling sounds typical for his age. A much more extensive study was carried out by Simon et al (1983), who studied 77 children with long-term tracheostomies ranging in age from 2 months to 7 years. Since many of these children were intellectually retarded, language development was interpreted relative to developmental rather than chronological age. Data from children whose tracheostomy tubes were removed when the child's developmental level was at a 'prelinguistic stage' (i.e. before single words or 'one-word' gestures are used) subsequently initiated speech development near the level appropriate for developmental age, and none of them were observed to go through the missed babbling stage.

Where decannulation occurred at a later age, Simon et al observed periods of phonological impairment after the absence or interruption of babbling experiences. However, of nine children who were assessed six or more months after decannulation, eight had verbal language and phonological skills commensurate with receptive functioning. Most of these children had communicated using sign language while the tracheostomy was in place, and all had had intensive speech therapy after decannulation.

Thus phonological difficulties did occur after prolonged tracheostomy but these proved to be temporary and it was concluded that there is no 'critical period' during which humans must vocalize in order to develop normal speech. One of the cases described by Ross (1982) leads to the same conclusion. This was a child of normal intelligence who had a tracheostomy tube inserted before 2 months of age, and removed at 21 months of age. The parents reported that the child did not vocalize prior to decannulation, but subsequently proceeded rapidly through all the normal stages of language development except babbling. When assessed using the Reynell Developmental Language Scales and an articulation test at 46 months of age the child was found to have normal speech and language skills.

Q2. Is speech perception independent of speech production?

The question of how people perceive a continuously varying acoustic waveform as a sequence of speech sounds is one that has puzzled scientists for many years. One might think it would be a fairly straightforward procedure for a scientist to perform an acoustic analysis of speech samples to discover patterns of acoustic features that corresponded to individual phonemes, but there are two difficulties. First, there is the segmentation problem: how to decide which part of the acoustic waveform corresponds to which sound? Figure 14.4 shows a sound spectrogram of eight monosyllabic words which differ only in the vowel.

The spectrogram is a visual representation of the component frequencies of speech. Time corresponds to the horizontal dimension, frequency to the vertical dimension, with the darkness of the mark indicating the relative intensity of each component frequency.

Consider the problem confronting anyone attempting to specify the acoustic characteristics of /h/. There is no obvious demarcation between the three phonemes in the spectrogram.

Second, there is the problem of how perceptual invariance is achieved. We perceive the same final sound in the words 'hid', 'had', 'head', and so on, but there is no constancy in the final portion of the speech waveform, even if we restrict consideration to a single speaker. The way in which an acoustic waveform is recognized depends on the phonetic context (in this case the preceding vowel). In a series of experiments using synthetic speech stimuli, Liberman and his colleagues showed that not only are different acoustic events perceived as the same consonant, depending on the phonetic context, but also a constant acoustic waveform may be perceived as different phonemes in different contexts (Liberman et al 1952, 1954). Furthermore, the acoustic characterisation of speech varies with age, sex and identity of speaker, and with rate and intonation of speech.

Attempts to resolve the problem of invariance in speech perception have taken two diametrically opposed directions. On the one hand we have theorists who continue to pursue invariance, arguing that if the phoneme does not have invariant acoustic correlates, then perhaps we need to consider larger units (e.g. words; Klatt 1981) or smaller units (e.g. distinctive features; Stevens 1981). Although these attempts have resulted in greater success than early work based on the phoneme, we are still a long way from specifying a set of procedures which will effect the transformation from acoustic waveform to a string of phonemes. If such procedures were specified, then it would be a simple matter to build computerized speech recognition devices. Despite intensive scientific efforts, the best computerized devices currently available are far less accurate than a 3-year-old child in recognizing speech.

Liberman et al (1967) attacked the problem of invariance from a completely different direction. Their solution to the lack of one-to-

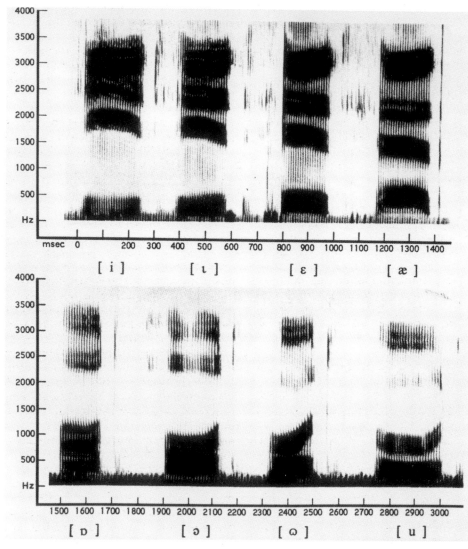

Fig. 14.4 A spectrogram of the words 'heed', 'hid', 'head', 'had', 'hod', 'hawed', 'who'd' as spoken in a British accent. (Reproduced with permission from Ladefoged 1975.)

one correspondence between acoustic signal and phoneme was not to abandon the phoneme as the unit of analysis, but rather to ask: if the acoustic waveform does not have a one-to-one relationship with speech sounds, can we find some other level of description which does?

Their solution lay with articulatory gestures. Whilst it is difficult even for experienced phoneticians to decode a spectrograph into speech, it is very much easier to deduce what has been said from a visual record of a sequence of articulatory configurations. The motor theory of speech perception maintained that speech is recognized by a process of matching an acoustic input to the articulatory configurations which would be needed to produce that acoustic signal.

From the time it was first formulated, the motor theory was criticized on logical grounds. In effect, it was argued, the motor theory solved nothing, since it did not explain how people are able to analyze an acoustic input in a way that would specify the articulatory gestures that would be necessary to produce that signal (Cole 1977). The problem of invariance is just as severe for the motor theory as for any other theory, since there is no one-to-one correspondence between acoustic signal and articulatory gesture, any more than there is between acoustic signal and phoneme. Furthermore, by making speech perception dependent upon speech production, the motor theory predicted that if speech production were impaired, then speech perception should be affected. As was pointed out in a series of case reports, the motor theory simply cannot be sustained in its original form in the face of congenitally speechless individuals with good speech perception and language comprehension skills (Lenneberg 1962, MacNeilage et al 1967, Fourcin 1975a,b).

This was not the only evidence to pose difficulties for the motor theory. Studies on infants demonstrating that ability to discriminate speech sounds precedes ability to produce such sounds were equally problematic (Palermo 1975). Such findings led Liberman & Mattingly to revise the motor theory in 1985. The current version of the theory postulates that knowledge of the motor correlates of speech sounds is innate. Thus the claim is that an anarthric child or a small baby has knowledge of how articulatory gestures relate to acoustic events. These children are not able to use this knowledge in their own speech production, but can use it for speech perception.

Although this modification enables the theory to cope with cases of adequate speech perception but inadequate speech production, it does leave the theory weakened. For a start, it makes it difficult to subject the theory to adequate test: there appears now to be no way in which the theory could be disconfirmed. Furthermore, there are reasons for regarding the postulate of innate knowledge of motor correspondences as implausible. We have to ask why it is that when children first start to speak they do not immediately use adult phonology, but go through a phase of using a restricted set of phonemes, often, for example, treating alveolar and velar plosives as a single sound (so that /d/ and /g/, and /t/ and /k/ are not distinguished in their speech production). Also, we know that people usually have difficulty in discriminating and in learning to produce speech sounds which are distinctive in another language but not in their own. For example, Japanese speakers of English find the distinction between /r/ and /l/ difficult. If knowledge of how speech sounds relate to articulatory gestures is innate rather than learned, why should this be so? In order to overcome this argument, one has to postulate, as Liberman & Mattingly do, that as one's native language is learned, some of the innate ability to relate speech sounds to their motor correspondences is lost. Thus a Japanese speaker at birth has the innate knowledge which allows him to discriminate /r/ and /l/, but then loses this because the distinction is not relevant in his language. Clearly, although the postulate of an innate ability to relate speech production and perception overcomes some of the problems confronting the motor theory, it makes it necessary to add further postulates to handle new difficulties.

The strongest argument against a motor theory, however, remains a logical one. The problem of invariance does not go away: it simply moves location. The perspective changes from that of discovering invariant relationships between acoustic cues and phonemes to that of finding invariant relationships between acoustic cues and articulatory gestures. Even if we accept that knowledge of the latter is innate, we remain ignorant about the nature of this innate knowledge.

Q3. Can language competence develop without performance?

How far can a child learn language just by listening to others speak? It seems logically possible that a child could develop an internalized representation of a language without needing ever to have spoken, just as it is possible to learn to distinguish musical from unmusical sequences even if one can neither sing nor play a musical instrument. Nevertheless, lack of practice in *producing* language is often given as an explanation for poor development of *receptive* language in children with expressive speech or language disorders. Goodstein (1968), for example, proposed that the poor quality of speech produced by cleft palate children leads to fewer rewards in speaking, with a consequent retardation of language skills and intelligence. Is this reasonable?

Contrary evidence from children with tracheostomies has already been discussed. Provided we restrict consideration to children who are neurologically and intellectually normal, language comprehension is unimpaired by prolonged inability to speak during infancy (Bowman et al 1972, Kaslon et al 1978, Tucker et al 1982, Singer et al 1985). Similarly, although impairment of receptive language is not uncommon in children with Moebius syndrome, this is usually associated with global developmental delay or hearing loss, and is far less likely in children with normal intelligence and hearing (Meyerson & Foushee 1978). Perhaps the most striking case of excellent language skills in the absence of articulate speech is the case of Richard Boydell, a cerebral palsied man with athetoid quadriplegia who was virtually anarthric. His first opportunity for effective communication with others came when he was given a foot-operated typewriter around the age of 30. Richard Boydell's account of his own history begins as follows:

> Like every child, I was born without language. Unfortunately, I was also born with cerebral palsy which, in my case, means that, although my intelligence is unimpaired, I have a very severe speech defect and no use in my hands and arms. (Fourcin 1975a; p. 263)

Fourcin describes how Richard Boydell as-

tounded everyone when, nine days after receiving his typewriter, he wrote an elegantly phrased letter to the manufacturers with a useful suggestion for the improvement of the machine. He subsequently became a professional computer programmer.

There is, however, one condition which does not conform to the general view that expressive speech disorders are associated with normal language functioning. An extensive literature on children with cleft palate, reviewed by Richman & Eliason (1982) and Nation & Wetherbee (1985), shows that there are small but reliable deficits in verbal functioning associated with cleft palate. Although the deficits reported vary from study to study, children with cleft palate tend to do more poorly on verbal than on nonverbal tests, they obtain lower verbal scores than matched control groups, and in some studies they are found to be deficient on receptive as well as expressive language measures. Investigators have attempted to relate this verbal deficit to factors such as type and degree of cleft, type of physical management, age at surgery, presence of middle ear disease and age at hospitalization, but no single variable has emerged as an adequate explanatory factor, although Goodstein (1961) noted that presence of other physical anomalies was linked to low language scores. A recent study by Hubbard et al (1985) concluded that conductive hearing loss associated with middle ear disease could not be responsible for low verbal IQ in cleft palate children.

The research on children with cleft palate seems to indicate that physical difficulty in speaking *can* impair development of more general language skills. How are we to reconcile this conclusion with the data from other speech-impaired groups? One possibility is that there is some hitherto undiscovered factor associated with cleft palate which is responsible for the verbal deficit. There is, however, an alternative possibility, which is that the apparent conflict arises from methodological differences between studies. There are two ways of addressing the question, 'does condition X impair language development?' One way is to consider whether children with X do, in general, score within accepted normal limits on language tests, and whether any children with X obtain above average scores. If the answer to both questions is 'yes' it is reasonable to conclude that X is compatible with normal language development. This reasoning was applied above in arguing that conditions such as long-term tracheostomy, Moebius syndrome and anarthria do not impair receptive language development. However, the research with cleft palate children indicates that it may be possible to answer 'yes' to these questions, when a more stringent test would reveal verbal deficits. Thus, as for the other conditions, it is true that on average children with cleft palate score well within normal limits on language and IQ tests, and that some of them obtain superior scores. The verbal deficit of this group is, however, revealed when we adopt the alternative research strategy, and compare a large sample of cleft palate children with a matched control group. The reason we get different results with the two methods is simply because the deficit is small. For example, suppose that the true effect of condition X is to depress IQ by five points. The mean IQ for children with X will be 95 rather than 100, but there would still be relatively few children with IQs below 80, and many children with X will obtain scores well above 100. Furthermore, if, as in our hypothetical example, the deficit is small relative to the variability within the population, a large sample will be needed to demonstrate it. In the example given above, one would need 70 subjects in each group to demonstrate a significant difference at the .05 level between children with and without X (assuming each group had a standard deviation of 15).

We may sum up by saying that research with cleft palate children suggests that physical difficulty in speaking *may* have a detrimental effect on more general aspects of language development. However, such an effect, if it exists, is a small one, and would be unlikely to cause clinically significant language disorders.

Language development and Piagetian theory

Although the principal concern of this chapter is with the impact of *speech* impairment on language development, it is worth noting here that cases such as that of Richard Boydell have a wider theoretical importance than this, as they also demonstrate the robustness of language development in the face of severe motor impairment.

Piaget proposed a theory of cognitive development in which the child is seen as passing through a series of stages, each developing out of and going beyond the previous one. The first of these stages, which precedes the development of language and is seen as a prerequisite for language, is the sensorimotor period, in which the child develops increasingly complex intellectual processes through interacting with the environment (Piaget 1952). In the first few weeks of life the infant does little more than make reflex responses to environmental and internal stimuli. These, however, then become progressively differentiated, so that, for example, the child adapts the sucking reflex depending on the stimulus encountered by the lips. As development proceeds, the child begins to co-ordinate information from different modalities, for example, vision and prehension, and to intentionally repeat actions that have resulted in specific effects. Later still, the child deliberately uses known means to try to achieve a particular goal, and also actively experiments by modifying known actions to observe their consequences. The intellectual accomplishments of the sensorimotor period are seen by Piaget and his followers as fundamental to the development of language. Children must first develop a practical intelligence, whereby they learn about cause and effect relationships and physical properties of the environment before they can go on to represent reality mentally and recapitulate actions in the past and anticipate actions in the future.

In the first manifestations of symbolic function, children may use an action associated with an object to stand for that object: later on they will progress to a verbal form instead.

Thus according to the Piagetian view, interaction between the child and the physical environment lays the foundations for language development.

Children with severe physical handicaps would seem, then, to provide a crucial test of Piagetian theory. As Mehler pointed out in a conference discussion in 1971, if a child were incapable of moving he should also be incapable of thinking or talking. Sinclair's (1971) response to this challenge was interesting. On the one hand she argued that Mehler was interpreting the term 'action' too literally: even if a child could only move his eyes and perceive moving objects, he would still be able to learn from correspondences between ocular movements and visual perceptions. However, she did grant that in this 'totally extreme and totally hypothetical' case, although the child would go through the same stages as any other child, this would be probably with much more difficulty and much more slowly.

The same issue resurfaced in 1975, when a conference was held near Paris to discuss the implications of Piaget's theory of language development, and to contrast it with Chomsky's 'innatist' approach. At one point, one of the discussants, Monod, suggested an empirical test of Piaget's theory:

> I am thinking of an experiment that is theoretically very simple: if the development of language in the child is closely related to sensorimotor experience, one can suppose that a child born paraplegic, for example, would have very great difficulties in developing his language. (Piattelli-Palmarini 1980; p. 140)

Chomsky agreed, pointing out that:

> If in fact the constructions of sensorimotor intelligence are a necessary condition for the development of language, then it should turn out that insofar as those sensorimotor constructions are impeded, the intelligence that leads to the acquisition of language should also be impeded; and if they are drastically reduced, language ought to be virtually eliminated. (Piattelli-Palmarini 1980; p. 170)

The participants seemed unaware of the case of Richard Boydell, who provides a clear counter-example to this prediction. More recently, Berninger & Gans (1986) gave psychological assessments to three severely cerebral palsied individuals, and found that one of them was above average in nonverbal intelligence and receptive vocabulary. A current study of cerebral palsied children provides further evidence that normal language can develop despite extremely limited ability to exert an action on external reality and explore its consequences (Bishop & Robson, in preparation). Using the Test for Reception of Grammar, a multiple choice test of understanding, we have found anarthric quadriplegic individuals who perform well within normal limits.

It is unlikely that such cases will force the Piagetians to alter their stance. In the course of the discussion with Monod, Inhelder predicted that fairly complete language development probably could occur in the face of severe motor disabilities, but, as Sinclair had done, she argued that this would be accounted for in terms of Piagetian theory by assuming that 'actions' need not be motor: they can be acoustical, visual, or tactile. However, as other discussants were quick to note, on this assumption the Piagetian theory starts to look very similar to Chomsky's 'innatist' view—and very different from what most people have typically understood Piaget to be saying, when, for example, he talks of sensorimotor intelligence as 'an entirely practical intelligence based on the manipulation of objects' (Piaget 1967b). The crucial difference between acoustical, visual and tactile experiences and motor experiences is that the motor system is the only system which the developing child can use in an exploratory way, so that in effect the child can act as experimenter, initiating an action and considering its sensory consequences. This hypothesis-testing aspect of the sensorimotor stage has always seemed to be crucial to Piaget's developmental theory, and is precisely the sort of experience that children like the young Richard Boydell were seriously deprived of early in life.

Nonverbal communication as a prerequisite for verbal development

A very different account of the preverbal origins of language development was proposed by Bruner (1978a), who stressed the continuity between what the child learned in nonverbal interactions with a caregiver, and the cognitive prerequisites of language. In contrast to Piaget, Bruner was less concerned about children's learning of relationships between their own actions and objects in the world than with interactions between children and their caregivers. According to Bruner, language acquisition is heavily dependent on the interaction between child and mother:

> Being a witness at the feast of language is not enough of an exposure to assure acquisition. There must be contingent interaction. (Bruner 1978a; p. 64)

Bruner describes many similarities between aspects of preverbal communication and early verbal communication between mother and child. Thus young infants learn to establish 'joint reference' with an adult by looking at the object the adult is focussing on. Later on they learn to direct another person's attention to an object of interest by pointing at it . From such early beginnings, dialogue-like exchanges can develop, where mother and child take turns to initiate and respond to topics of interest. Bruner is not talking exclusively about learning conversational competence: he argues that many of the concepts learned in preverbal communicative interactions are crucial to later mastery of syntax and semantics. Many early games between mothers and children involve giving and taking objects: he maintains that these enable the child to grasp

the linguistically relevant concepts of agent and recipient.

Bruner, like Piaget, adopts observational studies as the main source of support for these views. The inevitable weakness of such an approach is that it does not allow one to determine whether or not the developmental sequence of A followed by B arises because A *is a necessary precondition for* B. Chomsky (1980b) points out that children acquire language before puberty: yet we do not conclude that mastery of language is a necessary prerequisite for pubertal changes to occur.

Children developing in exceptional circumstances can provide interesting test cases in such circumstances. If anyone were tempted to take Chomsky's example seriously, we could challenge them with instances of post-pubertal individuals who failed to develop language.

Children with severe physical handicaps do, in a similar way, allow us to test the validity of some of the causal relationships implicit in Bruner's formulation. It would be naive to suggest that a severely handicapped child does not communicate nonverbally with its mother. Direction of gaze to establish shared reference is likely to be particularly well developed in a physically handicapped child who can neither speak nor point. But preverbal interactive games and gestural communication will be severely restricted, and such a child is far closer to being 'a witness at the feast of language' than an able-bodied toddler. The fact that normal understanding of language can develop despite such limitations leads one to question just how crucial these early forms of interaction are in the mastery of syntax and semantics.

A demonstration that written language is grammatically and semantically complex (Fourcin 1975a), or that there is good understanding of grammatically complex sentences (Bishop & Robson in preparation) does not, of course, entail that a person is linguistically quite normal apart from inability to speak. Bruner may be right insofar as he is talking about conversational competence. Thus a child with limited ability to interact by nonverbal means may prove to be poor at initiating or maintaining conversations, perhaps failing to take into account the need to take turns, or to ensure that the listener appreciates what the speaker is referring to. At present, this is virtually impossible to evaluate. The communication aids available to physically handicapped children with speech impairments are not conducive to natural conversations, because they operate so slowly as to make rapid exchanges impossible.

Q4. Can speechless and dysarthric children use inner speech?

What is the function of language? The obvious answer is that we use language to communicate with others. But is this a complete answer? Most people readily admit to a subjective sensation of talking silently to themselves during a range of mental operations such as memorizing telephone numbers, carrying out mental arithmetic, or planning a course of action. Soviet psychologists were among the first to be interested in this non-communicative function of language as a tool for thought. They were interested in two basic questions. First, what is the relationship between this 'inner speech' (or 'internal speech') and overt speech, and second, what is the role of inner speech in mental operations? Sokolov (1972) favoured the view that inner speech develops from overt speech. He noted that when young children are given a complicated problem to solve, they talk to themselves while solving it, even if no-one else is present. As they grow older, they whisper rather than talking aloud. Eventually, they remain silent. Sokolov argued that what is observed is a developmental progression for the use of speech in thought. At first, overt external speech is used, but as the child grows older, speech processes become internalized. Sokolov maintained that measureable micro-movements of the tongue could be observed as subjects silently read grammatically complex texts or solved arithmetical problems. An alternative way to test whether inner speech

was implicated in a task was by attempting to block inner speech to see if this impairs performance. Luria (1966) describes Russian studies in which children were required to solve problems or to write whilst holding the tongue between the teeth, or opening the mouth wide with the tongue in a fixed position. Other studies required subjects to repeat some well-learned verbal material while performing mental tasks. Luria noted that performance of adults was less likely than that of children to be impaired by these procedures, but he suggested that this was because keeping the tongue in a fixed position abolishes only the grosser forms of internal speech, but does not necessarily prevent finer and more contracted movements from occurring. Thus the early Russian work led to the conclusion that inner speech develops from overt speech and is implicated in many forms of mental activity.

Inner speech and short-term memory

The bulk of current research on inner speech has concentrated on its role in short-term memory performance. Interest in this topic by Western experimental psychologists was engaged when Conrad (1964) noted that errors in recalling sequences of *written* consonants tended to be *phonologically* similar to the correct item, so that, for example, B would be confused with D, P, or G. Conrad & Hull (1964) subsequently went on to show that phonologically similar letter strings such as P B T D G are harder to recall than distinctive strings such as F J Z Y H. It seems then that when given a sequence of written letters to remember, people do not just memorize the visual appearance of the letters, but convert the written form into a speech-based representation. This effect, which has been variously termed the 'acoustic similarity effect', the 'phonemic similarity effect' and the 'phonological similarity effect' has been frequently replicated and is also found when the test materials are written words or nameable pictures (see Baddeley, 1986, for a review). Baddeley et al (1975) discovered further evidence for some form of verbal representation of written materials in memory. They found that ability to recall a list of words depends not just on phonological similarity, but also on the time it takes to pronounce items. A list consisting of long words, such as 'university' or 'aluminium' is harder to recall than a list of short words such as 'sum' or 'hate'. This has been termed the 'word length effect', and was interpreted in terms of a model which assumed that a person mainains a list of items in memory by a rehearsal process that involves circulating them through an 'articulatory loop'. This is seen as analogous to a tape loop on a tape-recorder. If one tried to record a sequence of words on a tape loop, the number of words recorded would depend on the length of the words. Just so, it is assumed that the articulatory loop is of fixed length, so that fewer long words than short words can be rehearsed using this system. The notion is that items are prevented from decaying in memory by the person repeatedly (and usually silently) regenerating an articulatory representation of each item in the sequence. Although many memory researchers do not use the term 'inner speech', the silent articulation thought to underly rehearsal would seem to have much in common with the phenomena studied by the Russian psychologists.

Further experiments were designed to see what would happen if people were prevented from using articulatory coding in memory. The usual procedure involved asking the subject to repeatedly vocalize some overlearned sequence, such as 'the the the . . .' or '1, 2, 3, etc.' This technique is called *articulatory suppression* or *concurrent articulation*. Since it is impossible to say two words at once, if the articulatory system is engaged in producing such irrelevant utterances, this will make it impossible to generate subvocal speech codes for the test items. As one would predict on this view, concurrent articulation depresses short-term memory performance and abolishes both the phonological similarity effect and the word length effect when written words are memorized (Baddeley 1986).

Hulme et al (1984) argued that differences in rate of articulation are sufficient to explain developmental changes in memory performance. They measured the speed at which children of different ages could repeat words they subsequently had to memorize, and found that memory span could be directly predicted from articulation rate. Their data agreed well with a model in which an articulatory loop of fixed temporal length is used to rehearse words. Young subjects, who articulate slowly, will be able to process fewer items through the articulatory loop than older subjects, who articulate faster.

Conrad (1979) was able to show that *quality* of articulation was also linked to use of inner speech. He used the size of the phonological similarity effect as an index of use of inner speech in studies of short-term memory in deaf teenagers. In general, the likelihood that a deaf person speaks intelligibly is related to the severity of the hearing loss, and Conrad showed that the use of inner speech was also strongly related to degree of hearing loss. Furthermore, if one restricted consideration to profoundly deaf subjects, all of whom would have virtually no ability to discriminate spoken sounds, there was a link between the quality of speech output and the use of inner speech. Most profoundly deaf subjects had highly unintelligible speech and did not use inner speech in short-term memory. However, there was a subset of subjects who, despite being profoundly deaf, did have moderately intelligible speech, and this subgroup was more likely to use inner speech in memory. This would seem good evidence that inner speech in memory uses common processes with overt speech. This study, in common with studies of normal development (Conrad 1971, Hitch & Halliday 1983), found that the longer a person's memory span, the greater the likelihood that he used inner speech.

Although the evidence reviewed so far seems to support the notion that short-term memory involves a form of inner speech based on articulation, it is not totally conclusive. Studies such as those of Hulme et al (1984) and Conrad (1979) provide evidence that articulation and memory span are strongly related, but, as these authors recognize, there are inherent limitations in such correlational studies. It could be argued that there is no causal relationship between articulation and memory span, and that the two things tend to be correlated simply because both depend on some other factor, such as verbal intelligence.

Certainly, some memory phenomena are hard to account for in terms of articulatory coding in memory. For instance, Baddeley (1986) noted that if subjects are given a spoken list of words to recall, the phonological similarity effect persists even under conditions of concurrent articulation. Now, if the phonological similarity effect arises because of articulatory coding, and concurrent articulation abolishes such coding, then one should observe no phonological similarity effect under such conditions. The fact that the effect persists indicates that it is not just a by-product of articulatory coding. Baddeley suggests that as well as using an 'inner voice' (i.e. an articulatory code) we may also use an 'inner ear', so that we can remember verbal material by a phonological representation that can be generated either directly by hearing words spoken, or indirectly via articulatory coding. Nevertheless, articulatory coding is seen as crucial for generating a phonological representation from visual materials, and for rehearsing material to prevent the memory from decaying with time.

The precise nature of the 'inner speech code' used in short-term memory may seem of only theoretical interest, but it has considerable relevance for children with organically-based speech disorders. We have shown that inner speech plays an important role in short-term memory. If, as is often argued, inner speech involves silently *articulating* to oneself, then this would mean that children who can speak only with difficulty or not at all would be unable to use inner speech for memory and reasoning.

There is, however, an alternative possibility. Inner speech may have little to do with one's own overt speech production. This seems plausible when we consider that it is possible to imagine *nonverbal* sounds that we ourselves are quite incapable of producing, such as an orchestra playing. If this is possible for music, why not for speech as well? It could be that what we do when we memorize lists of items is to generate some auditory or phonological image of the words, which does not derive at all from our own articulation. On this view, the phonological similarity effect arises because the images of phonologically similar words are more confusable than those for phonologically distinct words. If articulatory coding is *not* implicated in inner speech, then, provided auditory perception is unimpaired, children with physical disorders of the speech apparatus would be able to use inner speech.

Studies from patients with *acquired* disorders have shown that although brain lesions which render patients speechless *can* impair inner speech (Levine et al 1982) they do not invariably do so. Nebes (1975) described a patient who was quite unable to speak after a stroke, but who showed evidence of inner speech in a range of tasks. She could indicate how many syllables a written word contained, could judge whether written words or pictures rhymed, and on a short-term memory task with visual presentation her errors tended to be confusions between phonologically similar items. Baddeley & Wilson (1985) tested memory in a man who had become anarthric after sustaining head injuries. They found that this patient had an average memory span, and showed a normal phonological similarity effect with both auditory and visual presentation. Thus despite being unable to articulate some patients show all the phenomena attributed to articulatory coding!

Baddeley (1986) suggested an explanation for these results. He proposed that when memorizing verbal materials, people generate appropriate motor programs for speaking the words, but do not execute these, so that memory is not in terms of actual muscle movements, but in terms of either the neural commands to muscles, or some specification of target positions of articulators. It could be argued that since adult patients with acquired anarthria had normal speech before they became ill, their ability to generate motor programs for articulation is intact, but brain damage interferes with implementation of these programs.

This explanation, however, predicts that *congenital* anarthria should have very different consequences from acquired anarthria. It does not seem feasible to suppose that a child who has never spoken has the ability to generate appropriate motor programs for articulation. If inner speech involves generating such motor programs, then congenitally anarthric children should be unable to use inner speech.

We are currently carrying out a study of memory in anarthric and dysarthric children and teenagers, and have found evidence of normal memory span performance by individuals who have been totally unable to speak *from birth* (Bishop & Robson, in preparation). As well as obtaining memory spans of normal length, we have found phonological similarity and word length effects of normal size in this group. Since these subjects never had the opportunity to learn the relationship between phonemes and their own articulatory gestures, this result is at odds with the view that implicates articulatory coding, even in terms of motor programs, in short-term memory.

It would seem that to make sense of the experimental data we must go beyond making a simple distinction between 'acoustic imagery' and 'articulatory coding' in memory and develop a much more detailed information-processing model of the stages involved in perceiving and producing speech. Our current interpretation is that when rehearsing material in memory people generate a code that is neither auditory nor articulatory, but is rather an abstract phonological code. If this idea is hard to grasp, consider the following. Two words with identical phonemic structure may nevertheless be quite distinct acoustically—for example, instances of the word 'cat' spoken with rising or falling intonation. Although we can easily *discriminate* between these stimuli, we interpret them as being instances of the same word, because in English tone is not a phonemically distinctive

feature. (There are languages where tone *is* a distinctive feature, and where native speakers would perceive just as much difference between these two versions of 'cat' as we would perceive between 'cat' and 'cap'). We must be able to convert acoustic verbal stimuli into an abstract phonological form in order to perceive that the same word is spoken when we hear it spoken with differing patterns of intonation, by different speakers, with differing amounts of background noise, and so on.

What happens then when we wish to repeat what we have heard? Can we directly convert each phoneme into appropriate articulatory movements? The answer is no. The articulatory correlates of a phoneme will vary considerably from one occasion to another, depending on the preceding and following phonemes, and such factors as whether one has a cigar in one's mouth when talking. Consider your own articulation of /s/ in 'sweet', 'soup', 'sat' and 'seat'. Lip position when producing this sound may be spread, neutral or rounded, depending on the following sounds. Clearly, we cannot simply have stored a set of motor movements which correspond to phonemes. There must be a more abstract level of representation in which a string of phonemes is represented which is then translated into articulatory movements. The motor movements corresponding to each sound will be computed taking into account the preceding and following articulatory configurations.

Thus both speech perception and speech production must involve an abstract level of phonological representation. We propose that this can develop quite adequately in individuals who have never spoken, provided speech perception is unimpaired and that it is this which is implicated in inner speech.

Q5. Do speech problems interfere with mastery of phonic skills in reading and writing?

Both theoretical research and practical experience lead to the conclusion that there are two ways in which one can go about the tasks of reading and writing in English. One way involves learning direct correspondences between complete letter strings and words: this process is the basis of the 'look and say' approach to reading. The alternative is to learn correspondences between letters and individual sounds, so that a word like 'seat is decoded by an indirect process which involves assigning the pronunciations S → /s/; EA → /i/; T → /t/, and then assembling the whole word /sit/. The phonic approach to reading involves learning such correspondences between letters and phonemes. Most contemporary educationalists would favour a combination of both approaches in teaching children to read and spell, rather than sole reliance on one or the other. The phonic approach has the advantage that it considerably reduces the overall amount of information which the child has to learn, and it provides a method of attack for totally unfamiliar words, which makes it particularly useful for the child learning to read. It has the disadvantage, however, that for the English language it is far from foolproof: many words have pronunciations which do not correspond to what would be expected on the basis of their spelling (e.g. 'one', 'two', 'four'), and many more words could be spelt in a variety of ways, each of which gives the correct phonology, but only one of which is correct (e.g. 'speech', 'speach', 'speatch', or even 'sbeech'). In order to be a competent reader and speller of English, one needs to have specific knowledge about the orthographic form corresponding to each word, as well as phonic skills.

The question of how the child develops phonic skills is closely allied to the topic of inner speech. When we consider children with speech problems, the critical question is whether one needs to be able to speak clearly in order to learn to relate letters to sounds. It seems reasonable to suppose that if the child has difficulty in producing distinctive forms of /s/ and /f/ it might be difficult to learn that S → /s/ and F → /f/.

The notion that articulatory processes might be implicated in phonic aspects of reading and writing is consistent with a study by Kimura & Bryant (1983), who investigated Japanese as well as English children. Japanese uses two writing systems. The Kanji system, derived from Chinese writing, is logographic, i.e. each symbol corresponds to a whole word and there is no relationship between the form of the symbol and its pronunciation. Thus there is no way Kanji could be read or written using a phonic strategy. Indeed, the same Kanji symbol can be used for different Chinese dialects, so that a single symbol will correspond to different pronunciations in different areas. The Kana system, on the other hand, uses symbols which correspond to a specific syllabic sound, so there is a direct relationship between the form of a word and its pronunciation. Japanese children learn both systems, mastering Kana fairly rapidly, but continuing to learn Kanji symbols throughout their schooldays.

Kimura & Bryant asked 7-year-old children to write words to dictation and to match written words to pictures, either silently or whilst performing a concurrent articulation task (in English this involved repeating 'icecream' rapidly). They found that for Japanese children, concurrent articulation had no effect on performance with Kanji words, but disrupted both reading and spelling of words in Kana.

For English children, however, concurrent articulation did not interfere with reading, but did disrupt spelling. It seems reasonable to draw two conclusions from this study. First, the processes of converting orthographic strings into phonological strings and vice versa are disrupted by concurrent articulation. Second, young children learning English seem to rely much more heavily on such phonic processes when spelling than when reading.

The use of the concurrent articulation technique in this study indicates a point of similarity with the memory research described in the previous section. Here again one is tempted to make the argument that if generating irrelevant articulation disrupts a particular process, then some form of articulatory coding is implicated in the normal operation of that process.

However, the results from our memory studies would suggest caution, indicating, as they do, that it is possible to generate a phonologically-based form of internal speech even if one cannot speak.

The question of interest, then, is: can one learn the letter-sound correspondences necessary to read and spell phonically even if one cannot produce speech sounds distinctively?

The impressive accomplishments of Richard Boydell (Fourcin 1975a) have already been mentioned. It is noteworthy that apart from producing clearly written prose without grammatical errors, he also spelt correctly. However, this does not constitute proof that one does not need to speak in order to appreciate letter-sound correspondences, for it could be argued that in this case spelling was achieved totally by a whole word approach, without any appreciation of letter-sound correspondences.

Bishop (1985b) investigated knowledge of letter-sound correspondences in seven dysarthric teenagers, who were compared with seven physically handicapped nondysarthric controls on three tasks. The first task involved judging homophony of written words and nonwords. Pairs of items such as 'fuse views', 'write right', 'gight gite', and 'chen jenn' were presented and the subject asked to judge if, when spoken, they would sound exactly the same or different. Performance on this task was very variable, with several subjects scoring at chance level on the nonword stimuli, but there was no difference between dysarthric and control subjects on this task, and some dysarthric subjects were very accurate with real word stimuli.

The second task was spelling of real words, where the prediction was that the dysarthric subjects would be relatively poor at spelling and/or give evidence of greater reliance on a whole word strategy than on the phonic approach. There was no evidence for this. Spelling ability was similar for dysarthric and control groups, and in both groups, spelling errors tended to bear close phonemic resemblance to the target word.

Finally, subjects were given monosyllabic nonwords to spell. Performance was far from perfect, though very well above chance level in both groups. There was no relationship between dysarthria and proficiency in this task, and analysis for individual dysarthric children of those sounds which were misspelt and those which were omitted or pronounced inconsistently showed no association between these.

In a subsequent study, we have obtained similar results with a new group of dysarthric young people, and have also shown that ability to spell real words and nonwords is compatible with congenital anarthria (Bishop & Robson, in preparation).

It can be concluded on the basis of these studies that phonic skills do not depend on ability to articulate. Provided a child's problem is restricted to speech output, and there is normal understanding of language, it seems that an abstract phonological code can develop normally and serve as an adequate basis for phonic skills.

It is interesting to contrast these findings with those obtained by Stackhouse (1982) and Snowling & Stackhouse (1983). These authors investigated reading and spelling skills in two groups of children with very different types of speech production problem. The first group consisted of children with speech problems associated with cleft palate, i.e. with a clear-cut physical disorder which accounted for their speech problems. Results with these children were not dissimilar to those obtained in Bishop's study of dysarthric subjects: there was no evidence that speech problems of these children interfered with their reading and spelling skills. This result contrasted sharply with those obtained for a group of children diagnosed as suffering from developmental verbal dyspraxia. These are children who have no detectable structural or neuro-motor abnormality to account for their speech disorder, but who have considerable difficulty in producing a correct sequence of phonemes. This small group of children had enormous difficulty even in repeating, let alone in spelling, nonwords, and their misspellings of real words bore little phonemic resemblance to the target word. Bishop (1985b) suggested that the phonological and spelling problems of these dyspraxic children arose from a common cause: failure to develop an abstract phonological code.

PRACTICAL IMPLICATIONS FOR EDUCATION AND TREATMENT

The overall conclusion from this review is an encouraging one. There are good theoretical grounds for supposing that problems with speech production should not just hinder communication, but should impair the child's ability to learn to understand language and use inner speech as a tool for thought. This proves not to be so. The available evidence shows that, provided hearing and intelligence are not impaired, inability to speak does not prevent development of language understanding and inner speech. There is no evidence that speechless or dysarthric children have disproportionate difficulty in learning to read and write using a phonic approach. Poor speech production ability is not an adequate explanation for poor speech perception in a child with an organically based speech disorder. Thus if a speechless child has difficulty in comprehending language, it is vital to investigate this further to see if some specific factor such as high frequency hearing loss (common in athetoid cerebral palsy) or low general intelligence is responsible.

It is important to note that the pattern of results described for children who have a physical basis for their speech disorder is quite different from that found for children who have difficulty in producing speech sounds correctly but who have no physical disorder involving the articulatory apparatus (e.g. Snowling & Stackhouse 1983).

The tragedy is that so many children with physical disorders of the speech apparatus have good language skills that they cannot use to express themselves. The main danger for those working in this field is that of concentrating solely on teaching of language form without concern for language function. Some people worry that if a child is encouraged to communicate in some non-standard fashion, such as sign language or Blissymbolics, this will impair their mastery of English, and that the first priority should therefore be to concentrate on speech, reading and writing. There is, however, no evidence for negative transfer between different forms of communication, whereas the benefits of enabling the child to communicate expressively are considerable (see, for example reports by English & Prutting (1975) and Kaslon et al (1978) on facilitating communication in children with tracheostomy). The development of electronic communication aids has been a boon, but one should beware of using these only as teaching aids in formal educational settings. One cerebral palsied boy was provided with a single-switch operated computer on which he learned to write, but was frustrated to find that the net effect of this was to *reduce* the amount of interaction with other people, as he would be seated in his classroom with school-work, whereas previously he required a great deal of one-to-one attention. Fortunately, he had the intelligence and language skill to write 'What's the use of writing things if nobody ever reads them?'

15

Five questions about language acquisition considered in the light of exceptional circumstances

K. Mogford and D. Bishop

In Chapter 1 we introduced five questions about language acquisition on which the study of exceptional circumstances might throw some light. We are now in a position to reconsider these questions in the light of the evidence provided in Chapters 2 to 14.

WHAT LANGUAGE INPUT IS NECESSARY FOR THE CHILD TO LEARN LANGUAGE?

The problem that we have to explain is how exposure to language input results in the child developing a grammatical system that makes it possible not just to imitate sentences spoken by adults, but to generate an infinite number of new, grammatical sentences. According to Chomsky (1959), the principles of learning advocated by behaviourists are quite inadequate to explain how the child learns language. If the child came to the language-learning task with no innate language-learning principles, then there is no way in which language could be learned by simple stimulus-response associations. One cornerstone of his argument is that the language input to the child provides an inadequate basis for language learning. However, in the late 1960s and 1970s some researchers began to question whether language addressed to children really was such an unsatisfactory source of information. Detailed observations indicated that when addressing children adults adopt a different style of speaking ('Motherese'), and that speech of adults to children is typically shorter and employs more exaggerated intonation patterns than speech between adults (see de Villiers & de Villiers 1978 for a review). Over the past decade the emphasis has shifted from looking purely at parental speech, to analyzing the whole communicative interaction between mother and child, including nonverbal as well as verbal communication. Rather than concentrating on the length and complexity of parental utterances, the focus has been on how parents structure communicative interactions with their children, for example, in responding to a child's gesture or utterance and encouraging continuation of the interaction (e.g. Harris et al 1986, Olson et al 1986).

This research has been used to argue for a reappraisal of Chomsky's views. He stressed that children learn language *despite* a restricted language input, concluding that innate language-learning abilities must play a substantial role in language acquisition. 'Motherese' studies, on the other hand, were used as evidence that specially structured language input was important in language-learning, and to play down the importance of the child's innate skills. However, there are two difficulties with this argument. First, there appears to have been confusion about what Chomsky meant when he described the input to the child as inadequate for language learning. Chomsky has been interpreted as saying that language addressed to children is full of false starts, hesitations, ungrammatical utterances and speech which is hard to disentangle from background noise. The 'Motherese' studies do not support this view, and thus, it has been concluded, Chomsky's premises are invalid. However, although Chomsky did mention that input to the child

was often 'degenerate' in the senses mentioned above, this was not the main foundation of his argument (Cromer 1980, Chomsky 1980c). The term 'poverty of the stimulus' refers rather to the fact that the deep structure which the child must learn to become a competent language-user is not transparently obvious from the surface structure of the sentences provided by parents, and further, the child must learn grammar from positive instances only: adults do not provide explicit examples of ungrammatical sentences and explain that these are wrong. The demonstration that adults use 'Motherese' to children in no way challenges this assertion. Indeed, it can be argued that in this respect, 'Motherese' provides a more impoverished stimulus than adult speech, because the child is exposed to only a limited range of short sentences.

Leaving this logical problem aside, the second difficulty for those concerned with the impact of the communicative environment on language development is that the evidence consists largely of demonstrations that adults modify their speech to children in ways which might be expected to facilitate language development. However, in practice it is difficult to establish just how much effect these behaviours do have (Newport et al 1977, Shatz 1982).

There are two ways of investigating the role of input in language acquisition within a normal population. First, one can look for correlations between language input and rate or type of language development. However, if there is a positive association between how the mother talks to the child and how the child develops, we cannot be certain that this reflects a causal chain from mother to child. It could be that the child's behaviour affects how the mother communicates. Or factors common to the genetic make-up or environment of mother and child may be responsible for the association (Hardy-Brown 1983). The best one can do with this approach is to demonstrate significant correlations over time between particular aspects of verbal input and specific features of child language which one would expect to be related on logical grounds, while at the same time showing no such close relationship for other aspects of behaviour. However, this technique remains logically inadequate to demonstrate causality (Rogosa 1980). Furthermore, to obtain reliable results with correlational methods while partialling out unwanted variables one needs far larger sample sizes than are typically used in this field (Hardy-Brown 1983) and, where adequate samples have been used, correlations between variables of interest have seldom been high (see Bates et al 1982 for a review of studies and a methodological critique).

A second and more satisfactory approach is to manipulate the input to the child to see how this affects verbal learning. However, although it is legitimate to modify input to children in ways which might be expected to enhance language development, it would hardly be ethical to use this approach to investigate the lower limits of input which are compatible with normal acquisition (although this has occasionally been tried notwithstanding—see Ch. 2). We can, however, profitably study naturally-occurring situations and consider what happens to language development when some or all of the normal communicative input is disrupted or different in quality for reasons which are clearly not caused by the child's behaviour, e.g. sensory impairment in the parent or child. Such studies allow us to ask the crucial question: how limited can communicative input be and still be compatible with language acquisition

There are two broad classes of circumstance in which communicative input to the child is altered in quality or quantity. First we have situations in which, for one reason or another, the language addressed to the child is abnormal. At one extreme we have children whose parents or other caregivers are so incompetent, malign or disturbed that the child is severely deprived of any normal human communication (Ch. 2). At the other end of the spectrum we have parents whose own ability to use oral language is limited, but who in other respects provide a normal, loving environment (Ch. 3). Also under this broad heading come children whose exposure

to one particular language is reduced because they are growing up in a bilingual environment (Ch. 4), and those who hear a normal quantity of language from adults, but for whom personalized communicative exchanges are reduced because they must share an adult's attention with a twin (Ch. 5).

The second group of circumstances are those where the input provided by an adult may be normal, but sensory impairments limit the child's ability to process all aspects of that input. Under this heading come mild and severe hearing losses (Chs. 6, 7 and 8) and visual handicap (Ch. 9).

These two sorts of influence may interact: thus the presence of a sensory impairment may influence how adults communicate with a child, and this in turn may affect language acquisition (see Ch. 9).

Factors affecting quality or quantity of communicative input from adult to child

Skuse (Ch. 2) is concerned with children whose gravely deficient verbal input occurs in the context of severe physical abuse and neglect. Quite apart from the extremely abnormal quality of communicative interactions experienced by most of these children, in simple terms of quantity their early verbal experience had been drastically reduced, so that for periods of months or years when normal children would be exposed to thousands of sentences every day, these children would hear little or no language. At discovery all the cases considered by Skuse were severely verbally retarded, proving the point, if any doubted it, that some minimum level of verbal input is necessary if the child is to learn language. What is much more remarkable, however, is the amount of recovery shown by some of these children once placed in a more normal environment, with some children catching up to reach the same language level as other children of their age. It should, however, be borne in mind that most of the case studies of extremely deprived children relied on clinical impression to assess ultimate language outcome. Not all investigators are able to carry out such a detailed investigation of language abilities as Curtiss (1977) did with Genie, but it is desirable to look at a range of language functions using objective measures wherever possible. It may be that in some cases the final level of language development achieved by the child, although impressive compared to the initial state on discovery, would prove to be less good on formal assessment than it appeared on clinical impression (cf. Ch. 13), or that conversely, as in Genie's case, expressive language gives a misleadingly low impression of verbal abilities.

As Skuse notes, what is striking about these cases is not just the good outcome obtained by some children, but also the variability in ultimate level achieved. He considers a range of environmental factors which might be expected to relate to language development, but no clear explanatory factor emerges. The answer, he concludes, may lie in constitutional differences between children. Children subjected to severe neglect and abuse are in no sense a random sample of the population. There are a number of reasons why we might expect a high rate of constitutional problems in such a group. First, a child who fails to develop normally is at particular risk of maltreatment. Itard, in his celebrated account of the Wild Boy of Aveyron assumed that Victor was a constitutionally normal child who lacked speech because he had been isolated from human contact for many years, but, even at the time Itard was writing, there was a considerable body of opinion that took the alternative view that Victor might have been abandoned precisely because he was abnormal from the outset (Lane 1977). Second, where a child's natural parents behave in a manner that is not only neglectful but also bizarre, as in the case of Genie, it is possible that there is a genetic predisposition to abnormal, possibly psychotic, behaviour in both parent and child. Third, physical abuse of young children often involves head injuries, so that the child's future development is compromised, not just by a grossly inadequate environment, but also by organic damage. Because the role of factors such as

these is difficult to ascertain, cases of poor outcome are much more difficult to interpret than instances of good outcome, which do provide clear evidence of the boundary conditions compatible with normal language development.

The children studied by Schiff-Myers (Ch. 3), like those described in Skuse's chapter, are exposed to limited quantity and quality of verbal language early in life. However, there the similarity ends. For hearing children of deaf parents the emotional and material environment is usually normal, and parents make every effort to communicate with their child, being limited only in the ability to do so through oral language. In this respect, this group provides a much less ambiguous test of the relationship between verbal input and language development with other factors held relatively constant. In particular, one can be certain that the limitations of the verbal input to the child have a clear external cause (deafness in a parent), and are not consequent on some constitutional abnormality in the child. Schiff-Myers demonstrates not only that normal language *can* develop despite severely limited oral language from parents, but that, provided no other disability is present, unimpaired language is the rule rather than the exception. Of course, it is not the case that these children hear no normal language. However, it seems that the quantity of clear and complex utterances they need to be exposed to is not substantial in order for language to be acquired, and that lack of consistency between the speech heard from a deaf parent and that from other sources does not interfere with acquisition. One might have expected that particular aspects of a deaf parent's speech, such as limited syntax, abnormal phonology, and atypical intonation patterns would be imitated by children, but this seldom proved to be the case. Also, one might have expected to find that there would be a relationship between age and outcome such that preschool children who did not attend nursery would show more adverse effects than older children who had more regular exposure to normal language at school. However, such a relationship did not clearly emerge from a review of published cases.

Results from these children indicate that oral language can be learned with considerably less verbal input than is usually available.

It would be interesting to extend studies of this kind to include parents with other kinds of selective verbal handicap, such as parents with an acquired aphasia or dysarthria. In most cases these parents would be at a disadvantage compared to congenitally deaf parents in not having an alternative means of communication, sign language.

The child in a bilingual environment has to contend with all the language-learning problems facing the monolingual child, but also has to develop two, possibly quite disparate, phonological, grammatical and sociocultural systems. The bilingual environment might be expected to hamper development for two reasons. First, the child must learn which parts of the input belong to which language. As Genesee points out in Chapter 4, instances of language mixing have been used as evidence that children initially fail to differentiate the two languages, treating everything they hear as belonging to a common language, which they encode in a single representation, only later making a distinction between languages. Genesee, however, examines the evidence critically and finds it wanting. He makes the bold claim that children have the perceptual abilities to differentiate between the phonological characteristics of languages from the earliest stages of language learning, and that even in their earliest utterances they may discriminate the contexts in which each language is used, and not treat words and structures from the two languages as if they were part of the same system. Mixing, he claims, can be partly accounted for in terms of an overlooked phenomenon: adults raising children bilingually frequently themselves produce utterances containing elements from two languages. There is obviously a considerable amount of research to be done on this topic. For example, does the rate of mixing depend on phonological similarities between the two

languages? Is mixing less frequent when the child is cared for by monolingual adults (e.g. parents and nursery staff), each speaking a different language? Whether or not Genesee's suggestion that bilingual children differentiate languages from the outset proves to be supported, there is no doubt that children who learn two languages simultaneously in the first years of life have no difficulty in keeping the languages apart after the age of 2 to 3 years.

The second aspect of a bilingual environment which might be expected to affect development is the fact that the total amount of exposure to any one language will be reduced, to the extent that the other language is used to communicate with the child. Thus if a child hears German at home and English at school the total amount of verbal input may be the same as for a monolingual child, but amount of exposure to English will be less than for the monolingual English child, and amount of exposure to German will be less than for the monolingual German child. If amount of language input is a critical determinant of rate of language development, we might expect the bilingual child, with fairly equal exposure to both languages, to learn both languages more slowly than a monolingual child. What is the evidence for this? McLaughlin (1984), reviewing the linguistic consequences of early bilingualism notes that, as well as being of theoretical interest, this question has important practical implications for parents who are considering raising their children bilingually. However, the research literature provides no simple answer: there is little consensus of views. At one extreme we have those who, following Ronjat's (1913) pioneering case study of his own child, maintain that early bilingualism has no disadvantages and may actually facilitate language learning. At the other extreme, Skutnabb-Kangas (1978) describes children whose bilingual experience results in a state she describes as 'semi-lingualism', where proficiency is achieved in neither language. McLaughlin concludes that the literature varies so greatly that almost all general statements are suspect. What is clear is that bilingual exposure can have different consequences for different children, suggesting that there are important intervening variables that have to be considered. He suggests that conditions of presentation of the two languages may be important, echoing the early views of Ronjat who stressed the importance of maintaining consistency between familiar speakers and a particular language. But as Genesee makes clear, bilingual adults use code-switching as part of their linguistic competence, and cannot always match this advice with their behaviour. It is also possible that the different conclusions drawn by different researchers are at least partly the result of variable criteria for assessing language proficiency: for example, measures of syntactic or phonologic skills might give a very different picture from estimates of vocabulary in a language.

Twins (Ch. 5) are of particular interest for the light they shed on the role of early mother-child interaction in language development. Mogford notes that the resources of the adult taking care of the children must be shared between two infants at the same developmental level. Thus although the language input to a twin may be the same as for a singleton in terms of the amount of heard speech, the relationship between that speech and the child's own behaviour will be less strong. If a mother makes her response contingent upon the behaviour of one twin she must at the same time ignore the other child. The extent to which mothers relate their speech to what their infant says and does has been isolated as one factor correlated with rate of language acquisition, and is regarded as more important than simple amount of speech produced in the presence of the child (e.g. Ellis & Wells 1980, Harris et al 1986). The data from twins is consistent with this view. Although normal language development is observed in many twin pairs, mild delays in language development are common. As Mogford points out, one must be cautious in interpreting this result, given the range of biological and environmental factors that could be responsible. There are, for instance,

positive relationships between language development in twins and indices of physical maturity, such as height. However, it is apparent that delayed language cannot be dismissed simply in terms of an increased rate of brain damage and low intelligence in twins: relationships with perinatal problems are weak, and the language deficit is too selective to be dismissed as part of a more general problem. We are still a long way from unravelling the complex chain of causation of language delay in twins, but it seems likely that the child's communicative environment is implicated to some extent. It is frustrating that studies of language development in twins typically adopt either a biological approach, looking for relationships between perinatal hazard, motor status or physical growth and language, or concentrate solely on the child's communicative environment. It would be useful to see studies that compared twins with singletons who were matched on some index of neurodevelopmental age, making it possible to consider the impact of the 'twin situation' once biological differences had been allowed for.

Factors affecting ability of the child to perceive communicative input

Even where a child's parents provide plentiful verbal stimulation, the quality of language received by the child may be degraded if hearing is impaired. Otitis media with effusion is an extremely common childhood ailment that might be expected to interfere with language acquisition for two reasons. First, while the middle ear is affected, perception of grammatically important speech segments may be impaired.

Second, it could be argued that because the condition fluctuates, verbal signals are perceived by the child in an inconsistent manner. In Chapter 6 Klein and Rapin consider the impact of mild temporary hearing loss on language learning: does such degradation of the verbal stimulus result in language impairments, or is there sufficient redundancy in language to make this unimportant? It is clear from their review that the data are somewhat conflicting. While it has been claimed that recurrent otitis media is associated with language delay, some studies find no such effect, and it seems that if there are genuine verbal impairments associated with this condition, they are relatively slight. (Whether age at which the child is affected is important is a question that will be considered below.)

When deafness is more severe, the picture is very different. In Chapter 7, Mogford considers what limitations are imposed on the acquisition of spoken language when little or no auditory information is available. She points out that although there is good evidence that visual information is used by normally-hearing children learning language, it does so by complementing the auditory information: sounds that are difficult to distinguish on an auditory basis are easy to tell apart visually, and vice versa. Visual information alone is not adequate for discriminating all speech sounds. Furthermore, the child must attend to a speaker's face in order to detect visual information, whilst auditory information imposes no such constraint. Although most deaf children have some residual hearing which may be utilized when hearing aids are provided, diagnosis is often late, and many children go through a long period where even this limited source of auditory information is denied them. Perhaps it should not surprise us therefore that children who must rely largely on visual cues learn spoken language only slowly and with great difficulty. One might imagine that it should be possible to bypass the auditory impairment by teaching deaf children via written language, but Mogford's review demonstrates the falseness of this assumption. Despite many years of exposure to the written word, most profoundly deaf children continue to have problems in understanding or using syntax appropriately. Mogford suggests that there may be a fundamental incompatibility between the temporal organization of an oral language and the way in which information is processed in the visual modality, which is better at organizing material on the basis of simultaneous, spatial characteristics.

Given the severe limitations on auditory input to profoundly deaf children, it seems that any language behaviour that does develop at the normal time must be preprogrammed and relatively independent of verbal input. Conventional wisdom has it that one of the earliest manifestations of language, babbling, does indeed develop normally in deaf children. Mogford re-examines the evidence and finds that while there is some truth in this notion, the situation is more complex than it seems at first sight, and the answer to the question 'do deaf children babble normally?' will depend on the age at which children are assessed and the definition of babbling employed. Certainly young deaf infants do vocalize, and their vocalizations bear some resemblance to those of hearing children, but the differences increase with age, with deaf children babbling less rather than more as they grow older and using a more restricted range of speech sounds.

Another piece of conventional wisdom questioned by Mogford is the assumption that profound deafness precludes the development of a phonological system. Current debate centres less on the question of whether or not profoundly deaf children can have a phonological system than on the extent to which their systems follow normal developmental patterns, on the relative contribution of visual and auditory information in establishing such a system, and specification of those variables which determine whether or not an individual child will be able to develop a phonological system adequate for intelligible speech.

However, although learning of some aspects of oral language is not precluded by profound deafness, the conclusion that must be drawn from Mogford's review is that visual input alone is inadequate for the acquisition of full competence in an oral language.

There is, however, plentiful evidence that deaf children can learn language visually, provided they have early and naturalistic exposure to a language suited to the visual medium, i.e. second generation deaf children whose parents use sign language (Ch. 8). Studies of natural sign languages indicate that they encode the same sorts of linguistic information as do spoken languages, but in very different ways, with spatial configurations playing an important role. One may ask how the different modality and structure of language input in sign language affects the course of language development. If children possess a language acquisition device specifically attuned to auditory-verbal input, then two predictions seem to follow. First, acquisition should be more natural and hence more rapid for spoken than for sign language. Second, ease of acquisition of sign language should depend on how similar the surface structure of sign language is to that found in a spoken language. Neither prediction is confirmed. One reliable and surprising finding is that acquisition of first words in sign occurs *earlier* than in spoken language (Orlansky & Bonvillian 1985), and later stages of acquisition show strong parallels with spoken language development, with ease of acquisition being determined more by linguistic complexity than by the extent to which signs are iconic, i.e. physically resembling their referents (see Ch. 8). An additional finding is that learning does not seem to be facilitated by the use of artificial sign languages that follow the surface structure of English (Bishop 1983b). This last conclusion is less well-founded than the others, because it could be argued that no fair comparison has been made: exposure to artificial sign systems typically starts much later than exposure to natural sign language, and those adults presenting the language are less skilled than native signers. It will be interesting to see if we ever arrive at the situation where fluent users of artificial sign languages teach their offspring to use the system as a first language. Our guess is that this situation is unlikely to arise: the hands are not well suited to represent the rapid sequence of signals involved in spoken syntax, and the eyes are not well adapted to perceive them (Studdert-Kennedy & Lane 1980). Even skilled users of artificial sign languages cannot communicate at the same speed as in speech,

so pressure will be created to alter the system away from English syntax to become closer to natural sign languages and rely more on spatial than sequential patterning.

Results on acquisition of sign language as a first language force us to conclude that the language acquisition device is not tied to auditory-verbal language, but utilizes language-learning procedures of a very general and abstract kind that can operate on input from the visual as well as the auditory modality, and has little difficulty in extracting structure from visuospatial as well as auditory-temporal patterns.

As Mills (Ch. 9) points out, it is not immediately obvious that visual handicap should influence language development, since this has no effect on auditory perception or production of speech. However, there are four ways in which blindness will affect the communicative input to the child.

1. Nonverbal communication with the blind child will be very different from that experienced by sighted children. Normal communicative interactions involve visual as well as auditory exchanges, and long before the child starts to speak, gestural and visual communication between mother and child can be observed. These early interactions have been assigned a crucial role in language development by several theorists (e.g. Bateson 1975, Bruner 1975a). For example, development of mutual gaze patterns by mother and infant is thought to pave the way for subsequent development of shared reference in conversation.

2. It is frequently assumed that young children learn much of their early vocabulary by noting that particular words and phrases occur in similar contexts. For example, the child notices that the word 'dog' is used when attention is focussed on a four-legged hairy animal. The blind child can, of course, relate what is said to non-visual sensory experiences, such as the sound, smell or touch of a dog. However, inability to perceive a referent which is noiseless and out of reach (trees, houses, boats, cats . . .) drastically limits the detectability of associations between words and what they refer to.

3. A more specific difference between the

language input of the blind and sighted child concerns the acquisition of phonology. Research on the development of phonology has focussed almost exclusively on auditory perception and motor aspects of speech production. However, Mills notes that the auditory cues in a speech signal are complemented by visual cues from the lips.

4. Adults talk differently to blind children than they do to children who can see them.

We can see, then, that there is a range of reasons why we might expect language to develop differently in blind and sighted children. So how does blindness affect language development? There seems to be no shortage of individuals ready to give confident answers. On the one hand, Chomsky (1980b) cites lack of language impairment in blind children to support his views of language acquisition. On the other hand, as Landau & Gleitman (1985) note in their Preface, it is now common to find many psycholinguists blithely asserting that language impairment is 'inevitable' in blind children. So what is the true position? Mills notes that several studies find that early verbal development *is* different or delayed in the context of a visual handicap. Nevertheless, it is evident that Chomsky's assertion is justified in two respects: first, whatever the *typical* outcome may be, it is evident that *some* congenitally blind children do develop language without apparent difficulty. To that extent, one may say that visual cues are not logically *necessary* for language acquisition. Second, where blindness does exert an effect, this is on the course, and possibly on the timing of language development, but as far as one can tell from the limited studies available, there is little impact on ultimate linguistic proficiency. Thus Mills showed, for example, that the lack of visual cues available to blind children influenced the course of phonological development, yet it did not result in disordered phonology in any of the three children she followed up. She also noted that in some cases, where abnormalities of language development were remarked in blind children, we should consider the possibility that this could result from the ways in which adults modify their speech to blind children, or they could

be the result of additional handicaps which often accompany blindness. Thus the inability to detect the *correlation* of sensory input from two different modalities, vision and hearing, has relatively small effects on language acquisition. One is forced to conclude that the language-learning system does not rely heavily on this particular source of information. Perhaps we should not be too surprised at this ability to learn language even when the terms do not have clear referents in our own perceptual experience. After all, many of the concepts referred to in language by sighted people have no perceptual correlates: e.g. 'need', 'nice', 'truth', 'until', 'perhaps', 'really' and many more.

Extremes of input compatible with language acquisition

Chomsky has been chided for stressing the inadequacies of language input experienced by children. Attention has been drawn to the way in which adults structure their communications with children to facilitate language learning. However, consideration of children learning in exceptional circumstances swings the pendulum back to support Chomsky. Irrespective of what sort of input the *average* child is exposed to, any theory of language acquisition must be able to explain how it is that a significant proportion of children learn language when the verbal input they receive is severely limited in quantity (Ch. 3), degraded and inconsistent in quality (Chs. 3 and 6), inconsistent in linguistic characteristics (Ch. 4), or is presented with limited contextual cues as to meaning (Ch. 9).

WHAT IS THE RELATIONSHIP BETWEEN COGNITION AND LANGUAGE?

Cognitive prerequisites for language development?

In the normal child, language acquisition takes place alongside numerous other sensory, motor and cognitive developments. The child's motor, perceptual and memory abilities increase; social awareness and logical reasoning develop. How far are these different developments inter-related, and how far is language logically dependent on other faculties?

Piaget has provided an influential theoretical framework for development which clearly links language to other aspects of cognition. The child is seen as progressing through a series of stages, each building on the last, with language developing as part of a more general ability to internalize, represent and symbolize external experience.

Theories of cognitive prerequisites of language are notoriously difficult to test. We know that in normal development our postulated prerequisite, A, regularly precedes the development of B: it is observation of such regularities that leads us to formulate our theory in the first place. But how can we prove that A is *necessary* to B? Most children develop their first tooth before learning to walk, yet there is no logical link between these developments: one does not need teeth in order to walk.

Even if it were practically possible to intervene and selectively disrupt one aspect of development, this would hardly be ethical. All one can do in order to test the logical link between one development and another is to look for naturally-occurring instances of dissociations between them. The best chance of finding such dissociations is if one considers individuals whose development is not proceeding along normal lines. For example, one might look at children whose overall development is severely retarded. Do they preserve the same temporal relationship between different aspects of behaviour? Rondal (Ch. 10) reviews work demonstrating that in general this is the case. Although there is heterogeneity of language profiles within the mentally-retarded population, one usually finds that language skills are either consistent with or lagging behind sensorimotor development.

The work described by Bellugi et al in Chapter 11, however, presents a different picture. Children with Williams syndrome show a dissociation between language development and supposed cognitive prerequisites. Thus, sophisticated use of language with complex syntax and adult-like vocabulary is found in individuals who demonstrate no evidence of concrete operational behaviour on Piagetian tasks, and whose overall level of mental development is below that of a 7-year-old.

Further challenge to Piagetian theory is provided by the evidence reviewed by Bishop in Chapter 14 on children with severe physical handicaps. Those working in a Piagetian framework have stressed the importance of development of actions in the sensorimotor stage as laying the foundations for language development. For example, Moerk (1975) explicitly states that development of cognitive as well as verbal structures proceeds from motor behaviour. Morehead & Morehead (1974) argue that children first learn the meanings of words through actions associated with objects and events, rather than through perception. They note that Piaget assigns perception a relatively unimportant role, stressing the importance of the sensorimotor schema as a *stable pattern of movement* together with a perceptual component geared to recognition. It follows that children who have little control of voluntary movements should be retarded in the development of thought and language. Educators working with children who have virtually no voluntary muscular control have long believed that some individuals have good intelligence despite being unable to demonstrate this in behaviour. This has now been demonstrated more objectively by systematic studies of cerebral palsied children, and by occasional individuals who have demonstrated remarkable talents once provided with a computer-based means of communication (see, for example, the autobiographical account by Nolan 1987). Thus, contrary to prediction, inability to talk and extremely limited ability to move need not impair language acquisition. Mills (Ch. 9) mentions that even when a child is both blind and cerebral palsied this need not result in language impairment.

The standard Piagetian defence against this sort of attack is to maintain that the evidence is irrelevant. Severely paralysed children are *not* incapable of passing through a sensorimotor stage. They do, after all, retain *some* motor control (for example, of eye movements), and may have relatively intact sensory systems (e.g. touch and taste, even if vision is impaired). However, the extreme restriction of voluntary motor control does make it inevitable that they will have far less experience of *correlations* between particular motor acts and associated sensations, and so opportunities to learn will be greatly reduced. If one interprets Piagetian theory to mean that the *range* and *amount* of sensorimotor experience is irrelevant, and it is necessary only that some minimal exposure to pairings of motor acts and their sensory consequences is required, then the theory remains compatible with data from handicapped children. However, this resolution is achieved only at the expense of reducing Piagetian theory to an innatist position (see Piatelli-Palmarini 1980).

It should be noted that cases of good language in children with severe motor impairments do not constitute a test of the notion that specific cognitive developments are prerequisites for language: it may well be that severely cerebral palsied children possess the cognitive skills regarded as characteristic of the sensorimotor stage, such as object permanence and ability to predict future position of an object before it moves. This has not been investigated. What is clear, however, is that normal ability to perform actions on the world and note their sensory consequences is not necessary for linguistic development.

So far we have considered the notion of cognitive prerequisites for language in global terms. Mills (Ch. 9) addresses the question at a more specific level. Blind children do not suffer from any general slowing of mental development unless an additional handicap is involved, but their dependence on the haptic and auditory modalities might be expected to affect the way they structure their world, and this in turn could affect language development. Where language is used to refer to concepts derived from visuospatial information, one would expect the blind child to follow a different course of development. As Cromer (1983) argues, research in this area is bedevilled by frequent failure to maintain a logical distinction between *conceptual* and *semantic* knowledge. If a child fails to use a word with the normally accepted meaning, this may be because: (a) the child lacks the underlying concept and so is unable to use the word appropriately—a *conceptual* deficit; or (b) the child has the underlying concept, but does not know the word which refers to that concept—a semantic deficit. Mills notes that blind children have been described as having specific difficulty in the acquisition of spatial deictic terms (such as this/that, here/there), and this has been explained in terms of delayed development of a spatial frame of reference, i.e. a conceptual problem. However, it could be that blind children develop an adequate frame of reference, but lack of visual information retards their learning of verbal labels referring to relative points in that space, i.e. their lack of ability to relate heard speech to visual contexts may result in a semantic deficit.

The studies of Landau & Gleitman (1985) provide fascinating examples of a third way in which semantic development may be affected in the blind: the child may develop a concept which is related to, though not identical to that used by sighted individuals, and use the word to refer to that. Where the accepted meaning of a word cannot correspond to anything in the child's experience, as with the verbs 'look' and 'see', the child interprets them in terms of another modality: Kelli, the child studied by Landau & Gleitman, used these terms to mean 'haptically explore' and 'haptically be aware of'.

How does language affect cognition?

We have concentrated so far on the question of how far language depends on underlying cognitive development, but psychologists have also shown great interest in the converse question: how does language affect cognition?

Mogford (Ch. 8) notes that the traditional approach to the study of language and thought involved the study of deaf children who were assumed to have little or no language. Where these children showed normal cognitive skills this was thought to provide evidence that such skills did not depend on language. However, this rationale involves a fundamental misapprehension, namely that deaf children lack language. Deafness does not preclude linguistic development, it rather affects the type of language which is learned and the way in which it is acquired. This does not mean that the study of cognitive development in deaf children is no longer of value, but only that the focus of interest has changed. Rather than asking 'does thought depend on language?' the question becomes 'how does the modality in which a language is learned affect both language and cognitive development?' For example, many profoundly deaf individuals do not show the normal phonological similarity effect in short-term memory for written words or pictures: their recall of sequences of similar-sounding words is no worse than recall of different-sounding words. However, there are exceptions, and even within the profoundly deaf one finds relationships between phonological proficiency and presence of a phonological similarity effect (Ch. 7). Even more intriguing is the demonstration that deaf persons who are native signers show an analogous effect, confusing items that are similar in hand configuration rather than those which are semantically related (Bellugi et al 1975, Poizner et al 1981).

Bishop (Ch. 14) considers how far cognition depends on overt, expressive language. She finds that cerebral palsied children are able to use inner speech in tasks involving memory, spelling, and rhyme judgements, even in cases where the child has never been able to speak. Thus there is good evidence that language is used for thought, but this use does not need to develop from speaking aloud.

HOW INDEPENDENT ARE DIFFERENT COMPONENTS OF THE LANGUAGE FUNCTION?

Studies of adults with acquired brain damage testify to the independence of different components of language: it is, for instance, possible to have disruption of grammatical expression while retaining good semantic skills, or conversely, to retain the ability to talk in long, fluent and complex sentences despite having lost much of the ability to produce or understand content words (see Saffran 1982 for a review). This does not, of course, mean that grammar and semantics develop from the outset as separate systems. It may be that these faculties differentiate into independent subsystems only after considerable language learning has taken place. For many years it was thought that the literature on acquired aphasia in children (Ch. 13) supported the notion that language skills were organized differently in adult and child because the pattern of language disturbances was different. The claim was that certain symptoms which are commonly observed in aphasic adults, particularly fluent aphasia with jargon and paraphasias, were rarely or never observed in children. However, recent reports have contradicted this belief, with jargon aphasia being reported in several children, including some as young as 5 or 6 years. We have insufficient data to know how the distribution of aphasic symptoms compares in adults and children. Although it appears likely that the frequency of different types of aphasia is heavily dependent on age, it does seem false to conclude that certain adult symptoms are not found in children, and the occurrence of aphasias in children which selectively impair some components of language while leaving others intact does point to a degree of independence of language functions from an early age.

When we consider conditions where neurological impairment is present from birth, we find the traditional view is that language development is typically delayed, but not otherwise abnormal. Down's syndrome is often thought of as the classic case of a condition which delays all aspects of language development, and limits the ultimate level of competence achieved, without disrupting the normal relationships between different components of language. Several authors have concluded that language acquisition in Down's syndrome is 'delayed' rather than 'different', resembling normal development in slow motion.

However, as Rondal (Ch. 10) points out, this conclusion is based on studies which analyze language in terms of fairly gross categories. Fine-grained analysis can give a very different picture. Also, one may get a very different impression if several aspects of language are considered simultaneously than if only one component is considered: individual linguistic abilities may follow a normal developmental course, but they may be out of synchrony with one another. Furthermore, while group studies may give the impression of a uniform lag in language development, there may be considerable variability from child to child. Similar arguments apply in the study of deaf children learning oral language: when one looks at broad measures such as order of acquisition of morphemes, then it seems that deafness results in delayed rather than deviant development, but when individual response patterns are examined in more detail there is evidence of comprehension strategies that are not found in hearing children of the same linguistic level (see Ch. 7).

When we turn to case studies of individual retarded children, we find some instances of extreme dissociations between mastery of syntax and semantics. Curtiss (1981b) described two intellectually retarded individuals who produced fluent, abundant and richly structured language, but whose comprehension of meaning was very poor. She contrasts these cases with Genie, who learned language only after a period of severe deprivation, and who showed almost the opposite pattern of impairment, with extremely limited expressive syntax, but good ability to understand and convey meaning. Cases like these demonstrate considerable independence of mechanisms subserving development of language form and those involved with meaning.

The syndrome of infantile autism presents us with perhaps the most striking cases of dissociation between different aspects of language development. As Fay's review (Ch. 12) makes clear, expressive language abilities of autistic children cover a wide spectrum, ranging from total mutism to fluent and syntactically complex speech. Problems in verbal comprehension appear to be universal, however. One of the more striking instances of a dissociation in linguistic skills is seen in hyperlexic children, who master the operations for transcoding written to spoken language despite understanding little of what they read. Children who show this skill, as well as those who are echolalic, demonstrate that an input signal (either heard speech or written language) can be translated into verbal output directly without apparently being processed in terms of meaning. Some older autistic individuals, such as the young man who describes his own problems on page 201, may learn to communicate meaningfully using long and complex sentences, but high-level aspects of language meaning and use continue to elude them. We are still a long way from understanding the underlying nature of language problems in autistic children, but what they do show us is that quite striking dissociations can occur between expressive and receptive skills, and between mastery of language form (phonology and syntax) on the one hand, and appreciation of language meaning and use on the other.

ARE THERE CRITICAL PERIODS FOR LANGUAGE DEVELOPMENT?

There is ample evidence throughout biology of instances where the impact of a particular environmental event depends critically on the time at which it occurs. For example, certain songbirds will learn to sing the appropriate song for their species only if they hear that song in the first few weeks of life; in other species sexual identity and social behaviour appear to be determined crucially by experiences in infancy. In each case, if early environmental experiences are absent or distorted, then this cannot be compensated for later on. Neurophysiologists have been particularly interested in studying the biological basis of age-dependent environmental sensitivities in the visual system, because of the possibility that some types of unexplained visual impairment (amblyopia) might be remediable if recognised and treated early enough. Studies with animals have confirmed that the way in which cells in the visual cortex develop depends on the type of stimulation they receive early in life, so that, for example, temporary loss of vision in one eye or a squint will result in permanently abnormal functioning of brain cells concerned with processing visual information, which cannot be remedied by later restoring normal vision (see Atkinson et al 1982 for a review). Such findings can be interpreted in terms of a general principle of neurological development which states that, while a neurological system is still immature, the nature of the input to that system will determine how it develops, but once biological maturity is achieved then the system is unlikely to be modified by environmental influences. The term *critical period* or *sensitive period* has been used to refer to the time window during which external influences have a significant effect.

The crucial question to be considered here is whether there is a critical period for language acquisition, as originally proposed by Penfield (1965) and Lenneberg (1967). The essential prediction from a critical period hypothesis is that the *timing* of any adverse experience will be crucial: after a certain age, variously estimated at 5 years (Krashen 1973) or puberty (Lenneberg 1967), ability to learn language diminishes, so that any language deficits still remaining at the end of this period are unlikely to be overcome. Three rather different sorts of evidence have been considered in evaluating the critical period hypothesis.

Reversal of environmental deprivation

The first is directly comparable to the studies carried out on experimental amblyopia, in that an alteration to the environment early in life is investigated to see if it has permanent consequences after the environment has been restored to normal. Under this heading come studies concerned with the effects of severe neglect and deprivation (Ch. 2), conductive hearing loss (Ch. 6), and tracheostomy (Ch. 14).

Cases of extreme deprivation in childhood have been used as evidence in evaluating the notion of a critical period for language development, but Skuse's review demonstrates the dangers of drawing general conclusions on the basis of isolated cases, when outcome is so variable and hard to predict. He notes that Genie, whose plight was not discovered until 13 years of age, and whose expressive language outcome was extremely limited, may well have had some constitutional abnormality. It is noteworthy also that her case has been used both as supportive evidence for the notion of a critical period, on the grounds that language learning was never complete (Curtiss 1981b), and as evidence *against* a critical period, on the grounds that considerable language learning did occur after puberty! (McLaughlin 1984).

If, following Krashen, we regard the upper boundary of a critical period as nearer 5 years of age than puberty, then other cases of severe deprivation are relevant. Mason's (1942) case, Isabelle, and the twins studied by Koluchova (1972, 1976) were not discovered until at least 6 years of age, yet they made impressive amounts of progress, achieving language levels which, at least on the basis of informal assessments, were within normal limits. Nor was there any evidence that a period in a normal environment early in life had any protective effect against later adverse circumstances: some of the children with the best outcomes had no such experience. As Skuse's review makes clear, the range of adverse circumstances implicated in cases of extreme deprivation make it difficult to relate outcome to any one factor, but neither age at discovery, nor previous experience of a normal environment, were of prognostic significance.

The notion of a critical period is often metioned in discussion of the effects of otitis media with effusion. By analogy with animal studies, it has been suggested that the negative impact of a period of hearing loss will be far greater early in life than later on. However, one cannot assume that what holds true for the mouse will also apply to humans. Dobbing & Sands (1979) have drawn attention to the tremendous inter-species variation in the maturity of the nervous system at birth, which is likely to be related to the timing of critical periods.

As Klein and Rapin discuss in Chapter 6, studies looking ·for language deficits associated with recurrent otitis media yield inconsistent findings. One reason might be that variable criteria are used to select subjects. Paradise (1981) argued that if one's aim is to look for evidence of a critical period, then the appropriate test involves comparing *normally-hearing* children with and without a *history* of recurrent otitis media. Yet many studies which purport to be relevant to this issue include subjects who have conductive hearing losses at the time of testing. The question of how much a mild conductive loss interferes with language processing is itself of interest, but it is not relevant to the critical period issue, which is concerned with whether a temporary period of impaired hearing can have irreversible long term effects *after hearing has been restored to normal.* Bishop & Edmundson (1986) showed that if one divided up studies into those that ensured experimental subjects had normal hearing at time of testing, and those that did not, then much of the variability in results could be explained. In general, the former type of study found fairly large language deficits, whilst the latter type found either no difference from a control group or very small effects.

This does not rule out the possibility that a critical period might operate. It could be that there is a critical period extending up to puberty, as suggested by Lenneberg, in which case we would expect children to be able to catch up after a period of conductive hearing loss, provided normal hearing was restored during childhood. Furthermore, otitis media usually fluctuates, so that periods of normal hearing are interspersed with periods of conductive hearing loss. It is possible that

even brief periods of normal hearing are sufficient for normal development to occur.

In some areas of functioning, normal development depends not just on the environment the organism is exposed to, but on the opportunities for interacting with that environment. Held & Hein (1963) showed that a kitten that was able to move about in an experimental environment developed normally, whereas an immobilized kitten exposed to the same visual stimuli did not develop normal perceptions. This raises the possibility that for language acquisition it may be important not just to hear normal language, but also to have the opportunity to produce speech at a critical period early in development. However, no support for this view emerges from studies of children with long-term tracheostomies (Ch. 14). These children are often denied the opportunity to speak for months or even years early in childhood, and may miss out on the babbling stage altogether. If there were a critical period for mastery of expressive phonology, one would expect that such an experience would have long-term adverse consequences, but the evidence goes against this prediction, with rapid recovery after decannulation being the rule, provided other handicaps are not involved.

Language learning at different points in life

A second line of evidence is concerned with the extent to which language learning is possible beyond what has been traditionally regarded as the upper limit of the critical period, i.e. puberty.

As Genesee points out in Chapter 4, proficiency in a second language is related to age at which it is learned. Children who are given naturalistic exposure to a second language in the preschool years usually learn to speak the language like a native, whereas those who encounter the second language later in life usually retain a difference in facility with the two languages, even though high levels of proficiency in the second language may be attained. These findings have been used to support the notion of a neurophysiologically-based critical period for language learning, but there are alternative explanations. Pre-existing linguistic knowledge can interfere with acquisition of a second language, and different cognitive mechanisms may come into play in older than in younger children.

There is tentative evidence that both profoundly deaf people learning oral language (Ch. 7) and individuals with Down's syndrome (Ch. 10) do continue to make progress in language development beyond adolescence, and this has been interpreted by some as evidence against a critical period for language acquisition. However, it would only act as such if we were to interpret the critical period notion in an extremely rigid fashion, maintaining that *no* language development should be possible beyond puberty. Even the strongest advocates of critical periods are unlikely to make such an absolute claim, as it could easily be dismissed by considering the cases of individuals who learn a new language in adulthood, or those who master a new technical vocabulary. What is crucial is not whether *any* verbal learning can take place after puberty, but whether the rate of learning declines, and whether different learning processes are implicated. Current data are inadequate to answer these questions.

Recovery from aphasia at different points in life

Much of the debate about critical periods in language development has centred around studies of recovery after focal brain damage (Ch. 13).

Lenneberg (1967) argued that there was an inverse relationship between age at injury and degree of recovery from acquired aphasia, so that the older the child, the less good the outcome, with complete recovery seldom being achieved for lesions acquired after puberty. In Chapter 13 the evidence is scrutinized, and some difficulties for Lenneberg's position are noted. As more cases have been described in adequate detail, it has become clear that the relationship between age at injury and outcome is far less clear-cut than

suggested by Lenneberg. Some children who acquire unilateral lesions as young as 5 or 6 years fail to make a full recovery; others who first become aphasic at 10 years or above progress well. Other factors than age at injury are clearly implicated, although they are not yet fully understood. Such evidence does not rule out a critical period hypothesis: it is possible that if we had sufficient cases to take into account all the variables associated with brain damage (e.g. locus and extent of lesion, etiology, and so on), then we would find a clearer relationship between age at injury and degree of recovery. However, it is probably mistaken to think in terms of a clear cut-off point, with good recovery below a certain age, and poor outcome otherwise. It seems more plausible to think in terms of a gradient, with a gradually diminishing facility for recovery throughout childhood (Woods & Carey 1979).

Maturity vs. learning as the basis for a critical period

Bishop (Ch. 13) considers how a biological basis for a critical period might operate, and concludes that ability to learn language may depend less on biological maturity per se, and more on the extent to which the brain is already committed to other functions. This line of argument is not dissimilar to that advanced by Genesee when he maintains that the factors that limit mastery of a *second* language may have less to do with neurophysiological maturity and more to do with the interference caused by pre-existing linguistic and cognitive knowledge. The claim is that ability to learn depends on how much has already been learned. Such an explanation remains highly speculative, but it would predict catch-up in language development after restitution of a normal verbal input in a child who had language delay after a period of deprivation, regardless of age (Chs. 2 and 6). A further prediction is that for any group of children of a given age, recovery from acquired aphasia will be best for those whose language development was most immature at time of injury. However, methodological problems of research in this area make it most unlikely that it will ever be possible to subject such a prediction to adequate test.

CAN WE SPECIFY NECESSARY AND SUFFICIENT CONDITIONS FOR LANGUAGE IMPAIRMENT?

It is common for theorists in the field of language acquisition to remark upon the amazing rapidity with which the normal child masters language. Many of the exceptional circumstances reviewed in this book lead one to the conclusion that language development is not only rapid, it is also remarkably robust. Children seem able to learn language against the odds in a range of adverse circumstances. This conclusion is all the more surprising for those of us who spend much of our professional time seeing children with 'specific language impairment' (also referred to as 'developmental language disorder' or 'development dysphasia'), i.e. children who fail to develop language normally for no apparent cause. By definition, these children's language difficulties cannot be explained in terms of intellectual retardation, hearing loss, adverse environment, or physical or psychiatric disorder. Thus on the one hand we have evidence that in many children language develops in the face of circumstances which might reasonably be expected to disrupt it. On the other hand, we frequently see children in whom language development goes awry for no obvious reason. Can we glean any information about likely causes from consideration of exceptional circumstances?

The role of verbal environment

In our experience, the commonest explanation put forward to account for specific language impairment by teachers and other professionals working with such children attributes slow verbal development to inadequate language input. One hears statements such as 'his parents don't talk to him, so of course he can't speak properly'. A related view is that

language disorders can arise when mothers spend insufficient time interacting with their child in the first few years of life. At a recent conference on child language disorders, Sheila Hollins, a child psychiatrist who is the mother of a language-impaired child, described how she was told by a pediatrician that, in view of the fact that she was working, it was not surprising that her son was not beginning to talk, and that if she was really concerned about the problem she should give up work and look after him full time.

As we have argued above, neither drastic reduction in quality and quality of oral language directed to the child (Ch. 3), nor the increased complexity of verbal input in bilingualism (Ch. 4), nor even severe verbal, material and emotional deprivation (Ch. 2) can be regarded as sufficient conditions for specific language impairment. Some children still develop normal language against overwhelming environmental odds. How then is it that people continue to argue that it is the verbal environment which is primarily responsible for language impairment in children? There are several strands to the answer.

First, there is frequent confusion between language impairment and use of minority language or dialect, so that to many people, 'working class language' is synonymous with 'deficient language' (Shafer 1978), and there is a consequent over-readiness to assume that parental language must be inadequate just because a child comes from a relatively disadvantaged social group.

This view has partly grown up because associations have been reported between social class and language development, and people have been impressed by the frequency with which such associations have been found without taking into account the *size* of reported effects. In short, there is a tendency to equate *statistical* significance with *clinical* significance. What needs to be understood is that when one says that a difference between two groups is statistically significant one is commenting on the *reliability* of the difference, not on its *size*. Those researchers who have looked at the magnitude of effects, as

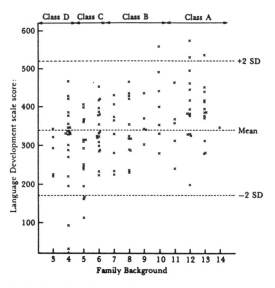

Fig. 15.1 Scatter diagram showing scores on a measure of overall language development vs. family background (an index similar to social class). Reprinted with permission from Wells (1985)

well as their statistical significance, have concluded that social class differences in language development are typically small and of no great importance. Wells (1985) brings the point home with a scatterplot showing the relationship between family background and language development obtained from the Bristol Child Language Study (Fig. 15.1). The correlation between family background and language development is highly statistically significant, but the overlap between the different classes is considerable, and the high correlation is largely due to the small group of children scoring more than two standard deviations above or below the mean. On a related point, Tizard et al (1980) found much greater variability in language competence within the same children in different situations than between children from different social backgrounds, suggesting that what looks like language deficiency in lower-class children might be the result of different strategies in using language in different situations.

However, social class is a very crude index, so perhaps we should not expect striking

effects. One thing that studies of mother-child interaction have taught us is that a wide range of complex factors are involved in successful interaction. We cannot assess a mother's communicative competence purely in terms of how much she speaks to her child, or how long her sentences are. Factors such as responsiveness to the child's communicative attempts may be more important, and the precise way in which communication is structured to achieve this responsiveness should change as the child develops. Our early ideas of what constitutes a poor communicative environment may prove to have been mistaken. For example, an articulate middle-class mother who is depressed, apathetic and unresponsive may provide a far less adequate environment for language-learning than a non-depressed woman of low intelligence and limited verbal skills who is responsive to her child's needs and interests.

Having said this, experimental studies doing more fine-grained analyses of mother-child interaction and language development have found it very hard to demonstrate reliable cause-effect relationships (Bates et al 1982). Furthermore, as with social class, where positive associations have been reported (e.g. Harris et al 1986) the effects are not large. As Mogford notes in Chapter 5, the substantial reduction of contingent interaction that typically arises when one parent is largely responsible for the care of twins is associated with language delay, but the amount of delay is not substantial and would seldom be regarded as of clinical significance. Of particular importance for our argument are studies looking at parent-child interactions in language-impaired children. Results have been inconsistent, and give no clear support to the notion that parental communicative behaviour is typically abnormal (Conti-Ramsden 1985). We may also note that many families contain both language-impaired and normally-developing children. In such cases the problem cannot be attributed to some general inadequacy of parental communication. In sum, while we cannot deny that grossly abnormal communicative behaviour in parents can blight language development in their offspring, we have to conclude that in the majority of cases of specific language impairment, behaviour of the parents is not an important causal factor.

We suspect that the tendency of professionals to attribute language impairments to lack of adequate communication at home has one further cause which has more to do with personal bias than scientific evidence. Environmental explanations are often regarded in a more positive light than biological ones. After all, the child's environment can be modified, whilst constitutional deficits can seldom be remedied. However, although arising from the best of intentions, such biases can do more harm than good if they lead us to accept environmental explanations without examining the evidence critically or considering alternative explanations. Parents of language-impaired children can only have guilt added to their distress and anxiety if they are led to believe that their child's problems are largely due to their failure to have provided an adequate communicative environment.

The role of auditory impairment

The notion that language impairment can arise as the result of hearing impairment is well founded in clinical experience and research studies. As we have seen in Chapter 7, profound deafness has severe consequences for acquisition of spoken language. More moderate levels of hearing loss affect the development of syntax and phonology and can result in a clinical picture not dissimilar to that of specific language impairment.

It therefore seems plausible that, although the diagnosis explicitly excludes cases whose disorder is attributable to hearing loss, specific language impairment may result from some auditory abnormality that makes it difficult for the child to process sounds, despite being able to hear them. Research on this topic has addressed the issue at two levels of explanation. First, we have etiologically-based investigations which are concerned with the possibility that hitherto undetected hearing loss at a critical period of language development might be responsible for persisting verbal deficits. Second, we have psychological studies that look for direct evidence of abnormal auditory processing in children with language difficulties, without making any assumptions about underlying causes of such abnormality.

Klein and Rapin (Ch. 6) review studies of the first kind. Many children have recurrent episodes of conductive hearing loss in early childhood due to otitis media, and such cases often go undetected. Over the past 10 years considerable interest has built up in the notion that repeated episodes of otitis media early in life may have long-term adverse consequences for language development, even after hearing has returned to normal (Downs 1985). Could recurrent otitis media be a sufficient cause of specific developmental language disorder? Bishop & Edmundson (1986) reviewed the evidence and concluded that otitis media depresses performance on verbal tests while the child is actively suffering from the disease, but these effects do not persist once hearing has returned to normal. They further noted that there is a danger of introducing spurious bias into studies of otitis media if, as their study suggested, doctors react differently to otitis media occurring in the context of normal development, and otitis media in the context of language disorder. When the child is language-disordered, the otitis media is regarded as a probable contributory factor and surgical treatment is recommended. If the otitis media appears to have no adverse consequences on language development, then more conservative treatment is adopted. The result will be that any sample of children selected on the basis that they are receiving hospital treatment for otitis media is likely to contain children who would not have been referred to hospital if they did not have a language disorder. If we then find a high rate of language problems in such a sample, we might conclude that this is evidence for a causal relationship between otitis media and language impairment. However, the real explanation may be that the presence of language impairment determines how otitis media is treated.

Although the evidence linking otitis media and language impairment is not strong, Klein and Rapin point out that we should beware of considering only simple-minded etiological models that consider only single causal factors in isolation. Perhaps recurrent otitis media has little impact on language development in an intelligent child with a good home background, but does have a negative influence in a child whose developmental environment is less ideal. Bishop & Edmundson (1986) produced tentative evidence suggesting that otitis media might indeed interact with other factors and play a role in the causation of language disorders in a child already at risk because of perinatal problems.

Even if the causal role of otitis media remains in question, the possibility remains that specific language impairments in children might be the result of problems in processing auditory stimuli. In a series of experimental studies, Tallal and her associates have provided evidence that language-impaired children are deficient at perceiving brief or rapid auditory stimuli (see Tallal & Piercy 1978 for a review of the early work). The stimuli do not need to be verbal, although the effect can be clearly demonstrated using synthethic speech (Tallal & Stark 1981). Tallal has argued that this is part of a more general neuropsychological deficit in producing and perceiving rapid stimuli in any sensory modality (Tallal et al 1985). The effect would be that language-impaired children would be able to tell if an auditory stimulus had occurred (i.e. they would pass pure tone audiometry), but they would have difficulty in discriminating between the rapidly changing auditory signals that occur in natural speech. The outcome would be not unlike that of a hearing loss. It is interesting to note that direct comparisons of comprehension of grammar by deaf children and children with normal hearing and severe comprehension problems reveal some strong similarities in pattern of performance (Bishop 1982). This raises the question of whether language-impaired children with severe comprehension difficulties could, like deaf children, reveal linguistic competence if provided with a natural sign language as first language (see Ch. 8). However, this experiment is unlikely to be carried out, as, despite the lack of experimental support (see Schiff-Myers Ch. 3, Bishop 1983b) the strong belief persists that signed and spoken forms of language are incompatible and likely to interfere with one another.

The role of brain damage

Damage to the left cerebral hemisphere in adulthood frequently results in selective language disturbance—aphasia. It therefore seems plausible that specific language impairment might arise from damage to the left hemisphere acquired early in life. Indeed, one can find parallels between the linguistic deficits observed in acquired adult aphasia, and patterns of verbal deficit in children with specific language impairment (Rapin & Allen 1983). Many language-impaired children have predominant difficulties with language form: phonology and syntax. In this respect they resemble cases of Broca's aphasia. Other children have been described who speak clearly and fluently in complex sentences, but the content of their language is unusual and inappropriate. One may see a parallel here with the fluent aphasias associated with posterior left-hemisphere lesions in adulthood. Do these similarities in symptoms reflect underlying similarities in brain pathology? If so, we should expect to find either a high rate of neurological disease in this group of children, or a raised incidence of perinatal problems which might cause brain damage. In general, the evidence for such a link is not strong (see Bishop 1987 for a brief review). Few children with specific language impairments have any history of brain disease or any hard neurological signs, and techniques such as CT scan or electroencephalography (EEG) reveal abnormalities only in a minority of children with particularly severe problems. Overall, the evidence for an acquired brain lesion as the cause of specific language impairment is slim.

Perhaps this should not surprise us. When we look at children who are known to have left-hemisphere lesions early in life, we find that they do not resemble children with specific language impairment. In Chapter 13 it was argued that focal brain damage acquired before language had developed tended to depress general intellectual ability rather than creating specific deficits in one area of functioning. Although lateralized brain damage acquired later in childhood could produce more classic aphasic symptoms, these usually resolved rapidly except in the oldest children, and long-term language deficits were seldom clinically obvious. Children who had apparently recovered from aphasia seemed able to speak using complex and appropriate language. Problems such as poor comprehension, weak vocabulary, and difficulties with reading and writing were, however, apparent on formal testing. This is a very different clinical picture from that found in most cases of specific language impairment.

Neurodevelopmental factors

However, destruction of brain tissue, as occurs in cases of head injury, infection, tumour or cerebrovascular disease, is not the only way in which the course of normal brain development can be affected. Both environmental and genetic influences can determine how the brain develops, even before the child is born. Demonstration that a child has no brain abnormality on CT scan does not necessarily mean that neurological development is entirely normal. A clear demonstration of this was provided by Kemper (1984) who reviewed post-mortem studies of individuals suffering from developmental *dyslexia*. These have revealed a number of neuroanatomical abnormalities in the left temporo-parietal region which appeared to have arisen early in fetal development when certain cells had failed to migrate to the normal position in the brain. The causes of this failure could not be established. We do know, however, that neurological development in the fetus can be impaired by in utero environmental influences (such as maternal malnutrition, disease, or drug-taking), and by genetic make-up.

There is, however, no evidence that specific language impairment is related to adverse prenatal environment, chromosomal anomaly or presence of a single major gene (see Bishop 1987 for a review). It is known, however, that these disorders do tend to run in families, and are much more common in boys than in girls, although there is no evidence of a dominant, recessive or sex-linked pattern of inheritance (Pennington & Smith 1983).

One possibility is that specific language development is the result of a delay in the maturation of certain areas of the central nervous system, determined at least in part by polygenic factors. Many aspects of physical development, such as limb growth, age at puberty, or dental development, are determined by the influence of multiple genes interacting with environmental factors. It seems plausible that brain development should be no exception, and it is possible that specific language impairment in children reflects an underlying immaturity of neurological development of those brain areas concerned with language development. At present, only indirect evidence exists for this speculative view (Bishop & Edmundson 1987).

Heterogeneity of language disorders and multifactorial causation

It is evident that we are still a long way from understanding what are the necessary and sufficient causes of specific language impairment in children. There are two points to bear in mind in future research on this topic. First, our results may be unclear because the phenomenon of interest is not homogeneous. Specific language impairment is defined largely by exclusion, and encompasses a range of problems with language. It is possible that we are dealing with a single underlying condition which is expressed in a variety of ways, but it may be that we are mixing together a range of different conditions with variable underlying causes, and that a clear picture will emerge only when we refine our classification. The second point to note is that we may be mistaken in looking for a single major cause of specific language impairment. Perhaps these disorders arise when a specific combination of adverse factors co-occur in a single child. Factors which on their own have no impact on language development might assume significance in combination. It is interesting to note that several of the chapters in this book conclude that while normal language development is *compatible* with a particular exceptional circumstance, the rate of language delay and disorder associated with that circumstance is nevertheless increased (see especially Chs. 3, 5, 6, 9 and 14). We should beware of assuming that because a particular factor has been shown to be compatible with normal language development it has no role to play in the causation of language disorder.

Appendix

A non-evaluative summary of assessment procedures

Our aim here is to provide basic information about test content for readers who may be unfamiliar with particular assessments referred to in this book. Publishers' details are provided, except where the procedure does not require test materials and is fully described in a book or journal. For more detailed description of these and other procedures, together with appraisal of psychometric characteristics, see Buros (1975), Darley (1979), Peterson & Marquardt (1981) and McCauley & Swisher (1984a).

Arizona Articulation Proficiency Scale
Author: J B Fudala
Date: 1963, 1970, 1974
Available from: Western Psychological Services, 12031 Wilshire Boulevard, Los Angeles, California 90025

The child is presented with a set of line drawings of objects and asked to name these. The tester records articulation errors. Scores are converted into a scale of articulatory proficiency by weighting misarticulations according to the frequency with which sounds occur in American speech. Norms are provided for children aged from 3;0 to 11;11.

Assessment of Children's Language Comprehension
Authors: R Foster, J J Giddon & J Stark
Date: 1969, 1973
Available from: Consulting Psychologists Press,

577 College Avenue, Palo Alto, California 94306.

A multiple choice test in which the child is asked to point to the stimulus item described by the tester. The number of main content words ('critical elements') increases as the test proceeds from one (i.e. single nouns, verbs, prepositions and modifiers) through two and three to a maximum of four (e.g. 'happy little girl jumping', 'boy standing in the house'). Some norms are available for children aged from 3;0 to 6;5.

Auditory Discrimination Test
Author: J M Wepman
Date: 1973
Available from: Language Research Associates, 175 East Delaware Place, Chicago, Illinois 60611

The test consists of 40 pairs of monosyllabic words differing by one sound, e.g. guile/dial. The tester reads each word pair to the child, who must judge if the two words presented are the same or different.

Bayley Scales of Infant Development
Author: N Bayley
Date: 1969
Available from: The Psychological Corporation, 304 East 45th St., New York 10017

Standardized scales for assessing development of children in the age range 2 to 30 months. The Mental Scale consists of 163 items measuring responses to visual and auditory stimuli, manipulation and play with objects and social interaction. The Motor Scale includes assessment of gross motor skills such as sitting, standing and walking, as well as fine-motor co-ordination in grasping objects of different sizes. The Infant Behavior Record is used to record aspects of emotional and social development.

Boehm Test of Basic Concepts
Author: A Boehm
Date: 1971, revised 1986
Available from: The Psychological Corporation, 304 East 45th St., New York 10017*

The child is given a record form showing a range of picture choices, and must mark with a pencil the correct choice in accordance with verbal instructions, e.g.: 'Look at the beads and strings. Mark the bead that has a string *through* it.' The test is suitable for children from kindergarten to 2nd grade level, corresponding roughly to the 4- to 8-year-old age range.

Carrow Elicited Language Inventory (CELI)
Author: E Carrow
Date: 1974
Available from: Teaching Resources Corporation, 100 Boylston St., Boston, MA 02116
British distribution: NFER-Nelson

The child is asked to imitate phrases and sentences of increasing grammatical complexity. Examples are: 'big girl', 'the lady will sit down', and 'if it rains, we won't go to the beach'. Performance is scored in terms of the number of errors made in repetition, and norms are provided for children aged from 3;0 to 7;11 years.

Clinical Evaluation of Language Functions (CELF)
Authors: E M Semel & E H Wiig
Date: 1980
Available from: Charles E Merrill Publishing Co., 1300 Alum Creek Drive, Columbus, Ohio 43216

A battery of 13 language subtests standardized in the USA on children aged from 6 to 18 years. Includes subtests assessing ability to comprehend language which varies in grammatical or conceptual complexity, and a range of measures of expressive ability and verbal fluency.

Crichton Vocabulary Scale
Author: J C Raven
Date 1950
Available from: NFER-Nelson, 2 Oxford Road East, Windsor, Berkshire

Designed as a supplement to Raven's Matrices, this is a vocabulary test where the child is told a word and asked to explain what it means. Suitable for children aged 4 to 14 years. Raw scores may be converted into percentiles.

Detroit Test of Learning Aptitudes (DTLA)
Authors: H Baker & B Leland
Date: 1967

---

* British address for Psychological Corporation: Harcourt Brace Jovanovitch, Foots Cray High St., Sidcup, Kent.

Available from: Tests division of Bobbs-Merril, 4300 West 62nd St., Indianapolis, IN 46468

Includes 19 subtests that measure reasoning and comprehension, practical judgment, verbal ability, time and space relationships, number ability, auditory attention, visual attention and motor ability. Subtests measuring language functions assess sentence repetition, ability to define words and provide antonyms, ability to say how word pairs are the same or different, comprehension of commands, and speed at generating words at random. The test has been standardized on children in the USA aged from 3 to 19 years.

Developmental Sentence Analysis

Author: L L Lee
Date: 1974
Available from: Northwestern University Press, 1735 Benson Ave., Evanston, Illinois 60201
Sources: Lee L (1966) Developmental sentence types: A method for comparing normal and deviant syntactic development. Journal of Speech and Hearing Disorders 31: 311–330.
Lee L, Canter S (1971) Developmental sentence scoring: A clinical procedure for estimating syntactical development in children's spontaneous speech. Journal of Speech and Hearing Disorders 36: 315–340.

Specifies a set of rules for analyzing grammatical development from a spontaneous language sample. Two procedures are used: Developmental Sentence Types (DST), which is used to analyse the very early stages of language development to see if the child has the elements necessary for basic sentence development. Developmental Sentence Scoring (DSS) is a procedure for analyzing complete sentences, examining the child's use of such structures as pronouns, verbal tenses, negatives and questions. Norms given for children aged from 2;0 to 6;11.

English Picture Vocabulary Test

Authors: M A Brimer & L M Dunn
Date: 1962, 1973
Available from: Education Evaluation Enterprises, Awre, Gloucester
Designed as an English version of the Peabody Picture Vocabulary Test (see below).

Full-Range Picture Vocabulary Test

Authors: Robert B Ammons & Helen S Ammons
Date: 1948
Available from: Psychological Test Specialists, PO Box 1441, Missoula, Mont. 59801
A short multiple-choice vocabulary test, which consists of 16 cards, each containing four line drawings. The testee is asked to select the picture that matches a word spoken by the tester. The 'Full-Range' designation refers to the fact that the test is designed to be suitable for the entire age range through from 2-year-olds to adults.

Gesell Developmental Schedules

Authors: A Gesell & C S Armatruda
Date: 1941
Available from: NFER-Nelson, 2 Oxford Road East, Windsor, Berkshire
Scales for assessing behaviour in children aged from 4 weeks to 6 years in four main areas: motor (consisting largely of walking and balance activities), adaptive (incorporating tests of eye-hand co-ordination such as building towers of blocks), language and personal-social.

Goldman-Fristoe-Woodcock Auditory Skills Battery

Authors: R Goldman, M Fristoe & R W Woodcock
Date: 1974
Available from: American Guidance Service, Publishers Building, Circle Pines, Minn 55014
Battery of twelve tests, in five groups as follows:
Selective attention: assesses ability to attend under increasingly difficult listening conditions.
Auditory discrimination: assesses ability to discriminate between sounds that are frequently confused.
Auditory memory: tests of recognition memory, memory for content and memory for sequences.
Sound symbol tests: seven subtests assessing abilities underlying the development of

written language skills, e.g. mimicry, spelling, sound blending.

The battery has been standardized in the USA, and is suitable for adults and children over the age of 3 years.

Goldman-Fristoe-Woodcock Test of Auditory Discrimination

Authors: R Goldman, M Fristoe & R W Woodcock
Date: 1970
Available from: American Guidance Service, Publishers Building, Circle Pines, Minn 55014

The test adopts a multiple-choice picture-pointing procedure, where the child must select the picture corresponding to a spoken word heard from a tape-recorder. Item arrays include foils depicting acoustically similar words (e.g. 'veil' vs 'nail'). The test consists of a training procedure, a quiet subtest, and a noise subtest. The training procedure is used to familiarize subjects with the test vocabulary. The quiet subtest has no background noise on the tape, whilst the noise subtest presents words against a background of cafeteria noise. The test is applicable to adults and to children aged from 3 years upwards.

Goodenough-Harris Drawing Test

Author: D B Harris
Date: 1963
Available from: NFER-Nelson, 2 Oxford Road East, Windsor, Berkshire and Harcourt Brace Jovanovich, New York

Provides criteria for rating the intellectual maturity of children's drawings of a man, woman or themselves.

Illinois Test of Psycholinguistic Abilities (ITPA)

Authors: S A Kirk, J J McCarthy & W D Kirk
Date: 1968 (revised edition)
Available from: University of Illinois Press, Urbana, Illinois 61801

This test is based on psycholinguistic model which distinguishes three dimensions on which communication can be described: channels of communication (auditory, visual, verbal and manual), psycholinguistic processes (reception, association and expression) and levels of organization (representational and automatic). Twelve subtests evaluate different combinations of these dimensions. These subtests are:

Auditory reception: a series of yes-no questions such as 'do dogs eat?', 'do sidewalks sprinkle?'

Visual reception: the child is presented with a single picture, and must then find a picture related in meaning from an array of four. For example, if the single picture shows a boy running, the choice is between a girl reading, a girl standing, a girl writing and a girl running (correct).

Visual sequential memory: a test pattern of one to eight chips with geometric designs must be remembered and reproduced by the child.

Auditory association: an analogy-type test where the child must complete sequences such as: 'Daddy is big, baby is ___ '.

Auditory sequential memory: the child must repeat series of digits of increasing length (presented at a rate of 2 per second).

Visual association: the child must select from an array of four pictures the one that goes with a target picture. For example, in one item the target is bone, and the four choices are pencil, rattle, pipe and dog (correct).

Visual closure: the child must find hidden figures in a drawing.

Verbal expression: five common objects are shown to the child who must describe each object as completely as possible.

Grammatic closure: the child is told a sentence, and must then complete a similar sentence with a different grammatical form.

Manual expression: pictured objects are shown to the child, who is asked to demonstrate the appropriate actions for each item.

Auditory closure: the tester speaks words with sounds omitted, and the child must supply the completed word, e.g. for 'da-y' the child should say 'daddy'.

Sound blending: the child is asked to identify words or nonsense words which are presented as a sequence of separate sounds or syllables.

Norms are provided for children from 2 to 10 years of age.

Language Assessment, Remediation & Screening Procedure (LARSP)
Authors: D Crystal, P Fletcher & M Garman
Sources: Crystal D, Fletcher P & Garman M (1976) The grammatical analysis of language disability. Edward Arnold, London.

Crystal D (1979) Working with LARSP. Edward Arnold, London

An unstandardized procedure for analyzing expressive grammatical development, suitable for children with language up to around the 4- to 5-year-old level. A chart is provided listing structures at clause, phrase, and word level which correspond to different stages of development. No summary score is given; the aim is to provide the therapist with a profile from which one can see areas of strength and weakness, and plan therapy to take the child from one stage of development to the next.

Leiter International Performance Scale
Author: R Leiter
Date: 1936, 1955, 1969
Available from: C H Stoelting Co., 1350 South Costner Ave., Chicago, Ill 60623

A nonverbal intelligence test suitable for use with deaf and language-disordered children as it does not require any verbal instructions. Blocks have to be matched against a picture strip on the basis of increasingly complex relationships. Thus the easiest items (2-year-old level) involve simple matching of colour or shape. Later items must be matched on the basis of two or three dimensions (e.g. colour, number and shape), or blocks must be assembled to make a particular pattern. Matching is on the basis of increasingly abstract relationships or fine perceptual distinctions at the upper end of the scale.

McCarthy Scales of Children's Abilities
Author: D McCarthy
Date: 1972
Available from: Psychological Corporation, 304 East 45th St., New York 10017

A general test of cognitive development for children aged from 2;6 to 8;6. Contains six scales: verbal, perceptual-performance, quantitative, general cognitive, memory, and motor.

Mean Length of Utterance (MLU)
Originator: R Brown
Date: 1973
Source: Brown R (1973) A first language: the early stages. Harvard University Press, Boston

A simple measure of grammatical maturity of expressive language which has been widely adopted in psycholinguistic research, although it is not a standardized assessment procedure. It is computed by taking each utterance in a language sample, counting its length in terms of morphemes (N.B. not words), and finding the average. Morphemes include grammatical inflections as well as words. The sentence 'the dogs ran quickly' contains four words, but seven morphemes, with 'dogs' credited as plural, 'ran' as past tense, and -ly as adverbial ending. Brown divided early language development into five arbitrary stages corresponding to MLU ranges.

Merrill-Palmer Scale of Mental Tests
Author: R Stutsman
Date: 1948
Available from: Harcourt Brace Jovanovich, New York

A predominantly nonverbal intelligence test, designed for use with children from 24 to 48 months of age. The speed and accuracy with which tasks are completed determines the age level credited to the child on many of the items, which include puzzles, formboards, building with cubes and pegboards. There are a few language items, including questions and repetition of words and phrases.

Northwestern Syntax Screening Test
Author: L L Lee
Date: 1971
Available from: Northwestern University Press, 1735 Benson Ave., Evanston, Illinois 60201
British distribution: NFER-Nelson

A screening test for receptive and expressive language suitable for children aged from 3;0 to 7;11. In the receptive part of the test the child is shown a plate of four pictures and asked to select the one to match a spoken sentence. In the expressive portion the child is shown a pair of pictures, and the tester speaks a sentence corresponding to each picture, e.g. 'The cat is behind the chair, the cat is under the chair.' The tester then points to one of the pictures, and the child is required to produce the appropriate sentence. Expressive responses are scored as incorrect if the child makes any change to the tester's spoken sentence.

Peabody Picture Vocabulary Test (PPVT)

Author: L M Dunn
Date:: 1965
Available from: American Guidance Service, Publishers Building, Circle Pines, Minn 55014

A test of receptive vocabulary, in which the testee is required to select a picture from an array of four to correspond to a word spoken by the tester. Norms are available for the age range 2;6 to 18 years.

Preschool Language Scale

Authors: I L Zimmerman, V G Steiner & R L Evatt
Date: 1969
Available from: Charles E Merrill Publishing Co., 1300 Alum Creek Drive, Columbus, Ohio 43216

Provides 'language ages' for auditory comprehension and verbal ability (as well as a composite language age). Receptive and expressive language functioning is assessed by four items at each age level, with age-levels ranging from 1;6 to 7 years. Various item types are used, ranging from asking the child to carry out commands, name objects and pictures, or provide information such as name and address.

Raven's Progressive Matrices

Author: J Raven
Date: 1960, 1963
Available from:NFER-Nelson, 2 Oxford Road East, Windsor, Berks.

A nonverbal test which assesses intelligence by a multiple-choice procedure where the child must select from six or eight items the part which best completes a meaningless

design. The Standard Progressive Matrices consists of 60 items grouped into five sets, and is suitable for adults and children from the age of 6 years upwards. The Coloured Progressive Matrices were designed for children aged from 5 to 11 years, and involve fewer items than the Standard Progressive Matrices.

Receptive-Expressive Emergent Language Scale (REEL)

Authors: K Bzoch & R League
Date: 1971
Available from: The Tree of Life Press, 1309 North East Second Street, Gainesville, Florida 32601

This scale, which is designed to identify very young children whose language development may be impaired, is administered primarily by interviewing a parent or other informant about a child's behaviour. For example, items include: 'Turns head deliberately toward the source of the voice' (Receptive: 3–4 months), 'Uses 3 or more words with some consistency' (Expressive: 11–12 months). Reported behaviours are scored as present, absent, or emergent, and results are combined to yield three total scores: a receptive language age, expressive language age, and a combined age. The scale is suitable for children in the age range 1 month to 3 years.

Reynell Developmental Language Scales

Author: J Reynell & M Huntley
Date: 1977 (Revised Edition), 1985
Available from: NFER-Nelson, 2 Oxford Road East, Windsor, Berks.

Consists of two scales, one for expressive language and one for comprehension, suitable for children in the age range 12 months to 7 years. Early items may be scored on the basis of parental report. The expressive scale assesses maturity of vocabulary and sentence structure, with picture materials and toys being used to elicit language in older children. Items on the comprehension scale, all of which require a nonverbal response, range from selective recognition of a word or phrase, through identification of common objects ('point to the cup') up to more difficult commands which use complex grammar and/or more abstract language (e.g. 'which pig is not outside the field?'; 'who used to go to school but doesn't now?').

Seguin Formboard
Author: F Seguin, H H Goddard & N Norsworthy
Date: 1911
Available from: C H Stoelting Co., 1350 South Costner Ave, Chicago, Ill 60623

An assessment of nonverbal maturity suitable for the age range 5 to 14 years. The child is presented with a formboard and a set of shapes which fit into the board. The speed with which all shapes are correctly placed in the board is converted into a mental age.

Sequenced Inventory of Communication Development
Authors: D L Hedrick, E M Prather & A R Tobin
Date: 1975
Available from: University of Washington Press, Seattle, WA 98105

Designed to assess communicative development in normal and retarded children from 4 months to 4 years of age. Samples a wide range of behaviours, using parental reports about children's behaviour at home as well as direct observation of the child. Includes a receptive scale, which assesses the child's responsiveness to environmental sounds and to speech, and an expressive scale which measures the child's use of prelinguistic behaviours such as expressive babble and imitation of play routines. In addition, instructions are given for taking a language sample and scoring it for a range of syntactic constructions.

Staggered Spondaic Word Test
Author: J Katz
Date: 1962, 1968
Available from: Auditec of St Louis, 330 Selma Ave, St Louis, MO 63119.

A test designed to assess central auditory functions, which uses overlapping dichotic spondaic words, i.e. two-syllable words presented so that each syllable has equal stress, e.g. 'cow-boy'. Words are presented, each to one ear, so that the second syllable of the first word is presented together with the first syllable of the second word. The testee is asked to repeat both words.

Stanford-Binet Intelligence Scale
Authors: L M Terman & M A Merrill
Date: 1960 (form L-M)
Available from: Riverside Publishing Co., 8420 Bryn Mawr Ave, Chicago, Illinois 60631

A scale for assessing intelligence in individuals from 2 years of age to adulthood. Items are graded by age level and cover a wide range of mental functions, including many items involving language. Examples of items include: identifying named body parts on a picture (2-year level), pointing to named pictures from an array (4-year level), copying a diamond (7-year level), making rhymes (9-year level), and repeating complex sentences (12-year level).

Templin-Darley Tests of Articulation
Author: M C Templin & F C Darley
Date: 1969 (2nd edition)
Available from: University of Iowa Bureau of Education Research and Service, Extension Division, C-20 East Hall, Iowa City, Iowa 52242

141 items are organized into nine overlapping subtests, so that the materials can be used flexibly, for example, just as a screening test, or just to assess ability to produce speech sounds requiring forceful oral breath pressure. Words are elicited from younger children by the use of pictures, whilst written materials are provided for children who can read.

Test for Auditory Comprehension of Language (TACL)
Author: Elizabeth Carrow
Date: 1973
Available from: Teaching Resources Corporation, 100 Boylston' St., Boston, Massachusetts 02116

A multiple choice testing the child's understanding of vocabulary and linguistic structure. Each item shows three line drawings, and the child must select the one to match a word, phrase or sentence spoken by the tester. The three pictures on each plate correspond to the test sentence (e.g. 'the girl is jumping') and distractors showing contrasting forms (e.g. 'the girl has jumped', 'the girl will jump'). The test is standardized on children aged from 3 to 6 years.

Test for Reception of Grammar (TROG)
Author: D V M Bishop
Date: 1973
Available from: D Bishop, Department of Psychology, University of Manchester, M13 9PL

A multiple choice test of comprehension of grammatical structure standardized on children aged from 4 to 13 years. A vocabulary pretest is provided to assess understanding of the individual nouns, verbs, and adjectives used in the main test, if necessary. Each item consists of four pictures, and the child must select the picture corresponding to a sentence spoken by the tester. A block of four items is used to test understanding of each of 20 grammatical constructions, ranging in difficulty from simple phrases and main clauses up to sentences with various types of subordinate clause (e.g. 'the book the pencil is on is red') and complex negation (e.g. 'the pencil is neither long nor red').

Test of Language Development
Authors: P L Newcomer & D D Hammill
Date: 1977
Available from: Empiric Press, Austin, Texas

A test of expressive and receptive language, standardized on children in the USA aged from 4;0 to 8;11. Includes the following subtests:

Grammatic completion: assesses the child's ability to provide the correct morphological ending for items such as: 'The dress belongs to the woman. Whose dress is it? It is the ___'.

Grammatic understanding: a multiple choice comprehension test with 25 items in which the child must select a picture to match a sentence spoken by the tester from an array including pictures showing semantically and grammatically contrasting sentences.

Picture vocabulary: a multiple choice vocabulary test with 25 items.

Oral vocabulary: the child is presented with 20 words to define.

Sentence imitation: a 30-item subtest designed to measure ability to repeat grammatically complex sentences verbatim.

Word discriminition: pairs of words differing by one phoneme (e.g. vale/dale) are presented to the child, who must say whether they are the same or different.

Word articulation: stimulus pictures and sentences are used to elicit spontaneous articulation of words that contain key speech sounds.

Token Test
Author: E de Renzi & L A Vignolo
Date: 1962
Source: De Renzi E, Vignolo L A (1962) The Token Test: a sensitive test to detect receptive disturbances in aphasics. Brain 85: 665–678.

The test consists of a series of auditory commands to manipulate a set of tokens varying in colour, size (big or small) and shape (circle or rectangle). In the first four sections of the test, difficulty is increased by lengthening the instructions, so that whereas in section 1 instructions are of the form 'Pick up the red circle', in section 4, we have items such as 'Pick up the small yellow circle and the large green rectangle'. In part 5, the grammatical complexity of the commands is manipulated, e.g. 'Put the red circle on the green rectangle'. The test was devised as a sensitive measure of receptive disturbances in adults with acquired aphasia, but it has also been used with children as young as 5 years, and norms have been published by Whitaker & Selnes (1978).

Utah Test of Language Development
Author: M J Mecham, J L Jex, J D Jones
Date: 1967
Available from: Communication Research Associates, PO Box 11012, Salt Lake City, Utah 84111

The tester gives the child instructions which

increase in complexity until the child fails eight consecutive items. Items range in content from asking the child to name colours and body parts, follow simple instructions such as 'give me the ball', respond to questions such as 'tell me the name of a colour that rhymes with head', and production of series such as counting to 50 and naming days of the week. Raw scores can be converted into language age scores ranging from 9 months to 16 years.

Vineland Social Maturity Scale

Author: E A Doll
Date: 1947, 1965
Available from: American Guidance Service, Publishers Building, Circle Pines, Minn 55014

This scale is designed to be given as an interview to parent or other caretaker. The questions concern the degree of social competence attained by the child, and cover six areas of performance: self-help (eating, dressing, etc.), locomotion, occupation (involving, for young children, the ability to keep oneself occupied), communication, self-direction and socialization. The scale spans the age range from birth to 25 years. A revision of this scale, called the Vineland Adaptive Behaviour Scales, was published in Britain in 1984 and is available from NFER-Nelson.

Wechsler Intelligence Scale for Children (WISC)

Author: D Wechsler
Date: 1974 (revised version, WISC-R)
Available from: The Psychological Corporation, 304 East 45th St., New York 10017

The most widely used standardized intelligence test in the USA, and probably also in Britain, suitable for children from 6 to 15 years. Six performance subtests (one optional) and six verbal subtests (one optional) yield a Performance IQ (PIQ), Verbal IQ (VIQ) and Full Scale IQ (FSIQ), the latter being based on scores on all subtests. The performance subtests, none of which requires any spoken language from the child, are:
Picture Completion: the child must find a missing detail from a picture.

Block Design: red and white patterned blocks are used to create visual designs of increasing complexity.
Picture Arrangement: picture sequences must be arranged to tell a sensible story.
Object Assembly: cut-out wooden pieces must be assembled to make an object.
Coding: the appropriate symbol must be written in under each of a sequence of numbers according to a key.
Mazes: the child has to draw in a path to lead out of a maze.

All the performance subtests are timed, with credit for fast completion of an item. The verbal subtests are:
Information: a series of questions testing general knowledge.
Similarities: the child must describe what a pair of words has in common.
Vocabulary: words are presented for the child to define.
Comprehension: questions requiring the application of common sense and knowledge of social rules, rather than specific learned facts.
Digit Span: series of digits of increasing length are presented at a rate of one per second for immediate repetition.

Wechsler Preschool & Primary Scale of Intelligence (WPPSI)

Author: D Wechsler
Date: 1967
Available from: The Psychological Corporation, 304 East 45th St., New York 10017

This intelligence test was designed as a downward extension of the WISC, suitable for children aged from 4 to 6 years. As in the WISC, subtests are divided to form verbal and performance scales. The five verbal subtests are analagous to those of the WISC, i.e. Information, Vocabulary, Arithmetic, Similarities and Comprehension. The performance subtests are Animal House (which taps some of the same skills as WISC Coding), Picture Completion, Mazes, Block Design and Geometric Design. This latter subtest is not similar to any of the WISC performance subtests: it involves copying geometric designs with pencil and paper.

Wide Span Reading Test
Author: Brimer
Date: 1972
Available from: NFER-Nelson, 2 Oxford Road East, Windsor, Berks.

A reading comprehension test consisting of 80 items covering the reading-age range from 7 to 16 years. The child is required to write down a word missing from a test sentence (e.g. 'He threw the key for her to ___ ', selecting the word from another complete sentence (e.g. 'He tried to lift the catch on the door to open it').

References

Abberton E, Fourcin A J, Hazan V 1986 Phonological competence with profound hearing loss. Speech, hearing and language: Work in progress, University College, London

Adelson E 1983 Precursors of early language development in children blind from birth. In: Mills A E (ed) Language acquisition in the blind child: normal and deficient. Croom Helm, London, and College Hill, San Diego

Alajouanine T, Lhermitte F 1965 Acquired aphasia in children. Brain 88: 653–662

Alekoumbides A 1978 Hemispheric dominance for language: quantitative aspects. Acta Neurologica Scandinavica 57: 97–140

Allen G D, Hawkins S 1978 The development of phonological rhythm. In: Bell A, Hooper J B (eds) Syllables and segments. North Holland, New York

Allen G D, Hawkins S 1980 Phonological rhythm: Definition and development. In: Yeni-Komshian G H, Kavanagh J F, Ferguson C A (eds) Child phonology: Vol 1. Production. Academic Press, New York

Als J, Tronick E, Brazelton T 1980 Affective reciprocity and the development of autonomy: the study of a blind infant. Journal of the American Academy of Child Psychiatry 19: 22–40

American Psychiatric Association 1980 DSM-III: Diagnostic and Statistical Manual of Mental Disorders, 3rd edn. APA, Washington DC

Andersen E S, Kekelis L S 1982 The role of visual perception in early caregiver-child communication: some input from the blind. Paper to the Seventh Annual Boston University Conference on Language Development (unpublished)

Andersen E S, Dunlea A, Kekelis L S 1984 Blind children's language: resolving some differences. Journal of Child Language 11: 645–664

Anderson R, Miles M, Matheny P A 1963 Communication evaluation chart from infancy to five years. Educators Publishing Service, Cambridge, Mass

Anglin J M 1970 The growth of word meaning. MIT Press, Cambridge, Mass

Annett M 1973 Laterality of childhood hemiplegia and the growth of speech and intelligence. Cortex 9: 4–33

Anon 1834 Caspar Hauser. The Penny Magazine of the Society for the Diffusion of Useful Knowledge III: 47

Aram D M, Ekelman B L, Rose D F, Whitaker H A 1985 Verbal and cognitive sequelae following unilateral lesions acquired in early childhood. Journal of Clinical and Experimental Neuropsychology 7: 55–78

Aram D M, Ekelman B L, Whitaker H A 1986 Spoken syntax in children with acquired unilateral hemisphere lesions. Brain and Language 27: 75–100

Archer L A 1977 Blissymbolics: a nonverbal communication system. Journal of Speech and Hearing Disorders 42: 568–579

Arnold R, Yule W 1985 The psychological characteristics of infantile hypercalcemia: A preliminary investigation. Developmental Medicine and Child Neurology 27: 49–59

Arnold W, Ganzer U, Kleinmann H 1977 Sensorineural hearing loss in mucous otitis. Archives of Otorhinolaryngology 215: 91–93

Ashton R, Beasley M 1982 Cerebral laterality in deaf and hearing children. Developmental Psychology 18: 294–300

Aslin R N, Pisoni D B, Jusczyk P W 1983 Auditory development and speech perception in infancy. In: Haith M M, Campos J J (eds) Infancy and the biology of development. Vol II of Carmichael's manual of child psychology (4th edn). Wiley, New York

Assal G, Campiche R 1973 Aphasie et troubles du langage chez l'enfant après contusion cérébrale. Neuro-Chirurgie 19: 399–406

Atkinson J, Barlow H B, Braddick O J 1982 The development of sensory systems and their modification by experience. In: Barlow H B, Mollon J (eds) The senses. Cambridge University Press, Cambridge

Atkinson M 1982 Explanations in the study of child language development. Cambridge University Press, Cambridge

Aviel A, Ostfeld E 1982 Acquired irreversible sensorineural hearing loss associated with otitis media with effusion. American Journal of Otolaryngology 3: 217–222

Baddeley A 1986 Working memory. Clarendon Press, Oxford

Baddeley A, Lewis V, Vallar G 1984 Exploring the articulatory loop. Quarterly Journal of Experimental Psychology 36A: 233–252

Baddeley A, Thomson N, Buchanan M 1975 Word length and the structure of short-term memory. Journal of Verbal Learning and Verbal Behavior 14: 575–589

Baddeley A, Wilson B 1985 Phonological coding and short-term memory in patients without speech. Journal of Memory and Language 24: 490–502

Baker L, Cantwell D P, Rutter M, Bartak L 1976 Language and autism. Spectrum, New York

Baldwin J M 1895 Mental development in the child and the race, 3rd edn. Macmillan, New York

Balkany T 1980 Otologic aspects of Down's syndrome. Seminars in Speech, Language and Hearing 1: 39–57

Ballantyne J, Martin J A M (eds) 1984 Deafness, 4th edn. Churchill Livingstone, Edinburgh

Baltaxe C A M 1984 Use of contrastive stress in normal, aphasic and autistic children. Journal of Speech and Hearing Research 24: 97–105

Baltaxe C A M, Simmons J Q 1977 Bedtime soliloquies and linguistic competence in autism. Journal of Speech and Hearing Disorders 42: 376–393

Baltaxe C A M, Simmons J Q 1981 Disorders of language in psychosis: Current concepts and approaches. In: Darby J K (ed) Speech evaluation in psychiatry. Grune and Stratton, New York

Barley Speechreading Test, CID Everyday Sentences 1971 In: Jeffers J, Barley M (eds) Speechreading (Lipreading). Charles C Thomas, Springfield, Ill

Baron-Cohen S, Leslie A M, Frith U 1985 Does the autistic child have a 'theory of mind'? Cognition 21: 37–46

Baron-Cohen S, Leslie A M, Frith U 1986 Mechanical, behavioural and intentional understanding of picture stories in autistic children. British Journal of Developmental Psychology 4: 113–125

Bartak L, Rutter M 1974 The use of personal pronouns by autistic children. Journal of Autism and Childhood Schizophrenia 4: 217–222

Bartak L, Rutter M 1976 Differences between mentally retarded and normally intelligent autistic children. Journal of Autism and Childhood Schizophrenia 6: 109–120

Bartel N, Bryen D, Keehn S 1973 Language comprehension in the moderately retarded child. Exceptional Children 39: 375–382

Bartolucci G, Albers R J 1974 Deictic categories in the language of autistic children. Journal of Autism and Childhood Schizophrenia 4: 131–141

Bartolucci G, Pierce S, Streiner D, Eppel P L 1976 Phonological investigation of verbal autistic and mentally retarded subjects. Journal of Autism and Childhood Schizophrenia 6: 303–316

Bartolucci G, Pierce S, Streiner D 1980 Cross-sectional studies of grammatical morphemes in autistic and mentally retarded children. Journal of Autism and Developmental Disorders 10: 39–50

Basser L S 1962 Hemiplegia of early onset and the faculty of speech with special reference to the effects of hemispherectomy. Brain 85: 427–460

Bates E 1976a Language and context. Academic Press, New York

Bates E 1976b Pragmatics and sociolinguistics in child language. In: Morehead D, Morehead A (eds) Normal and deficient child language. University Park Press, Baltimore

Bates E 1979 The emergence of symbols. Academic Press, New York

Bates E, Camaioni L, Volterra V 1975 The acquisition of performatives prior to speech. Merrill-Palmer Quarterly 21: 205–226

Bates E, Benigni L, Bretherton I et al 1977 From gesture to the first word: on cognitive and social prerequisites. In: Lewis M, Rosenblum L (eds) Interaction, conversation and the development of language. Wiley, New York

Bates E, Bretherton I, Beeghly-Smith M, McNew S 1982 Social bases of language development: a reassessment. In: Reese H W, Lipsitt L P (eds) Advances in child development and behavior 16: 7–75

Bates E, Snyder L (in press) The cognitive hypothesis in language development. In: Uzgiris I, Hunt J M (eds) Research with scales of psychological development in infancy. University of Illinois Press, Urbana, Ill

Bateson M C 1975 Mother-infant exchanges: the epigenesis of conversational interaction. Annals of the New York Academy of Sciences 263: 101–113

Baumeister A 1967 Problems in comparative studies of mental retardates and normals. American Journal of Mental Deficiency 71: 869–875

Beilin H 1975 Studies in the cognitive basis of language development. Academic Press, New York

Bellugi U 1968 Linguistic mechanisms underlying child speech. In: Zale E (ed) Language and language behavior. Appleton-Crofts, New York

Bellugi U 1980 The structuring of language: clues from the similarities between signed and spoken language. In: Bellugi U, Studdert-Kennedy M (eds) Signed and spoken language: biological constraints on linguistic form. Verlag Chemie, Weinheim

Bellugi U 1987 The acquisition of a spatial language. In: Kessell F (ed) The development of language and language researchers: essays in honor of Roger Brown. Erlbaum, Hillsdale, NJ

Bellugi U, Klima E S, Siple P 1975 Remembering in signs. Cognition 3: 93–125

Bellugi U, Klima E 1982 The acquisition of three morphological systems in American Sign Language. Papers and Reports on Child Language Development 21: 1–35

Bellugi U, Klima E S, Lillo-Martin D, O'Grady L, Vaid J 1986 Examining language dominance through hand dominance. Presentation at the 11th Annual Boston University Conference on Child Language Development, October (unpublished)

Bellugi U, Klima E S, Poizner H 1987a Sign language and the brain. In: Plum F (ed) Language, communication, and the brain (in press)

Bellugi U, Sabo H, Vaid J 1987b Spatial deficits in children with Williams Syndrome. In: Stiles-Davis J, Kritchevsky M, Bellugi U (eds) Spatial cognition: Brain bases and development. Erlbaum, Hillsdale, NJ

Bench J, Bamford J (eds) 1979 Speech-hearing tests and the spoken language of hearing impaired children. Academic Press, London

Benda C E 1949 Mongolism and cretinism. Grune and Stratton, New York

Benda C E 1960 The child with mongolism. Grune and Stratton, New York

Bennett F C, La Veck B, Sells C J 1978 The Williams elfin facies syndrome: the psychological profile as an aid in syndrome identification. Pediatrics 61: 303–305

Bennett F C, Ruuska S H, Sherman R 1980 Middle ear

function in learning disabled children. Pediatrics 66: 254–260

Bergman C R 1976 Interference vs. independent development in infant bilingualism. In: Keller G D, Teschner R V, Viera S (eds) Bilingualism in the bicentennial and beyond. Bilingual Press, New York

Bernard-Opitz V 1982 Pragmatic analysis of the communicative behavior of an autistic child. Journal of Speech and Hearing Disorders 47: 99–109

Berninger V W, Gans B M 1986 Language profiles in nonspeaking individuals of normal intelligence with severe cerebral palsy. Augmentative and Alternative Communication 2: 45–50

Berry M F, Eisenson J 1956 Speech disorders: principles and practices of therapy. Peter Owen, London

Bess F H 1983 Hearing loss associated with middle ear effusion: workshop on effects of otitis media on the child. Pediatrics 71: 640–641

Bess F H 1986 Audiometric approaches used in the identification of middle ear disease in children. In: Kavanagh J F (ed) Otitis media and child development. York Press, Parkton, Maryland

Bess F H, Tharpe A M 1984 Unilateral hearing impairment in children. Pediatrics 74: 206–216

Bettelheim B 1967 The empty fortress—infantile autism and the birth of the self. Free Press, New York

Bever T 1970 The cognitive basis for linguistic structures. In: Hayes J (ed) Cognition and the development of language. Wiley, New York

Bigelow A 1981 Early language of a blind child. Paper to Canadian Psychological Association Conference, Toronto (unpublished)

Bigelow A 1982 Early words of blind children. Paper to International Conference on Infant Studies, Austin, Texas (unpublished)

Bigelow A, Bryan A 1982 The understanding of spatial prepositions 'in', 'on' and 'under' in blind and sighted preschool children. Paper to the Canadian Psychological Association Conference, Montreal (unpublished)

Birns S L 1986 Age at onset of blindness and development of space concepts: from topological to projective space. Journal of Visual Impairment and Blindness 80: 577–582

Bishop D V M 1981 Plasticity and specificity of language localization in the developing brain. Developmental Medicine and Child Neurology 23: 251–253

Bishop D V M 1982 Comprehension of spoken, written and signed sentences in childhood language disorders. Journal of Child Psychology and Psychiatry 23: 1–20

Bishop D V M 1983a Test for Reception of Grammar. Available from author at Department of Psychology, University of Manchester, U.K.

Bishop D V M 1983b Comprehesion of English syntax by profoundly deaf children. Journal of Child Psychology and Psychiatry 24: 415–434

Bishop D V M 1983c How sinister is sinistrality? Journal of the Royal College of Physicians of London 17: 161–172

Bishop D V M 1983d Linguistic impairment after left hemidecortication for infantile hemiplegia? A reappraisal. Quarterly Journal of Experimental Psychology 35A: 199–207

Bishop D V M 1985a Age of onset and outcome in 'acquired aphasia with convulsive disorder' (Landau-Kleffner syndrome). Developmental Medicine and Child Neurology 27: 705–712

Bishop D V M 1985b Spelling ability in congenital dysarthria: evidence against articulatory coding in translating between phonemes and graphemes. Cognitive Neuropsychology 2: 229–251

Bishop D V M 1987 The causes of specific developmental language disorder ('developmental dysphasia'). Journal of Child Psychology and Psychiatry 28: 1–8

Bishop D V M 1988 Can the right hemisphere mediate language as well as the left? A critical review of recent research. Cognitive Neuropsychology (in press)

Bishop D V M, Edmundson A 1986 Is otitis media a major cause of specific developmental language disorders? British Journal of Disorders of Communication 21: 321–338

Bishop D V M, Edmundson A 1987 Specific language impairment as a maturational lag: evidence from longitudinal data on language and motor development. Developmental Medicine and Child Neurology 29: 442–459

Black N 1985 Glue ear: the new dyslexia. British Medical Journal 290: 1963–1965

Black J A, Bonham-Carter R E 1963 Association between aortic stenosis and facies in severe infantile hypercalcaemia. Lancet 2: 745–749

Blanchard I 1964 Speech pattern and etiology in mental retardation. American Journal of Mental Deficiency 68: 612–617

Bloom L 1970 Language development: form and function in emerging grammars. MIT Press, Cambridge, Mass

Bloom L 1973 One word at a time: the use of single-word utterances before syntax. Mouton, The Hague

Bloom L, Hood L, Lightbown P 1974 Imitation in language development: If, when and why. Cognitive Psychology 6: 380–420

Bloom L, Lightbown P, Hood L 1975 Structure and variation in child language. Monographs of the Society for Research in Child Development 40(2)

Bloom L, Rocissano L, Hood L 1976 Adult-child discourse: Developmental interaction between information processing and linguistic knowledge. Cognitive Psychology 8: 521–552

Bluestone C D 1978 Morbidity, complications and sequelae of otitis media. In: Harford E R, Bess F H, Bluestone C D (eds) Impedance screening for middle ear disease in children. Grune and Stratton, New York

Bluestone C D 1982 Otitis media in children: to treat or not to treat? New England Journal of Medicine 306: 1399–1403

Bluestone C D 1983 Complications and sequelae of otitis media: workshop on effects of otitis media on the child. Pediatrics 71: 639–652

Bluestone C D, Beery Q C, Paradise J L 1973 Audiometry and tympanometry in relation to middle ear effusions in children. Laryngoscope 83: 594–604

Bohannon J N 1985 Theoretical approaches to language acquisition. In: Berko Gleason J (ed) The development of language. Merrill, Columbus, Ohio

Bonnaterre P J 1800 Historical notice on the Sauvage de L'Aveyron. Translated in The Wild Boy of Aveyron (Lane H). George Allen and Unwin, London

Bornstein M H, Ruddy M G 1984 Infant attention and maternal stimulation: Prediction of cognitive and linguistic development in singletons and twins. In: Bouma H, Bouwhuis D G (eds) Attention and performance X: Control of language processes. Erlbaum, London

Boucher J 1976 Articulation in early childhood autism. Journal of Autism and Childhood Schizophrenia 6: 297–302

Bowman S A, Shanks J C, Manion M W 1972 Effect of prolonged nasotracheal intubation on communication. Journal of Speech and Hearing Disorders 37: 403–406

Boxx J 1979 A semantically-based language assessment and intervention programme for the young language-impaired child. Workshop presented to Queensland Branch of Australian Association of Speech and Hearing, Brisbane (unpublished)

Bradley R H, Caldwell B M 1976 Early home environment and changes in mental test performance in children from 6–30 months. Developmental Psychology 12: 93–97

Brain R 1941 Visual disorientation with special reference to lesions of the right cerebral hemisphere. Brain 64: 244–272

Braine M D S 1976 Children's first word combinations. Monographs of the Society for Research in Child Development 41(1)

Brandes P J, Ehinger D M 1981 The effects of early middle ear pathology on auditory perception and academic achievement. Journal of Speech and Hearing Disorders 46: 301–307

Brelje H W 1971 A study of the relationship between articulation and vocabulary of hearing impaired parents and their normally hearing children. Doctoral dissertation, University of Portland, Oregon

Brennan M 1975 Can deaf children acquire language? An evaluation of linguistic principles in deaf education. American Annals of the Deaf 120: 463–479. Reprinted in Supplement to the British Deaf News. February 1976

Briggs L A 1986 A case study of language impaired twins. Dissertation submitted for the degree of BSc in Speech, University of Newcastle upon Tyne

Broca P 1863 Localisation des fonctions cérébrales: Siége du langage articulé. Bulletin de la Société d'Anthropologie 4: 200–204

Broca P 1865 Sur le siége de la faculté du langage articulé. Bulletin de la Société d'Anthropologie 6: 377–393

Broen P 1972 The verbal environment of the language-learning child. ASHA Monograph 17, Washington DC

Brookhouser P E, Goldgar D E 1987 Medical profile of the language-delayed child: otitis-prone versus otitis-free. International Journal of Pediatric Otorhinolaryngology 12: 237–271

Brookhouser P E, Hixon P K, Matkin N D 1979 Early childhood language delay: The otolaryngologist's perspective. Laryngoscope 89: 1898–1913

Brooks D N 1985 Acoustic impedance measurement as screening procedure in children: discussion paper. Journal of the Royal Society of Medicine 78: 119–121

Brooks D N 1986 Otitis media with effusion and academic attainment. International Journal of Pediatric Otorhinolaryngology 12: 39–47

Brown J W 1975 The problem of repetition: A study of 'conduction aphasia' and the 'isolation' syndrome. Cortex 11: 37–52

Brown J 1984 Examination of grammatical morphemes in the language of hard-of-hearing children. Volta Review 86: 229–238

Brown R 1968 The development of wh questions in child speech. Journal of Verbal Learning and Verbal Behavior 7: 279–280

Brown R 1973 A first language. Harvard University Press, Cambridge, Mass

Brownlee R C Jr, De Loache W R, Cowan C C Jr, Jackson H P 1969 Otitis media in children: incidence, treatment and prognosis in pediatric practice. Journal of Pediatrics 75: 636–642

Brumark A 1986 Personal communication, University of Stockholm

Bruner J 1975a The ontogenesis of speech acts. Journal of Child Language 2: 1–19

Bruner J S 1975b From communication to language: A psychological perspective. Cognition 3: 255–287

Bruner J 1978a Learning how to do things with words. In: Bruner J S, Garton A (eds) Human growth and development. Clarendon Press, Oxford

Bruner J S 1978b From communication to language: a psychological perspective. In: Markova I (ed) The social context of language. Wiley, New York

Bruner J 1983 Child's talk: learning to use language. Norton, New York

Buddenhagen R G 1971 Establishing vocal verbalizations in mute mongoloid children. Research Press, Champaign, Ill

Burling R 1978 Language development of a Garo and English-speaking child. In: Hatch E (ed) Second language acquisition: a book of readings. Newbury House, Rowley, Mass

Burlingham D 1952 Twins: A study of three pairs of identical twins with 30 charts. Image Publishing, London

Burlingham D 1961 Some notes on the development of the blind. Psychoanalytic Study of the Child 19: 121–145

Burlingham D 1964 Hearing and its role in the development of the blind. Psychoanalytic Study of the Child 26: 95–112

Buros O K 1975 (ed) Intelligence: tests and reviews. Gryphon Press, Highland Park, NJ

Byers R K, McLean W T 1962 Etiology and course of certain hemiplegias with aphasia in childhood. Pediatrics 29: 376–383

Cabanas R 1954 Some findings in speech and voice therapy among mentally deficient children. Folia Phoniatrica 6: 34–37

Caparulo B, Cohen D 1977 Cognitive structures, language and emerging social competence in autistic and aphasic children. Journal of the American Academy of Child Psychiatry 16: 620–645

Carrel R E 1977 Epidemiology of hearing loss. In: Gerber S E (ed) Audiometry in infancy. Grune and Stratton, New York

Carrow E 1975 Test for auditory comprehension of language. Learning Concepts, Texas

Carter H 1962 The historie of Herodotus of Halicarnassus (translated and introduced by Carter H) Oxford University Press, Oxford

Carter R L, Hohenegger M K, Satz P 1982 Aphasia and speech organization in children. Science 218: 797–799

Casselbrant M L, Brostoff L M, Flaherthy M R, Bluestone

C D, Cantekin E I, Doyle W J, Fria T J 1985 Otitis media with effusion in preschool children. Laryngoscope 95: 428–436

Cazden C 1965 Environmental assistance to the child's acquisition of grammar. Doctoral dissertation, Harvard University

Chapman R S, Kohn L L 1978 Comprehension strategies in two and three year olds: animate agents or probable events? Journal of Speech and Hearing Research 21: 746–761

Chase J B 1972 Retrolental fibroplasia and autistic symptomatology. American Foundation for the Blind, New York

Cheskin A 1982 The use of language by hearing mothers of deaf children. Journal of Communication Disorders 15: 145–153

Chomsky C 1969 The acquisition of syntax in children from 5 to 10. MIT Press, Cambridge, Mass

Chomsky N 1957 Syntactic structures. Mouton, The Hague

Chomsky N 1959 Review of Skinner (1957). Language 35: 26–58

Chomsky N 1965 Aspects of the theory of syntax. MIT Press, Cambridge, Mass

Chomsky N 1966 Topics in the theory of generative grammar. Mouton, The Hague

Chomsky N 1968 Language and mind. Harcourt Brace, New York

Chomsky N 1978 On the biological basis of language capacities. In: Miller G A, Lenneberg E (eds) Psychology and biology of language and thought. Academic Press, New York

Chomsky N 1980a On cognitive structures and their development: a reply to Piaget. In: Piattelli-Palmarini (ed) Language and learning: the debate between Jean Piaget and Noam Chomsky. Routledge and Kegan Paul, London

Chomsky N 1980b Discussion of 'Schemes of action and language learning' by Jean Piaget. In: Piattelli-Palmarini (ed) Language learning: the debate between Jean Piaget and Noam Chomsky. Routledge and Kegan Paul, London

Chomsky N 1980c Rules and representations. Behavioral and Brain Sciences 3: 1–61

Civelli E M 1983 Verbalism in young blind children. Journal of Visual Impairment and Blindness 77: 61–63

Clahsen H 1986 Verb inflections in German child language: acquisition of agreement markings and the functions they encode. Linguistics 24: 79–121

Clark E V 1973a What's in a word? On the child's acquisition of semantics in his first language. In: Moore T E (ed) Cognitive development and the acquisition of language. Academic Press, London and New York

Clark E V 1973b Non-linguistic strategies and the acquisition of word meaning. Cognition 2: 161–182

Clark E 1978 From gesture to word; on the natural history of deixis in language acquisition. In: Bruner J S, Garton A (eds) Human growth and development: Wolfson College lectures 1976. Oxford University Press, Oxford

Clark R 1974 Performing without competence. Journal of Child Language 1: 1–10

Clark R 1977 What's the use of imitation? Journal of Child Language 4: 341–358

Clarke A D B Personal communication

Clarke A M, Clarke A D B 1976 Early experience: Myth and evidence. Open Books, London

Clarke-Stewart A 1977 Child care in the family: A review of research and some propositions for policy. Academic Press, New York

Clausen J 1968 Behavioral characteristics of Down's syndrome subjects. American Journal of Mental Deficiency 73: 118–126

Clopton B M 1980 Neurophysiology of auditory deprivation. In: Gorlin R J (ed) Morphogenesis and malformation of the ear. Liss, New York

Cohen D, Sade J 1972 Hearing in secretory otitis media. Canadian Journal of Otolaryngology 1: 27–29

Cole R A 1977 Invariant features and feature detectors: some developmental implications. In: Segalowitz S J, Gruber F A (eds) Language development and neurological theory. Academic Press, New York

Coleman J R, O'Connor P 1979 Effects of monaural and binaural sound deprivation on cell development in the anteroventral cochlear nucleus of rats. Experimental Neurology 64: 553–566

Coleman S, Stedman J 1974 Use of a peer model in language training in an echolalic child. Journal of Behavioral Therapy and Experimental Psychiatry 5: 275–279

Collignon R, Hecaen H, Angelergues R 1968 A propos de 12 cas d'aphasie acquise de l'enfant. Acta Neurologica Belgica 68: 245–277

Collis G M, Bryant C A 1981 Interactions between blind parents and their young children. Child Care, Health and Development 7: 41–50

Collis G M, Schaffer H R 1975 Synchronisation of visual attention in mother-infant pairs. Journal of Child Psychology and Psychiatry 16: 315–320

Colton R E 1973 A study of pure tone thresholds and intelligence in institutionalized and non-institutionalized Down's syndrome. Dissertation Abstracts International 34: 2420

Commission of the European Communities 1979 Childhood Deafness in the European Community

Condon W S, Sander L W 1974 Neonate movement is synchronized with adult speech: interactional participation and language acquisition. Science 183: 99–101

Conel J L 1939–1967 The postnatal development of the human cerebral cortex (in 8 volumes). Pergamon, Oxford

Conrad R 1964 Acoustic confusion in immediate memory. British Journal of Psychology 55: 75–84

Conrad R 1971 The chronology of the development of covert speech in children. Developmental Psychology 5: 398–405

Conrad R 1979 The deaf schoolchild: language and cognitive function. Harper and Row, London

Conrad R, Hull A J 1964 Information, acoustic confusion and memory span. British Journal of Psychology 55: 429–432

Conti-Ramsden G 1985 Mothers in dialogue with language-impaired children. Topics in Language Disorders 5: 58–68

Cooper R L, Rosenstein J 1966 Language acquisition of deaf children. Volta Review 68: 58–67

Corney G 1975 Placentation. In: Macgillivray I, Nylander P P S, Corney G (eds) Human multiple reproduction. Saunders, London

Corrigan R 1979 Cognitive correlates of language: differential criteria yield differential results. Child Development 50: 617–631

Cowie V A 1970 A study of the early development of mongols. Pergamon, Oxford

Cox M V 1986 The child's point of view. Harvester, London

Critchley E 1967 Language development of hearing children in a deaf environment. Developmental Medicine and Child Neurology 9: 274–280

Crome L, Stern J 1967 Pathology of mental retardation. Churchill, London

Cromer R 1973 Conservation by the congenitally blind. British Journal of Psychology 64: 241–250

Cromer R F 1980 Commentary: Empirical evidence in support of non-empiricist theories of mind. Behavioral and Brain Sciences 3: 1618

Cromer R F 1983 The implications of research findings on blind children for semantic theories and for intervention. In: Mills A E (ed) Language acquisition in the blind child: normal and deficient. Croom Helm, London

Crothers B, Paine R S 1959 The natural history of cerebral palsy. Harvard University Press, Cambridge, Mass

Crystal D 1984 Who cares about English usage? Penguin Books, Harmondsworth, Middlesex

Crystal D, Fletcher P, Garman M 1976 The grammatical analysis of language disability: A procedure for assessment and remediation. Edward Arnold, London

Culbertson J L, Gilbert L E 1986 Children with unilateral sensorineural hearing loss: cognitive, academic and social development. Ear and Hearing 7: 38–42

Cull J G, Hardy R E 1973 Language meaning among deaf and hearing students. Perceptual and Motor Skills 36: 98–101

Culler F L, Jones K L, Deftos L J 1985 Impaired calcitonin secretion in patients with Williams syndrome. Journal of Paediatrics 107: 720–723

Cummins J 1976 The influence of bilingualism on cognitive growth: a synthesis of research findings and explanatory hypotheses. Working Papers on Bilingualism 9: 1–43

Cummins J 1981 The role of primary language development in promoting educational success for language minority students. In: Office of Bilingual, Bicultural Education, California State Department of Education (ed) Schooling and language minority students: a theoretical framework. Evaluation, Dissemination, and Assessment Center, California State University, Los Angeles

Cunningham C 1986 Patterns of development in Down's syndrome. Paper presented at the 3rd International Conference on Down Syndrome, Brighton, England (unpublished)

Curtiss S 1977 Genie: a psycholinguistic study of a modern-day 'wild child'. Academic Press, London

Curtiss S 1981a Feral children. In: Wortis J (ed) Mental retardation and developmental disabilities. Vol XII. Brunner/Mazel, New York

Curtiss S 1981b Dissociations between language and cognition: cases and implications. Journal of Autism and Developmental Disorders 11: 15–30

Curtiss S, Prutting C A, Lowell E L 1979 Pragmatic and semantic development in young children with impaired hearing. Journal of Speech and Hearing Research 22: 534–552

Curtiss S, Yamada J 1981 Selectively intact grammatical development in a retarded child. UCLA Working Papers in Cognitive Linguistics 3: 61–91

Cutler A, Fodor J A 1979 Semantic focus and sentence comprehension. Cognition 7: 49–59

Cutsforth T D 1932 The unreality of words to the blind. The Teachers Forum 4: 86–89

Cutsforth T D 1951 The blind in school and society. American Foundation for the Blind, New York

Dales R J 1969 Motor development in twins during the first 3 years. Journal of Genetic Psychology 114: 114–115

Dalzell J, Owrid H L 1976 Children with conductive deafness: A follow-up study. British Journal of Audiology 10: 87–90

Damasio A R, Geschwind N 1984 The neural basis of language. Annual Review of Neuroscience 7: 127–147

Darley F L 1979 Evaluation of appraisal techniques in speech and language pathology. Addison-Wesley, Reading, Mass

Davis E A 1937 The development of linguistic skill in twins, singletons and sibs, and only children from 5–10. University of Minnesota Institute of Child Welfare, Monograph 14

Davis J 1974 Performance of young hearing-impaired children on a test of basic concepts. Journal of Speech and Hearing Research 17: 342–357

Davis J M 1977 Reliability of hearing-impaired children's responses to oral and total presentations of the Test of Auditory Comprehension of Language. Journal of Speech and Hearing Disorders 42: 520–527

Davis J M 1986 Effects of mild and moderate hearing impairments in language, educational and psychosocial behaviour in children. Journal of Speech and Hearing Disorders 51: 53–62

Davis K 1940 Extreme social isolation of a child. American Journal of Sociology 45: 554–565

Davis K 1947 Final note on a case of extreme isolation. American Journal of Sociology 52: 432–437

Day E J 1932 The development of language in twins. 1. A comparison of twins and single children. 2. The development of twins: their resemblances and differences. Child Development 3: 179–199, 298–316

DeMyer M K, Barton S, DeMeyer E, Norton J A, Allen J, Steele R 1973 Prognosis in autism: A follow-up study. Journal of Autism and Childhood Schizophrenia 3: 199–246

DeMyer M K, Barton S, Alpern G D et al 1974 The measured intelligence of autistic children. Journal of Autism and Childhood Schizophrenia 4: 42–60

Demott R M 1972 Verbalism and affective meaning for blind, severely impaired and normally sighted children. New Outlook for the Blind 66: 1–8

Dennis M, Kohn B 1975 Comprehension of syntax in infantile hemiplegics after cerebral hemidecortication: left-hemisphere superiority. Brain and Language 2: 472–482

Dennis M, Lovett M, Wiegel-Crump C A 1981 Written language acquisition after left or right hemidecortication in infancy. Brain and Language 12: 54–91

Dennis M, Whitaker H A 1976 Language acquisition following hemidecortication: linguistic superiority of the left over the right hemisphere. Brain and Language 3: 404–433

Dennis W 1941 Infant development under conditions of restricted practice and of minimal social stimulation. Genetics of Psychology Monographs 23: 143–189

Dennis W 1973 Children of the creche. Appleton-Century-Crofts, New York

Dermody P, Mackie K 1983 Problems in establishing tympanometric screening criteria: Experience with a language/learning population. Australian Journal of Communication Disorders 11: 41–50

Despert J L 1946 Discussion—Kanner L Irrelevant and metaphoric language in early infantile autism. American Journal of Psychiatry 103: 242–246

Deuchar M 1983 Is British Sign Language an SVO language? In: Kyle J, Woll B (eds) Language in sign: an international perspective on sign language. Croom Helm, London

De Villiers J G, De Villiers P A 1973 A cross-sectional study of the acquisition of grammatical morphemes in child speech. Journal of Psycholinguistic Research 2: 267–278

De Villiers J G, De Villiers P A 1978 Language acquisition. Harvard University Press, Cambridge, Mass

De Villiers P A, De Villiers J G 1974 On this, that, and the other: nonegocentrism in very young children. Journal of Experimental Child Psychology 18: 438–447

Dewey M, Everard M 1975 The autistic adult in the community. Proceedings of the National Society for Autistic Children Annual Conference, San Diego, California

Diaz R 1983 Thought and two languages: the impact of bilingualism on cognitive development. In: Norbeck E, Price Williams D, McCord W (eds) Review of Research in Education Vol 10. American Educational Research Association, Washington DC

Dobbing J (ed) 1984 Scientific studies in mental retardation. RSM/Macmillan, London

Dobbing J, Sands J 1979 Comparative aspects of the brain growth spurt. Early Human Development 3: 79–83

Dobie R A, Berlin C I 1979 Influence of otitis media on hearing and development. Annals of Otology, Rhinology and Laryngology 88 (3 Pt 2 suppl 60): 48–53

Dodd B 1976a The phonological systems of deaf children. Journal of Speech and Hearing Disorders 41: 185–198

Dodd B 1976b A comparison of the phonological systems of mental age matched normal, severely subnormal and Down's syndrome children. British Journal of Disorders of Communication 11: 27–42

Dodd B 1980 The spelling abilities of profoundly prelingually deaf children. In: Frith U (ed) Cognitive processes in spelling. Academic Press, London

Dodd B 1983 The visual and auditory modalities in phonological acquisition. In: Mills A E (ed) Language acquisition in the blind child: normal and deficient. Croom Helm, London, and College Hill, San Diego

Dodd B 1987a Lip-reading, phonological coding and deafness. In: Dodd B, Campbell R (eds) Hearing by eye: The psychology of lip-reading. Erlbaum, London

Dodd B 1987b The acquisition of lip reading skills by normally hearing children. In: Dodd B, Campbell R (eds) Hearing by eye: the psychology of lip-reading. Erlbaum, London

Dodd B, Hermelin B 1977 Phonological coding by the prelingually deaf. Perception and Psychophysics 21: 413–417

Dokecki P R 1966 Verbalism and the blind: a critical review of the concept and the literature. Exceptional Children 32: 525–530

Doll E A 1966 Preschool attainment record (Research ed). American Guidance Service, Circle Pines, Minn

Dore J 1974 A pragmatic description of early language development. Journal of Psycholinguistic Research 3: 343–350

Douglas J E, Sutton A 1978 The development of speech and mental processes in a pair of twins: a case study. Journal of Child Psychology and Psychiatry 19: 49–56

Down J L H 1866 Observations on an ethnic classification of idiots. London Hospital Reports 259

Downs M P 1985 Effect of mild hearing loss on auditory processing. Otolaryngologic Clinics of North America 18: 337–344

Drach K N 1969 The language of the parent: a pilot study. In: The structure of linguistic input to children. Working paper no 14, Language Behavior Research Laboratory, University of California at Berkeley

Drillien C M 1958 A longitudinal study of the growth and development of prematurely and maturely born children. II Physical development. Archives of Disease in Childhood 33: 423–443

Du Bose R F, Langley M B 1978 The developmental activities screening inventory. Teaching Resources Corporation, Boston

Duchan J F (ed) 1982 Communication problems of autistic children: The role of context. Topics in Language Disorders 3(1)

Duchan J, Erickson J 1976 Normal and retarded children's understanding of semantic relations in different verbal contexts. Journal of Speech and Hearing Research 19: 767–776

Dunlea A 1982 The role of visual information in the emergence of meaning. Doctoral dissertation, University of Southern California

Dunlea A 1984 The relationship between concept formation and semantic roles: some evidence from the blind. In: Feagans L, Garvey C, Golinkoff R (eds) The origins and growth of communication. Ablex, Norwood, NJ

Dunn J, Kendrick C 1982 The speech of two- and three-year-olds to infant siblings: 'Baby talk' and the context of communication. Journal of Child Language 9: 579–595

Dyer C, Hadden A 1981 Delayed echolalia in autism: Some observations on differences within the term. Child: Care, Health, and Development 7: 331–345

Egan D 1975 Delayed milestones. British Journal of Hospital Medicine 13: 623–629

Egland G O 1955 Teaching speech to blind children with cerebral palsy. New Outlook for the Blind 49: 282–289

Eibl-Eibesfeldt D 1972 Similarities and differences between cultures and expressive movements. In: Hinde R A (ed) Non-verbal communication. Cambridge University Press, Cambridge

Fimas P D, Clarkson R L 1986 Speech perception in children: are there effects of otitis media? In: Kavanagh J F (ed) Otitis media and child development. York Press, Parkton, Maryland

Eisen N G 1962 Some effects of early sensory deprivation on later behavior: the quondam hard-of-hearing child. Journal of Abnormal and Social Psychology 65: 338–342

Eisenberg L 1956 The autistic child in adolescence. American Journal of Psychiatry 112: 607–612

Ellis R 1986 Understanding second language acquisition. Oxford University Press, Oxford

Ellis R, Wells G 1980 Enabling factors in adult-child discourse. First Language 1: 46–62

Elonen A S, Zwarensteyn S B 1964 Appraisal of developmental lag in certain blind children. Journal of Pediatrics 65: 599–610

Elstner W 1955 Erfahrungen in der Behandlung sprachgestörter blinder Kinder. Bericht über die Blindenlehrerfortbildungstagung in Innsbruck. Verlag des Bundesblindenerziehungsinstitutes, Vienna

Elstner W 1983 Abnormalities in the verbal communication of visually-impaired children. In: Mills A E (ed) Language acquisition in the blind child: normal and deficient. Croom Helm, London, and College Hill, San Diego

Elston R C, Blockage C E 1978 An examination of the fundamental assumptions of the twin method. In: Nance W E, Allen G, Parisi P (eds) Twin research: Progress in clinical and biological research: Psychology and methodology. Liss, New York

English S T, Prutting C A 1975 Teaching American Sign Language to a normally hearing infant with tracheostenosis. Clinical Pediatrics 14: 1141–1145

Enticknap L E 1957 A picture vocabulary test. Thesis, University of Queensland

Erin J N 1986 Frequencies and types of questions in the language of visually-impaired children. Journal of Visual Impairment and Blindness 80: 670–674

Falconer D S 1960 Introduction to quantitative genetics. Oliver and Boyd, Edinburgh

Fant L R Jr, Schuchman J S 1974 Experiences of two hearing children of deaf parents. In: Fine P (ed) Deafness in infancy and early childhood. Medcom, New York

Fantini A E 1978 Bilingual behavior and social cues: case studies of two bilingual children. In: Paradis M (ed) Aspects of bilingualism. Hornbeam Press, Columbia, SC

Farr V 1975 Prognosis for the babies, early and late. In: Macgillivray I, Nylander P P S, Corney G (eds) Human multiple reproduction. Saunders, London

Fay W H 1966 Childhood echolalia in delayed, psychotic and neuropathologic speech patterns. Folia Phoniatrica 18: 68–71

Fay W H 1967a Childhood echolalia: A group study of late abatement. Folia Phoniatrica 19: 297–306

Fay W H 1967b Mitigated echolalia of children. Journal of Speech and Hearing Research 10: 305–310

Fay W H 1971 On normal and autistic pronouns. Journal of Speech and Hearing Disorders 36: 242–249

Fay W H 1973 On the echolalia of the blind and of the autistic child. Journal of Speech and Hearing Disorders 38: 478–489

Fay W H 1982 The development of yes and no answers in autistic children. Topics in Language Disorders 3: 24–32

Fay W H, Butler B V 1968 Echolalia, IQ and the developmental dichotomy of speech and language systems. Journal of Speech and Hearing Research 11: 365–371

Fay W H, Coleman R O 1977 A human sound transducer/reproducer: Temporal capabilities of a profoundly echolalic child. Brain and Language 4: 396–402

Fay W H, Schuler A L 1980 Emerging language in autistic children. University Park Press, Baltimore

Felix S W 1978 Some differences between first and second language acquisition. In: Waterson N, Snow C (eds) The development of communication. Wiley, Chichester

Ferguson C A, Yeni-Komshian G H 1980 Introduction. In: Yeni-Komshian G H, Kavanagh J E, Ferguson C A (eds) Child phonology, Vol 2. Academic Press, New York

Ferrer H P 1984 Impedance measurements in the diagnosis of otitis media with effusion. In: Lim D J, Bluestone C D, Klein J O, Nelson J D (eds) Recent advances in otitis media with effusion. Decker, Philadelphia

Fior R 1972 Physiological maturation of auditory function between three and thirteen years of age. Audiology 11: 317–321

Fischer S 1973 Verb inflections in American Sign Language and their acquisition by the deaf child. The Salk Institute

Fischler R S, Todd N W, Feldman C M 1985 Otitis media and language performance in a cohort of Apache Indian children. American Journal of Diseases in Children 139: 355–360

Fishbein S 1978 School achievement and test results for twins and singletons in relation to social background. In: Nance W E, Allen G, Parisi P (eds) Twin research: progress in clinical and biological research: psychology and methodology. Liss, New York

Fisher K, Share J, Koch R 1964 Adaptation of Gesell developmental scales for evaluation of development in children with Down's syndrome. American Journal of Mental Deficiency 68: 642–666

Fok A, Bellugi U, Van Hoek K, Klima E S 1987 The formal properties of Chinese languages in space. Paper for International Conference on Psychological Aspects of the Chinese Language, Chinese University of Hong Kong (in press)

Foldi N S, Cicone M, Gardner H 1983 Pragmatic aspects of communication in brain-damaged patients. In: Segalowitz S J (ed) Language functions and brain organization. Academic Press, New York

Fourcin A J 1975a Language development in the absence of expressive speech. In: Lenneberg E, Lenneberg E (eds) Foundations of language development vol. 1. Academic Press, New York

Fourcin A J 1975b Speech perception in the absence of speech productive ability. In: O'Connor N (ed) Language, cognitive deficits, and retardation. Butterworths, London

Fowler A E 1987 The development of language structure in children with Down syndrome. In: Cicchetti D, Beeghly M (eds) Down syndrome: the developmental perspective. Cambridge University Press, New York (in press)

Fraiberg S 1974 Blind infants and their mothers: an examination of the sign system. In: Lewis M, Rosenblum L (eds) The effect of the infant on its caregiver. Wiley, New York

Fraiberg S 1977 Insights from the blind: comparative

studies of blind and sighted infants. Basic Books, New York, and Souvenir Press, London

Fraiberg S, Adelson A 1973 Self-representation in language and play: observations of blind children. The Psychoanalytic Quarterly 42: 539–562. Reprinted in Lenneberg E H, Lenneberg E (eds) Foundations of language development. A multidisciplinary approach, Vol 2. Academic Press, New York

Fraser C, Bellugi U, Brown R 1963 Control of grammar in imitation, comprehension and production. Journal of Verbal Learning and Verbal Behavior 2: 121–135

Fraser G R 1971 Genetic approaches to the nosology of deafness. In: Bergsma D (ed) The clinical deliniation of birth defects: Part IX: Ear. Williams and Wilkins, Baltimore

Freeman B A, Parkins C 1979 The prevalence of middle ear disease among learning impaired children. Clinical Pediatrics 18: 205–212

Freeman B, Ritvo E, Miller R 1975 An operant procedure to teach the echolalic autistic child to answer questions appropriately. Journal of Autism and Childhood Schizophrenia 5: 169–176

Freud S 1897 Die Infantile Cerebrallaehmung. (Infantile cerebral paralysis). Translated by Russin L A, 1968. University of Miami Press, Coral Gables

Freud S 1965 New introductory lectures on psychoanalysis. W W Norton, New York

Fria T J, Cantekin E I, Eichler J A 1985 Hearing acuity of children with otitis media with effusion. Archives of Otolaryngology 111: 10–16

Frith U, Frith C 1974 Specific motor disabilities in Down's syndrome. Journal of Child Psychology and Psychiatry 15: 293–301

Fry D B 1966 The development of the phonological system in the normal and the deaf child. In: Smith F, Miller D A (eds) The genesis of language: a psycholinguistic approach. MIT Press, Cambridge, Mass

Fuller L J, Thompson W R 1960 Behaviour genetics. Wiley, New York

Furth H G 1966 Thinking without language: Psychological implications of deafness. Free Press, New York

Garber N B, David L E 1975 Semantic considerations in the treatment of echolalia. Mental Retardation 13: 8–11

Gardner R C 1986 Social psychology and second language learning: the role of attitudes and motivation. Edward Arnold, London

Garman M 1983 The investigation of vision in language development. In: Mills A E (ed) Language acquisition in the blind child: normal and deficient. Croom Helm, London, and College Hill, San Diego

Garvey C 1977 Play with language and speech. In: Ervin-Tripp S, Mitchell-Kernan C (eds) Child discourse. Academic Press, New York

Gass S M, Madden C G 1985 Input in second language acquisition. Newbury House, Rowley, Mass

Gates A I, Chase E H 1926 Methods and theories of learning to spell tested by studies of deaf children. Journal of Educational Psychology 17: 289–301

Gates G A 1983 Socioeconomic impact of otitis media: workshop on effects of otitis media on the child. Pediatrics 71: 639–652

Gates G A, Paradise J L, Birck H G et al 1985 Recent advances in otitis media with effusion: Management.

Annals of Otology, Rhinology and Laryngology 94 (suppl 116): 27–29

Geers A, Moog J 1978 Syntactic maturity of spontaneous speech and elicited imitations of hearing impaired children. Journal of Speech and Hearing Disorders 43: 380–391

Genesee F 1981 A comparison of early and late second language learning. Canadian Journal of Behavioral Sciences 13: 115–128

Genesee F 1985 Beyond bilingualism: social psychological studies of French immersion programs in Canada. Canadian Journal of Behavioral Sciences 16: 338–352

Genesee F 1987 Learning through two languages: studies of immersion and bilingual education. Newbury House, Cambridge, Mass

Gesell A 1950 The first five years of life. Methuen, London

Gibson D 1966 Early developmental staging as a prophecy index in Down's syndrome. American Journal of Mental Deficiency 70: 825–828

Gibson D 1981 Down's syndrome. The psychology of mongolism. Cambridge University Press, Cambridge

Gilbert J H V 1982 Babbling and the deaf child: A commentary on Lenneberg et al (1965) and Lenneberg (1967). Journal of Child Language 9: 511–515

Gill J M 1983 and 1987 International register of research on visual disability. Research Unit for the Blind, Brunel University, Uxbridge

Gleitman L R 1983 Biological dispositions to learn language. In: Demopoulos W, Marras A (eds) Language learning and concept acquisition. Ablex Publishing Corporation, Norwood, NJ

Goddard H H 1916 Feeblemindedness: its causes and consequences. Macmillan, New York

Goetzinger C P, Harrison C, Baer C J 1964 Small perceptive hearing loss: its effect in school-age children. Volta Review 64: 124–131

Goldfield B A, Snow C E 1985 Individual differences in language acquisition. In: Berko Gleason J (ed) The development of language. Merrill, Columbus, Ohio

Goldman P S 1972 Developmental determinants of cortical plasticity. Acta Neurobiologica Experimentalis 32: 495–511

Goldman P S 1976 An alternative to developmental plasticity: heterology of CNS structures in infants and adults. In: Stein D G, Rosen J J, Butters N (eds) Plasticity and recovery of function in the central nervous system. Academic Press, New York

Goldschmid M L, Bentler P M 1968 Concept assessment kit: Conservation. Educational and Industrial Testing Service, San Diego

Göllesz V 1972 Uber die Lippenartikulation der von Geburt an Blinden. In: Hirschberg S, Szepe G Y, Vass-Kovoics E (eds) Papers in interdisciplinary speech research: proceedings of the Speech Symposium, Szeged. Akademiai Kiado, Budapest

Goodglass H, Kaplan E 1972 Assessment of aphasia and related disorders. Lea and Febiger, Philadelphia

Goodluck H 1986 Language acquisition and linguistic theory. In: Fletcher P, Garman M (eds) Language acquisition, 2nd edn. Cambridge University Press, Cambridge

Goodman R 1986 Hemispherectomy and its alternatives in the treatment of intractable epilepsy in patients with infantile hemiplegia. Developmental Medicine and Child Neurology 28: 251–258

Goodstein L D 1961 Intellectual impairment in children with cleft palates. Journal of Speech and Hearing Research 4: 287–294

Goodstein L D 1968 Psychosocial aspects of cleft palate. In: Spriestersbach D C, Sherman D (eds) Cleft palate and communication. Academic Press, New York

Goodz N S 1987 Parental language mixing in bilingual families. Psychology Department, Dawson College, Montreal

Gopnik A, Meltzoff A N 1985 From people, to plans to objects. Journal of Pragmatics 9: 495–512

Gosher-Gottstein E R 1979 Families of twins: A longitudinal study of coping. Twins: Newsletter of the International Society for Twin Studies. 4–5: 2

Greenfield P M, Smith H 1976 The structure of communication in early language development. Academic Press, New York

Gregory S 1986 Advising parents of young deaf children: Implications and assumptions. In: Harris J (ed) Child psychology in action. Croom Helm, London

Gregory S, Mogford K 1981 Early language development in deaf children. In: Woll B, Kyle J, Deuchar M (Eds) Perspectives on British sign language and deafness. Croom Helm, London

Gregory S, Mogford K, Bishop J 1979 Mothers' speech to young hearing-impaired children. Journal of the British Association for Teachers of the Deaf 3: 42–43

Griffiths P 1986 Early vocabulary. In: Fletcher P, Garman M (eds) Language acquisition, 2nd edn. Cambridge University Press, Cambridge

Grunwell P 1982 Clinical phonology. Croom Helm, London

Guttman E 1942 Aphasia in children. Brain 65: 205–219

Haden R, Penn C 1985 The twin situation and its effects on syntax and interactional language over time. British Journal of Disorders of Communication 20: 19–30

Hakimi-Manesh Y, Mojdehi H, Tashakkori A 1984 Short communication: effects of environmental enrichment on the mental and psychomotor development of orphanage children. Journal of Child Psychology and Psychiatry 25: 643–650

Hakuta K 1974 Prefabricated patterns and the emergence of structure in second language acquisition. Language Learning 24: 287–297

Hakuta K 1986 Mirror of language. Basic Books, New York

Hall A P 1979 A developmental study of cognitive equivalence in the congenitally blind. Doctoral dissertation, University of California at Berkeley

Hallett C P 1982 The screening and epidemiology of middle ear disease in a population of primary school entrants. Journal of Laryngology and Otology 96: 899–914

Halliday M A K 1975 Learning how to mean. Edward Arnold, London

Hanson V L, Liberman I Y, Shankweiler D 1984 Linguistic coding by deaf children in relation to beginning reading success. Journal of Experimental Child Psychology 37: 378–393

Hardy-Brown K 1983 Universals and individual differences: disentangling two approaches to the study of language acquisition. Developmental Psychology 19: 610–624

Harley R 1963 Verbalism among blind children. American Foundation for the Blind, New York

Harris D B 1963 Children's drawings as measures of intellectual maturity, a revision and extension of the Goodenough Draw-a-Man Tests. Harcourt, Brace and World, New York

Harris M, Jones D, Brookes S, Grant J 1986 Relations between the non-verbal context of maternal speech and rate of language development. British Journal of Developmental Psychology 4: 261–268

Hartley G 1986 Personal communication

Haspiel G S 1965 Communication breakdown in the blind emotionally disturbed child. New Outlook for the Blind 59: 98–99

Hatch E (ed) 1978 Second language acquisition: a book of readings. Newbury House, Rowley, Mass

Hay D A, O'Brien P J 1981 The interaction of family attitudes and cognitive abilities in the La Trobe twin study of behavioural and biological development. In: Gedda L, Parisi P, Nance W E (eds) Twin research: Progress in clinical and biological research: Intelligence, personality and development. Liss, New York

Hay D A, O'Brien P J 1983 The La Trobe Twin Study: a genetic approach to the structure and development of cognition in twin children. Child Development 317–318

Hebb D O, Lambert W E, Tucker G R 1971 Language, thought and experience. Modern Language Journal 55: 212–222

Hecaen H 1976 Acquired aphasia in children and the ontogenesis of hemispheric functional specialization. Brain and Language 3: 114–134

Hecaen H 1977 Language representation and brain development. In: Berenberg S R (ed) Brain, fetal and infant. Martinus Nijhoff, The Hague

Hecaen H 1983 Acquired aphasia in children: revisited. Neuropsychologia 21: 581–587

Held R, Hein A 1963 Movement produced stimulation in the development of visually guided behavior. Journal of Comparative and Physiological Psychology 56: 872–876

Hellspong L 1986 Personal communication, University of Stockholm

Henderson F W, Collier A M, Sanyal M A, Watkins J M, Fairclough D L, Clyde W A Jr, Denny F W 1982 A longitudinal study of respiratory viruses and bacteria in the etiology of acute otitis media with effusion. New England Journal of Medicine 306: 1377–1383

Hermelin B, O'Connor N 1970 Psychological experiments with autistic children. Pergamon, Oxford

Hingtgen J N, Churchill D W 1969 Identification of perceptual limitations in a mute autistic child. Archives of General Psychiatry 21: 68–71

Hitch G, Halliday M S 1983 Working memory in children. Proceedings of the Royal Society of London (B) 302: 325–340

Hoemann H W, Andrews C E, Florian V A, Hoemann S A, Jensema C J 1976 The spelling proficiency of children. American Annals of the Deaf 121: 489–493

Hoffman-Lawless K, Keith R W, Cotton R T 1981 Auditory processing abilities in children with previous middle ear effusion. Annals of Otology 90: 543–545

Holm V A, Kunze L H 1969 Effect of chronic otitis media

on language and speech development. Pediatrics 43: 833-839

Hood P N, Perlstein M A 1955 Infantile spastic hemiplegia. II. Laterality of involvement. American Journal of Physical Medicine 34: 457–466

Hook E 1981 Down syndrome. Its frequency in human populations and some factors pertinent to variation in rates. In: de la Cruz F, Gerald P S (eds) Trisomy 21 (Down syndrome). University Park Press, Baltimore

Howie V M, Ploussard J H, Sloyer J 1975 The 'otitis-prone' condition. American Journal of Diseases in Children 129: 676–678

Howlin P 1984 The acquisition of morphemes in autistic children: A critique and replication of the findings of Bartolucci, Pierce and Streiner 1980. Journal of Autism and Developmental Disorders 14: 127–136

Hubbard T W, Paradise J L, McWilliams B J, Elster B A, Taylor F H 1985 Consequences of unremitting middle-ear disease in early life: otologic, audiologic and developmental findings in children with cleft palate. New England Journal of Medicine 312: 1529–1534

Hudson R A 1980 Sociolinguistics. Cambridge University Press, Cambridge

Hughes A, Trudgill P 1979 English accents and dialects. Edward Arnold, London

Hulme C, Thomson N, Muir C, Lawrence A 1984 Speech rate and the development of short-term memory span. Journal of Experimental Child Psychology 38: 241–253

Hurford J R, Heasley B 1983 Semantics: a coursebook. Cambridge University Press, Cambridge

Huttenlocher J, Eisenberg K, Strauss S 1968 Comprehension: relation between perceived actor and logical subject. Journal of Verbal Learning and Verbal Behavior 7: 527–530

Ignelzi R J, Bucy P C 1968 Cerebral hemidecortication in the treatment of infantile cerebral hemiatrophy. Journal of Nervous and Mental Diseases 147: 14–30

Imedadze N 1978 On the psychological nature of child speech formation under conditions of exposure to two languages. In: Hatch E (ed) Second language acquisition: a book of readings. Newbury House, Rowley, Mass

Ingram D 1974 Phonological rules in young children. Journal of Child Language 1: 97–106

Ingram D 1975 If and when transformations are acquired by children. In: Data D P (ed) Developmental psycholinguistics: Theory and appplications. Georgetown University Press, Washington DC

Ingram D 1976 Phonological disability in children. Elsevier, New York

Ingram D 1978 The role of the syllable in phonological development. In: Bell A, Hooper J (eds) Syllables and segments. North Holland, New York

Ingram D 1981 Procedures for the phonological analysis of children's language. Unversity Park Press, Baltimore

Inhelder B, Piaget J 1964 The early growth of logic in the child. Routledge and Kegan Paul, London

Iran-Nejad A, Ortony A, Rittenhouse R 1981 The comprehension of metaphorical uses of English by deaf children. Journal of Speech and Hearing Research 24: 551–556

Itard J 1801, 1806 In: Malson L (ed) (translated by White J) The wild boy of Aveyron. N L B, London 1972

Jakobson R 1968 Child language, aphasia, and phonological universals. Janua Lingaurum, Series Minor, 72. Mouton, The Hague

Jan J E, Freeman R D, Scott E P 1977 Visual impairment in children and adolescents. Grune and Stratton, New York

Jarvella R, Lubinsky J 1975 Deaf and hearing children's use of language describing temporal order among events. Journal of Speech and Hearing Research, 18: 58–73

Jensema C J, Karchmer M A, Trybus R J 1978 The rated speech intelligibility of hearing impaired children: Basic relationships and a detailed analysis. Gallaudet College, Washington

Jerger J 1970 Clinical experience with impedance audiometry. Archives of Otolaryngology 92: 311–324

Jerger J F 1986 Issues in immittance screening: controversies in screening for middle ear disease and hearing loss in children. Pediatrics 77: 62–63

Jerger S, Jerger J, Alford B R, Abrams S 1983 Development of speech intelligibility in children with recurrent otitis media. Ear and Hearing 4: 138–145

Johnson R C, Abelson R B 1969 Intellectual behavioral and physical characteristics associated with trisomy translocation and mosaic types of Down's syndrome. American Journal of Mental Deficiency 73: 852–855

Johnston C, Prior M, Hay D 1984 Prediction of reading disability in twin boys. Developmental Medicine and Child Neurology 26: 588–595

Jones K L, Smith D W 1975 The Williams elfin facies syndrome: a new perspective. Journal of Pediatrics 86: 718–723

Jones M L, Quigley S P 1979 The acquisition of question formation in spoken English and American sign language by two hearing children of deaf parents. Journal of Speech and Hearing Disorders. 44: 196–200

Junefelt K 1987 Personal communication, University of Stockholm

Jusczyk P 1981 Infant speech perception: a critical appraisal. In:Eimas P D, Miller J L (eds) Perspectives on the study of speech. Erlbaum, Hillsdale, NJ

Jusczyk P 1982 Auditory versus phonetic coding of speech signals during infancy. In: Mehler J, Walker E, Garrett M (eds) Perspectives on mental representation. Erlbaum, Hillsdale, NJ

Kagan J, Kearsley R, Zelazo P 1978 Infancy: its place in human development. Harvard University Press, Cambridge, Mass

Kahn J 1975 Relationship of Piaget's sensorimotor period to language acquisition of profoundly retarded children. American Journal of Mental Deficiency 79: 640–643

Kanner L 1943 Autistic disturbances of affective contact. Nervous Child 2: 217–250

Kanner L 1946 Irrelevant and metaphorical language in early infantile autism. American Journal of Psychiatry 103: 242–246

Kanner L 1971 Follow-up study of eleven autistic children originally reported in 1943. Journal of Autism and Childhood Schizophrenia 1: 119–145

Kaplan G J, Fleshman J K, Bender T R, Baum C, Clark P S 1973 Long-term effects of otitis media: A ten year cohort study of Alaskan Eskimo children. Pediatrics 52: 577–585

Kaslon K W, Grabo D E, Ruben R J 1978 Voice, speech, and language habilitation in young children without laryngeal function. Archives of Otolaryngology 104: 737–739

Kastein S, Gillman A E 1976 The interaction of emotional stress and language development: case studies of three visually-impaired children. Journal of Communication Disorders 9: 135–141

Kastein S, Hendin J 1951 Language development in a group of children with spastic hemiplegia. Journal of Pediatrics 39: 476–480

Kataria S, Goldstein D J, Kushnick T 1984 Developmental delays in Williams ('Elfin Facies') syndrome. Applied Research in Mental Retardation 5: 419–423

Kavanagh J F (ed) 1986 Otitis media and child development. York Press, Parkton, Maryland

Keeler W R 1958 Autistic patterns and defective communication in blind children with retrolental fibroplasia. In: Hoch P H, Zubin J (eds) Psychopathology of communication. Grune and Stratton, New York

Keenan E O 1974 Conversational competence in children. Journal of Child Language 1: 163–183

Kekelis L S, Andersen E 1984 Family communication styles and language development. Journal of Visual Impairment and Blindness 78: 54–64

Keller-Cohen D 1981 Input from the inside: the role of a child's prior linguistic experience in second language learning. In: Andersen R (ed) New dimensions in second language acquisition research. Newbury House, Rowley, Mass

Kelly J P 1985 Auditory system. In: Kandel E R, Schwartz J H (eds) Principles of neural science, 2nd edn. Elsevier, New York

Kemp N J 1981 Social psychological aspects of blindness: a review. Current Psychological Reviews 1: 69–89

Kemper T L 1984 Asymmetrical lesions in dyslexia. In: Geschwind N, Galaburda A M (eds) Cerebral dominance: the biological foundations. Harvard University Press, Cambridge, Mass

Kennard M A 1936 Age and other factors in motor recovery from precentral lesions in monkeys. American Journal of Physiology 115: 138–146

Kertesz A 1983 Localization in neuropsychology. Academic Press, New York

Kim C 1969 Social interaction of like-sex twins and singletons in relation to intelligence, language and physical development. Journal of Genetic Psychology 114: 203–214

Kimura Y, Bryant P 1983 Reading and writing in English and Japanese: a cross-cultural study of young children. British Journal of Developmental Psychology 1: 143–154

Kinsbourne M, Hiscock M 1977 Does cerebral dominance develop? In: Segalowitz S J, Gruber F A (eds) Language development and neurological theory. Academic Press, New York

Klatt D H 1981 Lexical representations for speech production and perception. In: Myers T, Laver J, Anderson J (eds) The cognitive representation of speech. North Holland, Amsterdam

Klee T M, Davis-Dansky E 1986 A comparison of unilaterally hearing-impaired children and normal hearing children and normal-hearing children on a battery of standardized language tests. Ear and Hearing 7: 27–37

Klein H 1981 Productive strategies for the pronunciation of early polysyllabic lexical items. Journal of Speech and Hearing Research 24: 389–405

Klein H 1984 Learning to stress: A case study. Journal of Child Language 11: 375–390

Klein J O 1984 Otitis media and the development of speech and language. Pediatric Infectious Disease 3: 389–391

Klein W 1986 Second language acquisition. Cambridge University Press, Cambridge

Klima E, Bellugi U 1979 The signs of language. Harvard University Press, Cambridge, Mass

Koch H L 1966 Twins and twin relations. Chicago University Press, Chicago

Kohn B 1980 Right-hemisphere speech representation and comprehension of syntax after left cerebral injury. Brain and Language 9: 350–361

Kokko E 1974 Chronic secretory otitis media in children: a clinical study. Acta Otolaryngologica (suppl) 327: 7–44

Koluchova J 1972 Severe deprivation in twins: a case study. Journal of Child Psychology and Psychiatry 13: 107–114

Koluchova J 1976 The further development of twins after severe and prolonged deprivation: a second report. Journal of Child Psychology and Psychiatry 17: 181–188

Krashen S 1973 Lateralization, language learning, and the critical period: some new evidence. Language Learning 23: 63–74

Krashen S 1981 Second language acquisition and second language learning. Pergamon, Oxford

Krashen S, Long M, Scarcella R 1979 Age, rate and eventual attainment in second language acquisition. TESOL Quarterly 13: 573–582

Kraus B, Clark G, Oka S 1968 Mental retardation and abnormalities of the dentition. American Journal of Mental Deficiency 72: 905–917

Kuczaj S A 1986 Discussion: On social interaction as a type of explanation of language development. British Journal of Developmental Psychology 4: 289–299

Kudrajavcev T, Schoenberg B S 1979 Otitis media and developmental disability: epidemiologic considerations. Annals of Otology, Rhinology and Laryngology 88 (5 Pt 2 suppl 60): 88–98

Kuhl P K 1986 Reflections on infants' perception and representation of speech. In: Perkell J S, Klatt D H (eds) Invariance and variability in speech processes. Erlbaum, Hillsdale, NJ

Lach R, Ling D, Ling A H, Ship M A 1970 Early speech development in deaf infants. American Annals of the Deaf 115: 522–526

Ladefoged P 1975 A course in phonetics. Harcourt Brace Jovanovich, New York

Lado R 1964 Language teaching: a scientific approach. McGraw-Hill, New York

Landau B 1983 Blind children's language is not 'meaningless'. In: Mills A E (ed) Language acquisition in the blind child: normal and deficient. Croom Helm, London, and College Hill, San Diego

Landau B, Gleitman L R 1985 Language and experience: evidence from the blind child. Harvard University Press, Cambridge, Mass

Landsell H 1969 Verbal and nonverbal factors in right-hemisphere speech: relation to early neurological history. Journal of Comparative and Physiological Psychology 69: 734–738

Lane H 1977 The wild boy of Aveyron. Allen and Unwin, London

Lansky P S 1986 Personal communication, Blind Children's Centre, Los Angeles

Largo R H, Howard J A 1979 Developmental progression in play behaviour of children between nine and thirty months. 1: Spontaneous play and imitation. Developmental Medicine and Child Neurology 21: 299–310

Launer P 1982 Acquiring the distinction between related nouns and verbs in ASL. PhD Dissertation, City University of New York

Lavery E B 1985 An investigation of the psychological effects of twinship on the development of identity concepts in normal same-sex twins. Dissertation submitted for the degree of BSc in Speech, University of Newcastle upon Tyne

Lawson L 1981 The role of sign in the structure of the deaf community. In: Woll B, Kyle J, Deuchar M (eds) Perspectives on British sign language and deafness. Croom Helm, London

Layton T L, Baker P S 1981 Description of semantic-syntactic relations in an autistic child. Journal of Autism and Developmental Disorders 11: 385–399

Layton T, Sharifi H 1979 Meaning and structure of Down's syndrome and nonretarded children's spontaneous speech. American Journal of Mental Deficiency 83: 439–445

Lee L 1966 Developmental sentence types: A method for comparing normal and deviant syntactic development. Journal of Speech and Hearing Disorders 31: 311–330

Lee L L 1971 Northwestern Syntax Screening Test. Northwestern University Press, Evanston, Ill

Lee L 1974 Developmental sentence analysis. Northwestern University Press, Evanston, Ill

Lee L, Canter S 1971 Developmental sentence scoring: A clinical procedure for estimating syntactical development in children's spontaneous speech. Journal of Speech and Hearing Disorders 36: 315–340

Lehmann M D, Charron K, Kummer A, Keith R W 1979 The effects of chronic middle ear effusion on speech and language development—a descriptive study. International Journal of Pediatric Otorhinolaryngology 1: 137–144

Leifer J, Lewis M 1984 Acquisition of conversational response skills by young Down syndrome and nonretarded children. American Journal of Mental Deficiency 84: 610–618

Lejeune J, Turpin R, Gautier M 1959 Le mongolisme, premier exemple d'aberration autosomique humaine. Année Génétique 2: 41–49

Leleux C, Lebrun Y 1981 Language development in two cases of left hemispherectomy. In: Lebrun Y, Zangwill O (eds) Lateralisation of language in the child. Swets and Zeitlinger, Lisse

Lenneberg E H 1962 Understanding language without ability to speak: case report. Journal of Abnormal and Social Psychology 65: 419–425

Lenneberg E H 1967 The biological foundations of language. Wiley, New York

Lenneberg E H, Nichols I A, Rosenberger E F 1962 Primitive stages of language development in mongolism. Proceedings of the Association for Research in Nervous and Mental Diseases 42: 119–137

Lenneberg E H, Rebelsky G F, Nichols I A 1965 The vocalisations of infants born to deaf and to hearing parents. Human Development 8: 23–37

Leonard L B, Newhoff M, Messalam L 1980 Individual differences in early child phonology. Applied Psycholinguistics 1: 7–30

Leopold W F 1939 Speech development of a bilingual child: a linguist's record. Vol 1: Vocabulary growth in the first two years. Northwestern University Press, Evanston, Ill

Leopold W F 1947 Speech development of a bilingual child: a linguist's record. Vol 2: Sound learning in the first two years. Northwestern University Press, Evanston, Ill

Leopold W F 1949a Speech development of a bilingual child: a linguist's record. Vol 3: Grammar and general problems in the first two years. Northwestern University Press, Evanston, Ill

Leopold W F 1949b Speech development of a bilingual child: a linguist's record. Vol 4: Diary from age two. Northwestern University Press, Evanston, Ill

Leopold W 1978 A child's learning of two languages. In: Hatch E (ed) Second language acquisition: a book of readings. Newbury House, Rowley, Mass

Levine D N, Calvanio R, Popovics A 1982 Language in the absence of inner speech. Neuropsychologia 20: 391–409

Levinson B, Osterweil L 1984 Autism: Myth or reality. Charles C Thomas, Springfield, Ill

Lewis M M 1968 The education of deaf children: the possible place of finger spelling and signing. HMSO, London

Lewis N 1976 Otitis media and linguistic incompetence. Archives of Otolaryngology 102: 387–390

LeZak R J, Starbuck H B 1964 Identification of children with speech disorders in a residential school for the blind. The Education of the Blind 31: 8–12

Liberman A M, Cooper F S, Shankweiler D P, Studdert-Kennedy M 1967 Perception of the speech code. Psychological Review 74: 431–461

Liberman A M, Delattre P, Cooper F S 1952 The role of selected stimulus-variables in the perception of the unvoiced stop consonants. American Journal of Psychology 65: 497–516

Liberman A M, Delattre P C, Cooper F S, Gerstman L J 1954 The role of consonant-vowel transitions in the perception of the stop and nasal consonants. Psychological Monographs 68: (no. 8) 1–13

Liberman A M, Mattingly I G 1985 The motor theory of speech perception revised. Cognition 21: 1–36

Lillo-Martin D 1986 Two kinds of null arguments in American Sign Language. Natural Language and Linguistic Theory 4: 415

Lillo-Martin D 1987 Children's new sign creations. In: Strong M (ed) Language learning and deafness. Cambridge University Press (in press)

Lillo-Martin D, Bellugi U, Poizner H 1985a Tests for American Sign Language. The Salk Institute for Biological Studies

Lillo-Martin D, Bellugi U, Struxness L, O'Grady M 1985b The acquisition of spatially organized syntax. Papers and Reports on Child Language Development

Lillo-Martin D, Bellugi U, Schemenauer D, O'Grady M 1986 What and where in language: the acquisition of spatial linguistic structures in ASL. The Salk Institute

Lindfors J W 1987 Children's language and learning. Prentice-Hall, Englewood Cliffs, NJ

Lindholm K J, Padilla A M 1978 Language mixing in

bilingual children. Journal of Child Language 5: 327–335

Linebarger M C, Schwartz M F, Saffran E M 1983 Sensitivity to grammatical structure in so-called agrammatic aphasics. Cognition 13: 361–392

Ling D 1972 Rehabilitation of cases with deafness secondary to otitis media. In: Glorig A, Gerwin K (eds) Otitis media: Proceedings of the National Conference: Callier Hearing and Speech Center. Charles C Thomas, Springfield, Ill

Ling D, McCoy R H, Levinson E D 1969 The incidence of middle ear disease and its educational implications among Baffin Island Eskimo children. Canadian Journal of Public Health 60: 385–390

Lockyer L, Rutter M A 1969 A five to fifteen year follow-up study of infantile psychosis III. Psychological aspects. British Journal of Psychiatry 115: 865–882

Lockyer L, Rutter M A 1970 A five to fifteen year follow-up study of infantile psychosis IV. Patterns of cognitive ability. British Journal of Social and Clinical Psychology 9: 152–163

Loew R 1982 Roles and reference. In: Caccamise F, Garretson M, Bellugi U (eds) Teaching American Sign. Language as a second/foreign language. National Association of the Deaf, Silver Spring, Maryland

Loew R 1983 Roles and reference in American Sign Language: A developmental perspective. PhD Dissertation, University of Minnesota

Longstreth L E 1981 Revisiting Skeels final study: a critique. Developmental Psychology 17: 620–625

Lous J 1987 Screening for secretory otitis media. International Journal of Pediatric Otorhinolaryngology 13: 85–97

Lous J, Fiellau-Nikolajsen M 1984 A five year prospective case-control study of the influence of early otitis media with effusion on reading achievement. International Journal of Pediatric Otorhinolaryngology 8: 19–30

Lovaas O I 1977 The autistic child: Language development through behavior modification. Irvington, New York

Lovaas O I, Berberich J B, Perloff B F, Schaeffer B 1966 Acquisition of imitative speech by schizophrenic children. Science 151: 705–707

Loveland K A 1984 Learning about points of view: spatial perspective and the acquisition of 'I/you'. Journal of Child Language 11: 535–556

Lovell K, Mitchell B, Everett I 1962 An experimental study of the growth of some logical structures. British Journal of Psychology 53: 173–188

Lovett M W, Dennis M, Newman J E 1986 Making reference: the cohesive use of pronouns in the narrative discourse of hemidecorticate adolescents. Brain and Language 29: 224–251

Lowe M 1975 Trends in the development of representational play in infants from 1–3 years—an observational study. Journal of Child Psychology and Psychiatry 16: 33–59

Lucas S A 1984 Auditory discrimination and speech production in the blind child. International Journal of Rehabilitation Research 7: 74–76

Ludlow C L 1980 Children's language disorders: recent research advances. Annals of Neurology 7: 497–507

Luria A R 1966 Human brain and psychological processes. Harper and Row, New York

Luria A R 1973 The working brain: an introduction to neuropsychology. Basic Books, New York

Luria A R, Yudovitch F 1959 Speech and the development of mental processes in the child. Staples, London

Lux G 1933 Eine Untersuchung über die nachteilige Wirkung des Ausfalls der optischen Perzeption auf die Sprache des Blinden. Der Blindenfreund 53: 166–170

Lynch G, Gall C 1979 Organization and reorganization in the central nervous system: evolving concepts of brain plasticity. In: Falkner F, Tanner J M (eds) Human growth, vol 3: neurobiology and nutrition. Balliere Tindall, London

Lytton H 1980 Parent-child interaction. The socialization process observed in twin and singleton families. Plenum, New York

Lytton H, Watts D 1981 The social development of twins in longitudinal perspective: How stable is genetic determination over age 2–9? In: Gedda L, Parisi P, Nance W E (eds) Twin research: Progress in clinical and biological research: Intelligence, personality, and development. Liss, New York

McAdoo W G, DeMyer M K 1977 Research related to family factors in autism. Journal of Pediatric Psychology 2: 162–166

McCaleb P, Prizant B M 1985 Encoding of new versus old information by autistic children. Journal of Speech and Hearing Disorders 50: 230–240

McCarthy D 1930 The language development of the preschool child. University of Minnesota Institute of Child Welfare, Monograph 4

McCarthy D A 1954 Language development in children. In: Carmichael L (ed) Manual of child psychology. Wiley, New York

McCauley R J, Swisher L 1984a Psychometric review of language and articulation tests for preschool children. Journal of Speech and Hearing Disorders 49: 34–42

McCauley R J, Swisher L 1984b Use and misuse of norm-referenced tests in clinical assessment: A hypothetical case. Journal of Speech and Hearing Disorders 49: 338–348

McCormick K, Dewart H 1986 Three's a crowd: early language of a set of triplets. Proceedings of the Child Language Seminar 1986: 286–287 Durham University

McCune-Nicolich L 1981 The cognitive bases of relational words in the single word period. Journal of Child Language 8: 15–34

MacDonald G W, Roy D L 1985 Williams Syndrome: a neuropsychological profile. Paper presented at the International Neuropsychological Society, San Diego (unpublished)

MacDonald K 1986 Developmental models and early experience. International Journal of Behavioral Development 9: 175–190

McFie J, Piercy M F, Zangwill O L 1950 Visual-spatial agnosia associated with lesions of the right cerebral hemisphere. Brain 73: 167–190

MacGillivray R 1968 Congenital cataract and mongolism. American Journal of Mental Deficiency 72: 631–633

McGinnis A R 1981 Functional linguistic strategies of blind children. Journal of Visual Impairment and Blindness 75: 210–214

McLaughlin B 1978 Second language acquisition in childhood. Erlbaum, Hillsdale, NJ

McLaughlin B 1981 Differences and similarities between

first- and second-language learning. In: Winitz H (ed) Native language and foreign language acquisition. Annals of the New York Academy of Sciences 379: 23–32

McLaughlin B 1984 Second-language acquisition in childhood: volume 1. Preschool children. Erlbaum, Hillsdale, NJ

McLaughlin B 1985 Second-language acquisition in childhood: volume 2. School-age children. Erlbaum, Hillsdale, NJ

McLeod J F 1985 An observational study of the interaction between a pair of 4 year old language disordered male twins and their mother. Dissertation submitted for the degree of BSc in Speech, University of Newcastle upon Tyne

MacNeilage P F, Rootes T P, Chase R A 1967 Speech production and perception in a patient with severe impairment of somesthetic perception and motor control. Journal of Speech and Hearing Research 10: 449–468

McNeill D 1970 The acquisition of language. Harper and Row, New York

Mahler M S, Furer M, Settlage C 1959 Severe emotional disturbances in childhood: Psychoses. In: Arieti S (ed) American handbook of psychiatry. Basic Books, New York

Malstrom P M, Silva M N 1986 Twin talk: manifestations of twin status in the speech of toddlers. Journal of Child Language 13: 293–305

Marcotte A C, LaBarba R C 1985 Cerebral lateralization for speech in deaf and normal children. Brain and Language 26: 244–258

Markides A 1970 The speech of deaf and partially hearing children with special reference to factors affecting intelligibility. British Journal of Disorders of Communication 5: 126–140

Maskarinec A S, Cairns G F, Butterfield E C, Weamer D K 1981 Longitudinal observations of individual infants' vocalisations. Journal of Speech and Hearing Disorders 46: 267–273

Mason M K 1942 Learning to speak after six and one half years of silence. Journal of Speech and Hearing Disorders 7: 295–304

Masters L, Marsh G E 1978 Middle ear pathology as a factor in learning disabilities. Journal of Learning Disabilities 11: 103–106

Matheny A P, Bruggemann C 1972 Articulation proficiency in twins and singletons from families of twins. Journal of Speech and Hearing Research 15: 845–851

Matsuda M M 1984 A comparative analysis of blind and sighted children's communication skills. Journal of Visual Impairment and Blindness 78: 1–5

Mavilya M P 1972 Spontaneous vocalization and babbling in hearing impaired infants. In: Fant G (ed) International symposium on speech communication abilities and profound deafness. A G Bell Association for the Deaf, Washington

Maxfield K E 1936 The spoken language of the blind preschool child: a study of method. Archives of Psychology 201

Mayberry R 1976 An assessment of some oral and manual language skills of hearing children of deaf parents. American Annals of the Deaf 121: 507–512

Mecham M J 1971 Verbal language development scale.

American Guidance Service, Circle Pines, Minn

Mehler J 1971 Discussion of paper by Sinclair. In: Huxley R, Ingram E (eds) Language acquisition: models and methods. Academic Press, London

Mehler J, Bertoncini J, Barriere M, Jassik-Gerschenfeld D 1978 Infant recognition of mother's voice. Perception 7: 491–497

Mehler J, Lambertz G, Jusczyk P, Amiel-Tison C 1986 Discrimination de la langue maternelle par le nouveau-né. Academie des Sciences 3: 637–640

Meier R 1981 Icons and morphemes: Models of the acquisition of verb agreement in ASL. Papers and Reports on Child Language Development 20: 92–99

Meier R 1982 Icons, analogues and morphemes: The acquisition of verb agreement in American Sign Language. PhD Dissertation, University of California, San Diego

Mein R, O'Connor N 1960 A study of the oral vocabularies of severely subnormal patients. Journal of Mental Deficiency Research 4: 130–143

Meisel J (in press) Early differentiation of languages in bilingual children. In: Hyltenstam K, Obler L (eds) Bilingualism across the lifespan: in health and pathology

Melnick M, Myrianthopoulos N C, Christian J C 1970 The effects of chorion type on variation in IQ in the NCPP twin population. American Journal of Human Genetics 30: 425–433

Menkes J H 1974 Textbook of child neurology. Lea and Febiger, Philadelphia

Menn L 1985 Phonological development: learning sounds and sound patterns. In: Berko Gleason J (ed) The development of language. Merrill, Columbus, Ohio

Menyuk P 1969 Sentences children use. MIT Press, Cambridge, Mass

Menyuk P 1979 Design factors in the assessment of language development in children with otitis media. Annals of Otology, Rhinology and Laryngology 88 (5 Pt 2 suppl 60): 78–87

Menyuk P 1986 Predicting speech and language problems with persistent otitis media. In: Kavanagh J F (ed) Otitis media and child development. York Press, Parkton, Maryland

Meyerson M D, Foushee D R 1978 Speech, language and hearing in Moebius syndrome: a study of 22 patients. Developmental Medicine and Child Neurology 20: 357–365

Meyerson M D, Frank R A 1987 Language, speech and hearing in Williams Syndrome: Intervention approaches and research needs. Developmental Medicine and Child Neurology 29: 258–270

Millar J M, Whitaker H 1983 The right hemisphere's contribution to language: A review of the evidence from brain-damaged subjects. In: Segalowitz S J (ed) Language functions and brain organization. Academic Press, New York

Miller J, Chapman R 1981 Research note: The relation between age and mean length of utterance in morphemes. Journal of Speech and Hearing Research 24: 156–161

Miller J, Chapman R, MacKenzie H (1981) Individual differences in the language acquisition of mentally retarded children. Paper presented at the Biennial Meeting of the Society for Research in Child Development, Boston (unpublished)

Mills A E 1983 Acquisition of speech sounds in the visually-handicapped child. In: Mills A E (ed) Language acquisition in the blind child: normal and deficient. Croom Helm, London, and College Hill, San Diego

Mills A E 1985 The acquisition of German. In: Slobin D I (ed) The crosslinguistic study of language acquisition. Erlbaum, Hillsdale, NJ

Mills A E 1986 The acquisition of gender: a study of English and German. Springer, Heidelberg

Mills A E 1987 The development of phonology in the blind child. In: Dodd B, Campbell R (eds) Hearing by eye: The psychology of lip-reading. Erlbaum, London

Mills A E, Meinecke C, Hattig H et al 1983 Die Rolle der Visuellen Information im Spracherwerb. DFG Abschlussbericht, University of Tubingen, FRG

Mills A E, Thiem R 1980 Auditory fusions and illusions in speech perception. Linguistische Berichte 68: 85–108

Miner L E 1963 A study of the incidence of speech deviations among visually-handicapped children. New Outlook for the Blind 57: 10–14

Mittler P 1969 Genetic aspects of psycholinguistic abilities. Journal of Child Psychology and Psychiatry 10: 165–176

Mittler P 1970 Biological and social aspects of language development in twins. Developmental Medicine and Child Neurology 12: 741–757

Mittler P 1971 The study of twins. Penguin, Harmondsworth, Middlesex

Moerk E L 1975 Piaget's research as applied to the explanation of language development. Merrill-Palmer Quarterly 21: 151–169

Mogford K 1987 Lip-reading in the prelingually deaf. In: Dodd B, Campbell R (eds) Hearing by eye: The psychology of lip-reading. Erlbaum, London

Mogford K, Gregory S 1982 The development of communication skills in young deaf children: picture book reading with mother. Paper given to the Psycholinguistics and Language Pathology Colloquium, University of Newcastle, November 1982 (unpublished)

Moll K L 1968 Speech characteristics of individuals with cleft lip and palate. In: Spriestersbach D C, Sherman D (eds) Cleft palate and communication. Academic Press, New York

Money J, Annecillo C, Kelley J F 1983 Growth of intelligence: failure and catch-up associated respectively with abuse and rescue in the syndrome of abuse dwarfism. Psychoneuroendocrinology 8: 309–319

Montague J C, Hollien H 1973 Perceived voice quality disorders in Down's syndrome children. Journal of Communication Disorders 6: 76–87

Montague J C, Hollien H 1974 Perceived voice quality disorders in Down's syndrome children. Training School Bulletin 71: 80–89

Moore D C, Best G F 1980 A sensorineural component in chronic otitis media. Laryngoscope 90: 1360–1366

Moore T 1968 Language and intelligence: a longitudinal study of the first 8 years—II. Environmental correlates of mental growth. Human Development 11: 1–24

Morehead D M, Ingram D 1976 The development of base syntax in normal and linguistically deviant children. In: Morehead D M, Morehead A E (eds) Normal and deficient child language. University Park Press, Baltimore

Morehead D M, Morehead A 1984 From signal to sign: a Piagetian view of thought and language during the first two years. In: Schiefelbusch R L, Lloyd L L (eds) Language perspectives—acquisition, retardation, and intervention. University Park Press, Baltimore

Mori A A, Olive J E 1978 The blind and visually-handicapped mentally retarded: suggestions for intervention in infancy. Journal of Visual Impairment and Blindness 72: 273–279

Morley M E 1970 Cleft palate and speech, 7th edn. Livingstone, Edinburgh

Morley M 1972 Development and disorders of speech in childhood, 3rd edn. Churchill Livingstone, Edinburgh

Mulford R C 1981 Talking without seeing: some problems of semantic development in blind children. Doctoral dissertation, Stanford University

Mulford R C 1983 Referential development in blind children. In: Mills A E (ed) Language acquisition in the blind child: normal and deficient. Croom Helm, London, and College Hill, San Diego

Mulford R C 1987 First word of the blind child. In: Smith M D, Locke J L (eds) The emergent lexicon: the child's development of a linguistic vocabulary. Academic Press, London

Munker G 1981 Inner ear hearing loss in acute and chronic otitis media. Advances in Otorhinolaryngology 27: 138–143

Munsinger H, Douglass A II 1976 The syntactic abilities of identical twins, fraternal twins and their siblings. Child Development 47: 40–50

Murphy J, Slorach N 1983 The language development of pre-preschool hearing children of deaf parents. British Journal of Disorders of Communication 18: 119–126

Murrell M 1966 Language acquisition in a trilingual environment: notes from a case-study. Studia Linguistica 20: 9–35

Myklebust H 1960 The psychology of deafness. Grune and Stratton, New York

Nakanishi Y, Owada K 1973 Echoic utterances of children between the ages of one and three years. Journal of Verbal Learning and Verbal Behavior 12: 658–665

Nation J E, Wetherbee M A 1985 Cognitive-communicative development of identical triplets, one with unilateral cleft lip and palate. Cleft Palate Journal 22: 38–50

Neale M M 1980 A description of the psycholinguistic abilities of a Williams syndrome population. Ph.D. dissertation, The American University

Nebes R D 1975 The nature of internal speech in a patient with aphemia. Brain and Language 2: 489–497

Needleman H, Menyuk P 1977 Effects of hearing loss from early otitis media on speech and language development. In: Jaffe B F (ed) Hearing loss in children. University Park Press, Baltimore

Nelson K 1973 Structure and strategy in learning to talk. Monographs of the Society for Research in Child Development 38

Nelson K 1981 Individual differences in language development: implications for development and language. Developmental Psychology 17: 170–187

Netsell R 1981 The acquisition of speech motor control: a perspective with directions for research. In: Stark R E (ed) Language behavior in infancy and early childhood. Elsevier/North Holland, New York

Newport E, Gleitman L, Gleitman H 1977 Mother, I'd

rather do it myself: Some effects and non-effects of maternal speech style. In: Snow C E, Ferguson C A (eds) Talking to children: Language input and acquisition. Cambridge University Press, Cambridge

Newport E, Ashbrook E 1977 The emergence of semantic relations in American Sign Language. Papers and Reports on Child Language Development 13: 16–21

Newport E, Meier R 1985 Acquisition of American Sign Language. In: Slobin D (ed) The cross-linguistic study of language acquisition. Erlbaum, Hillsdale, NJ

Newson J, Newson E 1975 Intersubjectivity and the transmission of culture. Bulletin of the British Psychological Society 28: 437–446

Nielsen H H 1966 Psychological study of cerebral palsied children. Munksgaard, Copenhagen

Nienhuys T G, Horsborough K M, Cross T G 1985 A dialogic analysis of interaction between mothers and their deaf or hearing preschoolers. Applied Psycholinguistics 6: 121–140

Ninio A, Bruner J 1978 The achievement and antecedents of labelling. Journal of Child Language 5: 1–15

Nolan C 1987 Under the eye of the clock. Weidenfeld & Nicolson, London

Noll J D 1982 Remediation of impaired resonance among patients with neuropathologies of speech. In: Lass N J, McReynolds L V, Northern J L, Yoder D E (eds) Speech, language and hearing. Vol II: Pathologies of speech and language. Saunders, Philadelphia

Norris M, Spaulding P J, Brodie F H 1957 Blindness in children. University of Chicago Press, Chicago

Northern J L, Downs M P 1984 Hearing in children, 3rd edn. Williams and Wilkins, Baltimore

Nylander P P S 1975 Factors which influence twinning rates. In: Macgillivray I, Nylander P P S, Corney G (eds) Human multiple reproduction. Saunders, London

Ochaita E, Rosa A, Pozo J I et al 1986 Language and concrete operational development in blind children. Paper to the Second European Developmental Psychology conference, Rome (unpublished)

O'Connor N, Hermelin B 1961 Visual and stereognostic shape of recognition in normal children and mongol and non-mongol imbeciles. Journal of Mental Deficiency Research 5: 63–66

O'Connor N, Hermelin B 1963 Speech and thought in severe subnormality. Pergamon, Oxford

O'Connor N, Hermelin B 1983 Peripheral and central handicap and encoding. Journal of Child Psychology and Psychiatry 24: 39–48

Oksaar E 1971 Code switching as an interactional strategy for developing bilingual competence. Word 27: 377–385

Oller D K 1986 Metaphonology and infant vocalization. In: Lindblom B, Zetterstrom R (eds) Precursors of early speech. Macmillan, Basingstoke

Oller D K, Kelley C A 1974 Phonological substitution processes of a hard of hearing child. Journal of Speech and Hearing Disorders 39: 65–74

Oller D K, Jensen T H, Lafayette R H 1978 The relatedness of phonological processes of a hearing-impaired child. Journal of Communication Disorders 11: 97–105

Olson M R 1983 A study of the exploratory behaviour of legally blind and sighted preschoolers. Exceptional Children 49: 130–138

Olson S L, Bayles K, Bates J E 1986 Mother-child interaction and children's speech progress: a longitudinal study of the first two years. Merrill-Palmer Quarterly 32: 1–20

Omwake E B, Solnit A J 1961 It isn't fair: the treatment of a blind child. Psychoanalytic Study of the Child 16: 352–404

Orlansky M D, Bonvillian J D 1985 Sign language acquisition: Language development in children of deaf parents and implications for other populations. Merrill-Palmer Quarterly 31: 127–143

Oster J 1953 Mongolism. Danish Science Press, Copenhagen

Owrid H L 1970 Hearing impairment and verbal attainment in primary school children. Educational Research 12: 209–214

Padden C 1983 Interaction of morphology and syntax in American Sign Language. PhD Dissertation, University of California, San Diego

Padilla A M, Liebman E 1975 Language acquisition in the bilingual child. Bilingual Review 2: 34–55

Palermo D 1975 Developmental aspects of speech perception: problems for a motor theory. In: Kavanagh J F, Cutting J E (eds) The role of speech in language. MIT Press, Cambridge, Mass

Paparella M M, Brady D R, Hoel R 1970 Sensori-neural hearing loss in chronic otitis media and mastoiditis. Transactions of the American Academy of Ophthalmology and Otolaryngology 74: 108–115

Paparella M M, Morizono T, Le C T et al 1984 Sensorineural hearing loss in otitis media. Annals of Otology, Rhinology and Laryngology 93: 623–629

Paparella M M, Bluestone C D, Arnold W et al 1985 Recent advances in otitis media with effusion: Otitis media: definition and classification. Annals of Otology, Rhinology and Laryngology 94 (suppl 116): 8–9

Pape K E, Wigglesworth J S 1979 Haemorrhage, ischaemia and the perinatal brain. Clinics in Developmental Medicine nos. 69/70. Heinemann, London

Paradise J L 1980 Otitis media in infants and children. Pediatrics 65: 917–943

Paradise J L 1981 Otitis media during early life: how hazardous to development? A critical review of the literature. Pediatrics 68: 869–873

Paradise J L, Rogers K D 1986 On otitis media, child development, and tympanostomy tubes: new answers or old questions? Pediatrics 77: 88–92

Parke K L, Shallcross R, Anderson R J 1980 Differences in coverbal behavior between blind and sighted persons during dyadic communication. Journal of Visual Impairment and Blindness 74: 142–146

Parsons C, Iacono T, Rozner L 1987 Effect of tongue reduction on articulation in children with Down syndrome. American Journal of Mental Deficiency 91: 328–332

Paterson A, Zangwill O L 1944 Disorders of visual space perception associated with lesions of the right cerebral hemisphere. Brain 67: 331–358

Paul R 1987 Communication in autism. In: Cohen D J, Donnellan A M (eds) Handbook of autism and atypical development. Wiley, New York

Pawlby S 1977 A study of the nature and structure of imitative sequences observed in interaction between mothers and their infants. In Schaffer H R (ed) Studies in Mother-infant interaction. Academic Press, London

Penfield W 1965 Conditioning the uncommitted cortex for language learning. Brain 88: 787–798

Penfield W, Roberts L 1959 Speech and brain mechanisms. Atheneum, New York

Pennington B F, Smith S D 1983 Genetic influences on learning disabilities and speech and language disorders. Child Development 54: 369–387

Perecman E (ed) 1983 Cognitive processing and the right hemisphere. Academic Press, New York

Perera K 1984 Children's writing and reading: analysing classroom language. Blackwell, Oxford

Peters A 1977 Language learning strategies: Does the whole equal the sum of the parts? Language 53: 560–573

Peters A 1983 The units of language acquisition. Cambridge University Press, Cambridge

Peterson H A, Marquardt T P 1981 Appraisal and diagnosis of speech and language disorders. Prentice-Hall, Englewood Cliffs, NJ

Peterson-Falzone S 1982a Articulation disorders in orofacial anomalies. In: Lass N J, McReynolds L V, Northern J L, Yoder D E (eds) Speech, language, and hearing, volume II: Pathologies of speech and language. Saunders, Philadelphia

Peterson-Falzone S 1982b Resonance disorders in structural defects. In: Lass N J, McReynolds L V, Northern J L, Yoder D E (eds) Speech, language, and hearing, volume II: Pathologies of speech and language. Saunders, Philadelphia

Petitto L 1983a From gesture to symbol: The relationship between form and meaning in the acquisition of personal pronouns in American Sign Language. PhD Dissertation, Harvard University

Petitto L 1983b From gesture to symbol: The relationship between form and meaning in the acquisition of ASL. Papers and Reports on Child Language Development 22: 100–107

Pfuderer C 1969 Some suggestions for a syntactic characterization of baby talk style. In: The structure of linguistic input to children. Working Paper No 14, Language-Behavior Research Laboratory, University of California at Berkeley

Phatate D D, Umano H 1981 Auditory discrimination of voiceless fricatives in children. Journal of Speech and Hearing Research 24: 162–168

Philips G M, Dyer C 1977 Late onset echolalia in autism and allied disorders. British Journal of Disorders of Communication 12: 47–59

Phillips J 1973 Syntax and vocabulary of mothers' speech to young children: age and sex comparisons. Child Development 44: 182–185

Piaget J 1926 Language and thought of the child. Routledge and Kegan Paul, London

Piaget J 1952 The origins of intelligence in children (translated by Margaret Cook). International Universities Press, New York

Piaget J 1967a Play, dreams and imitation in childhood. Routledge and Kegan Paul, London

Piaget J 1967b The mental development of the child. In: Elkind D (ed) Six psychological studies (by Jean Piaget, translated by Anita Tenzer). University of London Press, London

Piaget J 1971 Biology and knowledge. Edinburgh University Press, Edinburgh

Piaget J, Inhelder B 1959 La genése des structures logiques élémentaires: classifications et sériations. Delachauex et Niestle, Neuchatel

Piattelli-Palmarini M 1980 Language and learning: the debate between Jean Piaget and Noam Chomsky. Routledge and Kegan Paul, London, and Harvard University Press, Cambridge, Mass

Pick A 1924 On the pathology of echographia. Brain 47: 417–429

Picton T W, Naylor M J, Durieux-Smith A, Edwards C G 1986 Brainstem auditory evoked potentials in pediatrics. In: Aminoff M J (ed) Electro-diagnosis in clinical neurology. Churchill Livingstone, New York

Pierce S, Bartolucci C 1977 A syntactic investigation of verbal autistic, mentally retarded and normal children. Journal of Autism and Childhood Schizophrenia 7: 121–134

Poizner H, Bellugi U, Tweney R D 1981 Processing of formational, semantic, and iconic information in American Sign Language. Journal of Experimental Psychology: Human Perception and Performance 7: 1146–1159

Poizner H, Klima E S, Bellugi U 1987 What the hands reveal about the brain. MIT Press/Bradford Books, Cambridge, Mass

Poplack S 1979 Sometimes I'll start a sentence in Spanish y termino en Espanol: toward a typology of code-switching. Working Paper No 4, Centro de Estudios Puertorriquenos, New York

Power D J, Quigley S P 1973 Deaf children's acquisition of the passive voice. Journal of Speech and Hearing Research 16: 5–11

Preisser D 1983 Prevalence of phonological processes in normal two-year-olds. Doctoral dissertation, University of Illinois

Presnell L 1973 Hearing-impaired children's comprehension and production in oral language. Journal of Speech and Hearing Research 16: 12–21

Preus A 1972 Stuttering in Down's syndrome. Scandinavian Journal of Education Research 16: 89–104

Prinz P, Prinz E 1979 Acquisition of ASL and spoken English in a hearing child of a deaf mother and hearing father: Phase I. Early lexical development. Papers and Reports on Child Language Development 17: 139–146

Prinz P, Prinz E 1981 Acquisition of ASL and spoken English by a hearing child of a deaf mother and a hearing father: Phase II. Early combinatorial patterns. Sign Language Studies 30: 78–88

Prizant B M 1983a Language acquisition and communicative behavior in autism: Toward understanding of the 'whole' of it. Journal of Speech and Hearing Disorders 48: 296–307

Prizant B M (ed) 1983b Seminars in Speech and Language 4(1)

Prizant B M 1984 Toward an understanding of language symptomology of visually-impaired children. In: Sykanda A W, Jan J E, Blockberger S J et al (eds) Insight in sight. Proceedings of the Fifth Canadian Interdisciplinary Conference on the visually impaired child. CNIB, Vancouver

Prizant B, Booziotis K Language acquisition strategies of a blind child. (in preparation)

Prizant B M, Duchan J F 1981 The functions of immediate echolalia in autistic children. Journal of Speech and Hearing Disorders 46: 241–249

Prizant B M, Rydell P J 1984 Analysis of functions of delayed echolalia in autistic children. Journal of Speech and Hearing Research 27: 183–192

Pronovost W, Wakstein M P, Wakstein D J 1966 A longitudinal study of speech behavior and language comprehension of fourteen children diagnosed atypical or autistic. Exceptional Children 33: 228–233

Provence S, Lipton R C 1962 Infants in institutions: a comparison of their development with family-reared infants during the first year of life. International University Press, New York

Quigley S P, King C M 1981 An invited article: Syntactic performance of hearing-impaired and normal individuals. Applied Psycholinguistics 1: 329–356

Quigley S P, Kretschmer R E 1982 The education of deaf children: Issues, theory and practice. Edward Arnold, London

Quigley S P, Paul P V 1984 Language and deafness. Croom Helm, London

Quigley S P, Power D J, Steinkamp M W 1977 The language structure of deaf children. Volta Review 79: 73–84

Rankin J M, Aram D M, Horwitz S J 1981 Language ability in right and left hemiplegic children. Brain and Language 14: 292–306

Rapin I 1979 Conductive hearing loss: effects on children's language and scholastic skills: A review of the literature. Annals of Otology, Rhinology and Laryngology 88 (5 Pt 2 suppl 60): 3–12

Rapin I, Allen D 1983 Developmental language disorders: nosologic considerations. In: Kirk U (ed) Neuropsychology of language, reading, and spelling. Academic Press, New York

Rasmussen T, Milner B 1977 The role of early left-brain injury in determining lateralization. Annals of the New York Academy of Science 299: 255–269

Record R G, McKeown T, Edwards J H 1970 An investigation of the difference in measured intelligence between twins and single births. Annals of Human Genetics, 34: 11–20

Redlinger W E, Park T 1980 Language mixing in young bilinguals. Journal of Child Language 7: 337–352

Reed J C, Reitan R M 1969 Verbal and performance differences among brain-injured children with lateralized motor deficits. Perceptual and Motor Skills 29: 747–752

Remick H 1973 Maternal speech to children during language acquisition. ERIC Clearing House for Linguistics, EDO72863, Washington DC

Reynell J 1978 Developmental patterns of visually-handicapped children. Child Care, Health and Development 4: 291–303

Richman L C, Eliason M 1982 Psychological characteristics of children with cleft lip and palate: intellectual, achievement, behavioral and personality variables. Cleft Palate Journal 19: 249–257

Richon G, Plee B 1976 A propos de la dichotomie verbal/non-verbal. Enfance 4–5: 495–509

Ricks D M 1975 Vocal communication in preverbal normal and autistic children. In: O'Connor N (ed) Language, cognitive deficits and retardation. Butterworths, London

Ricks D M, Wing L 1975 Language, communication and the use of symbols in normal and autistic children. Journal of Autism and Childhood Schizophrenia 5: 191–220

Rigrodsky S, Prunty F, Glovsky G 1961 A study of the incidence, types and associated etiologies of hearing loss in an institutionalized mentally retarded population. Training School Bulletin 58: 30–44

Rimland B 1964 Infantile autism. Appleton-Century-Crofts, New York

Risley T, Wolf M 1967 Establishing functional speech in echolalic children. Behavioural Research and Therapy 5: 73–88

Ritvo E R, Freeman B J 1977 National Society for Autistic Children definition of the syndrome of autism. Journal of Pediatric Psychology 2: 146–148

Ritvo S, Provence S 1953 Form perception and imitation in some autistic children: Diagnostic findings and their contextual interpretation. Psychoanalytic Study of the Child 8: 155–161

Riva D, Cazzaniga L 1986 Late effects of unilateral brain lesions sustained before and after age one. Neuropsychologia 24: 423–428

Roberts J E, Sanyal M A, Burchinal M R, Collier A M, Ranney C I, Henderson F W 1986 Otitis media in early childhood and its relationship to later verbal and academic performance. Pediatrics 78: 478–480

Rogosa D 1980 A critique of cross-lagged correlation. Psychological Bulletin 88: 245–258

Rogow S M 1972 Language acquisition and the blind retarded child: a study of impaired communication. Education of the Visually Handicapped 4: 36–40

Rondal J A 1975 Développement du langage et retard mental: une revue critique de la littérature en langue anglaise. L'Année Psychologique 75: 513–547

Rondal J A 1978 Maternal speech to normal and Down's syndrome children matched for mean length of utterance. In: Meyers C (ed) Quality of life in severely and profoundly mentally retarded people: research foundations for improvement. Monograph of the American Association on Mental Deficiency

Rondal J A 1985a Langage et communication chez les handicapés mentaux. Mardaga, Brussels

Rondal J A 1985b Linguistic and prelinguistic development in moderate and severe mental retardation. In: Dobbing J, Clarke A D B, Corbett J A, Hogg J, Robinson R O (eds) Scientific studies in mental retardation. The Royal Society of Medicine/Macmillan Press, London

Rondal J A (in press) Parent-child interaction and the process of language acquisition in severe mental retardation: beyond the obvious. In: Marfo K (ed) Mental handicap and parent-child interaction. Praeger Press, New York

Rondal J A, Lambert J L 1983 The speech of mentally retarded adults in a dyadic communication situation: Some formal and informative aspects. Psychologica Belgica 23: 49–56

Rondal J A, Lambert J L, Sohier C 1980 L'imitation verbale et non-verbale chez l'enfant retardé mental mongolien et non-mongolien. Enfance 3: 107–122

Rondal J A, Ghiotto M, Bredart S, Bachelet J F 1987 Age-relation, reliability and grammatical validity of measures of utterance length. Journal of Child Language 14: 433–446

Ronjat J 1913 Le développement du langage observé chez un enfant bilingue. Champion, Paris

Rose R J, Uchida I A, Christian J C 1981 Placentation effects on cognitive resemblance of adult monozygotes. In: Gedda L, Parisi P, Nance W E (eds) Twin research: Progress in clinical and biological research: Intelligence, personality and development. Liss, New York

Rosenblatt D 1977 Developmental trends in infant play. In: Tizard B, Harvey D (eds) Biology of play. Clinics in developmental medicine No 62. SIMP/Heinemann, London

Ross G S 1982 Language functioning and speech development of six children receiving tracheotomy in infancy. Journal of Communication Disorders 15: 95–111

Rowland C 1983 Patterns of interaction between three blind infants and their mothers. In: Mills A E (ed) Language acquisition in the blind child: normal and deficient. Croom Helm, London, and College Hill, San Diego

Ruben R J, Rapin I 1980 Plasticity of the developing auditory system. Annals of Otology 89: 303–311

Ruben R J, Downs M P, Jerger J, Fiellau-Nikolajsen M, Paparella M M, Ranney J B 1985 Otitis media: impact and sequelae. Annals of Otology, Rhinology and Otolaryngology 94 (suppl 16): 31–32

Rudel R G 1978 Neuroplasticity: implications for development and education. In: Chall J S, Mirsky A F (eds) Education and the brain. University of Chicago Press, Chicago

Rudel R G, Teuber H, Twitchell T E 1974 Levels of impairment of sensori-motor functions in children with early brain damage. Neuropsychologia 12: 95–108

Russell E W 1975 A multiple scoring method for the assessment of complex memory functions. Journal of Consulting and Clinical Psychology 43: 800–809

Rutter M 1974 The development of infantile autism. Psychological Medicine 4: 147–163

Rutter M 1981 Maternal deprivation reassessed. Penguin Books, Harmondsworth, Middlesex

Rutter M 1985 Infantile autism and other child psychoses. In: Rutter M, Hersov L (eds) Child and adolescent psychiatry: modern approaches. Blackwell, Oxford

Rutter M, Lockyer L 1967 A five to fifteen year follow-up study of infantile psychosis, I. Description of sample. British Journal of Psychiatry 133: 1169–1182

Rutter M, Greenfield D, Lockyer L 1967 A five to fifteen year follow-up study of infantile psychosis, II. Social and behavioural outcome. British Journal of Psychiatry 113: 1183–1199

Rutter M, Chadwick O, Shaffer D 1983 Head injury. In: Rutter M (ed) Developmental neuropsychiatry. Churchill Livingstone, Edinburgh

Ryan J 1975 Mental subnormality and language development. In: Lenneberg E H, Lenneberg E (eds) Foundations of language development (Vol 2). Academic Press, New York

Sachs J, Brown R T, Salermo R A 1972 Adults' speech to children. Paper given at the International Symposium on First Language Acquisition, Florence, Italy (unpublished)

Sachs J, Bard B, Johnson M L 1981 Language learning with restricted input: Case studies of two hearing children of deaf parents. Applied Psycholinguistics 2: 33–54

Sachs J, Devin J 1976 Young children's use of age appropriate speech styles in social interaction and role-playing. Journal of Child Language 3: 81–98

Sachs J, Johnson M L 1976 Language development in a hearing child of deaf parents. In: von Raffler-Engel W, Lebrun Y (eds) Baby talk and infant speech. Swets and Zeitlinger, Lisse, Netherlands

Saffran E M 1982 Neuropsychological approaches to the study of language. British Journal of Psychology 73: 317–337

St James-Roberts I 1981 A reinterpretation of hemispherectomy data without functional plasticity of the brain: I. Intellectual function. Brain and Language 13: 31–53

Sak R J, Ruben R J 1981 Recurrent middle ear effusion in childhood. Implications of temporary auditory deprivation for language and learning. Annals of Otology 90: 546–551

Sarno M T 1980 Review of research in aphasia: recovery and rehabilitation. In: Sarno M T, Hook O (eds) Aphasia: assessment and treatment. Masson, New York

Satz P, Bullard-Bates C 1981 Acquired aphasia in children. In: Sarno M T (ed) Acquired aphasia. Academic Press, New York

Saunders W H, Meyerhoff W L 1980 Physical examination of the ear. In: Paparella M M, Shumrick D A (eds) Otolaryngology, Volume II. The ear, 2nd edn. Saunders, Philadelphia

Savic S 1979 Mother-child verbal interaction: the functioning of completions in the twin situation. Journal of Child Language 6: 153–158

Savic S 1980 How twins learn to talk. A study of the speech development of twins 1–3. Academic Press, London

Scarr-Salapatek S 1976 An evolutionary perspective on infant intelligence: species patterns and individual variations. In: Lewis M (ed) Origins of intelligence. Plenum, New York

Schachter J 1986 Second language acquisition and its relationship to universal grammar. University of Southern California, Los Angeles

Scheerer M, Rothmann E, Goldstein K 1945 A case of 'Idiot Savant': An experimental study of personality organization. Psychological Monographs 58(4): 1–63

Scheidt P C, Kavanagh J F 1986 Common terminology for conditions of the middle ear. In: Kavanagh J F (ed) Otitis media and child development. York Press, Parkton, Maryland

Schieffelin B K 1985 The acquisition of Kaluli. In: Slobin D I (ed) The crosslinguistic study of language acquisition. Volume 1: the data. Erlbaum, Hillsdale, NJ

Schiff N 1976 The development of form and meaning in the language of hearing children of deaf parents. Doctoral dissertation, Columbia University (unpublished)

Schiff N 1978 Communication of two-year olds changes with listener's linguistic needs. Paper presented to National Convention of the American Speech and Hearing Association, San Francisco (unpublished)

Schiff N 1979 The influence of deviant maternal input on the development of language during the preschool years. Journal of Speech and Hearing Research

22: 581–603; erratum 1980 23: 222

Schiff N, Ventry I M 1976 Communication problems in hearing children of deaf parents. Journal of Speech and Hearing Disorders 41: 348–358

Schiff-Myers N 1982 Sign and oral language development of preschool hearing children of deaf parents in comparison with their mothers' communication systems. American Annals of the Deaf 127: 322–330

Schiff-Myers N B, Klein H B 1985 Some phonological characteristics of the speech of normal-hearing children of deaf parents. Journal of Speech and Hearing Research 28: 466–474

Schirmer B R 1985 An analysis of the language of young hearing-impaired children in terms of syntax, semantics and use. American Annals of the Deaf 130: 15–19

Schlanger B, Gottsleben R H 1957 Analysis of speech defects amongst the institutionalized mentally retarded. Journal of Speech and Hearing Disorders 22: 98–103

Schreibman L, Carr E 1978 Elimination of echolalic responding to questions through the training of a generalized verbal response. Journal of Applied Behavior Analysis 11: 453–463

Schuler A L 1979 Echolalia. Issues and clinical implications. Journal of Speech and Hearing Disorders 44: 411–435

Schuler A L, Baldwin M 1981 Nonspeech communication and childhood autism. Language, Speech and Hearing Services in Schools 12: 246–257

Schwartz T J 1983 Social cognition in visually impaired and sighted children. Journal of Visual Impairment and Blindness 7: 377–381

Selfe L 1977 Nadia: A case of extraordinary drawing ability in an autistic child. Academic Press, London

Seliger H 1984 Processing universals in second-language acquisition. In: Eckman F R, Bell L H, Nelson D (eds) Universals of second language acquisition. Newbury House, Rowley, Mass

Semzowa M I 1961 Besonderheiten der Erkenntnistätigkeit blinder Kinder im jüngeren Schulalter. Die Sonderschule 6: 336–340

Seron X 1981 Children's acquired aphasia: is the initial equipotentiality theory still tenable?. In: Lebrun Y, Zangwill O (eds) Lateralisation of language in the child. Swets and Zeitlinger, Lisse

Sersen E, Astrup C, Floidstad I, Wortis J 1970 Motor conditional reflexes and word associations in retarded children. American Journal of Mental Deficiency 74: 495–501

Seymour H N, Miller-Jones D 1981 Language and cognitive assessment of black children. In: Lass N J (ed) Speech and language: advances in basic research and practice, vol. 6. Academic Press, New York

Shafer R E 1978 A cross-national study of teacher-language attitudes in England and the United States. In: Campbell R N, Smith P T (eds) Recent advances in the psychology of language: language development and mother-child interaction. Plenum, New York

Shaffer T, Ehri L 1980 Seriators' and nonseriators' comprehension of comparative adjective forms. Journal of Psycholinguistic Research 9: 187–204

Shapiro T 1977 The quest for a linguistic model to study the speech of autistic children. Journal of the American Academy of Child Psychiatry 16: 608–619

Shapiro T, Kapit R 1978 Linguistic negation in autistic and normal children. Journal of Psycholinguistic Research 7: 337–351

Share J B 1975 Developmental progress in Down's syndrome. In: Koch R, de la Cruz F (eds) Down's syndrome: Research, prevention and management. Brunner/Mazel, New York

Share J B, French R W 1974 Early motor development in Down's syndrome children. Mental Retardation 12 (December): 23

Shatz M 1982 On mechanisms of language acquisition: Can features of the communicative environment account for development? In: Wanner E, Gleitman L R (eds) Language acquisition: the state of the art. Cambridge University Press, Cambridge

Shatz M 1985 An evolutionary perspective on plasticity in language development: a commentary. Merrill-Palmer Quarterly 31: 211–222

Shields J 1980 Genetics and mental development. In: Rutter M (ed) Scientific foundations of developmental psychiatry. Heinemann, London

Shillito J 1964 Carotid arteritis: a cause of hemiplegia in childhood. Journal of Neurosurgery 21: 540–551

Shriberg L D, Smith A J 1983 Phonological correlates of middle ear involvement in speech-delayed children: a methodological note. Journal of Speech and Hearing Research 26: 293–297

Shurin P A, Pelton S I, Donner A, Klein J O 1979 Persistence of middle ear effusion after acute otitis media in children. New England Journal of Medicine 300: 1121–1123

Sibinga M S, Friedman J J 1971 Restraint and speech. Pediatrics 48: 116–122

Silverman S R 1971 The education of deaf children. In: Travis L E (ed) Handbook of speech pathology and audiology. Appleton, New York

Simmons A A 1962 A comparison of the type-token ratio of spoken and written language of deaf and hearing children. Volta Review 64: 417–421

Simon B M, Fowler S M, Handler S D 1983 Communication development in young children with long-term tracheostomies: preliminary report. International Journal of Pediatric Otorhinolaryngology 6: 37–50

Simon B M, Handler S D 1981 The speech pathologist and management of children with tracheostomies. Journal of Otolaryngology 10: 440–448

Simon N 1975 Echolalic speech in childhood autism. Archives of General Psychiatry 32: 1439–1446

Sinclair A, Sinclair H, De Marcellus O 1971 Young children's comprehension and production of passive sentences. Archives de Psychologie 41: 1–22

Sinclair H 1971 Sensorimotor action patterns as a condition for the acquisition of syntax—discussion. In: Huxley R, Ingram E (eds) Language acquisition: models and methods. Academic Press, London and New York

Sinclair-de-Zwart H 1967 Acquisition du langage et développement de la pensée. Dunal, Paris

Singer L T, Wood R, Lambert S 1985 Developmental follow-up of long-term tracheostomy: a preliminary report. Developmental and Behavioral Pediatrics 6: 132–136

Siple P 1985 Plasticity, robustness and language

development: an introduction to research issues relating sign language and spoken language. Merrill-Palmer Quarterly 31: 117–126

Skarakis E A, Prutting C A 1977 Early communication: Semantic functions and communicative intentions in the communication of the preschool child with impaired hearing. American Annals of the Deaf 122: 382–391

Skeels H M 1966 Adult status of children with contrasting early life experiences: a follow-up study. Monographs of the Society for Research in Child Development 31: 3

Skinner M W 1978 The hearing of speech during language acquisition. Otolaryngologic Clinics of North America 11: 631–650

Skuse D 1984 Extreme deprivation in early childhood I. Diverse outcomes for three siblings from an extraordinary family. Journal of Child Psychology and Psychiatry 25: 523–541

Skutnabb-Kangas T 1978 Semilingualism and the education of migrant children as a means of reproducing the caste of assembly line workers. In Dittmar N, Haberland H, Skutnabb-Kangas T, Teleman V (eds) Papers from the first Scandinavian-German symposium on the language of immigrant workers and their children. Universitetscenter, Roshilde, Denmark

Slobin D 1966 The acquisition of Russian as a native language. In: Smith F, Miller D A (eds) The genesis of language: a psycholinguistic approach. MIT Press, Cambridge MA

Slobin D 1973 Cognitive prerequisites for the development of grammar. In: Ferguson C A, Slobin D (eds) Studies of child language development. Holt, Rinehart and Winston, New York

Slobin D I (ed) 1985 The crosslinguistic study of language acquisition. Erlbaum, Hillsdale, NJ

Smith A 1972 Dominant and nondominant hemispherectomy. In: Lynn Smith W (ed) Drugs, development and cerebral function. Charles C Thomas, Springfield, Ill

Smith A 1981 On the organization, disorganization and reorganization of language and other brain functions. In: Lebrun Y, Zangwill O (eds) Lateralization of language in the child. Swets and Zeitlinger, Lisse

Smith B 1977 Phonological development in Down's syndrome children. Paper presented at the 85th Annual Convention of the American Psychological Association, San Francisco (unpublished)

Smith B L 1987 The emerging lexicon from a phonetic perspective. In: Smith M D, Locke J L (eds) The emergent lexicon: the child's development of a linguistic vocabulary. Academic Press, New York

Smith B, Oller K 1981 A comparative study of pre-meaningful vocalizations produced by normally developing and Down's syndrome infants. Journal of Speech and Hearing Disorders 46: 46–51

Smith N V 1973 The acquisition of phonology. Cambridge University Press, Cambridge

Smith N 1982 Some observations concerning pre-meaningful vocalizations of hearing-impaired infants. Journal of Speech and Hearing Disorders 47: 439–442

Snow C E 1972 Mothers' speech to children learning language. Child Development 43: 549–565

Snow C 1977a The development of conversation between mothers and babies. Journal of Child Language 4: 1–22

Snow C E 1977b Mothers' speech research: from input to interaction. In: Snow C E, Ferguson C A (eds) Talking to children. Cambridge University Press, New York

Snow C E 1986 Conversations with children. In: Fletcher P, Garman M (eds) Language acquisition, 2nd edn. Cambridge University Press, Cambridge

Snow C, Hoefnagel-Hohle M 1978 Age differences in second language acquisition. In: Hatch E (ed) Second language acquisition: a book of readings. Newbury House, Rowley, Mass

Snowling M, Stackhouse J 1983 Spelling performance of children with developmental verbal dyspraxia. Developmental Medicine and Child Neurology 25: 430–437

Sokolov A N 1972 Inner speech and thought (translated by G T Onischenko). Plenum, New York

Sparks S N 1984 Birth defects and speech-language disorders. College-Hill Press, San Diego

Spitz R A 1957 No and yes. International Universities Press, New York

Spitzer R, Rabinowitch J, Wybar K 1961 A study of the abnormalities of the skull, teeth and lenses in mongolism. Canadian Medical Association Journal 84: 567–572

Sridhar S N, Sridhar K K 1980 The syntax and psycholinguistics of bilingual code mixing. Canadian Journal of Psychology 34: 407–416

Stackhouse J 1982 An investigation of reading and spelling performance in speech disordered children. British Journal of Disorders of Communication 17: 53–60

Stampe D 1969 The acquisition of phonemic representation. Proceedings of Vth Regional Meeting of the Chicago Linguistic Society: 443–444

Stein Z, Susser M 1985 Effects of early nutrition on neurological and mental competence in human beings. Psychological Medicine 15: 717–726

Stengel E 1947 A clinical and psychological study of echo reactions. Journal of Mental Science 93: 598–612

Stengel E 1964 Speech disorders and mental disorders. In: de Reuck A V S, O'Connor M (eds) Disorders of language. Little Brown, Boston

Stevens K N 1981 Constraints imposed by the auditory system on the properties used to classify speech sounds: data from phonology, acoustics and psychoacoustics. In: Myers T, Laver J, Anderson J (eds) The cognitive representation of speech. North Holland, Amsterdam

Stinchfield S M 1944 Moto-kinaesthetic speech training applied to visually-handicapped children. Outlook for the Blind 38: 4–8

Stoel-Gammon C, Otomo K 1986 Babbling development of hearing-impaired and normally hearing subjects. Journal of Speech and Hearing Disorders 51: 33–40

Strange W 1986 Speech input and the development of speech. In: Kavanagh J F (ed) Otitis media and child development. York Press, Parkton, Maryland

Strauss E, Verity C 1983 Effects of hemispherectomy in infantile hemiplegics. Brain and Language 20: 1–11

Strazzulla M 1953 Speech problems of the mongoloid child. Quarterly Review of Pediatrics 8: 268–272

Stubbs M 1983 Discourse analysis: the sociolinguistic analysis of natural language. Blackwell, Oxford

Studdert-Kennedy M, Lane H 1980 Clues from the differences between signed and spoken languages. In:

Bellugi U, Studdert-Kennedy M (eds) Signed and spoken language: biological constraints on linguistic form. Verlag Chemie, Weinheim

Supalla T 1982 Structure and acquisition of verbs of motion and location in American Sign Language. PhD Dissertation, University of California, San Diego

Supalla T, Newport E 1978 How many seats in a chair? The derivation of nouns and verbs in American Sign Language. In: Siple P (ed) Understanding language through sign language research. Academic Press, New York

Swain M 1972 Bilingualism as a first language. PhD dissertation, University of California, Irvine

Swain M 1977 Bilingualism, monolingualism and code acquisition. In: Mackey W, Andersson T (eds) Bilingualism in early childhood. Newbury House, Rowley, Mass

Swain M 1985 Communicative competence: some roles of comprehensible input and comprehensible output in its development. In: Gass S M, Madden C G (eds) Input in second language acquisition. Newbury House, Rowley, Mass

Swain M, Wesche M 1975 Linguistic interaction: case study of a bilingual child. Language Sciences 37: 17–22

Swisher L 1976 The language performance of the oral deaf. In: Whitaker H, Whitaker H A (eds) Studies in neurolinguistics. Vol II. Academic Press, London

Tabouret-Keller A 1962 Vrais et faux problèmes du bilinguisme. In: Cohen M, Rezine I, Kocher F, Brauner A, Lentin L, Tabouret-Keller A (eds) Etudes sur le langage de l'enfant. Les Editions du Scarabee, Paris

Tager-Flusberg H 1981a On the nature of linguistic functioning in early infantile autism. Journal of Autism and Developmental Disorders 11: 45–56

Tager-Flusberg H 1981b Sentence comprehension in autistic children. Applied Psycholinguistics 2: 5–24

Tager-Flusberg H 1985 Putting words together: morphology and syntax in the preschool years. In: Berko Gleason J (ed) The development of language. Merrill, Columbus, Ohio

Tager-Flusberg H 1986 The semantic deficit hypothesis of autistic children's language. Australian Journal of Human Communication Disorders 14: 51–58

Tait M, Wood D 1987 From communication to speech in deaf children. Child Language Teaching and Therapy 3: 1–17

Tallal P, Piercy M 1978 Defects of auditory perception in children with developmental dysphasia. In: Wyke M (ed) Developmental dysphasia. Academic Press, London

Tallal P, Stark R E 1981 Speech acoustic-cue discrimination abilities of normally developing and language-impaired children. Journal of the Acoustical Society of America 69: 568–574

Tallal P, Stark R E, Mellits E D 1985 Identification of language-impaired children on the basis of rapid perception and production skills. Brain and Language 25: 314–322

Teasdale T W, Owen D R 1984 Heredity and familial environment in intelligence and educational level—a sibling study. Nature 309: 620–622

Teele D W, Klein J O, Rosner B A and the Greater Boston Otitis Media Study Group 1984 Otitis media with effusion during the first three years of life and development of speech and language. Pediatrics 74: 282–287

Templin M C 1950 The development of reasoning in children with normal and defective hearing. University of Minnesota, Minn

Teuber H, Rudel R G 1962 Behaviour after cerebral lesions in children and adults. Developmental Medicine and Child Neurology 4: 3–20

Thelin J W, Thelin S J, Keith R W, Novak K K, Keenan W J 1979 Effect of middle ear dysfunction and disease on hearing and language in high risk infants. International Journal of Pediatric Otorhinolaryngology 1: 125–136

Thompson A M 1986 Adam—a severely deprived Colombian orphan: a case report. Journal of Child Psychology and Psychiatry 27: 689–695

Tizard B, Carmichael H, Hughes M, Pinkerton G 1980 Four-year-olds talking to mothers and teachers. In: Hersov L A, Berger M, Nicol A R (Eds) Language and language disorders in childhood. Pergamon, Oxford

Tizard B, Hughes M 1984 Young children learning: talking and thinking at home and at school. Fontana, London

Todd P H 1975 A case of structural interference across sensory modalities in second language learning. Word 27: 102–118

Todd P, Aitchison J 1980 Learning language the hard way. First Language 1: 122–140

Tomasello M, Farrar M 1984 Cognitive bases of lexical development: object permanence and relational words. Journal of Child Language 11: 477–495

Tomasello M, Mannle S, Kruger A C 1986 Linguistic environment of 1-2-year-old twins. Developmental Psychology 22: 169–176

Tos M 1980 Spontaneous improvement of secretory otitis and impedance screening. Archives of Otolaryngology 106: 345–349

Trehub S 1973 Auditory-linguistic sensitivity in infants. PhD dissertation, McGill University, Montreal

Tucker H M, Rusnov M, Cohen L 1982 Speech development in aphonic children. Laryngoscope 92: 566–568

Tweney R D, Hoemann H W, Andrews C E 1975 Semantic organisation in deaf and hearing subjects. Journal of Psycholinguistic Research 4: 61–73

Udwin O, Yule W, Martin N D T 1986 Age at diagnosis and abilities in idiopathic hypercalcaemia. Archives of Disease in Childhood 61: 1164–1167

Urwin C 1978 The development of communication between blind infants and their parents: some ways into language. Doctoral dissertation, University of Cambridge

Urwin C 1983 Dialogue and cognitive functioning in the early language development of three blind children. In: Mills A E (ed) Language acquisition in the blind child: normal and deficient. Croom Helm, London, and College Hill, San Diego

Vaid J, Schemenauer D, Bellugi U, Poizner H 1984 Hand dominance in a visual—gestural language. Presentation to the Body for the Advancement of Brain, Behavior, and Language Enterprises, Niagara Falls, Ontario, Canada (unpublished)

Van Dongen H P, Loonen M C B 1977 Factors related to prognosis of acquired aphasia in children. Cortex 15: 131–136

Van Dongen H R, Loonen M C B, Van Dongen K J 1985

Anatomical basis for acquired fluent aphasia in children. Annals of Neurology 17: 306–309

Van Hoek K, O'Grady L, Bellugi U 1987 Morphological innovation in the acquisition of American Sign Language. Papers and Reports on Child Language Development 26 (in press)

Van Hout A, Evrard P, Lyon G 1985 On the positive semiology of acquired aphasia in children. Developmental Medicine and Child Neurology 27: 231–241

Van Hout A, Lyon G 1986 Wernicke's aphasia in a 10-year-old boy. Brain and Language 29: 268–285

Vargha-Khadem F, O'Gorman A M, Watters G V 1985 Aphasia and handedness in relation to hemispheric side, age at injury, and severity of cerebral lesion during childhood. Brain 108: 677–696

Velten H V 1943 The growth of phonemic and lexical patterns in infant language. Language 19: 281–292

Ventry I M 1980 Effects of conductive hearing loss. Fact or fiction. Journal of Speech and Hearing Disorders 45: 143–156

Vernon M 1974 Effects of parents' deafness on hearing children. In: Fine P (ed) Deafness in infancy and early childhood. Medcom, New York

Vihman M 1982 The acquisition of morphology by a bilingual child: a whole-word approach. Applied Psycholinguistics 3: 141–160

Vihman M 1985 Language differentiation by the bilingual infant. Journal of Child Language 12: 297–324

Vihman M M, Macken M A, Miller R et al 1985 From babbling to speech: a re-assessment of the continuity issue. Language 61: 397–445

Vihman M, McLaughlin B 1982 Bilingualism and second language acquisition in preschool children. In: Brainerd C, Pressley M (eds) Verbal processes in children. Springer-Verlag, New York

Visch-Brink E G, Van de Sandt-Koenderman M 1984 The occurrence of paraphasias in the spontaneous speech of children with an acquired aphasia. Brain and Language 23: 258–271

Volterra V 1981 I segni come parole: La communicazione dei sordi. Boringhieri, Rome

Volterra V, Taeschner T 1978 The acquisition and development of language by bilingual children. Journal of Child Language 5: 311–326

Von Armin G, Engel P 1964 Mental retardation related to hypercalcemia. Developmental Medicine and Child Neurology 6: 366–377

Von Tetzchner S, Martinsen H 1980 A psycholinguistic study of the language of the blind 1: verbalism. International Journal of Psycholinguistics 7: 49–61

Vygotsky L 1962 Thought and language. MIT Press, Cambridge, Mass

Vygotsky L S 1978 Play and its role in the mental development of the child. In: Cole M, John-Steiner V, Scribner S, Souberman E (eds) Mind in society. Harvard University Press, Cambridge, Mass

Waddington C H 1977 Tools for thought. Jonathan Cape, London

Wallace I F, Gravel J S, Ruben R J, McCarton C C (in press) Otitis media and language development

Wardrip-Fruin C, Peach S 1984 Developmental aspects of the perception of acoustic cues in determining the voicing feature of final stop consonants. Language and Speech 27: 367–379

Warren D H 1977 Blindness and early childhood development. American Foundation for the Blind, New York

Warren D, Anooshian L, Bollinger J G 1973 Early vs. late blindness: the role of vision in spatial behaviour. Research Bulletin No 26, American Foundation for the Blind, New York

Waterman P, Shatz M 1982 The acquisition of personal pronouns and proper names by an identical twin pair. Journal of Speech and Hearing Research 25, 149–154

Watts D, Lytton H 1981 Twinship as handicap:fact or fiction? In: Gedda L, Parisi P, Nance W E (eds) Twin research: Progress in clinical and biological research: Intelligence, personality and development. Liss, New York

Webster D B 1983a Auditory neuronal sizes after a unilateral conductive hearing loss. Experimental Neurology 79: 130–140

Webster D B 1983b A critical period during postnatal auditory development of mice. International Journal of Pediatric Otorhinolaryngology 6: 107–118

Webster D B, Webster M 1977 Neonatal sound deprivation affects brain stem auditory nuclei. Archives of Otolaryngology 103: 392–396

Webster D B, Webster M 1979 Effect of neonatal conductive hearing loss on brainstem auditory nuclei. Annals of Otology 88: 684–688

Weinberg B, Zlatin M 1970 Speaking fundamental frequency characteristics of five- and six-year-old children with mongolism. Journal of Speech and Hearing Research 13: 418–425

Welch P, Black K N, Christian J C 1978 Placental type and Bayley developmental scores in 18-month-old twins. In: Nance W, Allen G, Parisi P (eds) Twin research: progress in clinical and biological research: psychology and methodology. Liss, New York York

Wells C O 1942 The development of abstract language concepts in normal and deaf children. University of Chicago Libraries, Chicago

Wells G 1979 Variation in child language. In: Fletcher P, Garman M (eds) Language acquisition: studies in first language development. Cambridge University Press, New York

Wells G 1985 Language development in the pre-school years. Cambridge University Press, Cambridge

Wernicke C 1874 Der aphasische Symptomenkomplex. Cohn and Wiegert, Breslau

Wesner C E 1972 Induced arousal and word recognition learning by mongoloids and normals. Perceptual and Motor Skills 35: 586

West J, Weber J A 1973 A phonological analysis of the spontaneous language of a 4-year-old hard-of-hearing child. Journal of Speech and Hearing Disorders 38: 25–35

Whitaker H A, Selnes O A 1978 Token test measures of language comprehension in normal children and aphasic patients. In: Caramazza A, Zurif E B (eds) Language acquisition and language breakdown. Johns Hopkins University Press, Baltimore

White L 1981 The responsibility of grammatical theory to acquisitional data. In: Hornstein N, Lightfoot D (eds) Explanation in linguistics: the logical problem of language acquisition. Longman, London

Whitehouse D, Harris J C 1984 Hyperlexia in infantile

autism. Journal of Autism and Developmental Disorders 14: 281–289

Wilbur R 1977 An explanation of deaf children's difficulty with certain syntactic structures in English. Volta Review 79: 85–92

Wilcox J, Tobin H 1974 Linguistic performance of hard-of-hearing and normal hearing children. Journal of Speech and Hearing Research 17: 286–293

Williams J C P, Barratt Boyes B G, Lowe J B 1961 Supravalvular aortic stenosis. Circulation 24: 1311–1318

Wills D M 1979 Early speech development in blind children. The Psychoanalytic Study of the Child 34: 85–117

Wilson B C, Wilson J J 1977 Early identification, assessment and implications for intervention. Paper presented at the American Academy for Cerebral Palsy and Developmental Medicine (unpublished)

Wilson I Q, Herrnstein R J 1986 Crime and human nature. Simon and Schuster, New York

Wilson P J E 1970 Cerebral hemispherectomy for infantile hemiplegia. Brain 93: 147–180

Wing J K 1976 Kanner's syndrome: a historic introduction. In: Wing L (ed) Early childhood autism: clinical, educational and social aspects, 2nd edn. Pergamon, Oxford

Wing L 1969 The handicaps of autistic children—A comparative study. Journal of Child Psychology and Psychiatry 10: 1–40

Wing L 1971 Perceptual and language development in autistic children: A comparative study. In: Rutter M (ed) Infantile autism: Concepts, characteristics and treatment. Churchill, London

Wing L 1976a Early childhood autism: Clinical, educational and social aspects, 2nd edn. Pergamon Oxford

Wing L 1976b Diagnosis, clinical description and prognosis. In: Wing L (ed) Early childhood autism: Clinical, educational and social aspects, 2nd edn. Pergamon, Oxford

Wing L 1981 Language, social and cognitive impairments in autism and severe mental retardation. Journal of Autism and Developmental Disorders 11: 31–44

Wing L, Gould J 1978 Systematic recording of behavior and skills of retarded and psychotic children. Journal of Autism and Childhood Schizophrenia 8: 79–97

Witelson S F 1985 On hemisphere specialization and cerebral plasticity from birth: mark II. In: Best C T (ed) Hemispheric function and collaboration in the child. Academic Press, Orlando.

Wode H 1976 Developmental sequences in naturalistic L2 acquisition. Working Papers in Bilingualism 11: 1–31

Wolff S, Chess S 1965 An analysis of the language of fourteen schizophrenic children. Journal of Child Psychology and Psychiatry 6: 29–41

Wood D J, Wood H A, Griffiths A J, Howarth S P, Howarth C I 1982 The structure of conversations with 6- to 10-year-old deaf children. Journal of Child Psychology and Psychiatry 23: 295–308

Wood H A, Wood D J 1984 An experimental evaluation of the effects of five styles of teacher conversation on the language of hearing-impaired children. Journal of Child Psychology and Psychiatry 25: 45–62

Woods B T 1980 The restricted effects of right hemisphere lesions after age one: Wechsler test data. Neuropsychologia 18: 65–70

Woods B T 1983 Is the left hemisphere specialized for language at birth? Trends in Neurosciences 6: 115–117

Woods B T, Carey S 1979 Language deficits after apparent clinical recovery from childhood aphasia. Annals of Neurology 6: 405–409

Woods B T, Teuber H 1978 Changing patterns of childhood aphasia. Annals of Neurology 3: 273–280

Workman S H 1986 Teachers' verbalizations and the social interaction of blind preschoolers. Journal of Visual Impairment and Blindness 80: 532–534

Worster-Drought C 1956 Congenital suprabulbar paresis. Journal of Laryngology 70: 453–463

Wundt W 1898 Volkerpsychologie. Volume 1: die Sprache. Wilhem Engelmann, Leipzig. 3rd edn. Translation in Bar-Aden A, Leopold W F (eds) Child language: a book of readings. Prentice-Hall, Englewood Cliffs, NJ

Yeni-Komshian G, Kavanagh J, Ferguson C A (eds) 1980 Child phonology. vol. 2. Perception. Academic Press, New York

Yoder D, Miller J 1972 What we may know and what we can do: Input toward a system. In: McLean J, Yoder D, Schietelbusch R (eds) Language intervention with the retarded: developing strategies. University Park Press, Baltimore

Young C, McConnell F 1957 Retardation of vocabulary development in hard of hearing children. Exceptional Child 23: 368–370

Zangwill O L 1962 Cerebral dominance and its relation to psychological function. Oliver and Boyd, Edinburgh

Zazzo R 1960 Les jumeaux: le couple et la personne. Presses Universitaires de France, Paris

Zazzo R 1978 Genesis and peculiarities of the personality of twins. In: Nance W E, Allen G, Parisi P (eds) Twin research: progress in clinical and biological research: psychology and methodology. Liss, New York.

Zigler E 1986 Research on personality structure in the retardate. In: Ellis N (ed) International review of research on mental retardation (Vol 1). Academic Press, New York

Zinkus P W, Gottliob M I 1980 Patterns of perceptual and academic deficits related to early chronic otitis media. Pediatrics 66: 246–253

Zinkus P W, Gottlieb M I, Schapiro M 1978 Developmental and psycho-educational sequelae of chronic otitis media. American Journal of Diseases of Children 132: 1100—1104

Zipf G K 1949 Human behavior and the principle of least effort. Hafner, New York

Zisk P, Bialer I 1967 Speech and language problems in mongolism. Journal of Speech and Hearing Disorders 32: 228–241

Zukow P G 1986 The relationship between interaction with the caregiver and the emergence of play activities during the one-word period. British Journal of Developmental Psychology 4: 223–234

Author index

Subject index